CONQUERING THE FEAR OF FREEDOM

Conquering the Fear of Freedom

Japanese Exchange Rate Policy Since 1945

SHINJI TAKAGI

OXFORD
UNIVERSITY PRESS

Great Clarendon Street, Oxford, OX2 6DP,
United Kingdom

Oxford University Press is a department of the University of Oxford.
It furthers the University's objective of excellence in research, scholarship,
and education by publishing worldwide. Oxford is a registered trade mark of
Oxford University Press in the UK and in certain other countries

© Shinji Takagi 2015

The moral rights of the author have been asserted

First Edition published in 2015

Impression: 1

Published in the United States of America by Oxford University Press
198 Madison Avenue, New York, NY 10016, United States of America

British Library Cataloguing in Publication Data
Data available

Library of Congress Control Number: 2014953974

ISBN 978-0-19-871465-1

Printed and bound by
CPI Group (UK) Ltd, Croydon, CR0 4YY

To My Wife

Preface

This book reviews Japan's exchange rate policy from the end of World War II to the present. It is a subject upon which much has been written. Many a chapter, section, or paragraph of the book discusses a topic to which an entire volume has been devoted. My main task, therefore, has been to tell a coherent story by synthesizing the existing literature, draw overarching lessons from Japan's experience, and identify outstanding issues for the future. I have provided greater institutional details than a typical economics book might. I have also referred to the political science literature where relevant, though without delving too much into the intricacy of political dynamics. The book not only describes how legal and institutional frameworks evolved but also discusses their domestic and international contexts. It also assesses the impacts and consequences of policy actions taken by drawing on the empirical literature where available. Japan was the world's second largest economy during much of the period considered; the country remains the largest net creditor nation. As such, a systematic review of how Japan has conducted its exchange rate policy during the sixty-plus years should be of interest to a number of economists, political scientists, and historians.

The title *Conquering the Fear of Freedom* is meant to capture the trajectory of Japan's policy shift over the years. It is descriptive of how Japanese authorities (the term generally refers to the Ministry of Finance but in some cases also to other government agencies and the Bank of Japan), starting from a system of draconian controls over all international financial flows, liberalized first current payments and then capital transactions before ultimately terminating virtually all state interference, even including foreign exchange market intervention. Throughout the book, the term exchange rate policy is used loosely to mean a set of policy measures designed to affect the yen's nominal or real value, usually in relation to the United States dollar. For the most part, the exchange rate policy tools discussed in the book include: exchange rate regime choice, exchange controls (measures that restrict the making of payments and transfers for current international transactions), capital controls (regulations on capital transactions), regulatory actions related to domestic financial markets, and foreign exchange market intervention.

Exchange rate policy does not take place in a vacuum. National policymakers take action against the background of domestic and international developments. Exchange rates are also influenced by many factors. This means that exchange rate policy cannot strictly be separated from the broader context of fiscal, monetary, trade, and other policies. Even so, this book is not about Japan's macroeconomic or international economic policy. It remains focused on exchange rate policy. Any discussion of broader macroeconomic or international context, though essential, is kept tangential. The narrower focus corresponds to the definition of "action to influence an exchange rate" provided in 1974 by the Executive Board of the International Monetary Fund, which limits such action to include, "besides exchange market intervention, other policies that exercise a temporary effect on the balance of payments and hence on exchange rates, and that have been adopted for that purpose."[1] The current book discusses fiscal, monetary, and other policies as part of exchange rate policy, but only when they were specifically intended to influence the balance of payments or the exchange rate directly.

The book consists of six main chapters, followed by a concluding one. I would like to think of each main chapter as a case study in international economic policy. Chapter 1 is about how Japan stabilized postwar inflation by unifying multiple exchange rates and establishing a link between foreign and domestic prices. Chapter 2 reviews Japan's use of exchange controls and how it established current account convertibility, while Chapter 3 likewise discusses Japan's experience with capital controls and how it sequenced capital account liberalization. Chapter 4 chronicles Japan's exit from a fixed exchange rate and its early experience with managing a flexible exchange rate. Chapter 5 covers Japan's attempt to promote greater international use of its currency. Finally, Chapter 6 reviews Japan's experience with foreign exchange market intervention. Important policy issues in international economics do not accommodate experimentation, so the experience of Japan in these instances can be seen as a type of policy experiment. The chapters roughly proceed in chronological sequence but, given their topic focus, the succeeding chapters necessarily overlap with each other.

It is hoped that the reader will find these topics to have, not just historical or national, but universal relevance. For example, Japan's postwar stabilization in the late 1940s could be placed in the large literature that has subsequently emerged on the topic. Japan's restrictive system of trade and payments could be a reminder of how much of the world operated in the 1950s when most currencies were inconvertible. Officials of large emerging market economies may see in Japan's experience parallels to their own policy challenges, as they liberalize the capital account and allow market forces to play a greater role in determining their exchange rates. Japan's use of market-based capital controls could offer perspectives on the ongoing debate on the effectiveness of such

---

[1] On the other hand, no policies "adopted for demand management purposes" or "for purposes other than balance of payments purposes" are regarded as action to influence the exchange rate. This view was expressed as part of commentary on a memorandum entitled "Guidelines for the Management of Floating Exchange Rates." See Executive Board Decision No. 4232-(74/67), 13 June 1974.

instruments and how to design them; and Japanese foreign exchange market intervention, as reviewed herein, may present virtually the final word on the effectiveness of sterilized intervention. The consequences of attempts by major industrial countries to coordinate macroeconomic policies in the 1980s should not be forgotten, given the profound impact they had on Japan and the rest of the world.

I have incurred heavy debts of gratitude in the preparation of this book. I am especially grateful to Yung Chul Park, who encouraged me to pursue this project; Adam Swallow of Oxford University Press, who immediately recognized the contribution a work of this kind could make to the literature; and the coauthors of joint work, whose findings I have liberally used as if my own: Taro Esaka, Akihiko Kawaguchi, Masahiro Kawai, Issei Kozuru, Val Lambson, Toshihiko Nagai, Hiroki Okada, and Shuichi Shimakura. Jonathan Giles read the first draft of the entire manuscript to provide critical comment and suggestions for improvement; Melinda Keefe copyedited an advanced version of the manuscript. A reviewer provided extremely helpful and constructive suggestions at the final stage. A large portion of this work was completed while I was Professor of Economics at the Graduate School of Economics, Osaka University. The disruption associated with my departure from academia and subsequent relocation to Washington in the spring of 2013 inevitably delayed the completion by several months. Last but not least, I must express deep gratitude to my wife of thirty-four years, Sue Lynn Bergmark, who patiently gave me the freedom to spend evenings, weekends, and holidays over nearly four months, from late 2013 to early 2014, as I finalized the work for publication. It is to her that this book is dedicated.

Shinji Takagi

Washington, DC
August 2014

Contents

List of Figures

List of Tables

List of Abbreviations

AA	Automatic Approval
ABCP	Asset-backed CP
ABS	Asset-based securities
ACJ	Allied Council for Japan
AFA	Automatic Fund Allocation
AIQ	Automatic Import Quota
AMRO	ASEAN+3 Macroeconomic Research Office
ASEAN	Association of Southeast Asian Nations (Brunei, Cambodia, Indonesia, Laos, Malaysia, Myanmar, the Philippines, Singapore, Thailand, and Vietnam)
ASEAN+3	ASEAN Plus Three (ASEAN, China, Japan, and Korea)
BA	Bankers' acceptance
BIS	Bank for International Settlements
BOJ	Bank of Japan
BTN	Brussels Tariff Nomenclature
CAB	Current account balance (a component of the monetary base)
CAL	Capital account liberalization
CASA	Civil Affairs Holding and Staging Area (US)
CD	Certificate of deposit
CMI	Chiang-Mai Initiative
CMIM	Chiang-Mai Initiative Multilateralization
CP	Commercial paper
CPI	Consumer price index
CSP	Civilian Supply Program (US)
DAC	Development Assistance Committee (OECD)
DVP	Delivery versus payment
EC	European Communities
ECB	Economic Counsel Board
EIB	Export–Import Bank of Washington
EMS	European Monetary System
EPU	European Payments Union
ERM	Exchange Rate Mechanism (EMS)
EROA	Economic Rehabilitation in Occupied Areas (US)
ESB	Economic Stabilization Board

ESS	Economic and Scientific Section (US)
ETF	Exchange-traded fund
Eximbank	Export–Import Bank of Japan
FA	Fund Allocation
FAZ	Foreign Access Zone
FB	Financing bill
FDI	Foreign direct investment
FEB	Foreign exchange budget
FEC	Far Eastern Commission
FRB	Board of Governors of the Federal Reserve System (US)
FRBNY	Federal Reserve Bank of New York
FY	Fiscal year
FYA	Free-yen account
FYD	Free-yen deposit
G5	Group of Five (France, Germany, Japan, the United Kingdom, and the United States)
G6	Group of Six (G5 plus Canada)
G7	Group of Seven (G5 plus Canada and Italy)
G10	Group of Ten (G7 plus Belgium, the Netherlands, Sweden, and Switzerland)
G20	Group of Twenty
GARCH	Generalized autoregressive conditional heteroskedasticity
GARIOA	Government and Relief in Occupied Areas (US)
GATT	General Agreement on Tariffs and Trade
GHQ	General Headquarters (US)
GDP	Gross domestic product
GNP	Gross national product
IGGI	Inter-Governmental Group on Indonesia
IMF	International Monetary Fund
IMM	International Money Market (Chicago Mercantile Exchange)
IQ	Import Quota
JDB	Japan Development Bank
JETRO	Japan External Trade Organization
JGB	Japanese government bond
J-REIT	Tokyo Stock Exchange-traded real estate investment trust
LATW	Lean-against-the-wind
LDP	Liberal Democratic Party

LIBOR	London Interbank Offered Rate
LTCB	Long-Term Credit Bank of Japan
M1	Narrow money (roughly, cash plus demand and current deposits)
M2	Broad money (roughly, M1 plus time deposits)
MA	Moving average
MIPRO	Manufactured Imports Promotion Organization
MFN	Most-favored-nation
MITI	Ministry of International Trade and Industry
MMC	Money market certificate
MOF	Ministry of Finance
MOSS	Market Oriented Sector Selective
NAC	National Advisory Council on International Monetary and Financial Problems (US)
ODA	Official development assistance
OECD	Organization for Economic Cooperation and Development
OECF	Overseas Economic Cooperation Fund
OEEC	Organization for European Economic Cooperation
OJEIRF	Occupied Japan Export–Import Revolving Fund
OOF	Other official flows
OPA	Office of Price Administration (US)
OPEC	Organization of the Petroleum Exporting Countries
OTC	Over-the-counter
PCS	Price computing system
PPI	Producer price index
PPP	Purchasing power parity
PRS	Price ratio system
PTM	Pricing-to-market
QEMP	Quantitative easing monetary policy
QQE	Quantitative and qualitative easing
RCEP	Regional Comprehensive Economic Partnership (ASEAN+3, Australia, India, and New Zealand)
RFB	Reconstruction Finance Bank
RND	Risk-neutral density
RPI	Retail price index
RTGS	Real time gross settlement
SCAP	Supreme Commander for the Allied Powers
SCAPIN	SCAP Instruction Note

SI	Savings-investment
SII	Structural Impediments Initiative
STRIPS	Separate trading of registered interest and principal securities
SWNCC	State–War–Navy Coordinating Committee (US)
TB	Treasury bill
T-bill	Treasury discount bill
TIBOR	Tokyo Inter-bank Offered Rate
TOPIX	Tokyo Stock Price Index
US	United States
VAR	Vector autoregressive
VEC	Vector error correction
VER	Voluntary export restraint
ZIRP	Zero interest rate policy

CURRENCY SYMBOLS

$	Dollar (United States dollar, unless otherwise noted)
£	Pound (British pound, unless otherwise noted)
SF	Swiss franc
¥	Yen

1

Exchange Rate-Based Stabilization: 1945–50

1.1. INTRODUCTION

Our review of Japanese exchange rate policy begins with the immediate post-World War II period of political and economic reconstruction. From September 1945 to April 1952, Japan was under Allied occupation. The occupation's initial objectives were to eliminate militarism and to restore democracy in Japan; economic reconstruction became an objective only later in the process. In order to execute this complex undertaking, General Douglas MacArthur, the first Supreme Commander for the Allied Powers (SCAP),[1] added to the general staff sections of his General Headquarters (GHQ) special staff sections in various branches of civil affairs, including the Economic and Scientific Section (ESS) responsible for economic, industrial, financial, and scientific affairs. The GHQ was reorganized in early October 1945 as GHQ/SCAP, with dual military and civil functions to perform (Martin 1948; Williams 1979).[2]

The Japanese Government remained intact. Unlike Germany, a system of military government was never established and indirect rule—based on the existing organs of the Japanese Government—was adopted.[3] Although the

---

[1] General MacArthur held the post of Supreme Commander during the first sixty-seven months of the occupation until he was dismissed and succeeded in April 1951 by General Matthew B. Ridgway.

[2] Staff size, while initially small, began to grow after 1946 and reached a peak of about 6,000 in 1948, of which about a third were local Japanese employees and only about 200 were military officers. The number of special staff sections was about a dozen, although sections were added or abolished throughout the occupation period (Takemae 1983).

[3] This had not been the original intention. Months before the end of the war, the United States Government had started to train officers for service with military government units at military government schools located at several universities and the Civil Affairs Holding and Staging Area (CASA) at Monterey, California. These officers were trained to govern Japanese nationals in conquered areas as troops continued to advance (Williams 1979). Most of these officers were never needed in Japan—the country's surrender came much more quickly than anticipated and without land battles on the mainland (Takamae 1983). Most of the officers trained in civil affairs were never called to go to Japan, and those who did (about a thousand) were incorporated into the GHQ/SCAP or the Eighth (and briefly Sixth) Army. Many of them left Japan after a brief stay (Ward and Shulman 1974).

occupation of Japan was formally an Allied affair,[4] it was almost exclusively an American operation.[5] Broad policy goals were formulated by the State–War–Navy Coordinating Committee (SWNCC) in Washington. The details of implementation were left to the GHQ/SCAP; they could be communicated to the Japanese Government either informally or more formally through memoranda (abbreviated SCAPINs) addressed to the Central Liaison Office of the Japanese Government.[6] Some actions were initiated by the Japanese bureaucracy, which maintained various committees to make policy proposals, though cabinet orders and legislative bills were subject to GHQ/SCAP approval prior to promulgation or submission to the Diet.[7]

At the beginning of the occupation, Japan's external trade and payments were placed under the strict control of the GHQ/SCAP; financial institutions were ordered to surrender all foreign exchange, precious metals, and foreign securities to be used for occupation purposes. In October 1945, occupation authorities allowed a minimal amount of imports "essential for the mainten-ance of the civil population" and for the protection of "American forces against starvation riots" (Kurihara 1946). These would be paid for by ap-proved exports, since the stated US policy was to "encourage the reliance by Japan on exports of goods with no military or security significance to procure the foreign exchange which she must have if she is to pay for the food, fertilizer, and other essential imports required to maintain a subsistence standard of living, and if the burden on the occupation forces is not to be increased."[8] Trade could only be conducted by the Japanese Government. For this purpose, a Foreign Trade Fund Special Account (*bōeki shikin tokubetsu kanjō*) was set up in March 1946, while a Board of Trade (*Bōeki-chō*) was established in April 1946. The GHQ/SCAP negotiated with foreign govern-ments to determine the contents, destinations, quantities, and prices of goods

---

[4] Formally, the Far Eastern Commission (FEC, established in February 1946) in Washington was to give directives to the US Government and the Allied Council for Japan (ACJ, established in April 1946) in Tokyo to advise the United States-appointed SCAP.

[5] First, the Americans began to implement post-surrender reforms well before the formal occupation apparatus was established in early 1946. Second, the United States had veto power over the decisions of the FEC and, in the absence of an FEC decision, had the authority to issue "interim" directives of its own to the Japanese Government. Third, the occupation forces were entirely made up of American troops, except for small British Commonwealth contingents. Fourth, the ACJ had only a nominal existence, to which the American occupation authorities paid little attention. A majority of its biweekly meetings are said to have lasted only for a few minutes (Martin 1948; Takemae 1983).

[6] Many of the original English-language documents cited in this and subsequent chapters are reprinted in MOF (1982).

[7] In August 1948, the requirements of prior approval were replaced, in the case of cabinet orders, by the submission of copies after they had been promulgated along with a certification that they were "in strict compliance with the directives of the Supreme Commander, the Constitution, and the laws of Japan" (Williams 1968).

[8] US Department of State, "Interim Plans for Control and Regulation of Japanese Trade with the United States," 1 March 1946. See US Department of State (1969), Appendix 38.

to be exported; the Board of Trade served as the sole authorized exporter in selling the goods to the GHQ/SCAP according to these terms. For imports, the Board of Trade purchased through the GHQ/SCAP goods procured by the US Army.

Japan ran a deficit in the trade and service account throughout the occupation period (see Table 1.1). A large part of the shortfall corresponded to official aid from the United States, which Japan received until the end of June 1951.[9] Initially, the aid was limited to a minimum necessary to prevent disease and social unrest,[10] but a new Government and Relief in Occupied Areas (GARIOA) program was created during US fiscal year (FY) 1947 (July 1946–June 1947) to allow the provision of food, petroleum, fertilizers, and medical supplies. Beginning with US FY 1949 (July 1948–June 1949), an Economic Rehabilitation in Occupied Areas (EROA) program was created to provide industrial raw materials and machinery needed for economic rehabilitation. US budgetary figures indicate that Japan received about $1.95 billion under GARIOA and EROA, including funds expended for administration (see Table 1.2).[11] Along with implementation of the Dodge Plan in April 1949, the GHQ/SCAP created a US Aid Counterpart Fund Special Account within Japan's national budget, into which the yen sales proceeds of goods provided under US assistance were paid (see Section 1.5.1 for additional details).[12]

This chapter reviews attempts implemented by Japanese and occupation authorities to stabilize inflation during 1945–50, paying particular attention to

[9] Because most of the assistance provided during the immediate postwar period was part of the military operations of the occupation forces, it is difficult to obtain the exact and separate figure for the amount of US funds received by Japan. According to one estimate, US aid provided to Japan during the postwar period amounted to about $2.3 billion—a small, though significant, sum when compared with the estimated aggregate total of $32.7 billion provided by the United States as foreign aid during the period July 1945–December 1951; of this total, Europe claimed $25.2 billion, including Marshall aid (MOF 1952).

[10] In fact, until the spring of 1946, virtually no food was provided to Japan under the Civilian Supply Program (CSP) of the US Army (MOF 1976b).

[11] The terms of US assistance to Japan were ambiguous. At the time of the congressional hearings on GARIOA appropriations in the spring of 1946, US authorities testified that US budgetary expenditures for Japan would become Japan's liabilities. This position was communicated to the Japanese Government in a GHQ/SCAP memorandum of July 1946, stating that the terms of repayment would be specified at a later date (Shōji Keizai Kenkyūkai 1963). An implicit understanding thus emerged, on both sides, that at least part of the funds provided under US assistance would become liabilities for Japan. As early as in October 1952, the US Government approached the Japanese counterpart to initiate a formal negotiation on the repayment of Japanese obligations under GARIOA and EROA. After a series of negotiations and a substantial lapse of time, it was agreed in 1962 that, of the total $1.95 billion (the Japanese figure on the receipt side was $1.8 billion) provided to Japan in economic assistance, $490 million would be Japan's liabilities. Over the fifteen-year period commencing in 1963, Japan paid about $580 million to the United States, including principal and interest.

[12] During the three-year period from April 1949 to March 1952, a total of $845 million (or ¥304.2 billion) was paid into the Counterpart Fund Special Account, which was used to finance industrial investment projects (MOF 1952).

Table 1.1. Japan's balance of payments, 1946–51 (in millions of US dollars)

	1946	1947	1948	1949	1950	1951
Exports	65.3	181.6	262.3	533.3	920.3	1,353.5
Imports	303.3	449.0	546.6	728.1	885.9	1,645.3
Trade balance	−238.0	−267.4	−284.3	−194.8	34.4	−291.8
Net service	−34.6	−91.0	−121.3	−160.2	−50.2	−173.9
Balance on trade and services	−272.6	−358.4	−405.6	−355.0	−15.8	−465.7
Military receipts	—	—	18.8	48.6	62.6	624.2
Private grants	1.6	0.4	0.6	4.0	69.1	15.8
Private capital	—	—	—	—	5.4	34.1
Errors and omissions	15.0	13.6	26.9	−53.6	49.1	8.3
Financing needs	−256.0	−344.4	−359.3	−356.0	170.4	216.7
Government grants and borrowing	197.8	409.9	488.5	553.9	263.9	152.6
Other financial flows	72.9	−49.0	−80.6	−34.4	−138.5	−6.6
Change in foreign exchange reserves	14.7	16.5	48.6	163.5	295.8	362.7

Source: MOF (1976b)

Table 1.2. United States assistance to Japan under GARIOA and EROA, fiscal years 1946–51[a] (in millions of US dollars)

	GARIOA	EROA	Administration	Total
1946	92.6	—	—	92.6
1947	287.3	—	12.7	300.0
1948	351.4	—	19.9	371.3
1949	426.2	97.5	25.5	549.2
1950	237.4	188.0	19.2	444.6
1951	182.6	—	15.0	197.6
Total	1,577.5	285.5	92.3	1,955.3

[a] US fiscal years

Abbreviations: GARIOA= Government and Relief in Occupied Areas; EROA= Economic Rehabilitation in Occupied Areas

Source: MOF (1952)

how, as the culmination of these efforts, a single exchange rate was established for the yen at ¥360 per US dollar. As much of the country's productive capital had been destroyed during the war, and with a critical shortage of imported raw materials, the period saw high and sustained inflation, which was exacerbated by the central bank financing of government spending. Inflation needed to be stabilized, price and other domestic economic controls eased substantially, and a market exchange rate established, before private-sector trade could be normalized. The successful economic stabilization of early 1949 eventually paved the way for the partial transfer of foreign exchange authority to the Japanese Government in November 1949 and the full resumption of private-sector exports and imports in December 1949 and January 1950, respectively.

Although the focus of this chapter is necessarily placed on measures related to macroeconomic stabilization, it is well to remember that these actions took place against the background of the occupation's comprehensive social, political, and economic reform agenda. Most notably, a major political reform was accomplished by the enactment in May 1947 of a new constitution, which established universal suffrage and parliamentary democracy. In the economic realm, the occupation, among other things, sought to (1) dissolve large business conglomerates known as the *zaibatsu*;[13] (2) abolish tenant farming by limiting large agricultural land holdings; and (3) democratize industrial relations by protecting the rights of workers (Nakamura 1986; Flath 2014). With what historians call the "reverse course" in American policy toward Japan, however, the reform orientation of the occupation began to be scaled down and its focus shifted to economic reconstruction.[14]

The rest of the chapter begins by reviewing features of Japan's postwar inflation, including the government-directed system of trade and payments, which became an important cause of inflationary finance. This is followed by an extended discussion of the series of unsuccessful stabilization measures authorities implemented from early 1946 to mid 1948. The chapter then considers how the reverse course in American policy toward the occupation of Japan led to a new approach to stabilization and discusses the origins, contents, and implementation of the Dodge Plan of early 1949. The chapter concludes by discussing the Dodge Plan as exchange rate-based stabilization—in which the establishment of a fixed exchange rate served as a nominal anchor—and by highlighting its economic features in light of recent literature.

1.2. FEATURES OF POSTWAR INFLATION

1.2.1. Real, Monetary, and Price Developments

During World War II, Japan lost an estimated ¥134 billion (about $9 billion, if converted at the initial military rate of ¥15 per US dollar established in September 1945) in national wealth,[15] which amounted to about 41.5 percent of the total. As a result of damage to the country's productive capacity,

[13] The policy, prepared well ahead of Japan's surrender in August 1945, was based on the perception widely held by Americans that the *zaibatsu* were vestiges of feudalism that had somehow contributed to Japan's military aggression (Hadley 1970; Flath 2014).

[14] The scope of *zaibatsu* dissolution was cut back, agricultural land reform became protracted, and tolerance towards the labor movement waned. In other areas, banking sector reform never really took off (Tsutsui 1988).

[15] The military rate, set at ¥15 per US dollar on 10 September 1945, was raised over time. For example, it was ¥50 in March 1947 and ¥270 in July 1948.

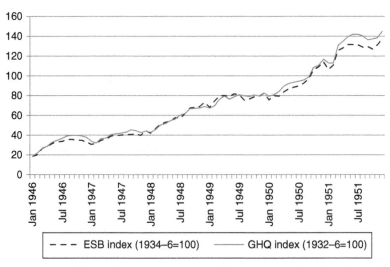

Figure 1.1. Manufacturing and mining production in Japan, relative to prewar level, January 1946–December 1951

Abbreviations: ESB=Economic Stabilization Board; GHQ=General Headquarters (of the Supreme Commander for the Allied Powers)
Source: ESB (1952)

cessation of raw material imports, and uncertainty surrounding the confiscation of industrial property for reparation, manufacturing production in the immediate postwar period stood at less than 20 percent of the prewar level (see Figure 1.1). Inflation, in part a natural consequence of the relaxation of wartime economic controls, was also fueled by expansionary monetary and fiscal policies. From August to November 1945, fiscal outlays for the repatriation of military personnel, severance payments for those on military duty, and payments for war goods under contract amounted to over ¥14 billion. From October 1945 through early 1946, commercial bank loans expanded to cover the costs of terminating production for military use. As a significant amount of bank deposits were withdrawn, the Bank of Japan (BOJ) extended credit to private financial institutions. The balance of BOJ notes increased by more than 40 percent from the end of September 1945 to the end of January 1946, while the narrow money supply (M1) rose by more than 10 percent during the same period (see Figure 1.2). Anticipating the imposition of a heavy property tax, moreover, those who held financial assets attempted to exchange them for goods.

Initially, occupation authorities stood aloof, stating that the "plight of Japan [was] the direct outcome of its own behavior, and the Allies [would] not undertake the burden of repairing the damage."[16] In November 1945, they

---

[16] "United States Initial Post-Surrender Policy for Japan," US Department of State (1969), Appendix 13.

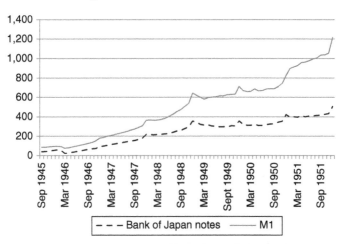

Figure 1.2. Monetary aggregates in Japan, September 1945–December 1951 (in billions of yen)

Source: Bank of Japan

prohibited any further government borrowing without permission; they ordered the Japanese Government to suspend all payments for military pensions and war-settlement claims.[17] The 24 November 1945 SCAP memorandum ordered any payment for claims arising from the "production or supply of war materials, from war damage or from the construction or conversion of war plants" to be suspended and instructed any claimant who had been paid since 15 August 1945 to redeposit the amount in a blocked account at the central bank. On the same day, a separate memorandum ordered the Japanese Government to terminate no later than 1 February 1946 "all payments . . . of any public or private pensions or other emoluments or benefits of any kind granted or conferred to any person" for war-related activities. These directives were given as much to "demonstrate to all Japanese that war is financially unprofitable" as out of concern for the inflationary consequences of government expenditure. But Washington was becoming alarmed by the situation and in November 1945 advised the SCAP that inflation would "substantially retard the accomplishment of the ultimate objectives of the occupation."[18]

Different pictures of Japan's postwar inflation experience emerge depending on whether the price level is measured by official or free/black-market prices (see Figure 1.3). According to the BOJ's wholesale price index, the price level rose from 346.6 in September 1945 to 20,825.1 in December 1948 (the last

---

[17] The Japanese Government had committed itself to pay some ¥56 billion in indemnity to war industries, insurance companies, and individuals (Kurihara 1946).

[18] Joint Chiefs of Staff 1380/15, transmitted to the SCAP on 3 November 1945, as referred to in Tsutsui (1988), p. 24. See also Kurihara (1946).

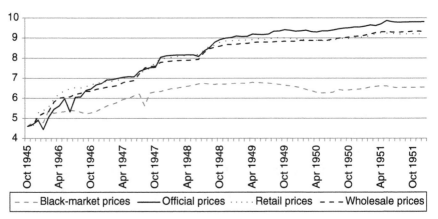

Figure 1.3. Monthly prices in Japan, October 1945–December 1951 (October 1945=100; expressed on logarithmic scale)

Source: ESB (1952)

month for which the consistent series are available), indicating a sixty-fold increase over three years and three months (10.5 percent per month or 126 percent per year if continuously compounded). Likewise, the BOJ's retail price index rose from 477.7 in September 1945 to the first peak of 37,386.9 in May 1949, representing a seventy-eight-fold increase over three years and nine months (9.7 percent per month or 116 percent per year). The index of official consumption goods prices rose from 3.21 in October 1945 to 315.38 in April 1949 when inflation began to subside, representing a ninety-eight-fold increase over three years and six months (10.9 percent per month or 131 percent per year). Regardless of the index used, the official prices rose at about 10 percent monthly or 116–31 percent annually.

In contrast, inflation measured by free or black-market prices was more modest: the index rose by about 8 times in three years and seven months, from September 1945 to April 1949. This represented a monthly increase of about 5 percent and a compounded annual increase of about 60 percent. The level of free-market prices was high to begin with, so stabilization involved aligning official with free-market prices, which had initially been about 30–40 times higher (see Figure 1.4). To the extent that official prices were not set for all goods and that the system of controlled prices was periodically adjusted upward, the use of official prices would seem to give an imperfect gauge of actual inflation. It even becomes problematic when examining the successful stabilization program of 1949, in which the price controls were lifted. While the Japanese economy was successfully stabilized during this period, the index of official consumption goods prices and the BOJ's wholesale price index actually rose—albeit slowly—by 20 percent and 10 percent, respectively, during the one-year period from June 1949 to June 1950. There was no

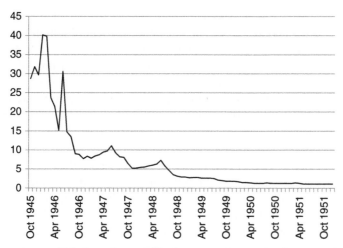

Figure 1.4. Ratio of black-market to official prices in Japan, October 1945–December 1951

Source: ESB (1952)

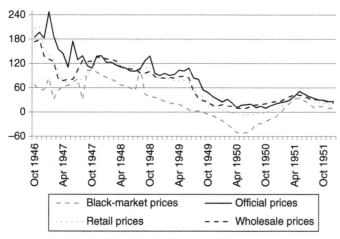

Figure 1.5. Monthly inflation in Japan, October 1946–December 1951 (in year-on-year logarithmic changes)

Source: ESB (1952)

deflation during the so-called deflationary period, if measured by official prices (see Figure 1.5).

With an average annual rate of 60–131 percent (depending on the index), Japan's postwar inflation does not qualify as a hyperinflation according to the standards set by the classical work of Cagan (1956), whose definition requires a sustained monthly rise in the price level of more than

50 percent.[19] Nor was it especially high relative to that of some countries during the same period. For example, China experienced a monthly increase in the wholesale price index of 78 percent from September 1945 to May 1949, while the price index rose by 3×10^{25} times in Hungary from July 1945 to August 1946 (Bomberger and Makinen 1983; Hu 1971). Even so, Japan's postwar inflation (especially if measured in official prices) was certainly "very high" inflation by the standards of Fischer et al. (2002), something only twenty-five countries experienced during 1960–96.[20] On a year-on-year basis, monthly inflation in official consumption goods prices never fell below 80 percent per annum from September 1946 to August 1949.

Japan's postwar experience with inflation was comparable to that of France and Italy after the end of World War II. Casella and Eichengreen (1993) describe the postwar inflations of France and Italy as the result of a distributional war of attrition between recipients of labor income and recipients of profits, interest, and rents. As these governments increased public-sector pay, provided public services at low costs, and gave subsidies to enterprises, the fiscal balance turned into deficit, especially when different interest groups all resisted higher taxes. Because the deficit was financed by central bank borrowing, inflation was the outcome. A similar characterization can be applied to Japan's postwar inflation. The Japanese Government too was unable to make distributional decisions during the immediate postwar period, thus resorting to easy central bank financing of pork-barrel spending. Casella and Eichengreen (1993) further argue that inflation in Europe came to a halt when the Marshall Plan reduced the magnitude of the concessions required from domestic interest groups. Likewise, the promise of US aid became one of the key ingredients of Japan's successful stabilization in early 1949.

1.2.2. Government Trade as a Source of Inflation

As it turns out, the way government-directed trade was set up—implicitly involving multiple exchange rates with subsidies for both exports and imports—became an important cause of inflationary finance. Given the large US-financed trade deficit, the system of government trade may seem to suggest that the Japanese Government sold more to the public than it purchased from them, thus earning profits on foreign trade. But this was not the case. On the

---

[19] To be precise, Cagan (1956) defines *hyperinflation* as an event that begins in the month inflation first exceeds 50 percent (per month) and ends in the month before the inflation rate drops below 50 percent (per month) for at least a year. Thus, the average monthly rate of inflation can be less than 50 percent.

[20] Fischer et al. (2002) define "very high" inflation as an episode that begins when the twelve-month inflation rate rises above 100 percent and ends with the first month before the twelve-month inflation rate falls below 100 percent and stays in that range for at least twelve months.

one hand, trade settlement in foreign exchange was made on the SCAP's special account, the details of which were not disclosed to the Japanese side (Ito 2009). On the other hand, domestic prices at which the Board of Trade sold and purchased goods to and from the GHQ/SCAP were independent of foreign prices at which the GHQ/SCAP (or the US Government) purchased or sold them abroad. Thus, there was no correspondence between the Foreign Trade Fund Special Account of the Japanese Government and the SCAP's special account for Japanese trade.

The delinking of the Foreign Trade Fund Special Account from the SCAP account meant that, ex post, Japanese trade entailed different exchange rates depending on the destination or source, exports or imports, and type of goods. For example, the overall (average) conversion rate in 1946 was ¥22.38 per US dollar for exports and ¥11.74 for imports; in 1948 it was ¥170.75 and ¥67.19, respectively (see Table 1.3). The conversion rate differed widely, depending on the commodity. For example, it ranged from about ¥109 to ¥1,078 for exports and from ¥9 to ¥1,107 for imports in 1948 in a representative sample of commodities (see Table 1.4). These were nothing but ex-post accounting rates, with little economic role. Even so, it is noticeable that, in line with the progressing inflation, the conversion rates depreciated over time for both exports and imports.

Given the structure of domestic prices, conversion rates were generally lower (the yen was more appreciated) for imports than for exports. Essentially, this amounted to implicit subsidies for both exporters and importers. To understand the implications of this, consider a hypothetical case of Japanese trade in which the value of imports ($1,000) exceeds the value of exports ($500) and the ex-post accounting rates are ¥400 and ¥100 per dollar for exports and imports, respectively; no transactions costs are assumed (see Table 1.5). In this example, the balance of trade deficit of $500 represents a net transfer of resources from the United States to Japan, but there is no counterpart within Japan. The GHQ/SCAP simply instructs the Japanese Government (Board of Trade) to procure for export a certain quantity of certain goods, while it delivers a certain amount of imports to the Board of

Table 1.3. Japanese trade and average yen–dollar conversion rates, 1946–8 (in millions of currency units; yen per US dollar)

	Exports			Imports		
	$ (1)	¥ (2)	(2)/(1)	$ (3)	¥ (4)	(4)/(3)
1946	129.4	2,896	22.38	305.6	3,587	11.74
1947	172.6	9,151	53.02	526.1	24,392	46.36
1948[a]	77.4	13,216	170.75	348.9	23,442	67.19

[a] January–June only

Sources: Economic Stabilization Board and Ministry of Finance, as summarized by Ito (2009), Table 1–9

Table 1.4. Yen–dollar conversion rates for selected exports and imports (yen per US dollar)

Exports (September 1948)		Imports (August 1948)	
Automobiles	506	Acetone	1,107
Automobile tires	482	Asphalt	255
Binoculars	490	Barley	118
Cameras	425	Bauxite	147
Caustic soda	206	Cotton (Egypt)	56
Cellophane	250	Cotton (India)	66
Cotton fabrics	227	Cotton (United States)	77
Cultured pearls	199	Iron ore	117
Electric motors	160	Lead	125
Electron tubes	452	Nickel	277
Fountain pens	448	Oil, diesel	370
Frozen tuna	374	Oil, gasoline	438
Harmonicas	388	Oil, kerosene	447
Industrial rubber belts	230	Paper pulp	154
Mercury	685	Rice	82
Microscopes	109	Rubber, crude	112
Photographic paper	532	Rubber, scrap	24
Ping pong balls	638	Scrap leather	9
Raw silk	376	Soybean	64
Sewing machines	422	Soybean flour	27
Sheet glass	668	Sugar, raw	102
Spinning machines	298	Sugar, refined	228
Storage batteries	365	Tin	272
X-ray film	1,078	Wheat	133
Zinc, electrowon	229	Wool	43

Source: Keizai Dōyūkai (1948), Tables 1 and 2

Table 1.5. Simplified representation of system of Japanese exports and imports under American occupation

	Foreign markets	GHQ/SCAP	Hypothetical accounting (exchange) rates	Board of Trade (Foreign Trade Fund Special Account)	Domestic markets
Hypothetical exports	$500	Procurement in kind	400 yen/dollar	Payments: ¥200,000	Receipts: ¥200,000
Hypothetical imports	$1,000	Delivery in kind	100 yen/dollar	Receipts: ¥100,000	Payments: ¥100,000
Balance	−$500	Assistance to Japan: $500	n.a.	−¥100,000	¥100,000

Abbreviation: GHQ/SCAP=General Headquarters of the Supreme Commander for the Allied Powers

Trade for distribution to the public, with no role for prices. What subsequently takes place in the domestic market has no link to the balance of trade.

Now, given the assumed accounting rates, the Board of Trade executes the order of the GHQ/SCAP by procuring goods for export by paying ¥200,000 while receiving ¥100,000 for selling the imported goods on the market. This means a deficit of ¥100,000 in the Foreign Trade Fund Special Account. As a counterpart of this, the Japanese public receives ¥200,000 and pays ¥100,000, for a profit of ¥100,000. The curious nature of this system becomes clear: even though there is a deficit in the external trade balance, the private sector earns a net profit. Needless to say, this is made possible by the corresponding deficit in the government account. A system of multiple exchange rates of this type necessarily involves subsidies. The American and Japanese authorities soon came to recognize that such a system could be inflationary and to believe that economic stabilization needed not only to rationalize domestic prices at stable levels but also to establish a single exchange rate and ultimately remove the government from the system.

1.3. FAILED ATTEMPTS AT STABILIZATION

As inflation picked up, the public began to exchange cash for goods. A widening differential between black-market and official prices emerged, making the official prices all but irrelevant for ordinary transactions. In response, on 18 September 1945, the Japanese Government sought to lift price controls on fresh foodstuffs in order to stimulate food supply but failed to receive concurrence from occupation authorities, who demanded that strict price controls continue. The shortage of foods and other necessities remained serious. On 3 October, the government tried again, announcing that it intended to terminate the rationing of all necessities, except for certain emergency goods, at official prices. This time, the GHQ/SCAP concurred, but only with respect to fresh foodstuffs; the price controls were to be tightened further with respect to other basic necessities. The rationing of fresh foodstuffs at controlled prices was terminated on 17 November, resulting in an increase of several times the previous price. The Japanese Government in late 1945 began to think seriously about controlling inflation, but no specific policy measures were taken until early 1946.

For the most part, the government's response during 1946–8 was to devise or intensify controls, as it had done during the wartime years. GHQ/SCAP officials appeared to be inclined to do the same. Many of them were New Deal reformers who believed in the virtue of government intervention; some were military officers with little prior knowledge of economics. The proclivity toward controls was reinforced in late 1946 when the wartime Office of

Price Administration (OPA) in Washington closed and a substantial number of its former economists and other officials joined the GHQ/SCAP. Bronfenbrenner (1975)—by referring to Galbraith (1946), who was OPA Deputy Administrator for Price Control during 1941-3—characterizes their recipe for stabilizing the price level as controlling "those individual prices most important in the ordinary man's market basket." This approach had considerable support in Japan, from a wide spectrum of political views.[21]

1.3.1. First Emergency Measures

On 16 February 1946, the Japanese Government announced the first of a series of anti-inflationary policy packages, known as "economic crisis emergency measures (*keizai kiki kinkyū taisaku*)." The package, implemented the next day, included a number of measures dealing also with finance and production, but its central piece was the "financial emergency measure ordinance (*kinyū kinkyū sochi rei*)." By this ordinance, as of 17 February 1946 (Sunday), all existing deposits were frozen. On 2 March (Saturday), old currency notes ceased to be legal tender and were replaced by new yen; depositors were required to convert their deposits into the new currency between 25 February and 7 March.[22] Moreover, regular workers were allowed to be paid in cash only up to ¥500 per month (considered to be the monthly cost of living for a standard household), beyond which salaries needed to be paid into frozen bank accounts. The head of a household was in principle allowed to withdraw only as much as ¥300 per month from the frozen accounts, with each dependent allowed to take out an additional ¥100 (from 30 March, everyone was uniformly permitted to withdraw only as much as ¥100).

The "price control ordinance (*bukka tōsei rei*)" of 3 March 1946 stipulated that a new system of price controls would be implemented the next day. The system, based on the monthly allowance of ¥500 for a standard household, set the official prices for grains, vegetables, and fresh fish in relation to the procurement price of ¥300 and the resale price of ¥250 for a *koku* (about 180 liters) of rice; it set the consumer prices of coal and pig iron, respectively, at ¥150 and ¥1,800 per ton. The idea was to keep the overall price level at 8 times the 1939 level, which meant that the prices of fresh foodstuffs and sundry household items were reduced to a third and a half of the prevailing levels. The unique feature of this system, compared to the previous efforts, was that it set a *structure* of prices rather than individual prices isolated from each other. The prices of goods that were not part of this structure, however, were

---

[21] In contrast, the business community back in the United States criticized the initial program of the GHQ/SCAP as "a pilot plant for a planned economy" (Bronfenbrenner 1975).

[22] The currency conversion resembled the Belgian monetary reforms of 1944 (Tsutsui 1988).

allowed to be set freely (whereas the past control orders had typically disallowed an increase in the price of any commodity).

At the same time, the government set out to establish an Economic Stabilization Board (ESB) and a Price Board as the planning and executing arms of the emergency measures (they would not actually become operational until 12 August).[23] These two agencies would be closely coordinated, with some officials holding joint appointments. Although the ESB would be the decision-making body for the price-control administration, actual approval and enforcement authority would be exercised by the Price Board through its local offices in eight major cities throughout the country. To ensure democratic accountability, economic stabilization councils would be established at the national and local levels, with representatives of the public. The councils were formed to promote public cooperation with the price-control directives, but they could also make recommendations to the government.

As a result of the emergency measures of February and March 1946, the outstanding balance of BOJ notes declined from ¥58.6 billion at the end of January to ¥23.3 billion at the end of March; the exchange of old yen for new yen itself had caused the balance of notes in circulation to decline from ¥61.8 billion on 18 February to ¥15.2 billion on 12 March (MOF 1976a). In contrast, the amount of current bank deposits increased from ¥38.5 billion to ¥54.6 billion over the same two-month period. But the impact was short-lived. From April, the balance of BOJ notes began to rise again and in September surpassed the previous peak (recorded in January). It continued to expand at the annual rate of 40 percent or more every month from then on until February 1949.

1.3.2. Fiscal Expansion Under Ishibashi

In May 1946, Shigeru Yoshida formed his first cabinet as prime minister, with Tanzan Ishibashi, a self-claimed Keynesian, as finance minister. Believing that the primary cause of inflation was the shortage of goods, Ishibashi argued that fiscal policy should be expanded to stimulate aggregate demand and that one did not need to worry about inflation as long as, with underemployed resources, production was increasing (Bronfenbrenner 1950). Thus, the FY 1946 budget saw a large increase in outlays, especially price subsidies to cover the difference between production costs and official prices. On 11 June, the cabinet made a decision to fundamentally revise the price controls of 2 March 1946; it further agreed that the official prices would be revised monthly

---

[23] According to the occupation authorities, Finance Minister Tanzan Ishibashi's opposition delayed the start of the ESB and the Price Board until mid August 1946. Memorandum prepared by Courtney Whitney, Chief of the SCAP Government Section, dated 1 May 1947, as found in Masuda (1998a).

thereafter. From June, the strict financial controls imposed in March were eased progressively; for example, people were authorized to use frozen deposits to make tax payments.[24] Further financial easing took place through the active promotion of bank lending.

On 1 August 1946, a Reconstruction Finance Department was established within the government-owned Industrial Bank of Japan. Given charge of the government's special account called the Reconstruction Finance Fund Special Account (*fukkō kinyu shikin tokubetsu kaikei*), it extended loans amounting to more than ¥4.1 billion during the next six months, until the Reconstruction Finance Bank (RFB, *Fukkō Kinyū Kinko*) was established in January 1947 and took over the government account. On 1 October 1946, the Temporary Goods Demand and Supply Adjustment Law took effect, which replaced the now-defunct National Total Mobilization Law of 1938 and opened the way for the government during peacetime to control a wide range of economic activities based on democratic principles, including government restrictions on the use of goods in short supply.

Economic policymaking was heavily influenced by Marxian economics, especially the glorified views of Soviet-style central planning that permeated the thinking of the national bureaucracy. Drawing on Karl Marx's *Das Kapital*,[25] economist Hiromi Arisawa developed the idea of the priority production system (*keisha seisan hōshiki*) in which Japan's scarce productive resources would be allocated on a priority basis to essential industrial goods, such as coal and steel (Okamura et al. 2009; also Kosai 1988). On 24 December 1946, the government put this idea into practice and, on 7 January 1947, gave priority to the basic industries in the allocation of credit. On 25 January 1947, the RFB began operation, providing priority-directed lending to key industries. In this system, the ESB formulated a quarterly production plan, upon which credit was allocated according to the strategic importance of each industry. As might be expected, the resulting allocation of resources totally lacked economic efficiency. The production of coal, steel, and other so-called "stabilization belt" goods (e.g.,

---

[24] Subsequently, the financial emergency measure ordinance was revised seven times and implementation rules changed an additional twenty-four times. For example, on 24 January 1947, the cash payment limit for monthly salaries was raised from ¥500 to ¥700; on 1 May 1947, the monthly cash limit for salary payment was removed while the monthly withdrawal limit was uniformly raised to ¥150 per person; on 21 July 1948, the deposit freeze was removed. Although the financial emergency measure ordinance would remain in force as a legal basis for financial control until July 1963, July 1948 marked its effective end as an anti-inflationary measure. See MOF (1976a).

[25] Marx, in the second volume of his work, postulates that an economy consists of two sectors: Department I to produce the means of production (capital goods) and Department II to produce the means of living (consumer goods). The view that Arisawa was influenced by Marx comes from economist Ryutaro Komiya, as quoted in Okamura et al. (2009). Kosai (1988) posits that the logic of priority production resembles the Ricardo effect of the Austrian school.

fertilizer, soda, and gas) expanded only at very high costs, causing government subsidies to increase.

RFB lending was extensive, with the balance amounting to nearly 25 percent of all loans at the end of March 1949. It was in part conceived as a way to mitigate the adverse impact of the SCAP-directed termination of war indemnity payments.[26] In May 1946, the GHQ/SCAP, considering the Japanese response to its November 1945 memorandum on the "elimination of war profits" totally inadequate, summoned Ishibashi and explained to him the American plan for "an extraordinary tax program." The tax program involved a capital levy to be applied to individuals owning assets worth more than ¥100,000 as of 3 March 1946 (when all financial assets were declared)[27] and a war indemnity tax to be applied to industries' war indemnity claims at 100 percent.[28] These measures were designed not only to reduce outstanding internal state obligations arising from the war but also to correct the excessive concentration of wealth and thereby to help strengthen democracy in Japan. The occupation authorities, however, viewed Ishibashi as uncooperative in delaying implementation of the tax program, targeted initially for the early summer of 1946.[29]

The GHQ/SCAP correctly regarded the RFB as a major obstacle to economic stabilization. Because the funding almost entirely came from the central bank, the monetary base expanded rapidly.[30] The occupation authorities felt that Ishibashi, delaying implementation of the extraordinary tax program, had

---

[26] In 1949, Joseph Dodge, financial advisor to the GHQ/SCAP, described the RFB as "a device to return to industry losses caused by cancellation of war indemnity claims on Government . . . Industry inclined to assume loans are gifts." Cable to the Department of the Army, 19 February 1949, quoted in Tsutsui (1988), p. 98.

[27] The capital levy was targeted at the 2–3 percent strata of Japanese society, with rates ranging from 10 percent on the first ¥10,000 of taxable wealth up to 90 percent on the excess above ¥15 million. Taxable individuals were to file returns on or before 15 February 1947, with payment due by 15 March 1947 (Shavell 1948). Corporations were exempted.

[28] By the war's end, the government faced a large debt of ¥80.9 billion, arising from war-damage insurance, contract termination, indemnities for government-ordered plant expansions, depreciation and obsolescence guaranties, and other claims generally classified as "war indemnities," as well as ¥24.8 billion of claims from private banks for industrial loans in default, all of which had been guaranteed by the government. With exemptions ranging between ¥20,000–50,000, a 100 percent tax was imposed at the source, which amounted to cancellation. The tax not only relieved the government of unpaid war obligations but also recaptured approximately ¥40 billion of claims that had been paid out between the war's end and the date of tax enforcement on 30 October 1946 (Shavell 1948).

[29] The War Indemnity Special Measure Law was enacted on 18 October 1946 and the Capital Levy Law on 11 November 1946. In nominal terms, the capital levy was a success. About 80 percent of the anticipated yield was declared by taxpayers' original assessment (Shavell 1948). Occupation authorities, however, thought that the delay (with ultimate enactment in the fall and collection in March 1947) had diminished the real value of the revenue through inflation and benefited the interests of large industrial groups.

[30] RFB borrowing would amount to more than 50 percent of the increase in BOJ notes during FY 1947–8 (MOF 1992, pp. 220, 270).

impeded stabilization of the Japanese economy and obstructed the achievement of "occupation economic objectives" and that this was motivated by "his sympathy for the interests of large industrial groups who stand to profit by inflation."[31] The GHQ/SCAP pressed Ishibashi to curtail nonessential bank loans throughout 1946, but it was not until the middle of January 1947 that he took a reluctant step to do so.[32] But reconstruction financing was not the only thing Ishibashi promoted to counter the impact of the extraordinary tax program. The Japanese Government also revised the financial emergency measure ordinance (11 August 1946), set up a new rediscounting facility at the BOJ for industrial and agricultural bills (30 August), and canceled the planned corporate property tax (30 October). In May 1947, Ishibashi was removed from public office by the occupation authorities for pursuing economic policies they considered to be out of harmony with the objectives of the occupation.[33]

1.3.3. Second Emergency Measures

Despite the priority scheme, production of steel and coal fell short of target, while other industries contracted, especially in the transportation and electric power sectors. According to the GHQ index, industrial production declined by more than 7 percent (the ESB index shows little change) from November 1946 to March 1947 (see Figure 1.1); on a year-on-year basis, the growth of production, starting from the initial pickup from the level of early 1946, decelerated throughout 1947 (see Figure 1.6). The adverse impact of financial disintermediation resulting from inflationary expectations may have offset

---

[31] A SCAP memo, dated 1 May 1947, as found in Masuda (1998a). In reality, it was small business owners who disproportionately benefited from inflation and the associated black-market activities (Bronfenbrenner 1955).

[32] A SCAP memo, dated 1 May 1947, as found in Masuda (1998a).

[33] As an official reason, the occupation authorities claimed that Ishibashi, as the editor and president of the *Oriental Economist*, had "supported military and economic imperialism in Asia, advocated Japan's adherence to the Axis, fostered belief in the inevitability of war with the Western Powers, justified suppression of trade unionism and urged the imposition of totalitarian controls over the Japanese people" (SCAP memo, dated 7 May 1948, as found in Masuda (1998a)). This was a concocted excuse that contradicted the conclusion of the Japanese Government screening committee, which the GHQ/SCAP disapproved. Because the *Oriental Economist* was one of the few remaining voices of reason and liberalism in wartime Japan, the GHQ/SCAP had wholeheartedly allowed publication to resume as early as October 1945. The GHQ/SCAP had attempted to remove Ishibashi from public office beginning in June 1946 when officials saw him display "in his first few weeks in office . . . an underlying lack of harmony with known policies of the Supreme Commander on financial and economic problems under the occupation" (SCAP/Government Section memo, dated 26 June 1946). This plan was not put into action immediately to avoid undermining the newly formed cabinet of Prime Minister Yoshida. By May 1947, Yoshida may have accepted the expulsion of Ishibashi, viewing his rising political influence as a personal threat (Masuda 1998b).

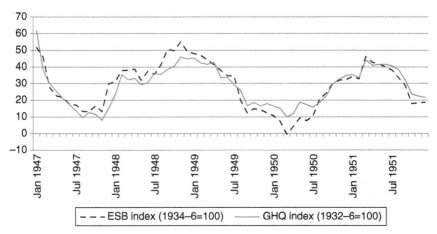

Figure 1.6. Growth in manufacturing and mining production in Japan, January 1947–December 1951 (in year-on-year logarithmic changes)

Abbreviations: ESB=Economic Stabilization Board; GHQ=General Headquarters (of the Supreme Commander for the Allied Powers)

Source: ESB (1952)

any positive impact of priority credit allocation on the key industries (Kasuya 1995). Under these circumstances, in March 1947, the GHQ/SCAP instructed the Japanese Government to immediately adopt strong and comprehensive economic and financial measures to overcome the economic crisis. In response, the government strengthened the role of the ESB, but specific measures needed to wait until the new coalition government of socialist Tetsu Katayama was formed on 1 June, after the general elections of April. On 11 June 1947, immediately after taking office, the Katayama cabinet declared that it would implement "emergency economic measures (*kinkyū keizai taisaku*)" to do more of the same things.

As the central pillar of the new control regime, a revised system of official prices was announced in several stages from 5 July through the end of September, with broad endorsement from the GHQ/SCAP. The new system set the national average industrial wage at ¥1,800 (27.8 times the average for 1934–6). Prices of basic goods were to be stabilized within a "corridor" determined in relation to prewar prices, with 60 and 65 times the 1934–6 average as the lower and upper bounds, respectively. Price subsidies were to be paid for basic goods whose prices would otherwise exceed the upper bound (¥12 billion was projected). Prices of manufacturing and mining products were set according to costs, while agricultural prices were set to maintain parity with the prices of nonagricultural goods in a typical consumption basket of agricultural households (called the parity method). Simply put, the plan was to maintain the prices of essential goods and the industrial wage below 65 and 28 times the prewar levels, respectively, by providing subsidies to firms to cover the losses if necessary.

The revision entailed an upward adjustment in official prices of about 2.3 times, which caused a portion of the goods previously diverted to black markets to return to official channels. While this package had the same control orientation of the first package, it stated the government's intention to promote exports and to achieve fiscal soundness, including by strengthening tax collection and taxing those who had profited from inflation and black-market activities. In July 1947, the Ministry of Finance (MOF) tightened controls on bank loans, stipulating that a ceiling would be set on the amount of loans each financial institution could extend, subject to certain exceptions (e.g., purchases of national or local government bonds and RFB debentures). Even so, black-market prices started rising again after a decline in August (see Figures 1.3 and 1.5). As the divergence widened between production costs and official prices, moreover, the amount of price subsidies and BOJ-funded RFB loans soared, which weakened the anti-inflationary impact of the package. With production stagnant and inflation unchecked, the Katayama cabinet was forced to resign in February 1948.

1.3.4. Revising the Price Structure

In June 1948, the new cabinet of Prime Minister Hitoshi Ashida set out to revise the structure of official prices in connection with the preparation of the FY 1948 budget, which had been much delayed by a political crisis. The revision followed the price-setting methodology of July 1947 and included the following provisions: (1) price subsidies of ¥51.5 billion (later raised by ¥11 billion) would be paid for the fourteen most important goods through the end of FY 1948 in order to contain the rise in official prices; (2) the national average industrial wage would be set at ¥3,700, with the price stability corridor at 110 times the 1934–6 average; (3) prices of manufacturing and mining products would be set according to production costs, while the parity method would be used to determine agricultural prices; and (4) as a result, the rise in prices of basic goods would be kept to 70 percent and the rise in prices of consumption goods to about 80 percent. The prices of ninety goods were announced on 22 June, 30 June, and 9 July to take effect on 10 July; those of the remaining goods were announced on 10 July to take effect the following day.

As an important feature of this package, the overall system of control was refined. The number of disaggregated commodity categories increased from 4,131 to 62,370; at the most aggregated level, the number increased from 69 before the package to 1,942 after the package (Tōyō Keizai Shinpōsha 1954). The revised price structure did narrow the gap between official and black-market prices (see Figure 1.4), with a significant moderation of black-market inflation. Without a supporting measure to ensure that the gap remained small, however, this may have been due to the significant recovery of production during 1948: manufacturing and mining production began to pick up in early 1948, rising from 40 percent to about 70 percent of the prewar level by the end of the year (see Figures 1.1 and 1.6).

Inflation remained high, though somewhat moderating. On a year-on-year basis, monthly inflation never fell below 100 percent in official prices and 30 percent (with a temporary surge to 108 percent in August) in black-market prices through late 1948 (see Figure 1.5). The government was compelled to raise the average industrial wage through arbitration in the fall and to raise the prices of staples by 1.3 times in January 1949. This effectively meant the end of the last in a series of attempts to stabilize inflation by means of price controls. This period saw some easing of the control apparatus, if not the price controls themselves. The Price Board in August removed reporting requirements from a number of goods and, for the remaining goods, decentralized administration by delegating authority to regional bureaus. This was followed by the abolishment on 8 October of price controls on 100 commodity categories (or more than 13,000 items at the disaggregated level).

1.3.5. Measuring the Effectiveness of Price Controls

Takagi et al. (1994) formally tested the effectiveness of the packages of price controls in arresting postwar inflation by estimating a monthly price-level determination equation, where the explanatory variables were the one-period lagged price level, money supply (M1 or the monetary base), expected inflation (proxied by a four- or five-month moving average of actual past, present, and future monthly inflation), industrial production, and dummy variables for the policy packages.[34] The financial measures were considered separately from the price-control packages, the effectiveness of which was considered collectively, such that four dummy variables were included covering the emergency financial measures of February 1946 and, for the three successive packages of price controls, the months of announcement (February 1946, June 1947, and June 1948), the months of implementation (March 1946, July 1947, and July 1948), and the subsequent months (April 1946, August 1947, and August 1948). The black-market price index was used as the price level.

Estimation of the equation by ordinary least squares for February 1946– September 1948 shows: (1) the coefficient of industrial production was numerically small and not statistically significant; (2) the coefficient of the money supply was statistically significant, but the implied speed of price adjustment was small (0.09–0.16, depending on the specification); and (3) none of the coefficients was statistically significant for the policy dummy

---

[34] The price level determination equation is derived from postulating a standard money demand function with a partial adjustment mechanism for the price level.

variables. Interestingly, the coefficients of the dummy variables for the financial emergency measures and the months when the price controls were announced were positive (though not statistically significant), suggesting the possibility that people rushed to the black markets to exchange cash for goods when they were informed of or anticipated these policies; the coefficients of the dummy variables for the other months were negative (though not statistically significant), suggesting that the measures may have had some moderate, though short-lived, impact on black-market prices.

1.4. A NEW APPROACH TO ECONOMIC STABILIZATION

1.4.1. Identifying the Underlying Causes of Inflation

The limited impact of attempts at stabilization through price controls is not surprising in view of the fact that none of these measures fundamentally addressed the root causes of the inflation. The econometric evidence cited above indicates that inflation was a monetary phenomenon; given the small speed of adjustment, moreover, it was not an explosive process driven by self-fulfilling expectations. This suggests that inflation could be stabilized by controlling the money supply, without necessarily requiring a radical currency reform. In the event, the money supply (whether measured by M1 or the monetary base) expanded unchecked throughout 1948, with an abrupt jump

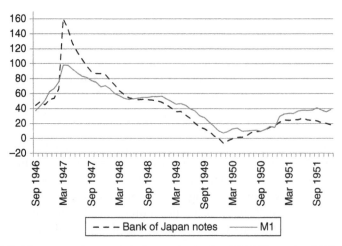

Figure 1.7. Money supply growth in Japan, September 1946–December 1951 (in year-on-year logarithmic changes)

Source: Bank of Japan

from around March 1947 to the end of the year (see Figure 1.7). The year-on-year rate of growth remained more than 60 percent for BOJ notes from February 1947 to March 1948; likewise, the rate of growth for M1 was greater than 60 percent from December 1946 to February 1948.

Contributing to the growth of the money supply were not only the RFB reconstruction loans and the price-differential subsidies but also the central bank financing of the deficit in the Foreign Trade Fund Special Account (see the example in Table 1.5). Given the chronic trade balance deficit (see Table 1.1), the system of government-controlled trade that existed in Japan could have generated a large surplus in the government account, but the implied conversion rates were generally smaller (or the yen was more appreciated) for imports than for exports (see Table 1.3). The deficit bias was reinforced by the fact that the Board of Trade was required to procure goods for export without delay at the GHQ/SCAP's order, which sometimes meant purchasing goods at black-market prices (Ito 2009). In addition, the Board of Trade bore the entire cost of administering the trade and payment system, including for handling, inventories, and processing. The special account deficit amounted to ¥1.4 billion for FY 1946 (which ended on 31 March 1947), ¥3.3 billion for FY 1947, and ¥6.6 billion for FY 1948 (Ito 2009), all of which were financed by the central bank.

1.4.2. The Reverse Course in American Policy

During 1947, a new consensus emerged in Washington on the role of American occupation, which historians call the "reverse course." With an impending fall of China to communism, some thought that action should be taken to rebuild Japan as an American ally in Asia. Long-term economic reform was therefore to be subordinated to short-term economic recovery, first to reduce the burden on the American taxpayer and later to help supply anticommunist forces in Asia (Bronfenbrenner 1955). The individual most responsible for implementing the reverse course in economic policy was William H. Draper, Jr., Under Secretary of the Army and a man with an investment banking background.[35] After his first visit to Japan in September 1947, Draper became critical of the reform orientation of the GHQ/SCAP's economic policy and decided to make "economic recovery the main objective" of US occupation policy. To communicate Washington's position to MacArthur and his reformers, "who were rather slow to appreciate the profound swing in American policy," in March 1948 Draper joined a "blue-ribbon mission" of prominent

---

[35] Draper became the first Under Secretary of the Army in September 1947 when the War and Navy Departments merged and the former became the Department of the Army within what was to become the Department of Defense.

businessmen to Japan, headed formally by Chemical Bank Chairman Percy Johnston (Schonberger 1989).

In May 1948, an interdepartmental mission (with no Army representation) on yen foreign exchange policy, headed by Ralph A. Young of the Federal Reserve Board, was dispatched to Japan. The American side recognized that the system of multiple exchange rates was a source of inflationary finance and feared that US assistance was thereby being wasted; a single exchange rate would help create a surplus in the Foreign Trade Fund Special Account corresponding to the trade deficit, hence eliminating an important source of inflationary finance. The Young mission recommended a ten-point stabilization plan that included establishment of a single exchange rate in the range of ¥270–330 per dollar before 1 October while emphasizing the need to achieve a balanced budget. MacArthur rejected these recommendations, arguing that introduction of a single exchange rate before full stabilization was achieved could accelerate inflation. On 28 June 1948, the National Advisory Council (NAC) on International Monetary and Financial Problems adopted the Young report after replacing the 1 October deadline with the phrase "as soon as administratively possible" (Schonberger 1989). The content of the Young report was not made public.

In the meantime, within Japan, economic stabilization remained a topic of intense discussion. A spectrum of views was expressed, with "immediate (*ikkyo*)" and "interim (*chūkan*)" stabilization at the two polar ends. The former advocated a big-bang approach to eliminating inflation through fundamental measures accompanied by currency reform; the latter referred to a gradualist approach to reducing inflation while increasing production. Government economists, mostly those based in the ESB, typically took the gradualist view and had already begun preparing a draft plan in the fall of 1947; at least three successive drafts, entitled "Realization of Interim Economic Stabilization," "Draft Program for Interim Economic Stabilization," and "Program of Interim Stabilization," were presented to the GHQ/SCAP during the months of May and June 1948. The main thrust of these plans was to achieve price stabilization gradually over a period of twelve to eighteen months while taking a sequence of measures to improve productivity, promote exports, improve public finances, and strengthen financial controls.

1.4.3. "Essentials of Economic Stabilization Program": July 1948

On 15 July 1948, the GHQ/SCAP communicated to the ESB an informal memorandum entitled "Essentials of Economic Stabilization Program." Accordingly, on 20 July, the cabinet approved the "Ten Principles of Economic Stabilization" based entirely on the 15 July memo. The GHQ/SCAP position, implicitly supporting the dominant gradualist view of the Japanese

Government, included the following ten elements: (1) developing important indigenous raw materials; (2) enforcing the allocation and rationing program and eradicating black-market activities; (3) improving the collection of food and increasing its allocation; (4) enforcing official prices, with prompt punishment of violators; (5) implementing flexible wage stabilization measures; (6) promoting a program to increase tax collection and vigorously prosecuting tax evaders; (7) redistributing taxes according to the principle of equity; (8) systematically reducing deficits in the special accounts; (9) improving the operation of foreign trade controls and establishing an appropriate agency within the government to manage foreign exchange; and (10) strengthening existing financial controls. MOF (1976a) speculates that the GHQ/SCAP plan, incorporating elements of the Young report in order to pay deference to Washington, was given to the Japanese authorities as a response to their own proposal for interim stabilization. Significantly, the establishment of a single exchange rate was missing from the program.

In September 1948, in addition to the existing GARIOA program, the US Government initiated the EROA program to provide industrial raw materials and machinery needed for economic rehabilitation. In order to ensure that the assistance was utilized efficiently, US authorities intensified their push for economic stabilization in Japan. In the meantime, the Ashida cabinet, weak and inept to begin with, was paralyzed by bribery charges and forced to resign in October. In November 1948, the GHQ/SCAP informed the newly installed cabinet of Shigeru Yoshida of what became known as the "three wage principles (*chingin san gensoku*)," designed to cut the vicious cycle of wage and price inflation. Specifically, occupation authorities prohibited the Japanese Government from using the following as a means of raising the wage rate: (1) RFB financing for deficit enterprises; (2) payment of subsidies to cover the difference between production costs and official prices if it caused the fiscal deficit to rise; and (3) an increase in official prices if it affected the general price level. Given the strong labor movement at the time, this was a difficult order for any Japanese politician to swallow. Yoshida dissolved the Diet on 23 December 1948 to strengthen his position (with an overwhelming Liberal Party victory, he would stay in office for another six years).

1.4.4. "Nine-Part Interim Directive on Stabilization": December 1948

By the summer of 1948, Draper had concluded that the greatest hindrance to Japan's industrial revival was the "rampaging inflation, which had yet to be brought under control by SCAP." He believed that, for this control to take place, an austerity program based on strict budgetary retrenchment and the promotion of exports would be necessary (Schonberger 1989; Tsutsui 1988).

On 19 December 1948, at Washington's order, the content of a "Nine-Part Interim Directive on Stabilization" was communicated to the Japanese Government. The directive, jointly prepared in Washington by the NAC and the National Security Council, was virtually identical to the Young report. This had been given to the GHQ/SCAP on 11 December (10 December in the United States) upon presidential approval. The content, expressed by MacArthur in a letter addressed to Prime Minister Yoshida and released to the public, included the following "Nine Commandments" (Bronfenbrenner 1950):

1) To achieve a true balance in the consolidated budget at the earliest possible date by stringent curtailing of expenditures and maximum expansion in total governmental revenues, including such new revenues as may be necessary and appropriate.

2) To accelerate and strengthen the program of tax collection and insure [*sic*] prompt, widespread and vigorous criminal prosecution of tax evaders.

3) To assure [*sic*] that credit extension is vigorously limited to those projects contributing to economic recovery of Japan.

4) To establish an effective program to achieve wage stability.

5) To strengthen and, if necessary, expand the coverage of existing price control programs.

6) To improve the operation of foreign trade controls and tighten existing foreign exchange controls, to the extent that such measures can appropriately be delegated to Japanese agencies.

7) To improve the effectiveness of the present allocation and rationing system, particularly to the end of maximizing exports.

8) To increase production of all essential indigenous raw material and manufactured products.

9) To improve the efficiency of the food collection program.

The tenth and concluding item then stated that the aim of these measures was "to pave the way for the early establishment of a single general exchange rate." The interim directive itself stated explicitly that this would be accomplished "within three months" of the implementation of the program, but this language was deleted from MacArthur's instructions to Yoshida released to the public.

The nine-part directive may not appear radically different from the earlier ten-part directive of July (or things the Japanese Government had said it would do but had failed to deliver during the past three years), but this directive was different in a fundamental way: it came as a presidential order from Washington. Significantly, it also explicitly spelled out that a single exchange rate would be established; balance was to be achieved, not in the general account (as had been in the past, with little substantive meaning), but in the consolidated national budget, including the special accounts and the activities of all government enterprises. The nine-part directive reflected Washington's disagreement with the GHQ/SCAP's gradualist approach. Washington also recognized that, given the harsh nature of some of the measures to be implemented, the Japanese Government could not implement the directive on its own. It thus used a carrot (financial assistance under EROA and GARIOA) and a stick (the authority of an occupying power) to compel government leaders to accept the big-bang approach.

1.5. THE DODGE STABILIZATION PLAN

1.5.1. The Dodge Plan of 1949–51

On 22 January 1949, the Japanese Government formulated an outline of comprehensive policy measures based on the nine-part directive and embarked upon preparing a budget for FY 1949. It was ten days later, on 1 February, that Detroit banker Joseph M. Dodge arrived on the scene, accompanied by General Kenneth C. Royall, Secretary of the Army, and Ralph Young of the Federal Reserve Board. President Harry Truman had asked Dodge to come to Japan in person to execute the order, after his experience with financial reforms in West Germany and to preempt expected opposition from MacArthur (Schonberger 1989). In his capacity as advisor to the GHQ/SCAP, Dodge instructed the Japanese Government to achieve a surplus in the consolidated fiscal account, terminate RFB financing, and suspend payment of price subsidies. After spending the first half of February gathering information, on 23 February Dodge began revising the FY 1949 budget that had been prepared by the Japanese Government. On 22 March, Dodge proposed a reworked budget plan, which the Japanese Government submitted to the Diet almost unaltered. On 20 April, the Diet passed the budget, with a planned net surplus of ¥156.7 billion (see Table 1.6).

The Dodge Plan, or the Dodge Line,[36] included the following elements: (1) all expenditure items would be explicitly budgeted, with no contingency items allowed; (2) national debt would be reduced as quickly as possible, including

---

[36] The origin of the term *line* is not clear. Martin Bronfenbrenner, an ESS economist who would later become a prominent American academic, took the word to mean "an official or public position." Bronfenbrenner (1950), in "Four Positions on Japanese Finance," contrasts the "Dodge Line" with three other competing views of what caused postwar inflation and what needed to be done to arrest it, namely, the "Ishibashi Line," the "ESB Line," and the "Communist Line." Later, Bronfenbrenner (1975), in "Inflation Theories of the SCAP Period," reclassifies the competing theories into six: Ishibashi Keynesianism, vulgar Marxism, Office of Price Administration (OPA) direct controls, sound finance fiscalism, banking school monetarism, and old

Table 1.6. Japan's national budgets, fiscal years 1946–50 (in billions of yen)

	1946	1947	1948	1949	1950
1. General account	0.0	0.0	0.0	0.2	0.0
Revenue	119.1	214.3	473.1	704.9	661.4
Expenditure	119.1	214.3	473.1	704.7	661.4
2. Special accounts	2.3	−1.2	0.6	28.1	41.5
Revenue	270.8	480.0	1,197.5	2505	1,740.1
Expenditure	268.5	481.2	1,196.9	2,476.9	1,698.6
3. State-owned enterprises	—	—	—	0.0	0.0
Revenue	—	—	—	1,314.0	1,416.6
Expenditure	—	—	—	1,314.0	1,416.6
4. Total (1+2+3)	2.3	−1.2	0.6	28.3	41.5
Revenue	389.9	694.2	1,670.7	4,524.0	3,818.2
Expenditure	387.6	695.4	1,670.1	4,495.7	3,776.6
5. Adjustment	−91.7	−49.7	−89.3	128.4	134.8
Of which: Debt issues	−104.1	−65.2	−104.2	−27.0	−5.3
Amortization	12.4	15.5	14.9	89.5	62.9
5. Net (4+5)	−89.3	−50.9	−88.7	156.7	176.3

Source: MOF, National Budget, 1949–51

full repayment of RFB debt of ¥109.1 billion using the capital expenditure of ¥30 billion, ¥62.4 billion from the US Aid Counterpart Fund (see item (4) below), and new national bond issues of ¥14.1 billion; (3) the issue of RFB bonds would be terminated, and no government borrowing would be carried over from one fiscal year to the next; and (4) a US Aid Counterpart Fund Special Account would be established under GHQ/SCAP control, in order to utilize US assistance effectively for economic independence. The Counterpart Fund, established on 30 April 1949, was intended to replace the role previously played by RFB financing.[37] It represented about 20 percent of the total budget for 1949–50, but for the first fiscal year, most of the budgeted ¥129.3 billion was used to redeem government debt, with less than 40 percent used for providing long-term, low-interest loans to the private sector.

In order to achieve balance in the Railroad and Telecommunications Special Accounts, train fares were raised by 60 percent and telecommunications fees by 50 percent. There was a large reduction in the government workforce, amounting to at least 5 percent of the total. On final settlement (not reported

Chicago School price flexibility. According to the latter classification, the Dodge Line incorporated the elements of sound finance fiscalism and banking school monetarism.

[37] This is how the Counterpart Fund worked: proceeds from the domestic sale of goods imported under US assistance were to be deposited in a special account, now separate from the Foreign Trade Fund Special Account, to be used for economic stabilization and reconstruction under GHQ/SCAP control. This was modeled after the way Marshall Plan aid was dispensed to Europe.

in the table), the consolidated fiscal balance, which had remained in deficit for three consecutive fiscal years (1946–8), turned into a surplus of ¥211.6 billion (or 6.9 percent of gross national product or GNP) in FY 1949. Moreover, whereas the government had recorded the net borrowing of ¥91.7 billion, ¥49.7 billion, and ¥89.3 billion during FY 1946–8, it redeemed ¥208 billion of debt during FY 1949. That is to say, from FY 1948 to FY 1949, the fiscal position improved by ¥300.3 billion (or 13.9 percent of 1948 GNP; 9.8 percent of 1949 GNP). The government's position vis-à-vis the private sector improved by as much as ¥597.6 billion (27.6 and 19.6 percent of 1948 and 1949 GNP, respectively), from a deficit of ¥178 billion to a surplus of ¥419.6 billion.

In October 1949, Dodge returned to Japan to revise the budget in line with new economic developments, including the recommendations of a GHQ/SCAP-requested tax mission headed by Carl Shoup. Because the FY 1950 budget was being prepared at the time, the second of Dodge's stabilization plans would effectively be implemented in terms of a fifteen-month budget covering January 1950–March 1951. Under the second program, the wage and civil service pay scales were maintained at the same level, economic controls were liberalized and rationalized, and some public corporations were dissolved. The scale of the FY 1950 budget was made smaller than the FY 1949 budget, with a budgeted increase in the surplus (see Table 1.6). On the initial budget basis, a surplus of ¥176.3 billion was budgeted, and ¥200.2 billion was allocated to redeem national debt. With the budgeted borrowing of ¥5.3 billion, this meant that the government's financial position vis-à-vis the private sector was to improve by ¥371.2 billion.[38]

1.5.2. The Single Exchange Rate

Following the enactment of the FY 1949 budget, the GHQ/SCAP announced that the official exchange rate of ¥360 per US dollar would take effect from 25 April. This action was meant not only as an anchor upon which stabilization was to be built but also to facilitate the resumption of private-sector trade. Limited private-sector exports had been permitted since 15 August 1947, but the lack of a market exchange rate became a hindrance to trade promotion. Although Japanese exporters were allowed to negotiate directly with foreign importers on possible trade deals, the GHQ/SCAP continued to set the dollar prices; domestic yen settlement through the Foreign Trade Fund Special Account was de-linked from the SCAP account through which dollar settlement was made. To promote Japanese exports, it became evident that traders needed

---

[38] With the outbreak of war on the Korean peninsula in mid 1950, the final budget saw ¥24.6 billion shifted out of debt amortization to create a special National Police Reserve of 75,000 men and to expand the Maritime Safety Board by 8,000 men.

to know (if not to be able to set) the yen and dollar prices that would determine the final receipts and payments when contracts were being negotiated.

As a possible solution, the authorities initially considered a "price ratio system (PRS)," under which: (1) they set minimum dollar prices ("price floors") and "price ratios" for different classes of commodities; (2) exporters and importers were free to set their own dollar prices (provided they were above the floors); and (3) the price ratios would be applied to determine the yen proceeds for Japanese exporters (Ito 2009). In the event, the GHQ/SCAP, knowing Washington's preference for a single exchange rate, abandoned the idea (PRS was a multiple exchange rate system) but instead allowed the Japanese Government to institute in September 1948 a scaled-down version named a "price computing system (PCS, *kakaku santei seido*)." The first set of conversion rates under the PCS were announced for fifty-two items on 15 October (see Table 1.7), followed by additional rates for more than six hundred items toward the end of November (MOF 1976b). Whatever the outcome, at least Japanese exporters had some certainty about the yen prices of their exports when they negotiated for a trade contract.

The PCS lasted only for six months, until the single exchange rate of ¥360 was established in April 1949. Dodge had earlier picked ¥330 as the unified rate for the yen, on the premise that it would sustain more than 80 percent of Japanese exports without subsidies. A similar figure (¥327.89) would have

Table 1.7. Selected yen–dollar conversion rates under price computing system, October 1948[a] (yen per US dollar)

Commodity	Conversion rate
Vitamin A	150
Agar	160
Sodium hydroxide	200
Frozen marine produce	260
Dried marine produce	280
Tea	330
Straw slippers	390
Fertilizers	390
Fountain pens	400
Bamboo products	430
Harmonicas	450
Pencils	500
Toys	500
Lanterns	550
X-ray film; photographic paper	600
Sheet glass	600

[a] Conversion rates were announced for fifty-two items in October; this was followed by the announcement of additional conversion rates for more than six hundred items in November

Source: MOF (1976b), Table 4–1

emerged if the wholesale price indices for both Japan and the United States with the base year of 1913 (when both countries were on the gold standard, before the commencement of World War I) had been used to calculate the purchasing power parity (PPP) exchange rate for the yen (Tōyō Keizai Shinpōsha 1954). Within the Japanese establishment, in January 1949 the MOF was arguing for the dollar rate of ¥330, the Board of Trade for ¥350–400, the BOJ for ¥300–50, the ESB for ¥220–350, the Ministry of Commerce and Industry for ¥350–400, and the business community for ¥400 (Ito 2009; Keizai Dōyūkai 1948). It appears that those concerned with economic stabilization desired a more appreciated level, whereas those wishing to promote exports favored a more depreciated one.

Although the FY 1949 budget had already been prepared on the assumed rate of ¥330, the NAC in Washington thought the yen should be set at a more depreciated level, possibly to maintain Japan's price competitiveness in light of an impending devaluation of the pound sterling.[39] After receiving the NAC recommendation, Dodge thought that any rate more depreciated than ¥330 would weaken industry incentives to rationalize; he nevertheless accepted ¥360 as useful for export promotion (Ito 2009). Dodge requested a delay in the announcement of the exchange rate until after the FY 1949 budget had been revised and legislated. Three days after the Diet passed its budget, on 23 April, the GHQ/SCAP informed the Japanese Government "to take the steps necessary to put into effect at 0001 hours, 25 April 1949, an official foreign exchange rate of 360 Japanese yen to one US dollar," which would "be the basis for all permitted foreign trade and exchange transactions."[40]

It is difficult to judge the propriety of the unified rate of ¥360 per dollar. The rate was about 10 percent depreciated from the weighted average conversion rate of ¥331 for exports in September 1948 and more than 300 percent depreciated from the weighted average conversion rate of ¥109 for imports in August 1948 (Keizai Dōyūkai 1948). However, the conversion rate for imports is not a good basis for making the judgment because the prices of essential imports (most imports were essential) were administratively kept low. Estimates of the PPP rate for the yen would be sensitive to the choice of base year and price index. For example, if the retail price index for Japan and the consumer price index for the United States had been used, the average PPP rate for 1948 would have ranged between ¥140–300 (see Table 1.8). Whatever the assessment of the initial level, it is certain that the continuing inflation eroded any advantage in Japan's price competitiveness, with the average PPP rate for 1949 rising to ¥494 if 1935 were used as the base year.

---

[39] The Pentagon explained in a secret cable to the GHQ/SCAP that the United Kingdom was planning to devalue the pound sterling shortly (Schonberger 1989). A 30-percent devaluation of the pound took place in September 1949.

[40] SCAPIN No. 1997.

Table 1.8. Estimating yen's purchasing power parity rate, 1948 and 1949 (yen per US dollar)

Base year	Average retail price index (RPI)[a] (1922=1.00)	Average consumer price index (CPI)[b] (1922=1.00)	Yen–dollar exchange rate in December	Average PPP rate for 1948 (Japanese RPI=97.14; US CPI=1.43)	Average PPP rate for 1949 (Japanese RPI=158.05; US CPI=1.42)
1922	1.00	1.00	2.07	140.0	230.6
1925	0.92	1.04	2.35	179.2	295.2
1930	0.66	0.99	2.03	207.4	341.8
1935	0.64	0.82	3.49	300.0	494.3

[a] Tokyo
[b] US cities
Sources: Bank of Japan; US Bureau of Labor Statistics

1.5.3. The Dodge Plan as Exchange Rate-based Stabilization

The Dodge Plan is often characterized as an austerity program that thrust Japan into depression, from which it could only recover with the help of special US procurement orders that came with the Korean War (Hamada and Kasuya 1993). The Japanese business community called the procurement order-driven expansion that started in mid 1950 God-sent, comparing it to the divine winds (*kamikaze*) that had saved Japan from the successive Mongol invasions under Kublai Khan in the thirteenth century. This view of the Dodge Plan was shared by contemporary observers, such as Bronfenbrenner (1950), who called it "more reminiscent of the 'Dismal Science' than of the 'Economy of Abundance'" and "imperfectly consistent with the policies which the national administration is contemporaneously applying in the continental United States." The "framing and implementing" of the Dodge Line, Bronfenbrenner continued, could be sought in Dodge's investment or banking background, and it was what US economic policy might also look like "in the future if financiers increase[d] their influence in its framing."

Even a cursory look at macroeconomic data suggests a different story (see Table 1.9). Real GNP, for example, grew by more than 20 percent from 1949 to 1950, with real personal consumption and real private investment expanding by 15 and 40 percent, respectively. Part of this, of course, reflects the significant economic pickup that followed the outbreak of the Korean War, but the economy was already expanding before that time. Real industrial production (the GHQ index), the only real macroeconomic series for which monthly data are available, had expanded by more than 15 percent from the first half of 1949 to the first half of 1950 (not reported in the table). It is true that public finances were significantly retrenched, but there was no conditionality as such on the

Table 1.9. Key macroeconomic indicators in Japan, 1947–51

	1947	1948	1949	1950	1951
National income accounts (in 1946 prices; annual percentage change in parentheses)					
Real gross national product	485.9 (2.7)	582.4 (19.9)	610.3 (4.8)	737.7 (20.9)	795.0 (7.8)
Real personal consumption	350.1 (5.1)	417.6 (19.3)	472.4 (13.1)	541.3 (14.6)	585.4 (8.1)
Real private investment	80.2 (14.2)	78.9 (−1.6)	56.1 (−28.8)	78.7 (40.2)	91.4 (16.2)
Industrial production (in annual percentage change)					
ESB index	25.4	52.4	33.6	17.8	37.9
GHQ index	21.9	43.4	34.1	23.1	40.9
Deflators (in annual percentage change)					
Overall	167.4	67.0	19.3	3.5	21.5
Consumption	161.2	60.9	15.0	−2.1	14.7
Investment	155.2	101.4	35.6	25.2	39.5
Trade (in millions of US dollars)					
Exports	181.6	262.3	533.3	920.3	1,353.5
Imports	449.0	546.6	728.1	885.9	1,645.3
US inflation (in percent per year)					
Consumer prices	14.4	8.1	−1.2	1.3	7.9
Wholesale prices	23.1	8.2	−5.1	3.8	11.4

Abbreviations: ESB=Economic Stabilization Board; GHQ=General Headquarters (of the Supreme Commander for the Allied Powers)

Sources: ECB (1953); ESB (1952); MOF (1976b); US Bureau of Labor Statistics; author's estimates

growth of money. The deceleration of money supply growth happened only as the sources of inflationary finance were eliminated, but real money balances actually rose vigorously throughout this period, even before mid 1950 (see Figure 1.8). Black-market inflation did decline to a negative range, but official price inflation, while declining, remained elevated as official prices were adjusted upward (see Figure 1.5).

These features—an expansion in output, consumption, and investment; declining but elevated inflation and (by implication) real exchange rate appreciation; and rising real money balances—are all well-known stylized facts of exchange rate-based stabilizations observed in Latin America from the late 1970s to the early 1990s (Easterly 1996; Kiguel and Liviatan 1992; Calvo and Vegh 1994).[41] The Dodge Plan had an important feature that distinguished it from a standard scheme: a single exchange rate was introduced in an essentially closed economy that had no current account convertibility. Even so, the single

---

[41] According to Hamann (1999), not all stylized facts consistently apply to countries outside Latin America. Nor do they seem to apply equally well to stabilization from moderate inflation, as typically attempted in industrial countries (Detragiache and Hamann 1999).

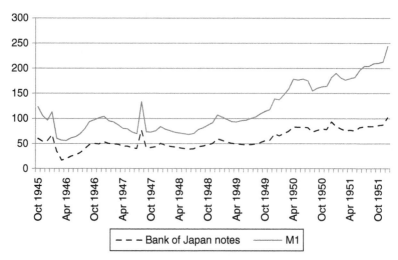

Figure 1.8. Real money balances in Japan, October 1945–December 1951 (end of month; billions of yen; December 1945 black-market prices)

Sources: ESB (1952); Bank of Japan

exchange rate served as a nominal anchor. Dodge, not totally bound by the Washington-drafted nine-part directive, deemphasized the plan's control aspect (Bronfenbrenner 1950). The elimination of official prices proceeded quickly after April 1949, with the GHQ/SCAP announcing on 8 August that official prices would be eliminated on 7,537 items. The pace of price decontrol was accelerated as black-market prices for some goods declined below official prices. By the end of 1949, the number of goods subject to government control was 61 percent of the peak.

Other aspects of economic controls were eased as well. For FY 1949, the ESB allocated only ¥20.2 billion in price subsidies, limiting them to steel, coal, nonferrous metals, fertilizers, and sodium hydroxide. With the scale of economic controls winding down, in June 1950 the ESB was downsized; the Price Board became a bureau within the ESB, with some functions transferred to the MOF. Thus, the orientation of the Dodge Plan was to strengthen the working of the market as the primary mechanism of resource allocation. In this, the establishment of the fixed exchange rate, together with the gradual opening of foreign trade, played a critical role as the benchmark for rationalizing the structure of domestic prices. Because exports expanded in 1950 in response to US military procurement orders, there was not a sharp deterioration in the trade balance, as is typically observed under an exchange rate-based stabilization. Still, the rapid expansion of imports in 1950 and 1951 attests to the applicability of the exchange rate-based stabilization paradigm to the experience of Japan under the Dodge Plan.

With the exchange rate as the nominal anchor, the initial contraction of the money supply may have been excessive because it failed to accommodate a pickup in demand for money without causing a decline in the price level. Market pressure for larger equilibrium real money balances may have been what prompted the Japanese authorities, with the implicit approval of the GHQ/SCAP (though not of Dodge), to ease monetary policy. On 17 May 1949, BOJ Governor Hisato Ichimada stated his intention to prevent a fall in prices (BOJ 1985). From June 1949 to April 1950, the BOJ actively purchased from commercial banks high-grade corporate bonds as well as RFB debentures maturing after August; on four occasions from August 1949 to April 1950, the BOJ lowered daily interest charges for general loans and bill discounting.[42] Any contractionary impact of the Dodge Plan was further mitigated because (1) the amount of price subsidies remained in real terms almost at the level of the previous year and (2) an income tax cut was implemented, as recommended by the Shoup mission, to rationalize the overall tax system.[43] The effective life of the Dodge Plan was brief, as it became "one of the first ideological casualties of the Korean War" (Bronfenbrenner 1975).

As noted, consistent with the post-stabilization experiences of most countries, real money balances (measured by black-market prices) rose in Japan during the period of the Dodge Plan (see Figure 1.8). But there had already been a moderate pickup in the growth of real money during the second half of 1948. This may mean that, with increasing US pressure for stabilization, the public was already beginning to adjust its inflationary expectations downward. Sargent (1982) argues that credible monetary and fiscal reforms are essential for successful stabilization because expectations can only change when economic agents are convinced of a regime change. In this respect, the Dodge Plan, imposed on Japan with the authority of an occupying power, had the credibility it required to be successful. The subsequent rise in real money balances was steady: from the end of 1949 to the end of 1951, the real balance of BOJ notes expanded by 46 percent and that of M1 by 76 percent. With stabilization thus achieved, and with the progressive easing of price and economic controls, the structure of prices in Japan began to link more closely with international prices. Japan was now ready to resume private-sector trade on a full scale.

---

[42] Dodge thought that monetary and credit policies could subvert the Dodge Plan. During his first trip to Japan, Dodge saw Ichimada as "a member of the pro-inflationist camp" of Ishibashi and sought to wrest one-man control of the BOJ by setting up a Policy Board. But to GHQ/SCAP officials the new Policy Board "seemed wholly ineffective in dovetailing financial policy with the stabilization program." Schonberger (1989), however, speculates that Dodge, "while maintaining an atmosphere of austerity, tolerated banking violations of stabilization principles because of a fear of economic collapse."

[43] The Shoup mission arrived in Japan in May 1949 at the request of the GHQ/SCAP and submitted its full report in mid September. It aimed to increase revenue while rationalizing the overall system in accordance with the principle of equity.

2

Achieving Current Account
Convertibility: 1949–64

2.1. INTRODUCTION

Establishment of a single exchange rate for the yen in April 1949—achieved in the context of economic stabilization—was only the first step toward normalizing Japan's external economic relations, which mostly remained in the hands of the state. Private-sector trade needed to resume on a full scale. At the instruction of US occupation authorities, in December 1949, the Foreign Exchange and Foreign Trade Control Law was enacted to provide a legal framework for trade and payments, thus allowing the full resumption of private exports (December) and private imports (January 1950). However, all international transactions in principle were made subject to government control; the yen remained an inconvertible currency for both current and capital account transactions, not only during the remainder of the occupation period (through April 1952),[1] but for another twelve years.

The restrictive system was conceived as a realistic mechanism for conserving scarce foreign exchange reserves. It was also a response to the reality of the world economy. At that time, there existed only a handful of convertible currencies, such as US and Canadian dollars;[2] even the currencies of Western Europe were not convertible.[3] In fact, throughout much of the 1950s, almost all the countries of the world maintained a restrictive trade and payments practice of one type or another (IMF 1950). With improved export performance

---

[1] The San Francisco Peace Treaty came into force on 28 April 1952, restoring Japan's national sovereignty and ending the Allied occupation.

[2] In the early 1950s, the International Monetary Fund had only nine member countries that, in accordance with Article VIII of its Articles of Agreement, refrained from imposing restrictions on the making of payments and transfers for current international transactions.

[3] In order to overcome the trade-restraining effect of inconvertible currencies, these countries established the European Payments Union (EPU) under the framework of the Organization for European Economic Cooperation (OEEC) as a vehicle for multilateral clearing of monthly trade imbalances between member countries. See Kawai and Takagi (2005).

and in response to the increasing convertibility of major currencies, the operation of Japan's system of foreign exchange and trade control became more flexible in the late 1950s. In April 1964, the system was fully liberalized with respect to the making of payments for current international transactions, about three years behind major Western European countries.

This chapter reviews Japan's trade and payments system that emerged in the aftermath of the Dodge stabilization, how it worked, and how it was used or modified over time in response to changing circumstances before full current account convertibility was achieved. In traversing the period 1949–64, it is important to remember that the operation of exchange rate policy was in some cases indistinguishable from that of trade policy. The nature of current account inconvertibility meant that trade control was exercised by rationing of foreign exchange. To discourage the import of a particular good, authorities could simply limit the allocation of foreign exchange to that activity; no import quota or tariff was required for this purpose. Itoh and Kiyono (1988) argue that "foreign exchange shortage" primarily dictated Japan's trade policy during this period. For this reason, Japanese authorities took measures to discourage imports (especially of luxuries) and to encourage exports. Foreign exchange allocation was therefore an integral tool of trade policy. To the extent that it favored certain industries, it was also a tool of industrial policy.[4] The restrictive system increasingly assumed that role as the foreign exchange constraint was eased over time.

Japan's exchange liberalization was nearly synonymous with trade liberalization as long as it involved relaxation of foreign exchange allocation rules for the import of goods and services, but trade liberalization was not complete in 1964 when full current account convertibility was achieved. This was so because tariffs and, in fewer cases, import quotas remained in place (see Section 2.7). While elimination of exchange restrictions was an international obligation Japan had assumed in 1952 when it became a member of the International Monetary Fund (IMF),[5] it had no commitment at the time to

---

[4] To promote certain export industries, the government provided a priority allocation of foreign exchange for the import of raw materials. In addition, it gave low-interest loans or discounting (through the central bank) to facilitate production and processing (1946–72) as well as allowed tax deductions on export earnings (1953–63). See Itoh and Kiyono (1988). How the government used some of these measures is discussed in the remainder of this chapter.

[5] Article VIII of the IMF's Articles of Agreement, under "General Obligations of Members," states in part: "No member shall, without the approval of the Fund, impose restrictions on the making of payments and transfers for current international transactions" (Section 2[a]) or "shall engage in . . . any discriminatory currency arrangements or multiple currency practices" (Section 3). Member countries, however, were allowed under the "Transitional Arrangements" of Article XIV to "maintain and adapt to changing circumstances the restrictions on payments and transfers for current international transactions that were in effect on the date on which it became a member" (Section 2). Japan availed itself of this provision when it became a member and retained Article XIV status through 31 March 1964.

dismantle barriers to all imports. Trade liberalization has proceeded rather slowly ever since because the Japanese bureaucracy, while accepting the general need to liberalize imports as the international responsibility of Japan as a developed nation and the necessary price it had to pay to expand exports, could not easily agree on which sectors of the economy to open up for competition from foreign imports. Komiya and Itoh (1988) attribute part of this inertia to what they call the *genkyoku* administrative system, in which each industry in Japan was overseen by an office, section, or department of the government. The *genkyoku* in charge of an industry considered itself responsible for maintaining order in that industry with a certain stable level of profits. Any change to the status quo was therefore resisted.

For the most part, the rest of the chapter abstracts from these and other microeconomic, resource allocation aspects of how Japan's restrictive system was managed. Rather, its focus is on the operation of the overall system in facilitating external transactions and influencing their volume or direction. After summarizing the main features of the trade and payments system of the early 1950s,[6] including the Foreign Exchange Budget (FEB) and the trade control apparatus, the chapter reviews how the system was employed to manage the balance-of-payments crises of 1952–3 and 1956–7. This is followed by an extended discussion of the major deregulatory changes of the late 1950s and the expansion of trade and foreign exchange market activity under the system. The chapter concludes by discussing the program of trade and exchange liberalization of the early 1960s, which culminated in the restoration of full current account convertibility for the yen in 1964.

2.2. THE TRADE AND PAYMENTS SYSTEM IN THE EARLY 1950s

2.2.1. The Foreign Exchange and Trade Control Law of 1949

Preparation began in early 1949 to transfer responsibility for managing foreign exchange reserves from the General Headquarters (GHQ) of the Supreme Commander for the Allied Powers (SCAP) to the Japanese Government and to set up a legal system of control over foreign trade and payments. In accordance with GHQ/SCAP directives, the Foreign Exchange Control Board was established on 16 March as a government agency responsible for managing foreign exchange; likewise, the Ministry of International Trade and

---

[6] This chapter attempts to follow the official, contemporary terminology of Wang (1953) in describing Japan's restrictive system in the early 1950s.

Industry (MITI) was established on 25 May and took over the functions previously performed by the Ministry of Commerce and Industry and the Board of Trade. The mandate given by the GHQ/SCAP to the Foreign Exchange Control Board was to "take the necessary steps promptly to establish coordinated control over the movement of foreign exchange and trade into and out of Japan." The SCAP directive further noted that "such controls . . . shall conform with the member nations" of the IMF.[7]

The Ministry of Finance (MOF) was already preparing its own plan to assume control of trade and payments (Asai 2012) in response to the July 1948 GHQ/SCAP memorandum "Essentials of Economic Stabilization Program," which stated the need "to improve the operation of foreign trade controls and tighten existing foreign exchange controls," thus intimating that the authority for foreign exchange and foreign trade control would be "delegated to Japanese agencies." Such a possibility became even more probable in December 1948, when the "Nine-Part Interim Directive on Stabilization" repeated the same phrase. After March 1949, the Foreign Exchange Control Board assumed responsibility for preparing the legislation while collaborating with representatives from the MOF and the MITI. The interagency team nearly completed drafting the law by the end of October 1949, but the work became deadlocked in a turf battle between the Board and the MITI (Asai 2012).

By this time, decisions had already been communicated by the GHQ/SCAP to Japanese authorities to resume private exports in December and private imports in January 1950.[8] The Japanese Government was thus placed under enormous pressure to finish preparing the trade and payments legislation. On 15 November 1949, the GHQ/SCAP presented an outline of the system prepared by an IMF technical mission,[9] which was little more than a set of general principles. A joint committee of GHQ/SCAP and Japanese officials

---

[7] SCAPIN No. 1968, dated 2 February 1949.

[8] The SCAP/Economic and Scientific Section (ESS) memorandum of 20 October 1949 instructed the MITI to submit a plan within ten days to resume private exports "not later than 1 December 1949"; likewise, the memorandum of 21 October gave similar instructions so that private imports could be resumed "on or before 1 January 1950."

[9] At the request of the GHQ/SCAP, the IMF mission arrived in October 1949 to provide advice on foreign exchange and trade control to GHQ/SCAP and Japanese officials. It was headed by Jan V. Mládek, a Czech national who, after having served as one of the IMF's first executive directors, was deputy director of the Operations Department (Horsefield 1969) and included Ernest A. Wichin. At the conclusion of their stay, Mládek and Wichin submitted a report, dated 18 November 1949 and entitled "Report on Exchange and Trade Controls in Japan," to General Douglas MacArthur. The report, as translated by the Foreign Exchange Control Board into Japanese, was subsequently published in the March 1950 issue of its *Monthly Bulletin* (pp. 1–24). In addition, technical advice was sought from William J. Logan, director general of the Allied-initiated Joint Export–Import Agency in West Germany, as well as a US Government-sponsored "Advisory Mission for International Trade" headed by Ormond Freile of the Department of the Army, which included experts from the Federal Reserve Bank of New York and the Departments of the Treasury, Commerce, and State (Asai 2012).

then supplied operational details for the outline and drafted a bill for Diet submission on 22 November, possibly incorporating elements of the earlier interagency work.[10] The Diet passed the bill in its original form, and the law immediately came into force on 1 December 1949, along with associated laws and cabinet orders.

2.2.2. The Operational Framework of Foreign Exchange and Trade Control

Given the haste with which it was prepared, the Foreign Exchange and Foreign Trade Control Law was a "skeleton." Besides setting out the Foreign Exchange Budget system (see Section 2.2.3), it left many of the details of how the law would be administered to separate cabinet orders. A typical article, for example, would give a list of transactions that were prohibited "unless permitted by a cabinet order." This provided the flexibility to allow substantive changes in the regime without requiring a legislative revision (Ozaki 1972). On 27 June 1950, the cabinet issued the Foreign Exchange Control Order.[11] The Foreign Investment Law, which took effect on 10 May 1950, assumed precedence over the Foreign Exchange Law in matters related to the import of long-term capital. The intent of Japanese authorities to create a liberal foreign investment regime was vetoed by MacArthur as unrealistic, given Japan's scarce foreign exchange reserves (Asai 2012).[12]

From November 1949 to the end of the occupation in April 1952, the GHQ/SCAP transferred control over foreign exchange reserves in several steps to Japanese authorities, starting with bookkeeping for the SCAP commercial account on 1 November 1949 (Ito 2009; Asai 2012). In preparation for resuming private imports, on 29 December, foreign exchange amounting to an equivalent of $67 million (consisting of 53 million US dollars and 5 million British pounds) was transferred to the Japanese Government. The management of US dollar reserves was transferred on 16 August 1951 and sterling reserves on 2 October 1951.[13] It was in anticipation of assuming control over

---

[10] Nobuhiko Ushiba (1950), head of the secretariat at the Foreign Exchange Control Board, characterizes the final outcome as being based on the Continental European system with British features.

[11] This incorporated advice received from G. C. Thorley of the British Treasury, who is said to have criticized the Foreign Exchange Law as a copy of the anachronistic Czechoslovakian law.

[12] Japanese authorities had hoped to make inflows through bond purchases and loans subject to notification only. Not only did the Foreign Investment Law make all inflows subject to prior approval, but it also did not guarantee the repatriation of principal for approved inflows until July 1952. As a result, Japan saw only limited private capital inflows during the 1950s (see Chapter 3).

[13] Reserves in "open accounts" (with countries under bilateral payments agreements) were transferred in stages from August 1951 as bilateral negotiations were concluded (in an open

dollar reserves seven days later that, on 9 August 1951, Japan applied for membership in the IMF (the membership would become effective in August 1952 following the restoration of national sovereignty in April).[14]

The Foreign Exchange Law and the associated statutes set forth the principle that all external transactions were prohibited unless expressly authorized, and they prescribed that an FEB be formulated to allocate foreign exchange for external payments. From 1 January 1950 to 31 March 1964, the Foreign Exchange Law was the legal framework, and the FEB the central tool, of Japan's restrictive trade and payments system. The key feature of the system was the use of exchange restrictions as a means of import control. When Japan accepted the obligations under Article VIII of the IMF Articles of Agreement on 1 April 1964, by removing virtually all exchange restrictions on the making of payments and transfers for current international transactions, it replaced the system of import control based on exchange restrictions with an alternative system based on import quotas.

During the period under review (1950–64), the MOF was responsible for general foreign exchange control. Following the dissolution of the Foreign Exchange Control Board and the Foreign Investment Commission on 31 July 1952 (as part of post-occupation administrative reforms),[15] the MOF also assumed responsibility for concentration of foreign exchange reserves, management of the Foreign Exchange Special Account, and administration of foreign investment control. The MITI performed foreign trade control and the licensing of imports and exports. The Bank of Japan (BOJ) was given charge of much of the routine day-to-day operation of the system as the agent of the national government. As the system of foreign exchange and trade control was liberalized over time, an increasing amount of approval authority was delegated to the BOJ and, in cases of automatic approval, to authorized foreign exchange banks.

2.2.3. The Foreign Exchange Budget (FEB)

The fundamental tool of foreign exchange and trade control was the Foreign Exchange Budget system (*Gaikoku Kawase Yosan Seido*). The FEB, which was

---

account, payments and receipts were netted out against each other over a specified period of time, with the final balance settled with hard currency—these bilateral clearing arrangements constituted exchange restrictions subject to IMF approval). The non-dollar, non-sterling balance of the SCAP commercial account was transferred on 28 April 1952 (the day the San Francisco Peace Treaty came into force), followed by the remaining open account balance on 30 April 1952.

[14] The application was approved on 28 May 1952. Japan joined the IMF on 13 August 1952 as the fifty-second member, a day ahead of West Germany.

[15] On this day, the Foreign Exchange Bureau was created within the MOF.

Table 2.1. Japanese foreign exchange budgets, fiscal years 1950–60[a] (in millions of US dollars)

	Merchandise			Invisibles		
	Initial	Final	Confirmed	Initial	Final	Confirmed
1950: Q1	141	172	139	—	—	—
1950: Q2	257	526	435	—	—	—
1950: Q3	386	526	437	—	—	—
1950: Q4	525	926	858	—	—	—
1951: Q1	456	465	310	—	—	—
1951: Q2	533	576	414	—	—	—
1951: Q3	653	660	465	—	—	—
1951: Q4	727	750	461	—	—	—
1952: S1	1,211	1,241	968	126	208	149
1952: S2	1,415	1,500	1,253	246	344	230
1953: S1	1,225	1,245	1,095	315	395	282
1953: S2	1,335	1,545	1,446	299	444	342
1954: S1	1,100	1,100	932	310	372	294
1954: S2	1,090	1,090	1,040	154	173	154
1955: S1	1,107	1,160	1,136	190	213	193
1955: S2	1,314	1,454	1,416	244	244	292
1956: S1	1,543	1,765	1,687	314	346	302
1956: S2	1,915	2,483	2,374	376	396	332
1957: S1	2,236	2,236	1,729	378	378	342
1957: S2	1,652	1,652	1,307	327	334	294
1958: S1	1,628	1,628	1,243	366	431	367
1958: S2	1,752	1,757	1,450	406	427	370
1959: S1	1,941	1,941	1,653	408	475	418
1959: S2	2,328	2,328	2,158	485	519	410
1960: S1	2,624	2,624	2,150	594	618	529
1960: S2	2,800	2,800	2,490	680	697	557

Abbreviations: Q=quarter (three months); S=semester (six months)

[a] Foreign exchange budgets were prepared quarterly through the end of fiscal 1951 (i.e., 31 March 1952) and semiannually thereafter (e.g., 1952: S2 refers to October 1952–March 1953)

Source: MOF, *Fiscal and Monetary Statistics Monthly*

first formulated for the January–March quarter of 1950 (or the fourth quarter of FY 1949), was initially determined quarterly. Beginning in FY 1952, the formulation of FEBs became semiannual (see Table 2.1).[16] The FEB, which required approval from the Cabinet Ministerial Council (*Kakuryō Shingikai*) under the chairmanship of the prime minister, prescribed foreign exchange payments based on anticipated foreign exchange receipts for the period concerned. Exchange receipts and payments for different types of commodities

---

[16] The Japanese fiscal year begins on the first of April and ends on the last day of March of the following year. Thus, fiscal year 1952 covers the twelve-month period from April 1952 through March 1953.

were initially classified into the dollar area, the sterling area,[17] and the open account area (see Section 2.2.7 for details). In order to provide flexibility in management, the FEB also included a reserve account for contingencies.

2.2.4. The Concentration Requirement

Under the system of foreign exchange concentration (*Gaika Shūchū Seido*) all residents were required, except under license, to surrender foreign means of payment and claimable assets acquired to authorized foreign exchange banks within ten days of acquisition.[18] Authorized foreign exchange banks would buy foreign exchange from their customers for the Foreign Exchange Special Account (or the Foreign Exchange Fund Special Account after April 1951), which had been separated out of the Foreign Trade Fund Special Account on 1 December 1949. In turn, foreign exchange banks were required to surrender the foreign exchange obtained to the Foreign Exchange Control Board. In April 1952, however, foreign exchange banks were permitted to hold dollar funds up to a designated amount as working balances, subject to BOJ approval. In June 1952, they were authorized to hold dollar deposits with foreign correspondence banks; this provision was extended to sterling deposits in March 1953 (Sakamoto 1960).

2.2.5. Foreign Exchange Receipts and Payments

In principle, all nontrade transactions between residents and nonresidents were prohibited unless expressly authorized. No authority was delegated to foreign exchange banks to approve payments except for transactions explicitly designated by the Ministerial Council. As to invisibles, transactions that would result in a receipt of funds from abroad could be conducted relatively freely and no license was required. Payments for services rendered by nonresidents, however, were subject to stricter control. The conclusion of a transportation contract in connection with imports required a license. Licenses to purchase foreign exchange had to be obtained from the MITI for payments directly connected to imports or exports, as well as for transactions involving patent

[17] The sterling area consisted of the United Kingdom, the Commonwealth (except Canada), British territories and colonies, and a few other countries (such as Burma, Jordan, and Libya). Members pooled their reserves in London and adopted common exchange and capital controls against non-sterling area countries. See Schenk (1994) on the operation of the sterling area system in the 1950s.

[18] In addition, money changers (e.g., travel agencies and hotels) and post offices were authorized to accept foreign currency notes, travelers' checks, and postal money orders. Although requirements were eased over time, the system itself was not abolished until 8 May 1972.

rights, other industrial property rights, and mining rights. In all other cases, licenses had to be obtained from the MOF. Although both inward and outward movements of capital were subject to control, outward movements were particularly severely restricted. Investments abroad were approved on a case-by-case basis. Issuance of securities abroad by a resident and issuance of securities in Japan by a nonresident were subject to license by the MOF. Subscription to foreign securities by a resident and subscription to domestic securities by a nonresident were similarly controlled.

2.2.6. Exchange Rates

On 1 December 1949, the US dollar and the pound sterling were designated as eligible currencies for use in external transactions (*shitei tsūka*). At this time, it was announced that the basic exchange rate (*kijun gaikoku kawase sōba*) was ¥360 per dollar (as previously established on 25 April 1949)[19] and that the arbitrage exchange rate (*saitei gaikoku kawase sōba*) was ¥1,008 per pound. In subsequent years, additional currencies were added to the list of designated currencies as Japan concluded new bilateral trade and payments treaties or as the currencies became transferrable, if not convertible (see Table 2.2). The government determined the rates at which the BOJ would buy or sell foreign exchange, as well as the interbank rates at which foreign exchange banks had

Table 2.2. Designated currencies for international transactions in Japan, 1949–64[a]

Date of designation	Currencies or comments
1 December 1949	US dollar; pound sterling
1 July 1954	Canadian dollar
2 August 1954	Swiss franc
1 October 1955	Deutsche mark
15 April 1956	Swedish krona
1 January 1957	French franc
1 June 1957	Dutch guilder
10 May 1958	Belgian franc
1 April 1959	Austrian schilling; Danish krone; Italian lira; Norwegian krone; Portuguese escudo
1 July 1960	Japanese yen
16 January 1962	all currency restrictions abolished for external payments
15 March 1964	Australian dollar (for external receipts)

[a] All currency restrictions were abolished for external receipts on 10 June 1971
Source: BOJ (1988)

[19] The rate of ¥360 per US dollar formally became the yen's parity at the IMF on 11 May 1953, some nine months after Japan had joined the organization on 13 August 1952.

to trade foreign currencies with each other. The Foreign Exchange Law stipulated that no transaction could take place outside the 1 percent limit of the basic or arbitrage exchange rate, in anticipation of Japan's future membership in the IMF (Okumura 1950). As to forward transactions, contracts could be concluded by a foreign exchange bank with its customers, another foreign exchange bank, or the BOJ. The government initially determined both the rates and the lengths of contracts, but it allowed market forces to play a larger role over time (see Section 2.6).

2.2.7. Methods of External Payment

Both the currency and the terms of payment (such as length of settlement period and currency of settlement, depending on the country of origin) were prescribed for different types of external transactions. In the prescription of currency, there were three standard methods of payment (*hyōjun kessai*), corresponding to the three designated currency areas: (1) settlement in sterling on a cash basis for countries with sterling payment agreements; (2) settlement through bilateral clearing accounts (called open accounts) expressed in US dollars for countries with special payment agreements (see Table 2.3); and

Table 2.3. Japan's bilateral clearing agreements, fiscal years 1949–61

End of fiscal year	Number of treaties	Countries added or terminated during previous year
1949	9	Brazil, Finland, French Union (including French Indochina), West Germany, Hong Kong, Indonesia, Netherlands, Thailand, and Taiwan added
1951	8	Hong Kong (September 1951) terminated[a]
1952	13	Argentina, Italy (January 1953), Republic of Korea (April 1950), Philippines (May 1950), and Sweden added
1953	14	Egypt (November 1953) added
1954	16	Turkey (February 1955) and Greece (March 1955) added
1955	14	West Germany (October 1955) and Italy (January 1956) terminated
1956	10	Sweden (April 1956), Thailand (April 1956), Argentina (June 1956), and French Union (January 1957) terminated
1957	6	Finland (April 1957), Netherlands (June 1957), Indonesia (July 1957), and Philippines (August 1957) terminated
1958	4	Brazil (October 1958) and Egypt (November 1958) terminated
1959	3	Turkey (August 1959) terminated
1960	2	Greece (April 1960) terminated
1961	1[b]	Taiwan (October 1961) terminated

[a] Hong Kong was fully included in the sterling area
[b] The last bilateral agreement, with Korea, was terminated in March 1966
Source: MITI, *Tsūshō Sangyōshō Nenpō*, annual issues

(3) settlement in US dollars on a cash basis for all others. As long as the standard method prescribed for a particular transaction was used, no additional approval was necessary to effect the payment. Otherwise, approval had to be obtained from control authorities.

2.3. THE SYSTEM OF TRADE CONTROL IN THE EARLY 1950s

2.3.1. Export Control

With the enactment of the Foreign Exchange Law, exports became freely permitted except for certain designated commodities, such as those of a strategic nature, those in domestic shortage, and those under barter contracts. Export control was also used from time to time to adjust Japan's trade relations with the sterling and open account countries in order to reduce the balance of inconvertible currencies. Export of some commodities to the dollar area was also placed under annual quota for political and other reasons—for example, the export of canned tuna to the United States. Except for these and other designated commodities, no license was required for exports provided that the certification of a foreign exchange bank was obtained to prevent capital flight through under-declaration and to ensure prompt settlement by a standard method.

To appreciate the way in which trade control procedures were used for exports, it is important to understand that Japan was securing a substantial portion of raw materials from the dollar area while its principal exports went to soft currency countries. As a result, Japan's merchandise trade balance could be in surplus with the sterling or open account areas when the balance was in substantial deficit with the dollar area (see, for example, the figures for FY 1951 and 1954 in Table 2.4). While the initial agreement with the United Kingdom (concluded in May 1948) had allowed Japan to convert sterling balances in excess of a certain designated amount into dollars every six months, this so-called "dollar clause" was abolished in April 1951. Sterling balances increased steadily from 1950 to 1952 (see Table 2.5).

For this reason, authorities sometimes used control procedures to discourage exports to the sterling area by placing certain goods under the licensing procedure or by shortening the period of execution for export contracts. At times, the discount rate for sterling area export bills was set higher than that for the dollar area, margins were increased for the buying rate of spot and forward sterling, and the length of forward contracts in sterling was reduced. On the other hand, to encourage exports to the dollar area, export proceeds

Table 2.4. Japan's exports and imports by currency area, fiscal years 1951–7 (in millions of US dollars)

		Exports	Imports	Balance
1951	Total	1,410	1,659	−249
	Dollars	309	933	−624
	Sterling	674	443	231
	Open	427	283	144
1952	Total	1,168	1,790	−622
	Dollars	440	957	−517
	Sterling	469	557	−88
	Open	259	276	−17
1953	Total	1,245	2,242	−997
	Dollars	453	1,160	−707
	Sterling	335	568	−233
	Open	457	514	−57
1954	Total	1,602	1,768	−166
	Dollars	530	1,006	−476
	Sterling	580	324	256
	Open	492	438	54
1955	Total	2,095	1,956	139
	Dollars	846	896	−50
	Sterling	781	613	168
	Open	468	447	21
1956	Total	2,494	2,782	−288
	Dollars	1,149	1,404	−255
	Sterling	1,013	998	15
	Open	332	380	−48
1957	Total	2,818	3,347	−529
	Dollars	1,300	1,793	−493
	Sterling	1,286	1,341	−55
	Open	232	213	19

Source: MOF, *Fiscal and Monetary Statistics Monthly*

from that area were sometimes accorded higher retention credits, which could preferentially be used to import goods on a specified list or for travel and other invisible expenses associated with the promotion of trade (see Section 2.3.4 for details).

The system of linking exports with preferred imports was another way of promoting certain exports. For example, during 1953–4, the export of ships, raw silk, whale oil, and plant equipment was linked with the import of Cuban sugar, which was cheaper than sugar from Taiwan or Indonesia. Because the domestic price of sugar was set much higher than the import cost of Cuban sugar, the profit from its sales provided a subsidy to expand the export of those designated commodities. In May 1954, however, the linking of raw silk with Cuban sugar was suspended because the export of silk had exceeded the target for the April–June period. This type of export–import link was altogether

Table 2.5. Japan's foreign exchange reserves, fiscal years 1949–63 (in millions of US dollars)

End of fiscal year	US dollars	Sterling	Open	Total (Old method)	Total (New method)[a]
1949	156	44	18	219	—
1950	464	55	42	561	—
1951	583	211	120	915	—
1952	768	249	122	1,138	—
1953	789	119	69	977	—
1954	648	214	192	1,054	—
1955	811	261	244	1,316	839
1956	1,063	91	267	1,421	738
1957	594	59	304	957	629
1958	—	—	—	—	974
1959	—	—	—	—	1,361
1960	—	—	—	—	1,997
1961	—	—	—	—	1,561
1962	—	—	—	—	1,863
1963	—	—	—	—	1,996

[a] The method of measuring foreign exchange reserves was substantially revised at the end of FY 1957, i.e., from April 1958; the new method subtracts from the previous concept (1) the balance in the open account, (2) the balance held by foreign exchange banks, and (3) Treasury deposits at foreign exchange banks; and adds (4) official gold holdings

Sources: MOF, *Fiscal and Monetary Statistics Monthly*; BOJ, *Economic Statistics of Japan*

abolished in 1955 in response to foreign criticism (Okazaki and Korenaga 1999b).

Japanese authorities also adopted a system of granting preferential treatment in the allocation of foreign exchange for the import of raw materials to those manufacturers who could fulfill their export quotas. Ratios were fixed between the raw materials allocated and the exports of finished products. As of November 1954, imports of six types of raw materials were linked to exports of final products: raw cotton to cotton textile products, wood to wood products, rayon pulp to artificial fiber products, iron and steel scrap to iron and steel products, lumber to plywood, and beef tallow to oil and fats (glycerin).

2.3.2. The Import Licensing System

Import licenses were granted within the framework of the FEB, which specified the maximum amounts for overall as well as individual imports. With minor exceptions (e.g., government imports), all goods required a license to be imported. Licenses were fairly freely granted for foodstuffs, basic raw materials, and specified machinery and equipment, but more severe restrictions were imposed on consumer goods, especially luxuries. All licensed imports were planned in the FEB and, for most commodities, portions were made public through the MITI's "import announcements (*yunyū kōhyō* or *yunyū happyō*)" from time to time. The first announcement by the MITI was made on 29 December 1949 for the January–March 1950 FEB. The budget for most invisibles was announced by the MOF.

There were two types of announcements. First, the type of announcement known as *yunyū kōhyō* was made once at the beginning of each budget period for some commodities. Second, for others, the type of announcement called *yunyū happyō* was applied, whereby disclosure was made in several installments during the period. This allowed authorities to make a better assessment of the flow of imports and prevailing domestic market conditions and also to minimize the possibility of disturbing the suppliers' markets. Regardless of type, the announcements would include information concerning: (1) the commodities for which application for license to import would be accepted; (2) the prescribed currency of settlement; (3) the import limit per applicant; (4) the opening and closing dates for license application; (5) the percentage of required guarantee money (to be explained in Section 2.3.3); (6) the foreign exchange allocation requirements; (7) the shipment area; (8) the settlement period; and (9) other relevant items.

Initially, regular imports covered by these announcements were licensed under two principal systems.[20] The first and most important instrument of import control involved direct allocation of exchange under the Fund Allocation (FA) system (*Gaika Shikin Wariate Sei*), which consisted of establishing quotas for the importation of particular goods from particular currency areas. In 1953, for example, the FA system applied to about 65 percent of all imports, covering foodstuffs, raw materials, and other essentials, primarily from the dollar area. For most FA goods, *yunyū happyō* was used as the type of import announcement,[21] and the MITI awarded import allocation certificates entitling importers to obtain the necessary exchange from authorized foreign exchange banks. A lump sum of exchange was allotted to each importer for a certain commodity to ensure proper supply of raw materials to selected industries. In their allocation decisions, authorities could take into consideration the applicants' production capacity, inventories, and shipment records.

The second import licensing system, the Automatic Approval (AA) system (*Jidō Shōnin Sei*), was first introduced in the July–September 1950 FEB and

---

[20] In addition, there was a minor system called "the First-Come, First-Served system" (*Senchakujun Sei*). Although this was more widely used at the beginning (Ozaki 1972), it became applicable to minor miscellaneous imports as well as those commodities that Japan was obliged to import under the provisions of certain trade and payments agreements. This licensing system, which covered only about 1 percent of total imports in 1953, was formally abolished in November 1956.

[21] *Yunyū happyō* became the only type of announcement for FA goods from the second FY 1950 FEB (October 1959) (BOT 1960).

applied to about 34 percent of all imports in 1953. For AA goods, *yunyū kōhyō* was the method of import announcement, and licenses were issued as long as the budgetary quota for a particular currency area was not fully committed. No quantitative limit was set for each commodity, only the limit for overall imports from a particular currency area. This system applied to goods that could not be easily allocated to specific industries.

The FA system increasingly came to serve as an instrument of industrial policy, especially from the late 1950s (BOT 1960). Okazaki and Korenaga (1999a, 1999b), explaining how the system worked, show that authorities devised and then strictly followed a foreign exchange allocation rule based on export performance and production capacity. In particular, based on detailed data for the wool-spinning industry, they show that the firm-level allocation of foreign exchange could be explained almost entirely by two variables, export performance and production capacity (with an R-squared of 0.967–97), for every FEB from the second half of FY 1953 to the second half of FY 1960. Thus, the system minimized the potential for corruption and rent seeking by removing room for arbitrariness. At the same time, by creating incentives for firms to increase production capacity and claim the rewards from exports, it served to promote private exports and investment.

2.3.3. Tools of Import Control

As a means of relaxing or tightening restrictions, goods were constantly shifted from one licensing system to another. To encourage imports from certain areas, for example, goods subject to direct allocation of exchange under the FA system could be moved to the AA list. To discourage imports from some areas, on the other hand, some goods could be withdrawn from the AA list and placed on the FA list. Non-quantitative measures for import control included financial incentives and the imposition of more strict terms of settlement. To encourage imports, for example, better import financing facilities—such as yen usance (time) bills or foreign exchange loans with a much lower rate of interest—were extended. To discourage imports, the application period or the terms of license were shortened.

The system of guarantee money was another tool of import control. Applicants for import licenses under the AA system were required to make a deposit of import guarantee money (*yunyū hoshōkin*), the amount of which was calculated by multiplying the value of the intended import goods by the percentage specified for the particular category of goods and the currency area from which they were being imported. In cases of cancellation, the deposit was in principle confiscated. To encourage or discourage imports, deposit requirements for particular items could be lowered or raised, either collectively or discriminately.

2.3.4. The Special Exchange Fund Allocation System

The Special Exchange Fund Allocation System (*Gaika Shikin Tokubetsu Wariate Seido*), called the Export Promotion Foreign Exchange System (*Yushutsu Shinkō Gaika Shikin Seido*) from November 1951 to August 1953, had its origin in the Foreign Exchange Credit System of July 1949, which was introduced on a nondiscriminatory basis for all currency areas. This was a Japanese version of the so-called retention quota system, which was widely used in many countries as a scheme of export promotion in the 1950s (IMF 1950). In the original system, exporters were given three different retention credits of 3, 6, and 10 percent on their proceeds, depending on the type of commodities exported. Retention credits could be used to make payments for certain commodities and services under a much simpler licensing procedure. All payments abroad to be effected with retention credits required prior approval of the BOJ in the case of nontrade payments and the MITI in the case of imports.

The system was suspended at the end of June 1951 but was reinstated in December 1951 (retroactive to 1 July 1951) as the Export Promotion Foreign Exchange System on a discriminatory basis. The old set of retained percentages (3, 6, and 10) was applied only to exports to the dollar area, while percentages for exports to other currency areas were set at 1, 3, and 6 percent. In July 1952, allocation of retention credits for exports to the sterling area and open account countries was suspended because of the excessive accumulation of sterling and open account dollar balances. At the same time, retention percentages for exports to the dollar area were raised to 5, 10, and 15 percent. The scope of eligible imports under the system was also expanded from "raw materials, machinery, instruments, and related commodities deemed to contribute to the promotion of exports" to "commodities deemed to contribute to the promotion of exports or the rehabilitation and stabilization of the economy."

In particular, retention credits could be used for the following purposes: (1) expenses for traveling or staying abroad connected with the promotion of trade; (2) advertising, research, and similar expenses associated with the promotion of trade; (3) freight, insurance premiums, and similar expenses associated with goods imported by the use of retention credits; (4) expenses associated with the establishment of branches in foreign countries; (5) goods deemed to contribute to the promotion of exports or the rehabilitation and stabilization of the economy; and (6) samples, catalogs, and other similar materials. In August 1953, the uniform rate of 10 percent was applied to all exports regardless of currency area, and the name of the system was changed to the Special Exchange Fund Allocation System.

2.4. THE RESTRICTIVE SYSTEM AS A TOOL FOR EXTERNAL ADJUSTMENT

2.4.1. The Balance-of-Payments Crisis of 1952–3

Japan's balance of payments deteriorated sharply in 1952 and 1953, partly because of stagnation in the world economy and import restrictions imposed against Japanese exports by members of the British Commonwealth and some open account countries, but more directly because of the sizable expansion of Japan's domestic demand (Narvekar 1957). While the overall merchandise trade deficit widened from $249 million in FY 1951 to $997 million in FY 1953, the deterioration was more pronounced for the sterling balance: the surplus of $231 million in FY 1951 turned to a deficit of $233 million in FY 1953 (see Table 2.4). Because the balance of sterling reserves had reached a critically low level by the middle of 1953, Japan purchased the sterling equivalent of $124 million in four installments from the IMF between September and December of that year.[22] Even with this drawing, the official holding of sterling declined by an equivalent of $130 million from the end of FY 1952 to the end of FY 1953 (see Table 2.5).

Measures were taken to reduce aggregate spending, stimulate exports, and achieve balance in trade with sterling area countries. In February 1953, authorities temporarily suspended the processing of applications for imports under the AA system from the sterling area. As previously stated, in August 1953, the system of retention credits was modified to remove disincentives against exporting to the sterling area, and the rate was set uniformly at 10 percent for all areas. Imports of less essential and luxury goods were made ineligible under the retention credit system. Credits arising from exports to the open account area were not permitted to be used for imports from the dollar and sterling areas.

In October 1953, the MITI removed sixty items from the exchange allocation system for the second half of FY 1953, including cocoa, coffee, alcoholic drinks, cosmetics, and some drugs. For FY 1954, moreover, authorities scaled down the FEB substantially: the foreign exchange allocation of $1.446 billion for imports in the second half of FY 1953 was reduced to $932 million and $1.04 billion, respectively, for the first and second halves of FY 1954 on a confirmation basis (see Table 2.1).[23] With the removal of additional items from the AA list in the first half of FY 1954, the proportion of imports covered

---

[22] Because Japan repurchased ¥22.2 billion with a payment of $61.6 million before making the fourth purchase, amounting to $61.6 million, its net purchase did not exceed $62.4 million.

[23] Initial figures could differ from confirmation figures because (1) there were lags in execution of import contracts, (2) additional funds were made available during the course of a given budget period, or (3) budgeted funds were not fully utilized for various reasons.

under the AA system declined from 33 percent of total imports in the second half of FY 1952 to 13 percent. On the other hand, imports covered under the FA system rose from 65 percent to 82 percent.

At the same time, Japanese authorities adopted measures to tighten special facilities for import financing, including shortening loan terms. In January 1954, they required that foreign exchange banks receive import guarantee money in cash and redeposit it with the BOJ for a prescribed period of time (initially twenty days; subsequently increased to three months), whereas the previous requirement had been simply that a letter of guarantee be sent by a foreign exchange bank to the BOJ. In April 1954, they raised the deposit requirements from 5 percent to 25 percent for imports under the AA system and from 1 percent to 5 percent for some imports under the FA system (to which the requirement had been applied during the previous year for the first time).

In April 1954, the scope of barter transactions was expanded. Previously, Japanese authorities had approved barter deals only when (1) it was necessary to cultivate new markets, or (2) it was difficult to expand exports to certain countries because of trade restrictions. Now, barter could be approved if deemed necessary to improve Japan's balance of payments. In July, authorities expanded the export insurance system and the system of preferential export finance, under which the BOJ applied lower interest rates to export advance bills and extended yen funds to Japanese commercial banks with export usance bills as collateral at rates prevailing in major financial markets abroad. To promote exports, part of the income received from exports was exempted from taxation, and items were added to the list of imports eligible under the retention credit system.

These restrictive measures were implemented in conjunction with broad deflationary macroeconomic measures consisting of monetary tightening (begun in October 1953) and fiscal austerity (adopted with the FY 1954 budget). Commercial bank lending was curtailed through the application of higher central bank penal rates as well as through the BOJ's window guidance. The number of instruments eligible for discount by the central bank was reduced, and the scale of the general account budget was cut in FY 1954, mainly through a reduction in the investment program, although the overall cash position of the government remained in deficit.

The Japanese balance of payments began to improve in the spring of 1954, and the overall balance turned to a surplus in the July–September quarter, followed by a surplus in the trade balance in the October–December quarter (Narvekar 1957). In April 1955, the restrictive measures therefore began to be relaxed. The deposit requirements, for example, were reduced to 5 percent for most imports under the AA system and to 3 percent for imports from the dollar area and 1 percent for imports from the sterling area under the FA system. The authorities also began to expand the scope of the AA system and the global quotas of the FA system (first introduced in April 1953 for pulp, barley, wheat, and a few other commodities), under which import allocation certificates were issued up to certain quotas for specified commodities without regard to the country of origin or the currency of settlement. At the same time, they remained cautious about relaxing restrictions on imports too much too fast, so they reduced the maximum term of import usance bills from six months to four months.[24]

2.4.2. The Balance-of-Payments Crisis of 1956–7

After improving further in 1955, Japan's external position began to deteriorate again in 1956 when the current account surplus of $205 million in 1955 turned to a deficit of $59 million. As in the previous crisis, Japan's problem showed up most seriously as a shortage of sterling balances because of Japanese policies of encouraging imports from the sterling area and open account countries and of encouraging exports to the dollar area. Because of the increased transferability of sterling, moreover, Japan had used sterling to make payments to the non-dollar area. The balance-of-payments difficulties occurred in 1956–7 despite the large increase in exports, suggesting that the primary cause was the expanding domestic demand associated with steady economic growth (Narvekar 1961). In fact, during this period, the Japanese economy was experiencing an investment boom, with private investment, national income, and industrial production all rising sharply in 1956 and early 1957. Wholesale prices rose, and the progress of import liberalization subsequent to the improvement in Japan's external position in 1954–5 contributed to a surge in imports as well. The balance-of-payments surplus of 1954–5 began to shrink in 1956, and a deficit emerged in the first half of 1957.

During this balance-of-payments crisis, authorities stated that existing restrictions on trade and payments would not be tightened in order to maintain the degree of liberalization that had thus far been achieved. In order to cope with the balance-of-payments problem, therefore, authorities initially used the macroeconomic tools of demand management (Narvekar 1961). The BOJ raised the discount rate twice, first in March and then in May 1957. Beginning with the FY 1957 budget (which took effect in April), authorities pursued a tight fiscal policy by curtailing the scale of government investment. Although an income tax cut was implemented in the budget, the central government ran a surplus in its cash position for that fiscal year. In June, Japan concluded an agreement to purchase $125 million from the IMF in order to finance part of the external deficit.[25]

---

[24] It was not until November 1960 that restrictions on import usance bills were relaxed.

[25] Japan made a drawing of $75 million in July and a drawing of $50 million in August.

In terms of trade control, Japanese authorities implemented only a few measures to restrict imports, most of which were financial (as opposed to quantitative). In May 1957, they tightened conditions for granting sterling usance bills to put them on an equal footing with dollar bills and raised interest rates on usance facilities. In June, the MITI raised the deposit rates of import guarantee money from 3–5 to 25 percent for imports under the AA system and from 1–3 to 5 percent for imports under the FA system and required that the deposit be made in cash for redeposit with the BOJ. There was some scaling down of FEBs for 1957, with a substantially reduced allocation for raw cotton and wool.[26]

Because of the macroeconomic adjustment program, which began in May 1957, a marked slowdown in economic activity emerged. The total value of imports for the second half of 1957 thus declined to a level comparable to the second half of 1955 so that even the smaller FEB was not fully utilized. While there was a deficit of $689 million in the balance of payments in the first half of 1957, there was a surplus of $187 million in the second half. As the balance of payments began to improve in the latter part of 1957, authorities began once again to ease restrictions. In December 1957, interest rates on usance bills were lowered. In May 1958, deposit rates of import guarantee money were lowered back to the levels that had prevailed before June 1957, and redeposit requirements with the BOJ were eliminated. Japan's trade and payments position further improved in 1958, and the adjustment program was terminated symbolically with the lowering of the discount rate on 18 June 1958.

2.5. MOVING TOWARD LIBERALIZATION OF THE SYSTEM

2.5.1. Changes in the Currency Area Classification

With the conclusion of less restrictive bilateral trade and payments agreements, new currencies were added to the list of designated currencies (see Tables 2.2 and 2.3) and adjustments were made in the classification of currency areas. In FY 1955, in part to comply with the IMF Executive Board

---

[26] Okazaki and Korenaga (1999b) discuss the confrontation that existed between the MITI and the MOF regarding the scaling down of FEBs for 1957. For the first half of FY 1957, the MITI argued for a large budget coupled with tight fiscal policy, while the MOF argued for a reduction in the budget as well. For the second half, given the improved balance-of-payments situation, the MOF argued for a significantly expanded budget, while the MITI asked for a smaller budget in order to adjust demand and supply conditions in industries. In both instances, the inter-ministry confrontation served to cut the FEB.

decision on bilateralism,[27] Japanese authorities began to abolish bilateral clearing account agreements in favor of settlement in US dollars, sterling, or selected major currencies. As a result, the number of such agreements steadily decreased from the peak of sixteen at the end of FY 1954. In addition to the Canadian dollar and the Swiss franc, which were added to the list of designated currencies in 1954, the deutsche mark and the Swedish krona became designated currencies when the new payments agreements took effect with West Germany (October 1955) and Sweden (April 1956), respectively.

By this time, the old three-currency-area classification had been changed to a six-currency-area classification: (1) the sterling area; (2) "specified area" countries, such as Argentina, Austria, China (Mainland), Denmark, Italy, Norway, the Portuguese Monetary Area, Sudan, and Thailand; (3) West Germany and Sweden; (4) Canada and Switzerland; (5) countries with bilateral clearing account agreements; and (6) all other countries on settlement in US dollars on a cash basis. With the increased transferability of sterling, category 2 was created in January 1956 for those countries with which sterling could be used as one of the possible means of payment (from late 1956 to early 1957, Finland, Uruguay, Cambodia, the USSR, Yugoslavia, and other Eastern European countries were added). With category 3 countries, settlements could be made either in the currency of the country or in sterling (the Belgian, French, and Netherlands monetary areas were later added). With category 4 countries, settlements could be made either in the currency of the country or in US dollars.

In December 1958, the six currency areas were again reclassified into three, namely: (1) the dollar settlement area; (2) the special settlement account area; and (3) all others (with which transactions were made principally in convertible currencies). In January 1959, the countries were further reclassified into two groups: (1) the special settlement account countries and (2) all others, with the result that the distinction between different designated currencies had been eliminated. Except with countries under bilateral clearing agreements, settlements with all other countries could be made in any of the designated currencies. This measure was taken in view of the restoration of external convertibility for thirteen major European currencies, which took effect on 29 December 1958, along with the dissolution of the European Payments Union (though full convertibility would not be achieved until February 1961).[28]

---

[27] In June 1955, the IMF issued an appeal to member countries to reduce and eliminate reliance on bilateralism as rapidly as practicable in order to establish "a multilateral system of payments in respect of current transactions between members." Executive Board Decision No. 433-(55/42), as found in IMF (2007), pp. 498–9.

[28] Under external (or nonresident) convertibility, authorities only permitted nonresidents' current earnings to be exchanged into any foreign currency. Otherwise, most of these countries continued to maintain restrictions on the making of payments and transfers for current transactions until they accepted the obligations under Article VIII of the IMF Articles of Agreement on 15 February 1961.

With the addition of other countries to the monetary areas of Western European countries, as many as thirty countries had established external convertibility by the beginning of January 1959 (IMF 1959).

At this time, only four bilateral clearing treaties were in effect, namely those with Turkey, Greece, Taiwan, and the Republic of Korea. By then, Japan had abolished bilateral treaties not only with European countries but also with such countries as Thailand, the Philippines, and Indonesia. The new payments agreements with the Philippines (stipulating settlement in US dollars on a cash basis beginning in August 1957) and with Indonesia (stipulating settlement in transferable pounds on a cash basis beginning in July 1957) had been negotiated in the context of reparations or economic cooperation treaties being concluded with the respective governments in May 1956 and January 1958 (Takagi 1995; see also Section 3.3.2 in Chapter 3). By the end of FY 1961, all bilateral clearing treaties were abolished, except with Korea (see Table 2.3).

2.5.2. Changes in the System of Export Control

Although the worsening balance-of-payments situation had led authorities to expand the scope of barter trade in April 1954, they revised the regulations again in October of that year, tightening the scope of barter trade (in which exports and imports were balanced transaction by transaction) in terms of geographical areas and the number of eligible items.[29] In November, the linking of exports to raw sugar and other preferred imports was abolished. The linking of exports to certain raw material imports remained in place, however, although the number of categories was reduced from six to four in April 1955, with the termination of links between scrap iron imports and exports of iron and steel products as well as between imports of timber and exports of plywood. The linking of beef tallow imports with exports of glycerin was abolished in April 1957.

In March 1955, the percentage of retention credits was reduced from 10 to 5 percent, in light of abuses in the system as well as the need to further normalize the system. In January 1957, the percentage was further reduced from 5 to 3 percent. Beginning in July, retention credits could no longer be applied to invisibles, such as foreign travel, advertisements, and expenses associated with the maintenance of foreign resident offices. On 1 October 1960, the Special Exchange Fund Allocation System (with retention credits) was abolished, and eligible imports under the system were transferred to the regular import licensing procedure.

---

[29] In principle, barter trade could be approved only if the country in question had no diplomatic relations or trade agreements with Japan or it had insufficient foreign exchange to purchase Japanese goods; barter contracts would not be approved if Japan had an open account settlement agreement with that country.

2.5.3. Changes in the Import Licensing System

In the latter part of FY 1955, Japan's balance of payments improved, prompting authorities to begin to liberalize imports by enlarging the overall FEB, widening the scope of the AA system, enlarging the global quota system, and introducing the non-dollar global quota system (in April 1956). While the global quota system had accounted for less than 2 percent of total imports in the April–October 1954 budget, it covered about 50 percent in the April–October 1956 budget, with another 8 percent accounted for by the non-dollar global quota system. The most restrictive and discriminatory system of individual licensing covered only 23 percent. In the second half of FY 1956, an additional thirty-one items were transferred from the FA system to the AA system.

With a deteriorating balance of payments, however, there was a setback to liberalization of the restrictive system in FY 1957 (see Section 2.4.2). As previously stated, during the adjustment program of 1957–8, authorities attempted to maintain the degree of progress made thus far in import liberalization by principally resorting to demand management policies. Although they did institute some restrictive measures mostly of a financial nature, they continued to expand the AA system and to increase the proportion of foreign exchange set aside as the global quota system, albeit within the context of overall tightening. In the first half of FY 1957, thirty-five more items were added to the AA list, and the global quota system was expanded to cover almost 70 percent of total imports within the FA system.

In response to the improved balance-of-payments situation and the resumption of external convertibility for major European currencies, authorities began to liberalize imports still further. In November 1959, the Automatic Fund Allocation (AFA) system (*Gaika Shikin Jidō Wariate Sei*) was introduced as an easy and flexible means of protecting certain domestic industries as imports were liberalized. Under the AFA system, the allocation of foreign exchange for the import of certain designated items, such as various types of machinery and equipment, could be automatic on application to the MITI without restrictions, unless it was thought that the importation of a particular item would be harmful to domestic producers or that it might have an adverse effect on the balance of payments. In practice, authorities used the AFA system as a buffer with which they transferred items from the FA system to the AA system.[30] Typically, if the transfer of a commodity from the FA system to the AFA system did not raise an issue in one semiannual FEB period, the commodity was transferred to the AA system in the next period.

---

[30] Because the AFA system operated like the AA system, authorities decided in January 1960 to apply the AA system's import deposit requirement to the AFA system.

By the end of the 1950s, exchange allocation certificates under the FA system were issued on a global basis for most commodities without regard to the country of origin or the currency of settlement. Under the AA system, the allocation of foreign exchange to import specified commodities was effectively free from restrictions as to total value because additional amounts were routinely replenished when the original appropriation in the FEB was exhausted. In fact, licenses for the specified commodities on the AA list were issued automatically by foreign exchange banks simply upon application. Except for a few commodities, discrimination on the basis of currency areas had also been eliminated for goods on the AA list.

2.6. FOREIGN TRADE AND FOREIGN EXCHANGE MARKET ACTIVITY

2.6.1. Expansion of Japan's Foreign Trade

Although the system of trade and payments was not free from government control, it was nonetheless under this system that the Japanese economy made a full recovery from the devastation of World War II. From 1952 to 1964, Japan's gross national product (GNP) expanded by 4.6 times, with an average real growth of 8.4 percent per year. Trade also expanded by as much as 8 times from 1950 to 1964 (see Figure 2.1). Japan did not achieve this simply by restoring the prewar markets for its traditional exports. In 1957, the

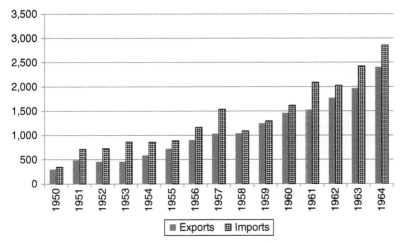

Figure 2.1. Japan's exports and imports, 1950–64 (in billions of yen)

Source: IMF, *International Financial Statistics*

proportion of metals, manufactures, machinery, and transport equipment was considerably higher, with a lower share of textiles. Also, North America and Southeast Asia took much larger shares of Japan's exports, whereas the share of the Far East was smaller. Narvekar (1960) estimates that over 70 percent of the 140-plus percent increase in exports from 1954 to 1957 could be explained by Japan's increased competitiveness, after correcting for the effect due to the growth and compositional change of world trade.

2.6.2. Expansion of Foreign Exchange Market Activity

The foreign exchange market emerged in Japan in July 1952 following the government decisions of preceding months to relax foreign exchange surrender requirements,[31] thereby allowing foreign exchange banks to maintain a limited open position in dollars. As the surrender requirements for sterling balances were relaxed in March 1953, the market expanded to include transactions involving the pound (BOJ 1973; Sumitomo Bank 1960; Tateno 1993). Even so, market activity remained limited as the Foreign Exchange Fund Special Account, acting through the BOJ as its agent, stood ready to buy and sell US dollars and British pounds at prescribed exchange rates with narrow margins. Initially, the BOJ directly transacted with foreign exchange banks at ¥0.35 above or below the basic rate, namely, at ¥360.35 and ¥359.65;[32] for the pound, the official selling and buying rates were ¥1,008.98 and ¥1,007.02, respectively. Under these circumstances, there was little scope for private market activity. Total turnover in Tokyo amounted to a mere $20 million during 1952 (see Table 2.6).[33]

The progressive withdrawal of government involvement, the introduction of wider margins, and the relaxation of surrender requirements all led to a growth of market activity (see Table 2.7 for a list of major actions affecting the dollar and sterling exchange rates).[34] On 12 January 1953, the MOF widened the margins and changed the official selling and buying rates of the US dollar

---

[31] Previously foreign exchange banks were required to sell any foreign exchange they might acquire to the Foreign Exchange Fund Special Account.

[32] In the customer market, the selling and buying rates for banks were set at ¥360.80 and ¥359.20, respectively.

[33] Osaka also had a foreign exchange market, which accounted for almost 30 percent of total turnover in the mid 1960s (Isobe 1966). Its importance diminished over time, though it still accounted for about 10 percent in 1969. There was a market in Nagoya as well, but the volume of turnover was negligible (BOJ 1973).

[34] The Foreign Exchange Fund Special Account did not buy or sell non-dollar, non-sterling currencies, making the pricing of forward contracts for all other designated currencies free (though the spot rates were officially set). From 10 September 1956, the setting of their spot rates was also made freely allowable, subject to the stipulation that they should remain within 1 percent on either side of the arbitrage exchange rate (MITI 1990).

Table 2.6. Japan's foreign exchange market, 1949–65

	Trading volume in Tokyo (in billions of US dollars)			Authorized foreign exchange banks (end of year)		
	Spot	Forwards and swaps	Total[a]	Domestic banks	Foreign banks	Total
1949	—	—	—	9	7	16
1950	—	—	—	20	8	28
1951	—	—	—	26	8	34
1952	0.02	—	0.02	29	8	37
1953	0.12	0.00	0.12	30	9	39
1954	0.09	—	0.09	32	9	41
1955	0.11	0.01	0.13	32	10	42
1956	0.21	0.03	0.24	32	10	42
1957	0.23	0.02	0.25	32	10	42
1958	0.24	0.05	0.29	32	10	42
1959	0.20	0.13	0.33	32	10	42
1960	0.30	0.30	0.60	44	10	54
1961	0.44	0.40	0.84	57	10	67
1962	0.82	0.89	1.71	59	10	69
1963	1.25	1.43	2.68	60	11	71
1964	1.87	1.89	3.76	64	12	76
1965	2.06	2.46	4.52	65	12	77
		Memorandum				
1970	4.76	6.74	11.50	70	16	86
1975	22.92	50.51	73.43	101	48	149
1980	211.84	367.38	579.22	122	64	186
1985	462.68	972.90	1,435.58	167	78	245
1990	2,495.66	3,466.87	5,962.53	218	92	310

[a] Numbers may not add up to total because of rounding
Source: Tokyo Foreign Exchange Market Practice Committee, as quoted in Tateno (1993), Tables 14–1 and 14–2

to ¥360.80 and ¥359.20, respectively. In September 1957, as the sterling payments crisis unfolded, the Foreign Exchange Fund Special Account ceased to buy or sell forward sterling, effectively liberalizing transactions in forward sterling contracts. In December 1957, the official exchange rates for sterling were allowed to be determined freely within 0.75 percent above or below the arbitrage rate of ¥1,008; on 14 August 1958, these 0.75 percent margins were widened to 1 percent and further to 1.5 percent on 12 September 1959 (Nakai 1961). In January 1959, the MOF removed all restrictions on spot and forward dealings in designated currencies by authorized foreign exchange banks, except for US dollars.

As to the US dollar exchange rate, on 12 September 1959, the official selling and buying prices were set at ¥361.80 and ¥358.20 (i.e., 0.5 percent on either side of the basic exchange rate), respectively (at this time, the margins for other currencies—including sterling, as noted above—were widened

Table 2.7. Major regulatory measures affecting official exchange rates in Japan, 1953–63

Date of action	US dollar		British pound	
	Spot	Forward	Spot	Forward
December 1949/January 1950	Prescribed margins of ¥0.35 (0.1 percent) on either side of basic rate of ¥360	1 percent per year for forward sales; forward rate set equal to spot rate for forward purchases	Prescribed margins of ¥0.98 (0.1 percent) on either side of arbitrage rate of ¥1,008	1 percent per year for forward sales; forward rate set equal to spot rate for forward purchases
12 January 1953	Prescribed margins widened to ¥0.80	n.a.	n.a.	n.a.
25 January 1954	n.a.	n.a.	Arbitrate rate to be determined by Minister of Finance based on market developments	n.a.
25 September 1957	n.a.	n.a.	n.a.	Government withdraws from forward transactions
9 December 1957	n.a.	n.a.	Prescribed margins widened to ¥7.56 (0.75 percent) on either side of arbitrage rate of ¥1,008	n.a.
14 August 1958	n.a.	n.a.	Prescribed margins widened to 1 percent	n.a.
12 September 1959	Prescribed margins widened to ¥1.80 (0.5 percent)	Government withdraws from forward transactions	Prescribed margins widened to 1.5 percent	n.a.
22 April 1963	Prescribed margins widened to 0.75 percent	n.a.	n.a.	n.a.

Sources: Sakamoto (1960); Nakai (1961); MITI (1990); Takagi (1997)

from 1 to 1.5 percent above or below the arbitrage rate). The determination of spot exchange rates in the retail market was liberalized, subject to the requirement that the rate stay within the 0.5 percent limit; spot rates for telegraphic transfers in US dollars were made freely quotable within 0.5 percent on either side. In the retail market, forward exchange rates for the US dollar were made freely quotable. Official transactions in forward dollars with foreign exchange banks were discontinued (Sumitomo Bank 1960). In April 1960, trading companies were permitted to hold US dollar and sterling deposits with authorized foreign exchange banks, to which no surrender requirements applied.

The establishment of non resident free-yen deposits (FYDs) in July 1960 increased the depth of the foreign exchange market by giving nonresidents the freedom to transact in yen (see Section 2.7.3; also Section 3.4.1 in Chapter 3). It also subjected the yen to greater volatility by increasing the volume of short-term capital flows. For example, the initial inflows of short-term capital were large enough to cause the yen to appreciate from ¥361.77 on 29 June to ¥358.22 on 11 July 1960—that is, from the upper limit to the lower limit of the range—in a matter of ten days (Sakamoto 1960). In order to allow the exchange rate to play a greater role in trade adjustment as imports were increasingly liberalized, on 22 April 1963 authorities further widened the margins from 0.5 to 0.75 percent[35] while allowing the rate to be freely determined within these limits. To enforce these limits, they introduced market intervention operations, whereby the BOJ, on behalf of the government, stood ready to step in whenever the exchange rate moved abnormally; the BOJ was also authorized to operate in the foreign exchange market "intra-marginally"—between the upper and lower limits—by using the Foreign Exchange Fund Special Account. The quotation of exchange rates by foreign exchange banks in the retail market was fully liberalized for all currencies, though banks voluntarily limited the additional margins charged to customers to ¥0.50 on either side (BOJ 1973; Isobe 1966).

The volume of trading in the Tokyo foreign exchange market expanded steadily as the Japanese economy grew and the restrictive system of trade and payments was progressively liberalized. Even so, it was not until after the collapse of the Bretton Woods system in 1971 and the floating of the yen in 1973 that the volume of trading saw a remarkable expansion. In June 1971, the MOF would ease restrictions on the holding of foreign currencies by residents (they needed to be surrendered within one month, instead of ten days) and eliminate the system of designated currencies authorized for use in international transactions (numbering fifteen at the time). In April 1972, the Tokyo dollar call market was established to meet the need for a market in foreign currency funds and, in May 1972, the foreign exchange surrender requirements were abolished altogether. With additional liberalization of market practices,[36] Tokyo would become the world's third largest foreign exchange market by the mid 1980s.

---

[35] This was in line with the practice in Europe, where most countries voluntarily used narrower margins than were allowed under Article IV of the IMF Articles of Agreement (1 percent on either side of parity) in order to minimize the margins against each other.

[36] The revised Foreign Exchange and Foreign Trade Control Law of 1980 fully lifted the entry and maturity restrictions in the Tokyo dollar call market. In 1985, market practices were changed to allow direct interbank trading and international broking, whereby domestic foreign exchange brokers could mediate trades with foreign markets.

2.6.3. Evolution of the Yen's Real Exchange Rate

The yen, pegged to the US dollar in early 1949 at the rate of ¥360, may have become quickly overvalued, given the several months of elevated inflation relative to the United States from 1949 to 1950 (see Section 1.5.2 in Chapter 1). How the yen's equilibrium exchange rate may have evolved subsequently is difficult to judge because Japan's trade and payments regime was tightly controlled. On the one hand, the fact that Japan ran a balance of trade deficit year after year may be an indication that the yen was overvalued through the mid 1960s when a surplus emerged. This view is consistent with the yen's black-market rate in Hong Kong, which was ¥400–50 per dollar during 1955 (Okazaki and Korenaga 1999b; Takagi 1997). The meticulous work of Fujino (1988) estimates the yen's purchasing power parity (PPP) rate in 1955 to have been ¥450–90 per dollar by using the base year of 1938.[37] In 1958, the Economic Planning Agency estimated that the PPP rate for the yen was ¥406 (Nihon Keizai Shimbunsha 1969). Komiya and Itoh (1988) maintain that, if the yen had not been overvalued, Japanese authorities would have had no need to introduce the zealous measures to promote exports and restrict imports that they did in the 1950s.

On the other hand, the trade deficit could just have been a reflection of the relatively more rapid growth of the Japanese economy; Japan was simply investing more than saving, given the higher rate of return on domestic investment than on foreign investment. Likewise, the more depreciated black-market rate could have only been an indication of the effectiveness of domestic rationing of US dollars. Whatever the initial overvaluation, however, it is probably safe to assume that Japan's faster productivity growth relative to the United States and other trading partners made the currency less over-valued as time wore on. With a fixed nominal exchange rate, real appreciation was possible only with a higher rate of inflation. This was indeed the case. For the period 1950–64 as a whole, the yen did appreciate in real terms by as much as 48 percent against the dollar and 18 percent against the pound, measured in terms of relative consumer prices (see Figure 2.2).

Japan has often been portrayed as a classic case of the celebrated Balassa–Samuelson effect (Balassa 1964; Samuelson 1964) whereby the currency of a faster growing economy appreciates in real terms. This is typically explained by higher productivity growth in the tradable goods sector, which raises the relative price of nontradable goods and thereby the consumer price index with a large share of services. Rogoff (1996) calls Japan the "canonical" example where a sustained appreciation of the real exchange rate against the US dollar

---

[37] Fujino (1988) further argues that, as a result of productivity gains, the yen was undervalued by the end of the Bretton Woods era in 1971.

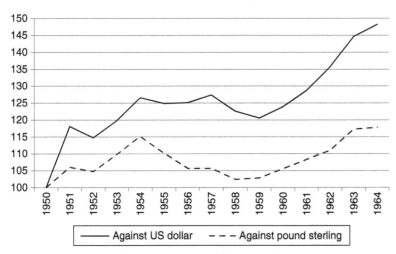

Figure 2.2. Yen's real exchange rates against US dollar and pound sterling, 1950–64 (based on consumer prices; 1950=100)

Source: IMF, *International Financial Statistics*

after World War II was due to an exceptionally large differential between productivity growth in the traded and nontradable goods sectors. For the period 1956–70, however, Imai (2010) notes that a larger portion of the yen's real appreciation reflected an increase in tradable goods prices and that the Balassa–Samuelson effect was therefore secondary. Unlike China, which achieved trade opening with a depreciating currency (Ito et al. 1997), it is significant that Japan's postwar reconstruction and expansion of trade occurred against the background of a currency that was appreciating in real terms and was also possibly overvalued initially.

2.7. TRADE AND EXCHANGE LIBERALIZATION IN THE EARLY 1960s

2.7.1. The "Plan for Trade and Exchange Liberalization"

The possibility of terminating transitional arrangements under Article XIV of the IMF Articles of Agreement (which allowed Japan to maintain "restrictions on payments and transfers for current international transactions that were in effect on the date on which it became a member") in favor of assuming the obligations of Article VIII was discussed between IMF staff and Japanese authorities as early as the summer of 1955. Japanese authorities were initially reluctant. In addition to what they considered to be Japan's still weak economic conditions, its lack of diplomatic relations or commercial treaties with many countries, the invocation of Article 35 of the General Agreement on Tariffs and Trade (GATT) by some countries to discriminate against Japanese goods,[38] and the heavy orientation of Japanese exports toward soft currency areas were among the reasons cited by the authorities.

Following the restoration of external convertibility for major European currencies in December 1958, however, there emerged an increased awareness within Japan of the benefits of a more open trade and payments system (Sumitomo Bank 1960). At the same time, with the US balance of payments deteriorating during 1958–9, Japan faced increasing external pressure to ease trade restrictions, particularly discriminatory practices against US products. At the annual meetings of the IMF and the GATT in 1959, for example, specific criticisms were directed against aspects of Japan's restrictive trade and payments system, such as the export–import linking devices, the barter deals, and the apparent lack of transparency in foreign exchange allocation rules. It was against this background that a Ministerial Council on the Promotion of Trade and Exchange Liberalization (*Bōeki Kawase Jiyūka Sokushin Kakuryō Kaigi*) was set up within the cabinet, with the prime minister as chairman, in order to discuss the objectives and timing of liberalization. In its inaugural meeting on 12 January 1960, it was decided that a program of liberalization would be formulated by the end of May.

On 24 June 1960, the government announced an "Outline of the Plan for Trade and Exchange Liberalization" (*Bōeki Kawase Jiyūka Keikaku Taikō*), which would be implemented over the following three years. In this program, imports were divided into four broad groups: (1) those to be liberalized within one year; (2) those to be liberalized within two to three years; (3) those to be liberalized within three years, if possible; and (4) those for which no schedule could be determined. It was announced that the import liberalization ratio (the proportion of imports under the AA and AFA systems in terms of the composition of imports in calendar year 1959, chosen as the base period) would increase from about 40 percent in April 1960 to about 80 percent within three years. All restrictions on payments for current invisibles would be removed within two years, and exchange controls connected with capital transactions would be gradually relaxed as circumstances permitted.

---

[38] When Japan was admitted as a full member of the Contracting Parties of the GATT on 9 September 1955, Article 35 was invoked against Japan by fourteen countries, namely, Australia, Austria, Belgium, Brazil, Cuba, France, Haiti, India, Luxembourg, the Netherlands, New Zealand, Rhodesia and Nyasaland, the Union of South Africa, and the United Kingdom. Subsequently, additional countries applied Article 35 to Japan. It was not until the early 1960s that the article was disinvoked by most countries, including Australia (1964), Belgium (1964), Cuba (1961), France (1963), Luxembourg (1964), the Netherlands (1964), New Zealand (1962), Rhodesia and Nyasaland (1963), and the United Kingdom (1963). See Komiya and Itoh (1988).

Table 2.8. Selected import liberalization measures in Japan, 1950–64

Date	Actions or comments
August 1950	Automatic Approval (AA) system introduced
January 1951	154 items announced on AA list
April 1953	Global quota system introduced within Fund Allocation (FA) system
January/April 1959	Of 231 AA items remaining on FA list for dollar area, 221 items moved to unrestricted AA list
November 1959	Automatic Fund Allocation (AFA) system introduced, with 48 items on list
January 1960	42 percent of imports liberalized
October 1960	44 percent of imports liberalized; in terms of AA list, remaining discrimination against dollar area abolished
April 1961	62 percent of imports liberalized
June 1961	63 percent of imports liberalized
July 1961	65 percent of imports liberalized
October 1961	68 percent of imports liberalized
December 1961	70 percent of imports liberalized
April 1962	Positive list of items on AA system replaced by negative list of items subject to restrictions, with 492 items; 73 percent of imports liberalized
October 1962	88 percent of imports liberalized, with 262 items on negative list
November 1962	88 percent of imports liberalized, with 254 items on negative list
April 1963	89 percent of imports liberalized, with 229 items on negative list
January 1964	92 percent of imports liberalized, with 189 items on negative list
April 1964	Almost 93 percent of imports liberalized, with 174 items on negative list

Restrictive trade practices were soon terminated. In September 1960, the Special Exchange Fund Allocation System (with retention credits) was abolished. In April 1961, the system of linking raw-material imports to exports was eliminated. On 1 July 1961, discrimination against the dollar area ceased to exist, with the removal of restrictions on dollar imports of soybeans and refined lard. As to import liberalization, more than 700 items were added to the list of goods under the AA system from October 1960 to July 1961, bringing the number of items on the AA list to 1,997, or 65 percent of total imports (see Table 2.8). In September 1961, the government formally began to accelerate by six months the implementation of the trade liberalization program by announcing that the import liberalization ratio would be raised from 65 percent in July 1961 to 90 percent by October 1962. Thus, from October 1961 to April 1962, more than 400 items were transferred from the FA system to the AA system, and more than 600 items were moved from the FA system to the AFA system, bringing the liberalization ratio to 73 percent.

In April 1962, all remaining restricted items (numbering 492) were placed on a negative list in terms of the Brussels Tariff Nomenclature (BTN). Previously, items freely importable had been on the so-called positive list, with imports of all items not included on the list subject to restrictions. In October 1962, the government liberalized 230 items, including crude oil, automobile tires and tubes, paper pulp, and ballpoint pens, thereby raising the liberalization ratio to 88 percent, or 2 percent short of the target announced in September 1961.[39] With subsequent measures, the liberalization ratio was raised to 92 percent, with 192 items on the negative list, by August 1963.

2.7.2. The Balance-of-Payments Crisis of 1961–2

A marked deterioration in the balance of payments emerged in early 1961 on account of a sharp increase in imports associated with steady expansion of the economy. The overall balance turned to a deficit of $399 million in 1961, compared with a surplus of $504 million in 1960. The trade balance also worsened, turning from a surplus of $268 million in 1960 to a deficit of $559 million in 1961. As a precautionary measure, monetary conditions were tightened in the second half of 1961. On 5 July, commercial banks were requested to curtail lending; on 22 July, the BOJ raised the discount rate by 0.365 percent, although the interest rates for export financing were lowered by 0.365 percent.

With little improvement in the balance of payments in sight, the BOJ raised the discount rate by an additional 0.365 percent on 29 September. Except for the rates for export financing, which were kept unchanged, all the principal lending rates were raised accordingly. The BOJ also increased penal rates for lending to commercial banks. On 1 October, the minimum cash reserve requirements for banks were raised for the first time since the introduction of the reserve requirement system in September 1959. In January 1962, Japan concluded a standby arrangement with the IMF for a period of one year for an amount equivalent to $305 million.[40]

In terms of import control, on 18 September 1961, authorities expanded the list of import items subject to the deposit of import guarantee money, increased the rates of deposit, and required that money placed with banks be redeposited with the BOJ. Now, the rates were 5 percent for most raw materials, 10 percent for office machines, and 35 percent for other categories. The Foreign Exchange Budget for the first half of FY 1962 was reduced by 10 percent from the previous period.

The balance-of-payments situation began to show signs of improvement in the first half of 1962. Judging that the objectives of the adjustment program had been achieved, authorities began to ease monetary policy in late 1962. The BOJ lowered the discount rate at the end of October and then again at the end of November. These measures were followed by further discount rate cuts in March and April 1963. On 1 November 1962, reserve requirements were lowered to their previous levels. From December 1962 through the summer of

---

[39] The shortfall of 2 percent was mainly accounted for by the exclusion of heavy oil (in consideration of the domestic coal industry).

[40] In the event, no drawing was made.

1963, the BOJ purchased securities in the market on a substantial scale in order to ease monetary conditions. On 8 October 1962, authorities reduced the deposit rate of import guarantee money for most raw materials from 5 to 1 percent and, on 13 December, further reduced the rates from 5 to 1 percent for most raw materials and most machines, from 10 to 1 percent for office machines, and from 35 to 5 percent for most other goods, as well as eliminating the requirement that the money be redeposited with the central bank. The FEB for the second half of FY 1962 was marginally increased.

2.7.3. Moving Toward Termination of the Restrictive System

The adjustment policy of 1961–2 had little effect on the progress of import liberalization, although it tightened import control somewhat through financial measures. In fact, despite the adjustment policy, successive measures were taken throughout this period to move toward termination of the restrictive system, including relaxation of the surrender requirements for foreign exchange, resumption of external convertibility for the yen, tariff reform, and liberalization of payments for invisibles. In April 1960, resident trading companies were authorized to maintain foreign currency deposits for as long as twenty days (this holding period would be extended to six months in June 1971). In June, authorities increased the ownership limit of Japanese firms by nonresident investors to 15 percent in nonrestricted sectors and 10 percent in restricted ones, subject to BOJ approval (previously, the limits had been 8 and 5 percent, respectively, since October 1956; see Section 3.5.1 in Chapter 3). The waiting period for the repatriation of proceeds from the sale of stocks by nonresidents was shortened over time and was abolished in April 1963.

On 1 July 1960, partial external convertibility was achieved for the yen by establishing FYDs (see Section 3.4.1 in Chapter 3). Free-yen accounts (FYAs) could be opened by nonresidents with any authorized foreign exchange bank in Japan, could be credited with yen proceeds from most current transactions, and could be converted into any of the designated currencies. In view of this, the yen became the fifteenth currency to be added to the list of designated currencies for international transactions (see Table 2.2). In June 1961, customs tariffs were revised for the first time since 1951, changing not only the tariff rates but also the tariff classification. With the adoption of the BTN, tariffs were raised, kept unchanged, or lowered, depending on the type of commodity. These changes were made not only to bring the tariff structure more in line with the prevailing composition of trade but also to protect certain domestic industries (in agriculture and manufacturing) against the impact of ongoing import liberalization, especially as exchange controls were about to be lifted.[41] There was another round of tariff rate changes in April 1962, in which some were raised and others were lowered.

The efforts at liberalization became more determined as eleven European countries, including the United Kingdom and West Germany, assumed the obligations under Article VIII of the IMF Articles of Agreement on 15 February 1961, and as Japan was invited to membership by the Council of the Organization for Economic Cooperation and Development (OECD) in July 1963.[42] In addition to import liberalization, restrictions on invisible transactions also began to be relaxed on a substantial scale. In November 1962, for example, contracts for chartering foreign aircraft and vessels for a period of less than one year were liberalized; payments for literary copyrights and advertising were liberalized up to a certain limit. In April 1963, restrictions on expenditures for business travel, television screening rights of foreign pictures, and services in Japan by nonresident artists and athletes were eased. In November 1963, restrictions were either eased or abolished for about forty of the eighty-two restricted items under the OECD codes for invisibles and capital, including payment for publishing and translation rights of books, maintenance expenses for personal property abroad, subscription to periodicals, musical records, and many other miscellaneous expenses.

As the number of restricted items declined, the FEB system lost more and more of its effectiveness as a tool for foreign exchange control. Moreover, because the remaining import restrictions were kept not for balance-of-payments purposes[43] but mostly for political or industrial policy reasons, Japanese authorities began to question the exchange restrictions entailed by the Foreign Exchange Budget system as a logical means of import restrictions. After accepting the obligations under Article VIII of the IMF Articles of Agreement, moreover, the restrictions would become subject to IMF approval. Thus, Japanese authorities made a decision in November 1963 to abolish the FEB system and replace the associated foreign exchange allocation system with an import approval system on a quantity basis, which would not involve restraint on current payments.

Effective 1 April 1964, Japan became the twenty-fifth IMF member country to accept the obligations under Article VIII and abolished the FEB system.[44]

---

[41] Where the rates were unchanged or lowered, the government was said to have no intention of permitting foreign goods to displace Japanese goods to any significant degree (Hunsberger 1964; Hollerman 1967). Overall, Komiya and Itoh (1988) assess the 1961 tariff revision as "mildly" protectionist.

[42] Following Diet approval, Japan's OECD membership became effective on 28 April 1964.

[43] In February 1963, Japan informed the GATT that it no longer claimed balance-of-payments justification under GATT Article 12 for maintaining import restrictions.

[44] At the same time, Japan obtained IMF approval to maintain two restrictions: the bilateral payments agreement with the Republic of Korea and the limit of $500 per person per trip per year for tourism.

As a precautionary measure against a run on the yen, on 11 March 1964 the IMF had agreed to a standby arrangement with Japan for a period of one year in an amount equivalent to $305 million under the first credit tranche.[45] The new import control apparatus involved three import approval systems, corresponding to the FA, AFA, and AA systems under the old trade control regime. Under the new Import Quota (IQ) system, covering goods on the negative list, importers received import quota certificates for approved imports from the MITI, which entitled them to receive import licenses from authorized foreign exchange banks upon application. Under the Automatic Import Quota (AIQ) system, import quotas for specified categories of goods were granted automatically by the MITI, and individual licenses could be automatically obtained from authorized foreign exchange banks.[46] Finally, under the Automatic Approval system, import licenses were issued freely by authorized foreign exchange banks without limit.

Takagi (1997)—by postulating that the restrictive system when used as a tool for import control would have raised the domestic prices of tradable goods relative to the import prices of similar goods—verifies that the system's effectiveness diminished over time. In particular, the author considers the wholesale price determination of several commodity groups, where explanatory variables included the import prices of comparable commodity groups and dummy variables for the adjustment packages of 1952–3, 1956–7, and 1961–2.[47] Estimation of this equation, based on monthly data for January 1951–December 1963, indicates that a statistically significant positive impact was found only for the first package of 1952–3. As to the effectiveness of the restrictive system as a tool for export promotion, Narvekar (1957, 1961) emphasizes Japan's increased competitiveness as a factor that helped it overcome the balance-of-payments crises. Given the nature of economic controls, it must have been easier to prevent imports from coming in than to promote exports out of the country.

---

[45] No drawing was made.

[46] The AIQ system was used as an administrative device for monitoring the developments in the import of newly liberalized goods, in a manner similar to the AFA system under the old regime.

[47] The regression equation is derived by postulating that a one-period change (from $t-1$ to t) in the wholesale price of an ith commodity group is determined by a fraction of the difference between the import price and the lagged wholesale price of the same commodity group (through a partial adjustment mechanism) and adjustment policy measures. The first dummy takes the value of unity for the twelve-month period from February 1953 (when authorities suspended the processing of applications for imports under the AA system for sterling area countries) and zero otherwise. The second dummy takes the value of unity for the twelve-month period from May 1957 (when authorities tightened the granting of sterling usance bills) and zero otherwise. The third dummy takes the value of unity for the twelve-month period from September 1961 (when authorities tightened import application procedures) and zero otherwise.

Although the Japanese Government could no longer use exchange restrictions as a tool for trade control, the structure of the trade and exchange control system itself remained virtually intact, albeit on a different legal basis. With tariffs and quotas, not to mention nontariff barriers, there was considerable room for further trade liberalization. Authorities continued to control capital transactions for balance-of-payments and industrial policy purposes. They were intent on using trade and foreign investment policies to protect certain agricultural and manufacturing sectors. With more than 90 percent of imports in the AIQ categories and the country's greatly improved balance-of-payments position, the trade and payments system was operationally much more liberal than it had ever been before. Even so, the legacy of the old system would survive for another sixteen years, until the revised Foreign Trade and Foreign Exchange Control Law took effect in December 1980.

3

Capital Account Liberalization: 1950–80

3.1. INTRODUCTION

Under the Foreign Exchange and Foreign Trade Control Law of December 1949, Japan restricted the freedom of cross-border capital transactions. Within the overall legal framework of the Foreign Exchange Law, the Foreign Investment Law of June 1950 regulated transactions that required approval, such as the acquisition of domestic equities by nonresidents, transfers of technology, and financial inflows with maturities of more than one year. The law was designed to provide legal protection for those foreign investments approved by the Foreign Investment Commission (or the Ministry of Finance (MOF) after August 1952) and to facilitate the repatriation of investment income, thus promoting capital and technology imports deemed beneficial to the Japanese economy. Even so, the volume of private capital flows was limited during the early years. For example, in terms of US dollars, inflows were less than $300 million from 1950 to 1956; outflows (including purchases of real assets abroad) were less than $40 million.[1]

Japan was not unique. The accepted wisdom during the early postwar years maintained that capital controls were necessary and useful instruments of economic management. Both main architects of the Bretton Woods system, John Maynard Keynes and Harry Dexter White, believed that countries should be protected from the disruptive impact of speculative international capital movements (Helleiner 1994; James 1996). Thus, Article VI, Section 3 of the Articles of Agreement of the International Monetary Fund (IMF) recognized the right of members to "exercise such controls as are necessary to regulate international capital movements." Capital account liberalization (CAL) among industrial countries proceeded in the 1960s in the context of the Organization for Economic Cooperation and Development's (OECD's) Code of Liberalization of Capital Movements. As Japan was invited to join the community of developed countries, it too subscribed to the emerging

---

[1] MOF, *Fiscal and Monetary Statistics Monthly*, No. 74, 1956, Table 31; No. 119, 1961, Table 42.

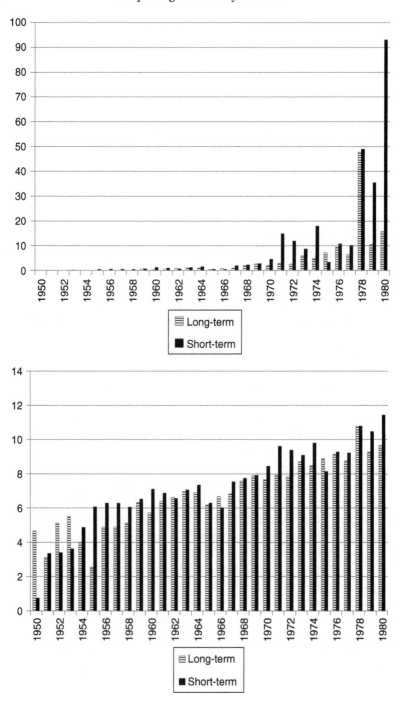

Figure 3.1. Japan's gross capital transactions, 1950–80[a] (a) in billions of US dollars; (b) on logarithmic scale

[a] Gross receipts and payments for 1950–3; gross changes in assets and liabilities for 1954–80
Source: MOF, *Fiscal and Monetary Statistics Monthly*

consensus endorsing free cross-border capital mobility (IEO 2005; Abdelal 2007),[2] and embarked—albeit judiciously—on capital account liberalization. Japan's volume of capital transactions remained small through the late 1960s (see Figure 3.1), but a steady rise is evident if transactions are expressed on a logarithmic scale (see the lower panel of the figure).

This chapter reviews Japan's experience with CAL from 1950 to 1980. Japan adopted a decidedly gradualist approach to achieving capital account convertibility, beginning with government-mediated flows. This was followed by short-term capital inflows in the early 1960s and foreign direct investment (FDI) from the late 1960s to the early 1970s. The liberalization of portfolio and other flows proceeded in the 1970s until the process was completed in December 1980, when the Foreign Exchange Law was revised to allow in principle all capital transactions to be conducted freely. After presenting an overview of the Japanese experience, the rest of the chapter discusses in sequence official and government-mediated capital flows, the management of short-term private flows, the liberalization of FDI, and the liberalization of portfolio and other flows. The final section reviews the content of the revised Foreign Exchange Law and assesses the economic impact of Japan's capital account liberalization.

3.2. AN OVERVIEW OF JAPAN'S CAPITAL ACCOUNT LIBERALIZATION: 1950–80

After enactment of the 1949 Foreign Exchange Law—which in principle prohibited all cross-border transactions—it took Japan thirty years to achieve full capital account convertibility. During the 1950s and 1960s, Japan's external current account balance swung widely, with a deficit as large as $1 billion, or 2 percent of gross national product (GNP), in 1961 (see Figure 3.2). In the absence of private capital flows, this meant that official flows constituted a substantial part of Japan's capital transactions, and the balance of payments often placed an upper limit (*kokusai shūshi no tenjō*, or a balance-of-payments ceiling) on the growth of domestic demand. In 1953 and again in 1957, Japan borrowed the sterling equivalent of $124 million and $125 million, respectively, from the IMF (see Section 2.4 in Chapter 2). Japan also received long-term loans from the World Bank and the Export–Import Bank of Washington (later renamed the Export–Import Bank of the United States).

---

[2] This consensus has been challenged by recent emerging market and global financial crises, which all revealed the risks inherent in the volatility of international capital flows. While the pendulum of professional opinion has definitely swung back, however, the debate on the benefits and costs of capital account liberalization remains unsettled. See IMF (2012).

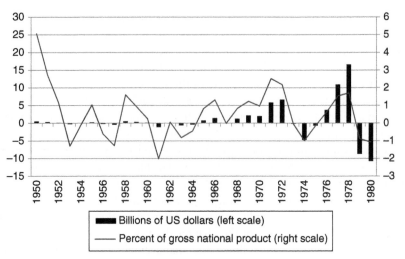

Figure 3.2. Japan's current account balance, 1950–80[a]

[a] National income, in place of gross national product, for 1950–4
Source: MOF, *Fiscal and Monetary Statistics Monthly*

Even though private capital flows were tightly controlled, gradual liberalization of the making of payments and transfers for current account transactions from the late 1950s (see Section 2.7 in Chapter 2)—which culminated in the establishment of current account convertibility in 1964—created considerable scope for conducting capital transactions. For example, subtracting changes in official foreign exchange reserves from the current account balance (which we assume was recorded more or less accurately) shows that the *implied* volume of capital flows began to increase from about 1960, when the yen became externally convertible (see Figure 3.3). This likely reflected, in addition to genuine short-term capital flows, disguised flows made possible through under- or over-invoicing of exports and imports, leads and lags between trade contracts and payments, and unreported payments for and receipts from invisibles.

Even so, the volume of gross capital transactions (as recorded in the balance of payments) barely kept pace with the volume of gross current transactions during the 1960s (see Figure 3.4). The value of gross current transactions (including exports, imports, and receipts from and payment for invisibles) expanded from around $3 billion in 1950 to $9.1 billion in 1960 and further to $43.8 billion in 1970, while gross short-term and long-term capital flows only rose from $110 million to $290 million and then to $1.8 billion during the same period. Although the expansion of capital transactions—starting from virtually nonexistent levels—represented a sixteen-fold increase, capital transactions only ranged between 1 and 8 percent of current transactions during 1950–70; capital transactions also fluctuated widely, both in terms of volume

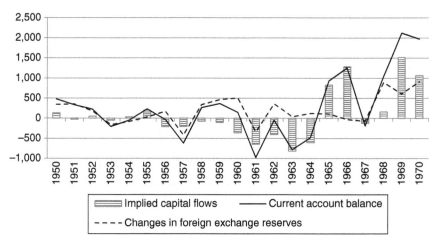

Figure 3.3. Japan's current account balance, changes in official foreign exchange reserves, and implied capital flows, 1950–70 (in millions of US dollars)[a]

[a] For changes in foreign exchange reserves and implied capital flows, a positive value means a net capital outflow from Japan

Source: MOF, *Fiscal and Monetary Statistics Monthly*, June 1972, pp. 2–3

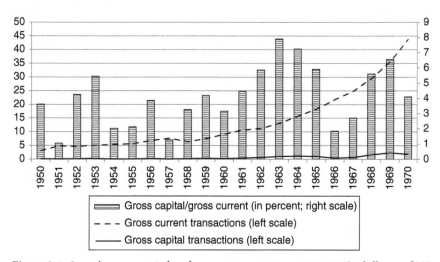

Figure 3.4. Japan's gross capital and current transactions, 1950–70 (in billions of US dollars, unless noted otherwise)

Source: MOF, *Fiscal and Moneary Statistics Monthly*

and relative to current transactions, whereas the growth of current transactions was steady throughout.

The liberalization of private capital flows involved the gradual easing of criteria for approving investment applications. In 1960, short-term private capital inflows were liberalized in connection with the establishment of external convertibility for the yen. Japanese authorities, however, developed various tools to manage short-term flows in response to balance-of-payments and exchange-rate developments through the end of the 1970s. With the gradual and judicious opening of the capital account, the public sector's share in capital flows declined. Following its accession to the OECD in 1964, Japan systematically liberalized FDI, beginning with inward FDI in 1967. Japan's strengthening external position from the late 1960s facilitated capital account opening. The pace of capital account liberalization, involving portfolio and banking flows, accelerated after the floating of the yen in 1973. Controls were often tightened or eased depending on how the exchange rate was moving (see Chapter 4), but the overall process was in the direction of greater capital account openness.

3.3. OFFICIAL AND GOVERNMENT-MEDIATED FLOWS

Official and other government-mediated capital flows constituted the dominant form of external capital transactions during the early postwar period, especially in short-term financing flows (see Figure 3.5). The size of official long-term capital flows appeared modest, but the private sector's external borrowing was often guaranteed by the government. The public sector was thus important in facilitating long-term capital transactions. In the early 1950s, the government also resumed repayment of external obligations incurred during the prewar and wartime years, although the scale of public-sector outflows remained limited until the late 1950s. Even then, the amount was small compared to the volume of long-term private capital outflows (the private sector as a whole remained a net borrower throughout this period).

3.3.1. Official Inflows in the 1950s and 1960s

On 13 August 1952, soon after the San Francisco Peace Treaty came into force in April, Japan joined the international financial community by becoming a member of the IMF and the International Bank for Reconstruction and Development (World Bank). In 1953, Japan received its first three loans from the World Bank, totaling $40 million, for the import of turbo generating units by three electric power companies (see Table 3.1). In 1953, Japan also concluded its first standby arrangement with the IMF in which it made a drawing of £44.3 million (equivalent to $124 million). Over subsequent years, Japan concluded two more standby arrangements with the IMF, in June 1957

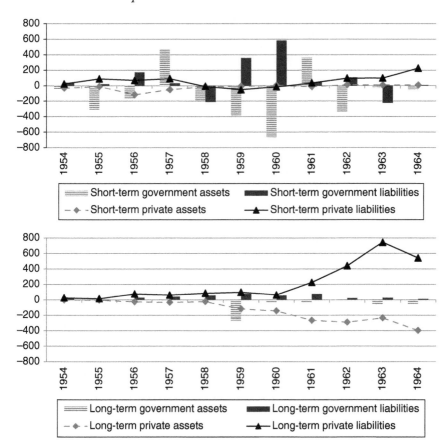

Figure 3.5. Changes in Japan's external assets and liabilities, 1954–64 (in millions of US dollars) (a) short-term assets and liabilities; (b) long-term assets and liabilities[a]

[a] Financial institutions are included in the government sector; a positive (negative) number means an inflow (outflow) of capital

Source: MOF, *Fiscal and Monetary Statistics Monthly*

and January 1962 (see Sections 2.4 and 2.7.2 in Chapter 2). The 1962 arrangement, in which no drawing was made, turned out to be Japan's final standby with the IMF. Beginning in 1956, Japan also received long-term loans from the Export–Import Bank of Washington (EIB).[3] From 1959 to 1965, about twenty

---

[3] Before this time, Japan had received short-term trade credits from the EIB for the import of American raw cotton. From May 1948 to December 1950, a credit line of $60 million was maintained with several US banks (including the EIB) for this purpose against the security of the Occupied Japan Export–Import Revolving Fund (OJEIRF), the so-called Gold Pot (Borden 1984; Schonberger 1989). From November 1951 to July 1955, the EIB authorized five cotton credits totaling $260 million in favor of the Bank of Japan (BOJ).

Table 3.1. Official loans to Japan, 1953–70[a] (in millions of US dollars; number of loans in parentheses)

Year[b]	World Bank	Export–Import Bank of Washington[c]
1953	40.2 (3)	—
1954	—	—
1955	5.3 (1)	—
1956	32.4 (3)	17.4 (2)
1957	7.0 (1)	55.9 (8)
1958	164.0 (7)	57.9 (6)
1959	54.0 (3)	20.2 (2)
1960	53.0 (3)	24.3 (3)
1961	132.0 (3)	92.2 (7)
1962	—	62.8 (6)
1963	75.0 (1)	90.0 (3)
1964	75.0 (2)	42.4 (4)
1965	125.0 (3)	69.3 (7)
1966	100.0 (1)	58.7 (5)
1967	—	91.1 (6)
1968	—	102.8 (6)
1969	—	145.2 (8)
1970	—	11.6 (2)
Total	862.9 (31)	942.0 (75)

[a] Some of these loans were recorded as private loans in the balance of payments
[b] The years in which the loans were authorized or contracted, which may not correspond to the years in which the loans were actually disbursed
[c] The name was changed to the Export–Import Bank of the United States in 1968
Source: MOF, *Fiscal and Monetary Statistics Monthly*

government and government-guaranteed bonds were floated in New York, London, Frankfurt, and Zurich.[4]

The World Bank and the EIB provided Japan with a significant amount of capital during the 1950s, accounting for more than 60 percent of the country's total capital inflows (MITI 1990). The electric power and steel industries received most of the loans (about 85 percent of the World Bank loans and over 70 percent of the EIB loans). Almost all of the World Bank loans were extended to the Japan Development Bank (JDB)—a government-owned financial institution—on behalf of private companies because it was thought inappropriate to give government guarantee (required by the World Bank)

---

[4] The first government bond of the postwar period was floated in New York in February 1959 for $30 million, the proceeds of which were used to finance the construction of a hydroelectric dam. This was followed by another government bond issue in May 1963. The first government-guaranteed bond, for the Nippon Telegraph and Telephone Public Corporation, was floated in New York in April 1961 for $20 million. Following the US imposition of an interest equalization tax in July 1963, Japan shifted its funding sources to European capital markets (MOF 1992; Volcker and Gyohten 1992).

directly to a private company. The EIB loans were guaranteed by either the JDB or one of Japan's major commercial banks.

After 1957, the World Bank eased its lending terms and expanded the scale of lending to Japan, making it the second largest borrower (behind India) for some time. After 1960, however, the World Bank began to tighten its lending terms to Japan as bank officials recognized Japan's increasing ability to borrow in the international capital markets. During this period, loans were almost exclusively extended to the Japan Highway Public Corporation and Japan National Railways for the construction of expressways and a high-speed rail system, respectively. All in all, Japan contracted thirty-one loans from the World Bank, totaling $863 million, during the period 1953–66. In terms of cash flows, Japan was a net borrower of World Bank funds through 1968; the cash flow turned negative in 1969 and remained so until July 1990, when the final installment was paid on the last loan contracted in 1966.

3.3.2. Reparation and Quasi-reparation Payments

Japan's beginning as a capital exporter can be traced to the payment of reparations and quasi-reparations to its World War II victims, which began with the first reparation agreement concluded with Burma in 1954 (Takagi 1995). While recognizing Japan's obligation to make reparations, the San Francisco Peace Treaty left the amount and form to be determined through bilateral negotiations. Many countries, including all the major powers, renounced their claims to reparations from Japan. Formal reparations were claimed only by four countries: Burma, the Philippines, Indonesia, and South Vietnam (see Table 3.2). Of these, the Philippines and South Vietnam were the only countries with which Japan signed reparation agreements under the terms of the San Francisco Peace Treaty. Bilateral reparation agreements with Burma (which was not a signatory to the treaty) and Indonesia (which signed but did not ratify the treaty) were concluded separately.

Japan agreed to provide economic assistance over 1965–77 to eight additional developing countries as a settlement for World War II, including Thailand, Laos, Cambodia, the Republic of Korea, Singapore, Malaysia, Micronesia, and Mongolia (see Table 3.2).[5] Although these countries had renounced their claims to formal reparations from Japan, the funds were clearly provided in the spirit of reparations, so they are usually referred to in Japan as "quasi-reparations." The reparation and quasi-reparation payments constituted a

---

[5] Official flows are currently classified as official development assistance (ODA) and other official flows (OOF), according to the criteria set out by the OECD's Development Assistance Committee (DAC). This chapter's discussion of official capital flows, however, does not strictly follow this distinction, especially when considering the early years.

Table 3.2. Japan's reparation and quasi-reparation payments (in millions of US dollars; in billions of yen)

Country	Amount		Payment period	
	US dollars	Yen[a]	From	To
(1) Reparation:				
Burma	200.0	72.0	April 1955	April 1965
Philippines	550.0	190.2[b]	July 1956	July 1976
Indonesia	223.0	80.3	April 1958	April 1970
South Vietnam	39.0	14.0	January 1960	January 1965
Total	1,012.0	356.5		
(2) Quasi-reparations:[c]				
Thailand[d]	15.0	5.4		
Original			July 1955	May 1959
Revised	26.7	9.6	May 1962	May 1969
Laos	3.0	1.0	Jane 1959	January 1965
Cambodia	4.5	1.5	July 1959	July 1966
Burma[e]	140.0	47.3[f]	April 1965	Apr 1977
Korea, Republic of	300.0	102.1	December 1965	December 1975
Singapore	—	2.9	September 1967	March 1972
Malaysia	—	2.9	September 1967	May 1972
Micronesia	—	1.8	May 1972	October 1976
Mongolia	—	5.0	August 1977	August 1981
Total	—	179.6		

[a] The yen figures are rounded to 100 million and may not add up to totals

[b] The planned amount, before appreciation of the yen, was ¥198 billion

[c] Includes grants only and excludes loans extended under bilateral treaties

[d] Thailand was a friendly nation during the war, and the treaty was meant to settle the claims arising from the "special yen" account the country had maintained at the Bank of Japan to receive payment for the local procurement of supplies by the Japanese Imperial Army (in May 1957, similar claims in French Indochina were settled with France for about ¥1.7 billion in pounds sterling and US dollars)

[e] Burma received both reparations and quasi-reparations because of a special clause in the original treaty that allowed the country to reserve the right to renegotiate reparations based on the amount Japan provided to other countries

[f] The planned amount, before appreciation of the yen, was ¥50.4 billion

Sources: Baishō Mondai Kenkyūkai (1963); MOF, *Fiscal and Monetary Statistics Monthly*; MOF, *Kokusai Kinyūkyoku Nenpō*

significant portion of Japanese financial flows through the early part of the 1960s, although they constituted on average 0.2 percent of GNP and never exceeded 2.1 percent of the general account budget (Cohen 1967; Hasegawa 1975). In addition, Japan paid small compensations to some industrial countries for war-related damages, most of which were paid between 1955 and 1961 (Baishō Mondai Kenkyūkai 1963).[6]

---

[6] Among them were the Netherlands (about ¥3.6 billion), Spain (about ¥2 billion), Sweden (about ¥500 million), Switzerland (about ¥1.1 billion), and the United Kingdom (about ¥500 million).

The total amount of reparation payments was approximately ¥357 billion (about $1 billion), and the provision of grants under bilateral economic and technical cooperation agreements amounted to about ¥180 billion. Some of the treaties also included the provision of official or private loans. For example, the first agreement with Burma (signed in 1954) included the provision of $20 million in private loans,[7] in addition to the grant of $200 million. Similarly, the agreement with the Philippines included the provision of $250 million in private loans and credits (in addition to the grant of $550 million), and the agreement with Indonesia included $400 million in private loans and investments as well as cancellation of the Indonesian trade deficit of $177 million. These and other payments are said to have helped promote the export of Japanese goods into these otherwise reluctant markets (Hasegawa 1975).

3.3.3. Extension of Official Loans and Grants

Japan concluded its first government-to-government loan agreement with India in February 1958 for ¥18 billion (or $50 million) in support of India's Second Five-Year Plan (see Table 3.3). In August 1958, Japan responded to the World Bank's call to participate in a five-country consortium on India (with Canada, the United Kingdom, the United States, and West Germany), organized under the bank's chairmanship, and agreed to provide an additional $10 million. Japan also joined a similar World Bank consortium on Pakistan (consisting of the same five countries) in October 1960, agreeing to provide a total of $105 million. During the rest of the 1950s and the first half of the 1960s, almost all of Japan's loans were extended to these two countries. These loans were initially implemented entirely through the Export–Import Bank of Japan (Eximbank).[8] Following establishment in 1960 of the Overseas Economic Cooperation Fund (OECF),[9] responsibility for executing Japan's official loans was divided between the two agencies.

---

[7] The loan agreement, however, was not executed because of a coup d'état in the fall of 1957.

[8] The Eximbank was originally established as the Export Bank of Japan in 1950, in order to assist domestic firms in their export of plants and capital equipment. In April 1952, the bank was allowed to finance private-sector imports as well, so the name was changed to reflect the additional line of operations. In August 1953, it was authorized to finance foreign investment as well as foreign projects; it was then authorized to extend direct loans to foreign governments and corporations in 1957. Beginning in 1965, responsibility for administering concessional loans with interest rates of less than 4 percent was given to the OECF (see Footnote 9).

[9] Created in December 1960, the OECF began its operations in March 1961. The OECF initially extended loans to Japanese firms engaged in projects in developing countries. It began in 1965 to join the Eximbank in extending direct loans to foreign governments. In July 1975, a policy was established to make a clear demarcation between the OECF and the Eximbank, giving the OECF sole responsibility for administering ODA loans.

Table 3.3. Japan's official loans to developing countries, 1958–65 (in millions of US dollars)

Year	Country	Amount[a]	Implementing agency
1958	India	50.0	Export–Import Bank of Japan (Eximbank)
1959	South Vietnam	7.5	Eximbank
	Paraguay	3.8	Eximbank
1961	India	95.0	Eximbank[b]
	Pakistan	20.0	Eximbank[b]
1962	Brazil	17.5	Eximbank
1963	Pakistan	55.0	Eximbank[b]
	India	65.0	Eximbank[b]
1964	India	60.0	Eximbank[b]
	Pakistan	30.0	Eximbank[b]
1965	Brazil	32.6	Eximbank
	Taiwan (Republic of China)	150.0	Overseas Economic Cooperation Fund (OECF)
	Republic of Korea	200.0	OECF
	India	60.0	Eximbank[b]
	Iran	17.0	Eximbank[b]
	Chile	6.2	Eximbank
	Argentina	10.2	Eximbank

[a] On a contractual basis
[b] Cofinancing with commercial banks
Source: MOF, *Fiscal and Financial Statistics Monthly*

In April 1965, Japan agreed to provide a total of $150 million to Taiwan (the Republic of China) to support its Fourth Four-Year Plan. In June 1965, Japan established a diplomatic relationship with the Republic of Korea after years of tough negotiations and agreed to provide $200 million in concessional loans and more than $300 million in private credits.[10] In May 1966, Japan agreed to provide a bridging loan of $30 million to support Indonesia in its balance-of-payments crisis; it hosted the first meeting of the Inter-Governmental Group on Indonesia (IGGI) in September 1966 and committed an additional $50 million in new credits and $10 million in grants. These and subsequent loans made Indonesia and Korea two of the largest recipients of Japan's official concessional loans from the latter part of the 1960s into the 1970s.

In 1980, Japan concluded its first official development assistance (ODA) loan agreement with the People's Republic of China. With a change in political climate, Chinese authorities had approached the Japanese Government in August 1979 with a request for a concessional loan of almost ¥1.4 trillion to finance major projects in economic infrastructure, such as hydroelectric power and railroads. Supporting China's economic modernization, Japan thus became the first non-socialist country to provide concessional financial assistance by agreeing in December to extend a ¥50 billion loan (the formal agreement was

[10] These were in addition to the quasi-reparations of $300 million, as noted in Table 3.2.

signed in April 1980).[11] In subsequent years, Japan provided a significant number of concessional loans, as well as a smaller number of grants, and remained by far the most significant supplier of development capital to China among the members of the OECD's Development Assistance Committee (DAC). The size of Japanese ODA, having surpassed that of the United Kingdom in 1972, would overtake West Germany in 1983, France in 1986, and temporarily the United States in 1989 when it reached almost $9 billion.

3.4. MANAGING SHORT-TERM FLOWS

3.4.1. Liberalizing Short-term Capital Flows

On 1 July 1960, Japan took the unusual step of allowing nonresidents to conduct short-term capital transactions freely through free-yen accounts (FYAs) established at a small number of commercial banks the MOF had authorized to do foreign exchange business in Japan. The step is unusual in the sense that it violated the conventional wisdom that, given their highly volatile nature, short-term capital flows should be the last to be liberalized in the process of capital account liberalization (Ishii et al. 2002). This view, however, was not widely held in the early 1960s.[12] For sure, Japanese authorities thought differently. With the economy expanding rapidly, they recognized that Japanese industry would benefit from controlled capital inflows. But rather than allowing the private nonfinancial sector to borrow directly from abroad, they viewed inflows intermediated through the highly regulated banking sector to be a safer means of augmenting domestic savings. Thus, Japan's slow process of CAL began with the liberalization of short-term capital inflows in 1960.

The decision to establish nonresident FYAs came about against the background of foreign pressure to liberalize Japan's restrictive trade and payments system, since the Japanese economy had recovered from the devastation of World War II and was experiencing a double-digit growth year after year. Pressure intensified after major Western European countries had restored external convertibility for their currencies at the end of 1958. In the meantime, the balance of foreign exchange reserves, which stood at barely $500 million in early 1958, rose steadily to over $1.3 billion by the end of 1959. It was under these circumstances that, in January 1960, the Japanese cabinet established a

---

[11] Japan had earlier agreed to provide trade credits to China on commercial terms.

[12] The literature on the so-called pace and sequencing of capital account liberalization did not fully develop until the late 1990s (e.g., Johnston et al. 1997). Korea's capital account liberalization followed a path similar to Japan's, which may have increased the country's crisis vulnerability; Korea experienced a major currency crisis in the fall of 1997 (Cho 2001; Kim et al. 2001).

ministerial committee to discuss measures to liberalize trade and payments and, after several months of deliberation, announced the Outline of the Plan for Trade and Exchange Liberalization in June 1960 (see Section 2.7.1 in Chapter 2). The first measure to be introduced under this scheme was the establishment of FYAs for nonresidents, along with authorization for the yen to be used for trade settlement purposes (MOF 1999b).

FYAs allowed nonresidents to keep the proceeds from current exports to Japan in yen and to take the deposits out of the country without formality. But this had far-reaching implications. Because accounts could be opened not only with yen proceeds from current exports to Japan but also with the sale of foreign exchange to onshore banks, nonresidents were given virtual freedom to bring short-term capital into Japan. Free-yen deposit (FYD) rates were subject to maximum ceilings stipulated by law, depending on the type and maturity. For example, the ceiling was 5.84 percent for time deposits with maturities of more than three months in the case of nonresident financial institutions; in the case of nonfinancial firms and individuals, the ceiling was 4.3 percent for three months, 5.5 percent for six months, and 6 percent for one year. Overseas branches of Japanese banks also participated in this market by transferring Eurodollar deposits, converting them into yen, and depositing the proceeds with the head offices.

With FYAs, authorized foreign exchange banks (then numbering twelve) could freely obtain short-term funds from abroad, making it meaningless to control other sources of short-term funding. Thus, in August 1960, the Japanese Government took a decision to lift the quantitative limit on the amount of unsecured foreign currency borrowing resident foreign exchange banks could obtain from foreign banks abroad. In September 1960, the government further eased the regulation controlling foreign exchange banks' open positions in spot foreign exchange, with the controls made applicable only to overall spot and forward positions. For all practical purposes, short-term capital inflows had been fully liberalized by this time (albeit through the banking system). On the outflow side, nonresidents could freely take yen out of the country as long as the funds had been parked as FYDs at authorized foreign exchange banks.

3.4.2. Instruments to Regulate Short-term Flows

Following the substantial liberalization of short-term capital flows (especially on the inflow side), authorities soon developed several regulatory instruments to manage surges in such inflows (see Table 3.4).[13] To the extent that some of these

---

[13] *Authorities* refers to the MOF, the BOJ, or both. The BOJ was not independent of the government, so making a distinction between the two is inconsequential. The BOJ made decisions only when the authority to do so had been delegated by, and only under approval from, the MOF.

Table 3.4. Instruments to regulate short-term capital flows in Japan, 1961–77

Instrument		When introduced	When abolished
1	Guideline interest rates	July 1961	July 1966
2.1	Liquidity requirement	June 1962	June 1972
2.2	Marginal liquidity requirement	January 1963	June 1965
3	Window guidance on monthly change in balance of foreign liabilities	July 1964	January 1972
4	Yen conversion limit	February 1968	June 1977[a]

[a] In June 1977 yen conversion limits were replaced by spot open position controls; the system itself was not abolished until June 1984

were market-based, they pre-dated by three decades the introduction of a market-based control (in the form of unremunerated reserve requirements) by Chile in the early 1990s. Authorities used these instruments to influence the size and direction of short-term capital flows, though they occasionally appealed to moral suasion and voluntary quantitative restraints when the pace of inflows was especially brisk (e.g., July 1961 and July 1962). These instruments were introduced one after another when authorities determined that something (more) needed to be done to moderate the surge in short-term capital inflows.

First, from July 1961 to July 1966, the BOJ announced maximum interest rate guidelines for short-term external borrowing by foreign exchange banks as a means of controlling short-term capital inflows (MOF 1992). Different guideline interest rates (*shidō kinri*) were designated for different maturities, which authorities changed from time to time in response to international and domestic market developments (see Figure 3.6 for two representative maturities). Though the level of interest rates was initially kept constant, in January 1963 the rates were cut as Japan experienced a surge in short-term capital inflows. Guideline interest rates were frequently changed during 1964 and 1965 (fourteen and twenty-two times, respectively). The level of market interest rates saw a secular decline relative to foreign interest rates. The system of guideline interest rates was abolished in July 1966, when authorities determined that interest rate arbitrage motives no longer existed for short-term borrowing.

Second, from June 1962 to June 1972, authorities required foreign exchange banks to keep a certain percentage of short-term external liabilities in liquid foreign assets (MOF 1992).[14] This measure was introduced against the background of a steady rise in the balance of FYDs in the first part of 1962, with no sign that the pace was abating. Initially, the liquidity requirement was set at 20 percent, which authorities subsequently raised or lowered to discourage or encourage short-term capital inflows (see Figure 3.7). As short-term inflows

[14] Short-term external liabilities included foreign currency deposits, call money, FYDs, and unsecured borrowing from foreign banks abroad, while liquid foreign assets included cash, deposits, call loans, foreign government securities, and bankers' acceptances.

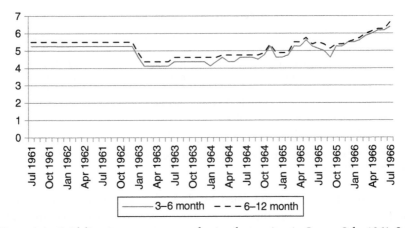

Figure 3.6. Guideline interest rates on foreign borrowing in Japan, July 1961–July 1966 (in percent per year)

Source: Inuta (2000), Table 2 (p. 302) and Table 3 (p. 305)

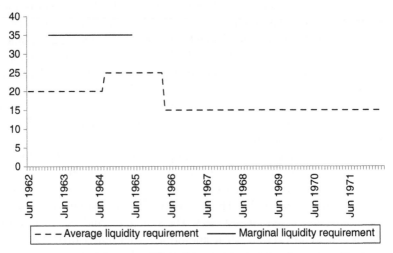

Figure 3.7. Average and marginal liquidity requirements on short-term foreign assets in Japan, June 1962–May 1972 (in percent)

Source: Inuta (2000), pp. 10–11

continued from January 1963 to June 1965, authorities introduced a marginal liquidity requirement of 35 percent, with the provision that additions to the existing balance of reserves be held in foreign currency securities issued by foreign governments or international organizations. The marginal liquidity requirement applied to any amount above the average December 1962 balance of foreign liabilities.

Faced with continued inflow pressure, in August 1964 authorities tightened their grip by raising the average liquidity requirement from 20 to 25 percent and by applying the marginal liquidity requirement to the amount beyond the July 1964 balance. As the pace of inflows moderated in the aftermath of the US Federal Reserve's decision to raise the discount rate from 3.5 to 4 percent in November 1964, the marginal liquidity requirement was abolished in June 1965. Net inflows then turned to net outflows in December when the Federal Reserve raised the discount rate further to 4.5 percent, prompting Japanese authorities in April 1966 to cut the average liquidity requirement to 15 percent. It is said that, after this point, the average liquidity requirement was no longer binding because it was smaller than the amount banks would have kept in any case for internal risk management (Inuta 2000). The liquidity requirement was abolished in June 1972 and replaced by statutory reserve requirements (see Section 3.4.3).

Third, from July 1964 to January 1972, Japanese authorities, recognizing the liquidity requirements' limited effectiveness in controlling short-term inflows, introduced a "window guidance" to persuade banks to keep the growth of short-term borrowing within monthly guidelines (MOF 1992). Initially, the guideline was calculated as the ratio of the balance of short-term liabilities at the end of June 1964 to the balance of foreign assets at the end of May, and a bank was required to maintain this liabilities/assets ratio in determining the balance of foreign liabilities at the end of July. Beginning in January 1965, a three-month average was used as the reference amount for foreign assets. That is to say, the balance of foreign liabilities at the end of January 1965 was to be determined in relation to the ratio of the balance at the end of December 1964 to the average monthly balance of foreign assets during September through November. Subsequently, authorities changed the reference balance from time to time in response to the strength or direction of capital flows. After August 1970, authorities applied the guidelines to net inflows (gross inflows less Eurodollar lending) to allow foreign exchange banks to engage in arbitrage transactions in the Eurodollar market.[15]

Finally, from February 1968 to June 1977, authorities imposed a limit on *yen conversion*, defined as the amount obtained by subtracting the balance of relevant foreign assets from the balance of relevant external liabilities.[16] The

---

[15] Authorized foreign exchange banks were permitted unconditionally to extend short-term Eurodollar loans in February 1970.

[16] Consider the following simplified representation of a commercial bank balance sheet:

Assets	Liabilities
Foreign currency assets (A)	Foreign currency liabilities (B)
	Nonresident FYDs (C)
Other assets	Other liabilities

The amount of yen conversion is equivalent to B + C − A. Beginning in December 1973, FYDs were excluded from the liabilities side except for the claims to overseas branches of Japanese banks.

yen conversion limit was introduced as window guidance in an environment where authorities were tightening monetary policy to reduce the widening current account deficit. By limiting the amount of foreign exchange funds banks could use to make domestic loans, authorities attempted to preserve the effectiveness of the tight monetary policy. The amount of yen conversion essentially refers to the amount of foreign borrowing (including foreign currency deposits and FYDs) that could be lent out to domestic borrowers.

Under this regulation, authorities determined the yen conversion limit for banks on a monthly average basis (initially 103 percent of the average balance during December 1967 and January 1968). This was effectively a reintroduction of the spot foreign exchange position control, which had been abolished in September 1961. At the same time, authorities tightened the scrutiny of resident foreign banks which, with limited access to domestic deposits, were not subject to yen conversion limits. During the tumultuous years of 1969–73 when the Japanese yen was under considerable appreciation pressure (see Section 4.3 in Chapter 4), authorities used yen conversion limits and the newly introduced marginal reserve requirement on FYDs (see Section 3.4.3) as the two principal means of managing short-term flows (see Table 3.5). In March 1970, yen conversion limits were applied to foreign banks for the first time (MOF 1992). During the rest of the 1970s, these two instruments were used from time to time to deal with appreciation or depreciation pressure on the yen under the flexible exchange rate regime.

After the foreign exchange market turmoil had passed, the yen faced depreciation pressure, especially in consequence of the quadrupling of oil prices (the first oil shock) in the latter part of 1973. The conversion limits were therefore eased by removing FYDs from application of the limits (except for head office–branch accounts) in December. In August 1974, the conversion limits for resident foreign banks were eased in order to encourage capital inflows. The limits, however, began to receive foreign criticism as arbitrarily inhibiting the freedom of capital flows. With the institution of reserve requirements on all foreign liabilities held by foreign exchange banks in November 1976, authorities felt that yen conversion limits were no longer needed. In June 1977, they replaced them with conventional spot open position controls, but the system itself was not terminated until June 1984 in the context of a Japan–US Yen/Dollar Agreement (Frankel 1984).

3.4.3. The Marginal Reserve Requirement

In June 1972, statutory reserve requirements replaced the opaque "window guidance" of the 1960s, under which most of the capital account regulations had been employed. In the meantime, yen conversion limits had also assumed

Table 3.5. Measures to control short-term capital flows in Japan, 1971–80

Phase	Measures, as applied to authorized foreign exchange banks
1. Tightening, August–September 1971	Requirement introduced to keep outstanding balance of free-yen deposits (FYDs) at or below 18 August balance (19 August 1971); base changed to 27 August balance (28 August 1971); application of yen conversion limit changed from monthly average balance to daily balance basis (7 September 1971)
2. Easing, December 1971–January 1972	Application of yen conversion limit reverts back to average monthly basis (21 December 1971); restrictions introduced in August 1971 abolished on maximum balance of FYDs (6 January 1972)
3. Tightening, May–July 1972	Application of yen conversion limit changed from monthly to daily (May 1972); 25 percent marginal reserve requirement imposed on FYDs based on 21 April–20 May 1972 balance (1 June 1972); marginal reserve requirement raised to 50 percent based on 21 May–20 June 1972 balance (1 July 1972)
4. Easing, December 1973	Marginal reserve requirement lowered from 50 to 10 percent based on 21 May–20 June 1972 balance (10 December 1973); yen conversion limit abolished for FYDs, except for head office-branch accounts (17 December 1973)
5. Easing, August–September 1974	Yen conversion limit for resident foreign banks eased (5 and 26 August); marginal reserve requirement lowered from 10 to 0 percent (11 September 1974)
6. Tightening, June 1977	Reserve requirement of 0.25 percent introduced on outstanding balance of FYDs (1 June 1977)
7. Tightening, November 1977	Marginal reserve requirement of 50 percent introduced based on 1–31 October 1977 balance (22 November 1977)
8. Tightening, March 1978	Marginal reserve requirement raised from 50 to 100 percent based on 1–28 February balance (18 March 1978)
9. Easing, January–February1979	Marginal reserve requirement lowered from 100 to 50 percent based on 1–28 February 1978 balance (17 January 1979); marginal reserve requirement further reduced to 0 percent (10 February 1989)

Sources: BOJ (1988); Fukao (1990); and Inuta (2000)

legal status in September 1971 amid an evolving currency crisis.[17] Thus, the reserve requirement on FYDs and yen conversion limits became part of the standard toolkit for managing short-term capital flows during the 1970s. When first introduced in June 1972, the reserve requirement was marginal at the rate of 25 percent, to be applied to the amount exceeding the average balance for 21 April–20 May 1972. When the Tokyo market reopened on

[17] Authorities had previously regulated banks with respect to short-term capital flows through administrative fiat. In September 1971, in the immediate aftermath of the currency crisis of August, they placed the regulations within the framework of a ministerial ordinance to eliminate room for legal challenge (Inuta 2000).

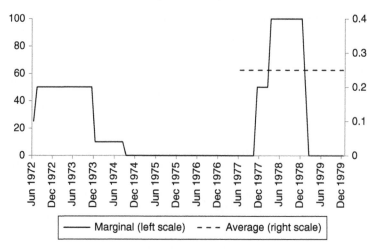

Figure 3.8. Reserve requirements on free-yen deposits, 1972–9 (in percent)

Source: BOJ, *Economic Statistics Monthly*, March 1986

29 June 1972 after a four-day suspension following the floating of the British pound, authorities raised the marginal reserve requirement to 50 percent to stem the inflow of short-term capital (see Figure 3.8). Following the first oil crisis, in December 1973, the marginal reserve requirement was lowered to 10 percent and, in September 1974, further down to zero.

When the yen began to experience moderate appreciation pressure in June 1977, authorities introduced an average reserve requirement (on outstanding FYD balances) at the very low rate of 0.25 percent (see Figure 3.8). As the yen continued to strengthen, the marginal reserve requirement was reintroduced in November 1977 at the rate of 50 percent; in March 1978, the requirement became prohibitive at 100 percent. Then, the yen began to depreciate in the fall of 1978, prompting authorities to reduce the marginal requirement to 50 percent in January 1979 and further down to zero a month later. In December 1980, the system of nonresident FYDs was abolished altogether when the new Foreign Exchange and Trade Control Law came into effect (see Section 3.7.2), making the distinction between residents and nonresidents all but meaningless.

It is inherently difficult to assess the effectiveness of a market-based control in influencing the volume of short-term capital flows because such a measure is typically imposed or intensified precisely when inflows surge. Without address- ing the endogeneity of a capital control, any assessment of effectiveness would be biased against concluding that the measure was effective. Esaka and Takagi (2013) applied the method of propensity score matching (based on a probit model of capital control intensification) and compared the volume of inflows between intensive capital control episodes and similar episodes (in terms of a propensity score) but without an intensive control. Their main finding is that, although an increase in the marginal reserve requirement modestly reduced the volume of FYA inflows during the 1970s, the impact was not statistically significant. It is possible that current receipts and payments served as a vehicle through which speculative capital found its way into onshore bank deposits.

3.5. FOREIGN DIRECT INVESTMENT

3.5.1. Early Measures

Japan's postwar legal framework did not explicitly recognize foreign direct investment (FDI) as such. The statute did not make a clear distinction between direct and portfolio investment and only stipulated that, regardless of the investment type, permission to engage in capital transactions would be granted based on the assessment of the merits of each case. Whether or not a particular transaction had FDI-like features, however, mattered in making that assessment. The notion of "managerial control," as implied by FDI, carried a favorable weight in the authorities' approval of foreign investment applications.

On the inflow side, the Foreign Investment Law freely allowed foreign residents to purchase newly issued domestic shares, upon notification to the authorities, provided they did not intend to take the dividends out of the country. Given the initially low foreign ownership limit in a domestic firm, no inward foreign investment would have been counted as FDI according to the contemporary criteria (normally a 10 percent threshold). More lenient approval criteria were applied to new shares because purchases of *new* shares implied a motive for management participation. Otherwise, inward capital transactions, including purchases of existing shares in the secondary market (a case of bona fide portfolio investment), were strictly controlled.

The liberalization of FDI-like investment involved the relaxation of criteria for approving portfolio investments motivated by management participation. In September 1952, for example, equity purchases by nonresidents became subject to automatic approval by the BOJ if the combined foreign equity ownership of a firm was 8 percent or less; or, in the case of nineteen restricted industrial sectors, 5 percent or less. These percentages were raised to 15 and 10 percent, respectively, in June 1960. In May 1961, the basis for approving foreign capital imports was changed from demonstration of merit (e.g., "beneficial" to the Japanese economy) to demonstration of lack of harm. A cabinet decision in March 1963 further simplified the procedures and relaxed the approval criteria. This was followed by a cabinet decision in July 1963 that established the principle that all inward FDI-type investment and technology imports would be approved as long as no harm could be demonstrated.

From October 1956 to July 1963, a special scheme known as the "Yen-Based Free Stock Acquisition System (*En Bēsu Kabushiki Jiyū Shutoku Seido*)" was in place (Itoh and Kiyono 1988; MOF 1999b). Designed to attract FDI without subsequently creating foreign exchange concerns, the system allowed foreign companies freely to set up wholly owned subsidiaries or joint ventures in Japan without presuming a guaranteed repatriation of dividends or principal. The system was so successful that as many as 290 foreign firms established operations in Japan under this scheme, including such prominent ones as the Coca-Cola Company, the Minnesota Mining and Manufacturing Company, Olivetti, the Pepsi-Cola Company, Standard Oil of New Jersey (Esso), and Xerox (Nihon Keizai Shimbunsha 1967; MOF 1992). The system was abolished on 1 July 1963 when it was learned that Article VIII of the IMF Articles of Agreement would oblige Japan to allow investment income to be repatriated freely, an obligation the country was about to accept in April 1964.

On the outflow side, the Japanese Government, in approving or disapproving investment applications, initially considered FDI to be any investment in a foreign entity in which the Japanese investor had either (1) a stake of 25 percent or more or (2) a stake of 10 percent or more plus a representative on the board. Subsequently, the concept of FDI was applied more widely to include any investment that met one of the following conditions: (1) a representative on the board; (2) provision of manufacturing know-how; (3) supply of raw materials; (4) purchases of finished products; (5) provision of financial assistance; (6) exclusive sales agency agreements; or (7) any other long-term economic relationship (Inuta 2000).

Purchases of securities issued by a foreign entity controlled by Japanese residents required approval from the MOF (or from the BOJ beginning in January 1964, if the amount was less than $50,000). Purchases made for the purpose of starting new production activities were routinely deliberated by an inter-ministerial committee (consisting of the Ministries of Finance, International Trade and Industry, Agriculture and Fisheries, Transportation, and Foreign Affairs, plus the Economic Planning Agency) before being submitted to the MOF for formal approval. Provision of credit to a foreign entity to secure long-term sources of raw material imports was also considered to be FDI and required approval from the Ministry of International Trade and Industry (MITI).

Despite these and other measures to relax controls on inward and outward FDI, the volume remained miniscule throughout the 1950s (see Figure 3.9). The systematic liberalization of FDI only began after Japan's accession to the OECD in 1964, but even then Japan was careful not to rush into opening the domestic market to foreign investors or allowing Japanese investors to access the foreign markets freely. Japan lodged reservations with the OECD on both inward and outward FDI as permitted,[18] for which Japan received increasing

---

[18] Japan lodged a total of eighteen (out of thirty-seven) reservations equally divided between List A (items for which commitment to liberalize was irreversible, once declared) and List B

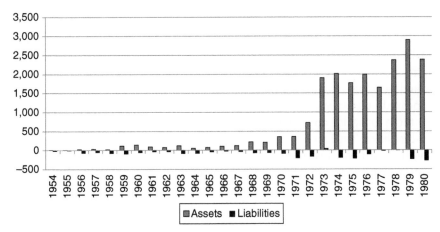

Figure 3.9. Foreign direct investment to and from Japan, 1954–80 (in millions of US dollars)[a]

[a] Calculated from international investment positions on a calendar-year basis; a positive (negative) value means an outflow (inflow) of capital

Sources: MOF, *Fiscal and Monetary Statistics Monthly*, 1954–64; *Kokusai Kinyūkyoku Nenpō*, 1965–80

external criticism, especially from the United States. Foreign complaints were directed not only at the number of controls Japan placed on foreign capital inflows but also at the slow pace of, and the lack of transparency in, the approval process.

3.5.2. Liberalization Under the OECD Code

The liberalization of inward FDI began in 1967 and continued until 1976 (although the formalities would remain until 1980). Concerned that Japanese firms might not be able to compete successfully with large foreign companies when they were allowed to come in, some in Japan called the impending liberalization of inward FDI the second Black Ships.[19] Partly as a defensive measure, several prominent private firms—notably in the machinery, steel, and automobile industries—merged to form larger companies between 1964 and 1970. The liberalization of outward FDI started two years later, in 1969, and continued until 1978 (with the formalities removed in 1980). The slower start probably reflected the fact that it was not the target of foreign criticism.

(items for which it could be reversed for compelling reasons), the most restrictive of any member country except for Portugal (twenty-eight reservations) and Spain (nineteen reservations). See Ozaki (1972) and Inuta (2000).

[19] The first Black Ships had carried Commodore Matthew Perry of the US Navy into Tokyo Bay in 1853, demanding that the Japanese open the country to the West.

3.5.2.1. Inward FDI

In 1967, Japan embarked upon a program of systematically liberalizing inward FDI subject to careful sequencing. In particular, authorities divided industrial sectors into three categories: (1) those for which investment applications would be approved automatically; (2) those for which applications would be approved automatically if foreign ownership were less than 50 percent; and (3) those for which applications would be approved or disapproved on a case-by-case basis. The first two types were called liberalized sectors (*jiyūka gyōshu*) and the third type restricted sectors (*hijiyūka gyōshu*). The process of liberalization involved transferring an increasing number of sectors from the third to the second and then to the first category. This process, however, did not apply to the acquisition of existing shares, for which a slower and more restricted approach was adopted. This represented the authorities' cautious attitude toward the possibility of a hostile takeover of Japanese firms by foreign investors. The program proceeded broadly in five stages, with the final stage completed in May 1976 (see Table 3.6).

The first round (July 1967) aimed to allow as much as 50 percent foreign ownership in thirty-three sectors and as much as 100 percent in seventeen others in the case of new firms.[20] The former included electric appliances, among others, while the latter included musical instruments, transportation equipment, chemicals, and small-scale shipbuilding. In the case of existing firms, the threshold for automatic approval was raised from 5 to 7 percent for individual ownership; for aggregate foreign ownership, the threshold was raised from 10 to 15 percent for nineteen restricted sectors and from 15 to 20 percent for others. Most foreign stakeholders reacted negatively, considering the measures to be too little too late.

The second round (March 1969) aimed to allow as much as 50 percent foreign ownership in 160 sectors and as much as 100 percent in 44 others in the case of new firms. Foreign stakeholders remained critical, considering that most of the liberalized sectors were unattractive. In their view, conspicuously missing from the list were various sectors within the automobile industry, as well as cosmetics and metals, which many had thought would be included (Inuta 2000).

The third round (September 1970) covered 524 sectors (50 percent ownership in 447 sectors, with 100 percent in 77 others), which now included banking, securities, machinery, chemicals, and transportation and distribution. In the case of existing firms, the aggregate foreign ownership threshold for automatic approval was raised from 20 to 25 percent in unrestricted sectors. These measures were followed, in April 1971, by the liberalization of FDI in the automobile industry (with six additional sectors). This came about

---

[20] With some exceptions, the classification followed the Japan Standard Industrial Classification, which identified a total of 1,211 sectors.

Table 3.6. Liberalization of inward foreign direct investment in Japan, 1967–76

	Number of liberalized sectors (for new firms)		Number of liberalized sectors (for existing firms)		
	Automatic approval for up to 50 percent foreign ownership	Automatic approval for up to 100 percent foreign ownership	Limit per foreign investor	Aggregate limit for all foreign investors	
				Restricted sectors[a]	Other sectors
Before 1 July 1967	n.a.	n.a.	5 percent	10 percent	15 percent
(1) First round, 1 July 1967	33 sectors	17 sectors	7 percent	15 percent	20 percent
(2) Second round, 1 March 1969	160 sectors	44 sectors	n.a.	n.a.	n.a.
(3) Third round, 1 September 1970	447 sectors	77 sectors	n.a.	n.a.	Less than 25 percent
(3A) Automobile industry, 1 April 1971	453 sectors (6 automobile-related sectors added)	n.a.	n.a.	n.a.	n.a.
(4) Fourth round, 4 August 1971	All other sectors, except for 7 sectors set aside for item-by-item approval	228 sectors	Less than 10 percent	n.a.	n.a.
(5) 1 May 1973	Automatic approval for 100 percent foreign ownership permitted in all but 5 sectors, subject to transition period of two to three years for 17 sectors		Removed entirely with consent of incumbent management, except in 22 (5+17) sectors		
(5A) 1 June 1975	Large-scale retailing becomes fully open		Restriction removed from large-scale retailing		
(5B) 1 May 1976	Automatic approval for 100 percent foreign ownership permitted in all but 4 sectors		Removed entirely with consent of incumbent management, except in 4 sectors		

[a] There were nineteen restricted sectors, including: water supply, electricity, gas, broadcasting, local railroad, light rail, telecommunication, sea shipping, port transportation, road shipping, civil aviation, fishery, mining, trust business, banking, mutual banking, long-term credit banking, authorized foreign exchange banking, and central banking (since the Bank of Japan is a joint stock company)
Source: Inuta (2000), pp. 237–9

in the context of the Japan–US automobile negotiations that had been held intermittently over 1967–9.

The fourth round (August 1971) adopted a "negative list" approach to the application of 50 percent foreign ownership in new firms. In particular, the government set aside seven sectors as subject to item-by-item approval while extending automatic approval for full ownership to 228 sectors and 50 percent ownership to all others. The sectors on the negative list included agriculture, petroleum refining and sale, leather manufacturing and sale, computers, information processing, large-scale retailing with more than seven stores, and real estate. The government, however, indicated that applications for FDI in the seven sectors, if made, would be favorably considered. The fourth-round measures were a compromise between the MOF (which in principle pushed for 100 percent foreign ownership in all sectors) and the MITI (which desired to keep the 50 percent limit in most) (Inuta 2000). For existing firms, the limit per foreign investor was raised to 10 percent, the contemporary threshold for equity investment to be counted as FDI.

The fifth and final round (May 1973) followed a decision made in early 1973 to fully open the FDI regime. It was thought that Japan's status as an economic superpower no longer justified any further delay in implementing the commitment made under the OECD code. The measure extended automatic approval for 100 percent ownership to all but five sectors (agriculture and fishery, mining, petroleum, leather products, and large-scale retailing with more than eleven stores); liberalization was to be achieved in a phased manner for seventeen sectors over 1974–6. The foreign ownership limit for existing shares was removed entirely except in twenty-two (five restricted plus seventeen transitional) sectors, provided that consent was obtained from the incumbent management.

The exclusion of large-scale retailing received criticism from foreign manufacturers, who thought that access to retailing was key to successfully marketing their products in Japan. Japanese authorities, on the other hand, were concerned that large foreign retailers, if allowed to enter the market, might wipe out small retail establishments. In March 1974, the Large-Scale Retail Store Law came into force, requiring large retail establishments, both domestic and foreign, to file a prior application with the MITI. With the protection of small retailers thus secured, on 1 June 1975 the retail sector was fully opened to FDI.

The liberalization of inward FDI was virtually complete in May 1976, when automatic approval was extended to all sectors in the case of new firms and the foreign ownership limit for existing firms was removed (with incumbent management consent) in all but four sectors (agriculture and fishery, mining, petroleum, and leather products). In April 1978, the administrative procedures for FDI applications were simplified, with automatic approval authority delegated to the BOJ (except when it was difficult to verify incumbent management consent). As a result, the typical length of an application process was shortened from about a month to two weeks. Even so, the volume of FDI or the number of FDI applications did not increase noticeably (see Table 3.7), in sharp contrast to the significant impact of the parallel liberalization on the volume of outward FDI (see the following text).

Table 3.7. Applications for inward foreign direct investment in Japan, 1965–80

	Number of applications (of which, new applications)	Value (in millions of US dollars)
1965	106 (—)	38.9
1966	133 (83)	32.7
1967	163 (76)	33.1
1968	192 (102)	50.6
1969	255 (120)	56.9
1970	361 (168)	75.3
1971	375 (204)	222.7
1972	634 (297)	176.3
1973	818 (416)	147.1
1974	633 (284)	179.5
1975	643 (257)	156.0
1976	670 (262)	183.8
1977	662 (248)	207.5
1978	663 (297)	212.6
1979	761 (308)	506.8
1980	684 (292)	327.9

Source: Inuta (2000), p. 296

3.5.2.2. Outward FDI

The systematic process of outward FDI liberalization also proceeded in five broad stages from 1969 to 1978. The liberalization involved raising the limit for automatic approval (made by the BOJ) and easing the qualification criteria for foreign entities receiving FDI (see Table 3.8).

The first round (October 1969) delegated approval authority to the BOJ for any FDI project of $300,000 or less in which the resident investor had an equity stake of 25 percent or more plus a full-time representative on the board. If the investment balance (defined as a sum of equity and loan positions) was $200,000 or less, there was the presumption that an application would be approved promptly and automatically.

The second round (September 1970) raised the automatic BOJ approval threshold from $200,000 to $1 million and relaxed the eligibility criteria to include a foreign entity in which the resident investor had an equity stake of 50 percent or more without board representation. In addition, automatic approval was granted to the establishment of unincorporated branches abroad when the amount was $1 million or less (whereas the first round had no provision for branch operations abroad). This raised the share of outward FDI applications subject to BOJ automatic approval to 78 percent of the total volume of outward FDI (Inuta 2000).

The third round (July 1971) was implemented as part of the first set of emergency economic measures announced as a cabinet decision on 4 June 1971 to

Table 3.8. Liberalization of outward foreign direct investment in Japan, 1969–78

Date	Limit for automatic approval (equity and debt position)	Eligibility criteria for foreign entities receiving investment[a]
Before October 1969	$50,000 (by Bank of Japan (BOJ) from 4 January 1964)	n.a.
(1) First round, 1 October 1969	$200,000	Japanese equity participation of 25 percent or more with full-time board representative
(2) Second round, 1 September 1970	$1 million	Japanese equity participation of 50 percent or more or of 25 percent or more but less than 50 percent with full-time board representative
(3) Third round, 1 July 1971	Unlimited	Japanese equity participation of 25 percent or more or of 10 percent or more but less than 25 percent with (1) board representation, (2) provision of manufacturing technology, (3) provision of raw materials, (4) purchase of final products, (5) provision of financial assistance, or (6) agreement of exclusive agency contract
(4) Fourth round, 8 June 1972		Japanese equity participation of 25 percent or more or of less than 25 percent with (1) board representation, (2) provision of manufacturing technology, (3) provision of raw materials, (4) purchase of final products, (5) provision of financial assistance, (6) agreement of exclusive agency contract, or (7) establishment of long-term economic relationship
(5) Fifth round, 1 April 1978	Purchases of securities in principle subject to notification to BOJ (no notification necessary for purchases less than ¥3 million)	

[a] Exceptions were made for the fisheries, cultured pearls, banking, and securities industries and where serious adverse impact was recognized for Japan's diplomacy, economy, and international cooperation

Source: Inuta (2000), Table 4, p. 125

counter appreciation pressure on the yen (see Section 4.3.1 in Chapter 4). The maximum threshold for automatic BOJ approval was removed. The criteria for eligible foreign entities were further relaxed to an equity stake of 25 percent or more when no board representation was involved. When a close economic relationship could be established, any investment in which the resident investor had an equity stake of 10 percent or more became subject to automatic BOJ approval, and the maximum remittance limit for foreign branches was abolished. These measures were believed to raise the share of outward FDI applications subject to BOJ automatic approval to more than 90 percent of the total volume (Inuta 2000). Purchases by residents of real estate abroad were placed under automatic approval by the BOJ, based on the demonstration of real demand.

The fourth round (June 1972) further relaxed the eligibility criteria for automatic approval by the BOJ to include any foreign entity—regardless of the size of the equity stake—with which the resident investor had (or was about to have) any long-term relationship. Extension of credit, however, remained subject to MITI approval. Purchases by residents of real estate abroad became subject to automatic approval by the BOJ, regardless of demonstration of real demand (the real demand requirements were reinstituted from January 1974 to June 1977 when the yen came under depreciation pressure).[21]

The fifth and final round (April 1978), which took place as part of the "measures to liberalize and simplify foreign exchange control" announced by the MOF in January 1978, replaced the automatic approval requirements with prior notification requirements to the BOJ, except for certain items.

These and other liberalization measures led to a rapid increase in the volume of outward FDI (see Table 3.9; see also Figure 3.9). While outward FDI during the 1950s had been limited to mining rights in Asia and the activities of trading companies in North America, the geographical reach of FDI expanded to Latin America, the Middle East, Africa, and Europe. Of the cumulative FDI outflows of $3.6 billion from 1951 to 1970, North America received $900 million (25 percent), Asia $780 million (22 percent), Europe $640 million (18 percent), and Latin America $560 million (16 percent), with the remainder allocated among the Middle East, Oceania, and Africa. In terms of sectoral breakdown, trade and services accounted for 39 percent, agriculture and mining (mainly related to the development of natural resources) 34 percent, and manufacturing 27 percent (Kojima 1973). These percentages continued roughly unchanged throughout the 1970s, with the share of manufacturing increasing somewhat at the expense of agriculture and mining.

Contemporary observers noted that Japan's manufacturing FDI, especially in Asia, typically involved the establishment of relatively small-scale subsidiaries as joint-venture partnerships with local interests (Nakajo 1980). Kojima (1973)—observing that a substantial proportion of FDI was undertaken by small and medium-sized firms in labor-intensive, declining industries—argues that production moved out of an industry in which Japan was losing comparative advantage to a country that was gaining.[22] The textile industry

---

[21] Beginning in December 1981, no approval or notification requirements existed for purchases by residents of real estate located abroad.

[22] In contrast, Kojima (1973, 1985) observes that, in the United States, the bulk of outward FDI was undertaken by large multinational firms with advanced technology and oligopolistic power. As a result, FDI tended to cause unemployment and promote measures to protect the remaining industries at home. Japanese-type FDI, on the other hand, tended to promote trade by allowing the country to move up the technological ladder while importing the goods it no longer

Table 3.9. Japan's outward foreign direct investment, fiscal years 1951–80 (on approval or notification basis; in millions of US dollars)

	Securities	Credit	Others[a]	Total
1951–60	122	94	67	283
1961	47	38	79	164
1962	39	31	28	98
1963	63	23	40	126
1964	67	39	13	119
1965	74	73	12	159
1966	74	122	31	227
1967	117	135	23	275
1968	199	328	30	557
1969	223	404	38	665
1970	296	570	38	904
1971	471	333	54	858
1972	1,781	252	305	2,338
1973	2,177	1,100	217	3,494
1974	1,262	1,098	35	2,395
1975	1,652	1,485	143	3,280
1976	1,487	1,882	93	3,462
1977	1,319	1,388	99	2,806
1978	2,038	2,383	177	4,598
1979	1,833	2,994	168	4,995
1980	2,295	2,184	214	4,693

[a] Others include establishment or expansion of foreign branches and real estate purchases
Source: Inuta (2000), p. 133

spearheaded the trend because it was the first to suffer from rising domestic labor costs.[23] Ogawa and Lee (1995), using data for six industries (textiles, chemicals, basic metal, machinery, electrical machinery, and transportation equipment) during 1960–88, find that production in an industry tended to move abroad as its vintage capital became unprofitable at export prices. The authors further identify the two oil shocks (1973–4 and 1979–80) and the two episodes of sharp yen appreciation (1977–8 and 1986) as critical events that raised local input costs and led to a rapid increase in manufacturing FDI. In this view, outward FDI was a way of preserving the value of vintage capital by

produced. Based on bilateral trade data for twenty major trading partners during 1985–95, Bayoumi and Lipworth (1998) confirm the positive, permanent impact of Japanese outward FDI on the volume of Japanese imports from recipient countries.

[23] In 1955, Japanese textile firms established their first cotton spinning and weaving operations overseas in Brazil and El Salvador, where the anti-Japanese sentiment prevalent in Asia during the immediate postwar years was absent. In the 1960s, FDI in the textile industry expanded to Asia (notably Taiwan) and Africa, while the early 1970s saw an acceleration of FDI activity in Asia (notably Korea and Indonesia), South America, and North America, where import restrictions against Japanese textile imports were tightened. See Yoshioka (1979).

applying the accumulated industry- and firm-specific intangible assets in a location with lower input costs.

3.6. PORTFOLIO AND OTHER INVESTMENTS

3.6.1. Portfolio and Other Inflows

Although the Foreign Investment Law did not make a clear distinction between FDI and portfolio inflows, FDI-like inflows received preference in the liberalization process. For example, purchases by nonresidents of *new* privately placed shares were freely allowed upon prior notification (upon ex-post notification beginning in April 1951), provided that the investor had no intention of repatriating the dividends abroad. Purchases of existing shares were permitted subject to approval, provided they involved a technology transfer (an indication of a FDI-like motive), with the provision that only the dividends (but not the liquidation proceeds) could be repatriated freely. Likewise, purchases of corporate bonds and extension of loans were permitted subject to approval, provided they involved a technology transfer or a stock acquisition (again an indication of an FDI-like motive). In principle, all other types of private inflows were not allowed.

In April 1951, the requirement that purchases of existing shares be part of an investment program involving a technology transfer was removed, making it possible for foreign investors to purchase shares in the secondary market for the first time. In July 1952, purchases of corporate bonds and extension of loans to residents were permitted subject to approval. These marked the beginning of a long process of liberalizing portfolio and other investment inflows (see Table 3.10). In September 1952, purchases of shares became subject to automatic approval by the BOJ if they did not raise foreign owner-ship above 8 percent in unrestricted sectors and 5 percent in restricted ones. In June 1960, foreign currency loans, as well as purchases of corporate bonds and beneficiary securities, became subject to approval by the BOJ, provided that the amount was less than $100,000. The automatic approval and ownership limits were raised progressively over time. In July 1963, foreign currency loans of less than $300,000 became subject to automatic approval. As noted previously, in July 1967 the foreign ownership limits were raised to 20 percent in unrestricted sectors and 15 percent in restricted ones, with the upper limit of 7 percent on a single investor.

Many liberalization measures concerned the ease with which liquidation proceeds could be repatriated (dividends could be freely repatriated for investments approved under the Foreign Investment Law). Although these were related to capital outflows, they affected the incentive of nonresidents to invest

Table 3.10. Selected measures in liberalization of portfolio and other inflows in Japan, 1951–67

Date	Measures[a]
3 April 1951	Prior notification requirements replaced by ex post notification requirements for purchases of new privately placed shares when repatriation of dividends not involved; purchases of publicly offered new shares permitted upon notification, when repatriation of dividends not involved; for purchases of existing shares, requirement that they be made part of investment program removed
1 July 1952	For purchases of privately placed new shares, repatriation of liquidation proceeds permitted, subject to minimum holding period of two years and five equal annual installments; purchases of corporate bonds and extension of loans subject to approval; for approved purchases of corporate bonds and beneficiary securities, repatriation of liquidation proceeds subject to five equal annual installments
30 September 1952	Purchases of shares subject to automatic approval by Bank of Japan (BOJ) if foreign ownership not raised above 8 percent in unrestricted sectors and 5 percent in restricted ones
27/30 October 1956	Acquisition by nonresident investors of stocks freely permitted if no repatriation involved (permitted subject to approval in restricted sectors)
1 June 1960	Ownership limit for automatic approval by BOJ raised to 15 percent in unrestricted sectors and 10 percent in restricted sectors, with limit of 5 percent per individual investor; stipulation for repatriation of liquidation proceeds eased to minimum holding period of two years with three equal annual installments; foreign currency loans subject to approval by BOJ if amount less than $100,000; purchases of corporate bonds and beneficiary securities subject to approval by BOJ if amount less than $10,000; repatriation of liquidation proceeds for beneficiary securities subject to three equal annual installments
1 May 1961	Stipulation for repatriation of liquidation proceeds eased further to allow lump sum payment, subject to minimum holding period of two years, for purchases of shares; for purchases of corporate bonds, repatriation of liquidation proceeds or principal freely allowed after minimum holding period of two years; minimum remaining maturity of corporate bonds for purchase by nonresidents reduced from five to two years; purchases of all publicly offered corporate bonds and beneficiary securities subject to approval by BOJ
1 August 1962	Minimum holding period for purchases of shares reduced to six months; minimum remaining maturity of corporate bonds for purchase by nonresidents reduced from two years to six months
1 April 1963	Repatriation of liquidation proceeds for shares freely allowed
1 July 1963	Foreign currency loans subject to approval by BOJ if amount less than $300,000 and maturity longer than three years
1 July 1967	Foreign ownership limit for automatic approval by BOJ raised to 20 percent in unrestricted sectors and 15 percent in restricted ones, with limit of 7 percent per individual investor

[a] Because the Foreign Investment Law did not make a distinction between direct and other investments, some of these measures applied to both

Source: Inuta (2000), pp. 160–5

in Japan. In July 1952, for example, liquidation proceeds were allowed to be repatriated, subject to a minimum holding period of two years and the requirement that they be made in five equal annual installments over five subsequent years. These terms were eased over time, with liquidation proceeds repatriated freely beginning in April 1963 if the purchases had been approved under the Foreign Investment Law. By the early to mid 1960s, small purchases of equity shares, corporate bonds, and beneficiary securities were freely permitted, with the repatriation of liquidation proceeds no longer subject to restrictions. The pace of inflows through loans picked up in the late 1950s, while equity inflows expanded sharply in the early 1960s (see Table 3.11).

The liberalization of portfolio and other inflows was halted or reversed during the currency crisis of 1971 (see Section 4.3.1 in Chapter 4). In March 1971, for example, the MOF virtually prohibited nonresidents from purchasing short-term government securities, whereas such transactions had previously been subject to automatic approval. Likewise, in May 1971, authorities prohibited purchases by nonresidents of unlisted bonds and investment trust certificates. With the subsequent weakening of the yen, however, the process of liberalization resumed. The restrictions on purchases of Japanese bonds (in place since March 1971) were lifted in August 1974. Controls were temporarily tightened again when the yen came under renewed appreciation pressure

Table 3.11. Portfolio and other inflows approved under Japan's Foreign Investment Law, 1950–67 (in millions of US dollars)

	Equities (of which, those involving management participation)	Loans[a]	Corporate bonds and beneficiary securities	Total
1950	1.8 (1.7)	0	0	1.8
1951	12.8 (11.8)	2.5	0	15.3
1952	9.8 (5.9)	30.7	0	40.6
1953	5.6 (3.8)	54.4	0.6	60.5
1954	4.2 (1.6)	13.5	0.1	17.8
1955	3.6 (1.9)	18.4	0	22.1
1956	9.2 (6.0)	132.8	0.1	142.1
1957	12.8 (7.7)	65.9	0.1	78.8
1958	9.4 (3.2)	261.0	0.1	270.5
1959	21.6 (10.5)	106.9	0.2	128.7
1960	57.0 (—)	146.0	0.4	152.1
1961	112.0 (63.9)	385.0	1.4	498.4
1962	125.0 (42.0)	277.0	0.8	402.8
1963	236.0 (54.0)	525.0	0.8	761.8
1964	85.0 (25.0)	595.0	3.0	683.0
1965	78.0 (44.0)	451.0	3.0	532.0
1966	112.0 (31.0)	335.0	2.0	449.0
1967	152.0 (33.0)	459.0	0.4	611.4

[a] These include loans from the World Bank and the Export–Import Bank of Washington
Source: Inuta (2000), Table 2, p. 181

in late 1977 and early 1978, but any remaining controls were lifted in February 1979.[24] In addition, stipulations for obtaining impact (general-purpose) loans from abroad were progressively eased from May 1979 to March 1980.

3.6.2. Portfolio and Other Outflows

Portfolio and other investment outflows were the last to be liberalized. In fact, purchases of foreign securities by residents (other than authorized foreign exchange banks) were totally prohibited until April 1970 when the steady balance-of-payments improvement placed upward pressure on the yen. On 16 April 1970, authorities allowed investment trusts to purchase listed foreign equities and bonds up to $100 million.[25] On 18 January 1971, the same authorization was extended to insurance companies for portfolio management purposes. These measures were followed by a decision, on 1 July 1971, to abolish the $100 million ceiling for investment trusts and securities companies and to allow individual investors to purchase listed foreign equities and bonds without limit through securities companies. On 1 November 1971, authorities allowed securities companies to purchase listed equities and bonds for their own accounts; they extended the same authorization to trust banks on 28 February 1972 and to major foreign exchange banks on 30 March 1972 (Inuta 2000).

From May to September 1972, these ad hoc measures were subsumed by a set of more comprehensive measures. First, authorities allowed all institutional investors to purchase foreign securities in the secondary market. Second, they allowed individual investors to purchase, in addition to listed securities, bonds issued by borrowers who had other securities listed at major exchanges for which prices were quoted. Third, they authorized over-the-counter (OTC) sales of foreign securities by domestic securities companies. Fourth, they established a procedure for the domestic sale of newly issued foreign bonds, up to half the total subscription (with private placements limited to institutional investors). On 17 November 1972, individual investors were allowed to purchase open-end investment trust securities, whether they were listed,

---

[24] From November 1977 to March 1978, public auction of short-term government bills was suspended. In March 1978, purchases of yen-denominated domestic bonds with remaining maturities of less than five years and one month were prohibited. This control was eased in January 1979 and then abolished in February.

[25] To qualify, a foreign security needed to be listed at the New York, London, Paris, Frankfurt, Amsterdam, Sydney, Zurich, or Toronto exchanges. The American and Luxembourg exchanges were added to the list in November 1971, followed by the Milan and Brussels exchanges in May 1972, when the security listing requirement became binding only for individual (not institutional) investors. The list was expanded to include the Wellington, Madrid, and Montreal exchanges in December 1973, and the NASDAQ, the Pacific, and several Asian exchanges in June and August 1977.

unlisted, newly issued, or traded in the secondary market (closed-end securities were regarded as ordinary equity investments). This last measure was implemented in view of the adoption in April 1972 by the OECD of standard rules for investment trusts. In October 1972, regulation for extending medium- and long-term loans by banks was relaxed.

The liberalization of outward portfolio and other investments proceeded in line with Japanese authorities' desire to promote capital outflows to ease upward pressure on the yen. This was temporarily halted or even reversed when the yen came under depreciation pressure following the first oil crisis. In January 1974, authorities asked foreign exchange banks, securities companies, insurance companies, and investment trusts voluntarily to refrain from increasing the net value of foreign securities investments; extension of medium- and long-term loans became subject to item-by-item approval. In August 1974, extension of medium- and long-term loans was prohibited in principle. The process of liberalization resumed in June 1975, when the voluntary restriction on foreign securities investments was lifted except for foreign exchange banks.

The liberalization of capital outflows continued. In November 1976, the regulation on the extension of medium- and long-term loans by banks was further relaxed. In March 1977, the voluntary restriction on foreign securities investments was lifted for foreign exchange banks. Extension of foreign currency-denominated medium- and long-term loans by major foreign exchange banks became subject to blanket approval in July 1978, and extending yen-denominated medium- and long-term loans was liberalized in October 1980. As a result of these and other measures, the balance of external portfolio and other assets steadily rose throughout the 1970s; there was a particularly noticeable sharp increase in the purchases of bonds after 1978, likely reflecting the major liberalization measure of April 1977 (see Table 3.12). The speculative nature of some of the capital flows was also evident, for example, in 1973 and 1979 when both purchases and sales surged in response to heightened exchange rate volatility.

3.7. ACHIEVING CAPITAL ACCOUNT CONVERTIBILITY

3.7.1. Completing Capital Account Liberalization

Japan took thirty years to achieve capital account convertibility by using three different approaches. First, short-term inflows (and outflows by nonresidents) were liberalized at a relatively early stage in 1960, although authorities subsequently developed largely market-based instruments to manage them. Second, following the ad hoc liberalization measures of the 1950s and early 1960s,

Table 3.12. Japan's outward portfolio investment, fiscal years 1970–80 (on settlement basis; in millions of US dollars)

Fiscal year	Equities		Bonds		Investment trust securities		Outstanding balance[a]
	Acquisitions	Sales	Acquisitions	Sales	Acquisitions	Sales	
1970	30	11	19	1	0	0	36
1971	136	26	311	99	0	0	354
1972	681	282	1,260	237	23	0	1,777
1973	977	621	1,194	478	310	105	3,038
1974	245	374	196	273	97	89	2,851
1975	537	550	202	85	176	176	2,954
1976	373	432	318	105	99	114	3,070
1977	195	212	3,456	378	47	47	5,849
1978	585	330	14,383	1,097	59	55	13,249
1979	1,226	1,146	17,850	4,597	174	214	17,189
1980[b]	639	791	25,095	5,651	204	168	20,108

[a] Net acquisitions do not add up to an increase in outstanding balance because of redemption, equity conversions, and other items
[b] Through the end of November 1980
Source: Inuta (2000), pp. 148–9

systematic liberalization of FDI began in the late 1960s, with the bulk of it taking place during 1967–76 for inflows and 1969–78 for outflows. The unique feature of FDI liberalization is that, once the process was initiated, it was never halted or reversed. Finally, liberalization of portfolio and other flows was an especially protracted process that initially involved easing of approval criteria for inward investment applications by nonresidents; purchases by residents of foreign securities for portfolio investment purposes were prohibited until 1970. While authorities gradually liberalized both outflows and inflows during the 1970s, they temporarily tightened controls to discourage inflows (out-flows) when the yen came under appreciation (depreciation) pressure.

When the yen began to strengthen in early 1975, however, authorities did not tighten controls on inflows (as they had previously done) because the active use of capital controls had been criticized for creating unnecessary unpredictability in economic decision-making. From this time on, exchange market pressure, if anything, acted to ease controls in one direction without necessarily tightening them in the other.[26] The program of allowing foreign public entities to raise bonds in the Tokyo market (suspended since late 1973) also resumed, with Finland and New Zealand raising ¥10 billion each in May and November 1975, respectively. At the end of June 1976, Japan notified the OECD that it would lift six of the fourteen reservations it had maintained under the OECD code, thereby eliminating all restrictions pertaining to: (1) purchases and sales by nonresidents of listed securities; (2) purchases and sales by nonresidents of unlisted securities; (3) extension by nonresidents of credit and loans to residents; (4) purchases abroad by residents of listed securities; (5) purchases abroad by residents of unlisted securities; and (6) extension by residents of credit and loans to nonresidents.[27]

As Japan faced mounting foreign criticism for its current account surplus, in June 1977 the MOF announced a program to remove remaining exchange and capital controls. On 1 June 1977, authorities lifted yen conversion limits while introducing a control on open spot positions. Beginning 13 June 1977, they substantially eased the BOJ approval criteria for the making of payments on invisible transactions;[28] almost all remaining payment formalities associ-ated with invisibles were eliminated in April 1978. Authorities took measures to increase the accessibility of the Japanese money market to foreign investors, and to liberalize short-term external lending by Japanese banks, purchases by Japanese residents of foreign currency bonds, and foreign bond issues in

---

[26] The period of yen strength from late 1977 to early 1978 was an exception.

[27] Beginning in early 1977, these transactions became subject to automatic approval by the BOJ.

[28] For example, foreign exchange banks were authorized to approve payment for educational and medical expenses abroad without limit; for all other invisible payments, the exemption limit for BOJ approval was raised from $1,000 to $3,000. Departing nonresidents were allowed to exchange yen for foreign currencies without limit subject to approval by foreign exchange banks.

Tokyo. Japanese authorities took advantage of the 1 November 1978 US Government action (see Section 4.5.1 in Chapter 4) and the subsequent weakening of the yen to further dismantle barriers to capital inflows, including reduction (January 1979) and then elimination (February 1979) of the marginal reserve requirement on FYDs and relaxation of restrictions on purchases by nonresidents of Japanese securities.[29]

3.7.2. The Revised Foreign Exchange Law

With the ad hoc, though progressive, liberalization of capital flows, there emerged a conflict between what the 1949 Foreign Exchange Law stated and what the government actually professed and practiced under the law. Since repatriation of principal and investment income was freely permitted, the Foreign Investment Law had become superfluous. Not only had the Foreign Exchange Law become increasingly outdated, but the way the government administered the law had become complex and opaque. Against this background, Prime Minister Takeo Fukuda thought it would make a "public relations" sense to project the image of Japan intent on liberalizing its trade and payments system (Horne 1985). In April 1978, the Japanese Government set up working groups within the MOF and the MITI to revise the law, aiming to submit the bill to the Diet in December. After having failed to be approved by the Diet twice (in May and August 1979) for reasons unrelated to the substance of the revision, the proposed bill was finally enacted into law on 11 December 1979. On 1 December 1980, the revised Foreign Exchange and Foreign Trade Control Law came into force, and with it the Foreign Investment Law was abolished.

The revised Foreign Exchange Law established the principle that all external transactions could be conducted freely unless explicitly prohibited. The law classified capital transactions into four categories: (1) transactions that required approval; (2) transactions that required prior notification but for which no government review was expected; (3) transactions that required prior notification and for which government review was expected; and (4) transactions that required neither approval nor notification. The first category represented transactions deemed controlled ex ante, such as foreign currency transactions between residents; deposit and trust contracts between residents and nonresidents; and issuance of Euroyen bonds by nonresidents in foreign

---

[29] On 23 January 1979, authorities reduced the maturity limit of domestic bonds that could be purchased by nonresidents subject to automatic approval from five years and one month to one year and one month; the maturity limit was entirely removed on 24 February. In May 1979, the government fully liberalized nonresident participation in the short-term *gensaki* (bond-repurchase) market.

countries. The law also allowed the government to impose "minimum necessary controls" for balance-of-payments or exchange-rate management purposes. The system of nonresident FYDs was abolished because the distinction between residents and nonresidents lost much of its relevance under the revised law. Significantly, foreign currency-denominated impact loans were liberalized, as a result of which short-term capital inflows expanded with far-reaching consequences for the still regulated domestic financial markets.

Most transactions fell under the second and third categories. The second category, for example, included inward FDI, which required prior notification of the MOF and the responsible minister.[30] Under normal cases, no government review was expected, but the foreign investor could not conclude the investment for thirty days, during which time the government could intervene. In the event of a potential problem, ministers could extend the probationary period from thirty days to as much as four months (five months if requested by the Foreign Exchange Council). If ministers judged that the investment would have a harmful impact, they could recommend alteration or even termination (beginning in July 1985, approvals were granted promptly upon receipt of an application in the majority of cases).

The third category included such transactions as outward FDI, external lending, debt guarantees by residents for securities issued by nonresidents in foreign countries, and acquisition by nonresidents of real estate in Japan—for which, in addition to the requirement of prior notification, a review by the government was to be expected as a matter of course. FDI was clearly defined as: (1) purchases of securities issued by, or lending of funds to, a foreign corporation established by a Japanese resident, made in order to establish a long-term economic relationship; or (2) payment of funds to establish or expand plants, branches, and other places of operation in a foreign country. For FDI, the law in principle replaced all existing provisions with a simple twenty-day advance notification requirement regardless of the type of investment. For portfolio and other investments, approval requirements for purchases of securities and extension of medium- and long-term loans by residents were replaced by prior notification requirements (with major foreign exchange banks exempted).

Authorized foreign exchange banks and designated securities companies played a critical role in the new control regime. Transactions that required neither approval nor notification—the fourth category of transactions—were those cross-border transactions intermediated by authorized foreign exchange banks or portfolio investments intermediated by designated securities companies. In fact, many of the transactions in the first category were made subject to control precisely to protect the integrity of the authorized foreign exchange

---

[30] In practice, foreign direct investors filed applications through the BOJ.

bank system. Otherwise, the overall system of inward and outward investments was quite liberal—subject, of course, to the condition that transactions be made through a bank or a securities company, thus allowing the government to monitor or intervene if necessary. In addition, the minister of finance retained power to limit foreign exchange banks' open positions in foreign exchange, specify requirements for their foreign exchange business, and prohibit them from paying interest on yen deposits held by nonresidents.

Nonfinancial institutions and wealthy individuals became almost totally free to acquire foreign financial assets under the revised Foreign Exchange Law, subject to two restrictions: (1) they had to make all foreign exchange transactions through authorized foreign exchange banks and make securities transactions through designated securities companies; and (2) as a corollary, they could not hold bank deposits in foreign countries beyond a certain limit. As compensation for the second restriction, they were permitted to hold foreign currency deposits with domestic financial institutions without limit. As a result of these and other measures, authorities virtually lost capital controls as an instrument of exchange rate policy. The only leverage they retained was the "prudential" regulations on foreign securities investment of financial institutions and institutional investors. To keep the momentum of CAL, and also to respond to institutional investors' desire to diversify their portfolios, Japanese authorities took steps to liberalize some of these prudential regulations in the early 1980s (see Section 5.1 in Chapter 5).

3.7.3. Assessing the Economic Impact of Capital Account Liberalization

It would be inappropriate to think of what happened in December 1980 as a onetime break in Japan's capital account regime. Though the enactment of the revised Foreign Exchange Law had symbolic significance, it was neither the beginning nor the end of a long, sustained, and gradual process of capital account liberalization (Chapter 5 presents a sequel). Even so, it was from the late 1970s and the early 1980s that Japan moved decisively toward achieving a high degree of capital account openness, which allowed Japanese residents to engage in capital transactions more freely. Fukao (2003) shows that the internationalization of Japanese financial markets did not progress very much during the 1970s despite the series of measures taken to liberalize cross-border capital flows. It was only in the 1980s that the volume of capital transactions expanded rapidly, irrespective of current transaction needs. Takagi (1994), by running a causality test of current receipts and payments vis-à-vis long-term capital flows based on quarterly data for Q1 1981–Q2 1992, finds that capital transactions were largely exogenous to current transactions during the post-liberalization period.

Fukao and Okina (1989) argue that greater capital mobility allows a larger and more persistent current account imbalance to result from divergent fiscal policies between two countries.[31] Capital mobility, by deepening the foreign exchange market and raising risk tolerance, allows the market to accommodate a larger portfolio shift with a smaller exchange rate movement. This means that, when divergent fiscal policies cause real interest rates to diverge, capital flows into the country with a higher real interest rate and allows the current account deficit to persist without forcing the real exchange rate to depreciate. Fukao and Okina (1989) appeal to this logic to explain why the yen remained weak in the early 1980s despite Japan's widening current account surplus, whereas in the 1970s a current account improvement was typically associated with an appreciating yen.

Another consequence of the greater capital mobility was the closer financial integration of Japan with the rest of the industrial world. In the early 1970s, capital controls were binding. Ito (1986) shows that the Euroyen interest rate deviated systematically from the *gensaki* rate according to the direction of capital controls. From late 1973 to early 1974, for example, the Euroyen rate exceeded the *gensaki* rate, indicating that the outflow controls were binding in the face of yen weakness; at the end of December 1973, the deviation was as large as 28.5 percent per year for three-month instruments (see Figure 3.10). On the other hand, in early 1975 and from late 1977 to early 1979, the reverse was true, suggesting that the inflow controls were binding. With the easing of capital controls, deviations declined over time and, for all practical purposes, disappeared in early 1979, when nonresident purchases of Japanese securities (February) and nonresidents' access to the *gensaki* market (May) were fully liberalized (Frankel 1984; Otani and Tiwari 1981). Any deviations were small relative to the estimated transaction costs (Ito 1986).

The 1980s also observed a closer link between Japanese and US stock prices compared to the 1970s. Gultekin et al. (1989), using weekly data for January 1977–December 1984, estimate a multifactor asset pricing model in which nominal returns were assumed to be a function of expected returns and risk factors. By estimating the nominal returns of a similarly constructed set of more than a hundred stocks for each country in terms of domestic and foreign interest rates and prices, the authors find that the pricing of risk was similar between Japan and the United States during 1981–4 but not during 1977–80. From this they conclude that the revised Foreign Exchange Law led to a closer integration of the two markets and allowed arbitrage to equate the prices of risk. Likewise, Campbell and Hamao (1992), based on monthly data for January 1971–March 1990, show that a greater portion of the excess stock market returns in the two countries (relative to the US Treasury bill rate)

---

[31] This is formally shown in a "textbook" two-country IS–LM model, which is augmented by asset market equilibrium with imperfect asset substitutability.

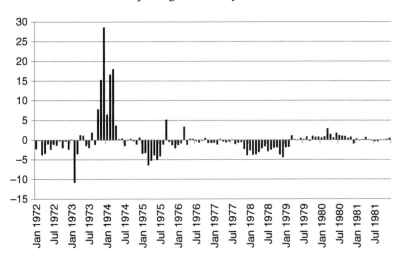

Figure 3.10. Deviations from covered interest parity between Euroyen and *gensaki* markets, January 1972–December 1981 (in percent per year)[a]

[a] Based on end-of-month data for three-month instruments; the Euroyen rate is estimated from the Eurodollar rate and the forward exchange rate; a positive number indicates that the Euroyen rate exceeds the *gensaki* rate
Source: Ito (1986), appendix table. Used by permission

reflected the influence of common variables during January 1981–March 1990, whereas the Japanese excess returns during January 1971–December 1980 hardly responded to any US variable. Fukao and Okubo (1984) obtain a similar result for the determination of the secondary yield of long-term Japanese government bonds.

Fukao and Hanazaki (1987) observe that the integration of Japanese financial markets was part of a global trend. The authors note that differentials between offshore and onshore interest rates had narrowed throughout the world while also noting the tendency for real interest differentials to narrow over time, especially for longer-term rates. Hutchison and Singh (1997) show, based on quarterly data for Q1 1981–Q3 1991, that short-term real interest rates in Japan and the United States were cointegrated. Although deviations from real interest rate parity fluctuated widely in the short run, an estimated vector error correction model shows that a deviation from equilibrium was eliminated within one to two years. These are strong results. Real interest rate arbitrage presupposes both purchasing power parity and uncovered interest rate parity, conditions not likely to hold except perhaps over a long period of time. While it thus requires a leap of faith to accept the implications of these findings at face value, taken in context, they add to the body of evidence showing that Japanese financial markets became highly integrated with those of other major industrial countries during the 1980s.

4

Managing Flexibility: 1971–90

4.1. INTRODUCTION

In the mid 1960s, tension emerged in the Bretton Woods system of fixed exchange rates as major countries developed chronic balance-of-payments imbalances. In November 1967, sterling was devalued by 14.30 percent. Likewise, in August 1969, the French franc was devalued by 11.11 percent, which precipitated a 9.29 percent revaluation of the deutsche mark eleven weeks later. As the cumulative payments deficits of the United States caused the supply of gold reserves to barely cover the country's external liabilities (Kenen 1969), the dollar came under attack, and the Gold Pool lost some $2.7 billion of gold during the first months of 1968 (Maisel 1973).[1] In March 1968, participating countries created a two-tier system in which they agreed to continue to buy and sell gold to each other at $35 per ounce but no longer support the price in the commercial market. As the gold convertibility of the US dollar was questioned, in 1969 forty-six countries converted dollars into gold; in 1970 sixty countries converted $630 million; and by early 1971 the US gold reserves stood at $11 billion, some $7 billion smaller than in 1960 (Scammell 1980).

Initially, Japan was not party to the currency turmoil sweeping the European markets. Even so, things obviously looked different. In the past, whenever the economy expanded rapidly, a deficit had emerged in the balance of payments. This time, Japan was experiencing a sustained economic expansion (with growth in excess of 12 percent in 1968 and 1969), but no deficit was emerging. At the fixed exchange rate of ¥360 per dollar, Japan's improved competitiveness had evidently led to a structural trade surplus beginning in about 1965 (see Figure 4.1)[2] and to a sustained current account surplus from 1968.

---

[1] The Gold Pool was established in November 1961 by the United States, the United Kingdom and six continental European countries to maintain the official gold price of $35 per ounce by providing sufficient gold to the private market. France withdrew in June 1967.

[2] It is estimated that Japan became a net creditor country in about September 1968 (Nihon Keizai Shimbunsha 1969).

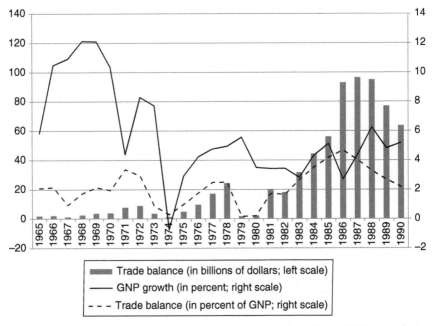

Figure 4.1. Japan's trade balance and real gross national product (GNP) growth (in billions of US dollars; in percent of GNP; year-on-year percentage rate of change)

Source: IMF, *International Financial Statistics*

Jorgenson et al. (1987) show that, by the late 1960s, Japan's industrial productivity had improved sufficiently to present a cost advantage over the United States in twenty-three out of the thirty sectors they examined, although technological parity had not yet been reached.[3] Because there was no external deficit, the government saw no compelling reason to restrain domestic demand, even though the economy was overheating. The decision to tighten monetary policy was delayed until September 1969,[4] but this was criticized abroad as contrary to the objective of promoting Japanese imports and limiting downward pressure on the dollar.

This chapter reviews Japan's exchange rate policy during 1971–90, when the yen appreciated against the dollar from ¥357.3 (the upper limit of 0.75 percent margins) to ¥134.4 (see Figure 4.2). Authorities used capital controls, market intervention, monetary and fiscal policies, and other measures to manage the ever fluctuating yen–dollar rate. The exchange rate and the current account

---

[3] These sectors included textiles, fabricated textiles, iron and steel, nonferrous metal, fabricated metal, machinery, electrical machinery, motor vehicles, transportation equipment, and precision instruments. The literature generally suggests that Japan's technological catch-up with the West was over by the early 1970s (McKinnon and Ohno 1997).

[4] Kuroda (2003) calls this the first time in postwar history that the Bank of Japan raised the discount rate for domestic considerations alone.

Figure 4.2. Yen–dollar exchange rate, January 1971–December 1990 (yen per dollar; end of period)

Source: IMF, *International Financial Statistics*

balance were the two main endogenous variables of relevance. Inevitably, the conduct of exchange rate policy became embedded in current account developments. This chapter, after giving an overview of exchange rate policy during the period, discusses in greater depth episodes of significant policy action, namely, the currency crises of 1971–3, the oil crises of 1973–4 and 1979–80, and the international policy coordination attempts of 1978 and 1985–7. The chapter concludes by reviewing the academic debate that ensued from the late 1980s about the impact of exchange rate changes on current account and price adjustments and by assessing the economic consequences of Japan's policy stance that, in retrospect, excessively subordinated domestic objectives to external considerations.

4.2. AN OVERVIEW OF EXCHANGE RATE POLICY: 1971–90

Over the period 1971–90, the yen–dollar exchange rate was subject to considerable swings, which involved eight major episodes of sustained appreciation or depreciation (see Figure 4.3). The swings were associated with current account developments, with a rising surplus triggering an appreciation and a fall in the surplus or an emerging deficit leading to a depreciation of the currency. During the sharpest and most sustained period of yen appreciation, from early 1985 to late 1987, Japan's quarterly current account surplus on

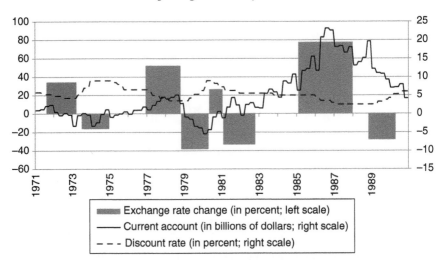

Figure 4.3. Magnitudes and durations of major appreciation and depreciation episodes in Japan, January 1971–December 1990[a]

Source: Datastream, London closing rates; IMF, *International Financial Statistics*; MOF, *Fiscal and Monetary Statistics Monthly*

goods and services widened from $6 to $18 billion (though no causality is implied by this association). Two depreciation episodes, from 1973 to 1974 and from 1979 to 1980, coincided with a weak current account position associated with substantial increases in the price of imported oil. Frequently, the counterpart of Japan's current account surplus was a US deficit. The conduct of exchange rate policy therefore became intertwined with bilateral trade frictions between the two countries.

4.2.1. Monetary Policy

In response to exchange rate developments, Japanese authorities resorted to various measures to moderate volatility or correct underlying macroeconomic imbalances (see Table 4.1). Monetary policy and foreign exchange market intervention were the standard tools. Figure 4.3 clearly shows that monetary policy was systematically tightened (loosened) when the yen was depreciating (appreciating). For example, during the period of yen weakness from 1973 to 1974, the Bank of Japan (BOJ) successively raised the official discount rate from 5.5 to 9.0 percent; in contrast, from 1976 to 1978, when the yen was appreciating, the discount rate was cut successively from 6.5 to 3.5 percent.

[a] Each shaded area represents a major appreciation or depreciation phase, with a positive (negative) number indicating an appreciation (depreciation) of the yen from trough (peak) to peak (trough), expressed as a logarithmic difference in basis points; the discount rate is an end-of-month figure expressed as percent per annum, while the current account is a quarterly figure expressed in billions of US dollars.

Table 4.1. Selected policy measures adopted during major appreciation and depreciation episodes in Japan, 1971–90

Episode (percentage change between peak and trough)[a]	Macroeconomic background	Monetary, fiscal, and trade measures	Intervention	Exchange and capital controls
(1) Appreciation (+34.16%): August 1971 to March 1973	Economic slowdown emanating from tight monetary policy to defend peg and subsequent yen revaluation; persistent and rising current account surplus	Aggressive monetary easing; supplementary budget, with import promotion scheme and voluntary export restraints (October 1972)	Dollar purchases	Tightening exchange regulations and controls on capital inflows (see Tables 4.3 and 4.4)
(2) Depreciation (−16.08%): July 1973 to December 1974	Reversal in speculative capital flows; emerging current account deficit following first oil crisis (fall 1973); sluggish growth with high inflation	Aggressive monetary tightening; fiscal restraint	Dollar sales to defend particular level (raised from ¥265 to ¥300 in January)	Tightening of outflow controls; easing of inflow controls
(3) Appreciation (+52.05%): December 1976 to October 1978	Rising current account surplus against economic recovery; interest rate differentials favoring yen; Japanese surplus receiving international criticism; international pledge by Japan to stimulate growth	Cautious and then substantial monetary easing; fiscal expansion (from fall 1977); administrative guidance to restrain exports and stockpiling of commodity imports (April 1978), followed by emergency imports (August 1978)	Limited intervention, followed by large dollar purchases from late 1977 to early 1978	Series of measures to tighten inflow controls and to ease capital outflows (see Table 4.6)
(4) Depreciation (−37.98%): October 1978 to April 1980	Declining current account surplus against economic expansion, followed by emerging current account deficit after second oil crisis (late 1979); interest rate differentials favoring dollar (especially after October 1979)	Consistent tightening of monetary policy (April 1979 to February 1980); fiscal tightening (from summer 1979)	Large coordinated intervention initially to support dollar (late 1978), followed by consistent dollar sales, reportedly large (spring and fall 1979) and coordinated (March 1980)	Easing of barriers to capital inflows (from January 1979); tightening of outflow controls (from October 1979)

(continued)

Table 4.1. Continued

Episode (percentage change between peak and trough)[a]	Macroeconomic background	Monetary, fiscal, and trade measures	Intervention	Exchange and capital controls
(5) Appreciation (+26.26%): April 1980 to January 1981	Dramatic turnaround in balance of payments, followed by current account surplus by summer 1980; deceleration of economic growth	Moderate monetary easing (from August 1980); modest fiscal easing (from mid 1980), involving restoration of earlier expenditure cuts	Yen sales (especially from fall 1980), coordinated in January 1981	New Foreign Exchange Law (December 1980), accompanied by further easing of controls on capital inflows
(6) Depreciation (−33.11%): January 1981 to October 1982	Decelerating growth (output contraction in Q4 1981); widening interest rate differentials favoring dollar; price stability; trade frictions over export practices; emerging current account surplus overshadowed by large capital outflows	Monetary easing to stimulate growth (from March 1980); modest fiscal stimulus (from March 1981) within tight fiscal space; import promotion measures (announced as part of four-point program in October 1981)	Limited intervention to support yen, coordinated in June, August, and October 1982	Series of liberalization measures on foreign investment by institutional investors, followed by moral suasion to restrict capital outflows (from March 1982)
(7) Appreciation (+77.37%): February 1985 to December 1987	Large and widening current account surplus, against pickup in growth	Short-term interest rates allowed to drift higher in October 1985; followed by substantial monetary easing, coordinated in 1986	Dollar sales, coordinated in February and fall 1985; in March 1986, intervention switched to purchasing dollars; large dollar purchases through end 1987, coordinated in April and May	n.a.
(8) Depreciation (−27.87%): November 1988 to April 1990	Strong economic expansion, with moderate decline in current account surplus	Monetary tightening from late 1989 to contain asset price inflation	Dollar sales, coordinated sporadically throughout 1989 and in early 1990	n.a.

[a] Approximated by a logarithmic difference in basis points

Sources: FRBNY, *Monthly Review,* 1971–6; FRBNY, *Quarterly Review,* 1977–90; Ohta (1982); Komiya and Suda (1983); Ito (1987); Funabashi (1988)

Easing of monetary policy was meant not only to moderate the inflow of capital, but also to reduce net exports by stimulating domestic demand. Active use of monetary policy was possible because the central bank was not independent of government oversight. The Ministry of Finance (MOF) had the authority to request or to veto a change in monetary policy.

Active use of monetary policy to manage the exchange rate has been confirmed by several empirical studies. First, Hutchison (1988) estimates a reaction function of the call rate in terms of several explanatory variables. The author, by using monthly data for March 1973–September 1985, finds that the exchange rate was virtually the only statistically significant explanatory variable but that, when the sample was divided into two subperiods, the finding holds only for the July 1978–September 1985 period. Second, De Andrade and Divino (2005) likewise find that, from the mid 1980s to the mid 1990s, the call rate responded significantly to deviations from purchasing power parity (a proxy for real exchange rate misalignment); the response was particularly strong for the August 1985–May 1987 period. Third, Danne and Schnabl (2008), estimating a similar reaction function by using monthly data for January 1974–March 1999, show that the call rate responded significantly to the deviation of the yen–dollar exchange rate from a five-year backward moving average but that inflation and industrial production were also significant determinants of monetary policy. The use of monetary policy became more intensive after the mid 1980s.[5]

The finding, common to all three studies, that the use of monetary policy somehow became more intense after the mid 1980s requires careful scrutiny. First, monetary easing in Japan after 1985 was coordinated with other countries, allowing the BOJ to cut the discount rate more aggressively. Second, use of monetary policy was even more intense under the Bretton Woods regime of fixed exchange rates, when policy was tightened (eased) whenever a deficit (surplus) emerged in the balance of payments. During the 1956–73 period, for instance, money supply (M2) growth fluctuated widely between 15 and 25 percent, with correspondingly wide swings in the growth of real gross national product (GNP) with a lag of a few quarters (Hamada and Hayashi 1985; Suzuki 1985). In contrast, after 1973, external balance became only one of the multiple objectives of monetary policy.

The multitasking of monetary policy occasionally posed a conflict, especially given the lack of central bank independence. At times, the BOJ found

---

[5] Danne and Schnabl (2008), in one of their specifications, obtain the result that the call rate was reduced when the yen appreciated but it hardly changed in times of depreciation. It is unwarranted, in light of the evidence presented in this section, to conclude that monetary policy in Japan was therefore asymmetric with respect to appreciation and depreciation. This particular finding of monetary policy asymmetry is likely an artefact of the way the exchange rate variable is defined. The secular appreciation of the yen observed during this period implies very few, if any, episodes of depreciation if it is defined in relation to the five-year moving average.

itself forced to sacrifice domestic stability for external objectives. During the period of yen weakness in 1983, for example, weak domestic economic activity called for easing monetary policy. But monetary easing would further stimulate capital outflows and weaken the yen, an outcome not palatable to the authorities when international attention was focused on Japan's widening current account surplus. In the event, higher short-term interest rates were kept unnecessarily long to support the yen (Fukao 1983). On the other hand, when the yen was depreciating from January 1981 to October 1982, monetary policy was eased to stimulate domestic demand, thereby accelerating the pace of capital outflows and pushing the yen further downward.

4.2.2. Foreign Exchange Market Intervention

Foreign exchange market intervention is a more flexible tool of exchange rate policy, though its effectiveness is less predictable. The MOF has not released official intervention data going back to the decades of the 1970s and 1980s, so we must estimate the amount and direction of official intervention from changes in the monthly or quarterly balance of official foreign exchange reserves, adjusted for interest income. The fact (though not the amount) of Japanese official intervention can be confirmed by accounts in the *Monthly Reviews* (through September 1976) or *Quarterly Reviews* of the Federal Reserve Bank of New York (FRBNY) if it was coordinated with US authorities. A typical pattern of intervention is evident in Figure 4.4: Japanese authorities sold (purchased) yen when it was "strong" ("weak") or appreciating (depreciating). That is, they followed a lean-against-the-wind (LATW) strategy. For example, when the yen appreciated by 7.5 percent during the fourth quarter of 1977, authorities sold an estimated $4.6 billion equivalent of yen; in contrast, they purchased an estimated $5 billion equivalent of yen during the first quarter of 1979 when the currency depreciated by 5.6 percent.

The pattern was neither exact nor consistent, suggesting that intervention decisions involved multiple considerations. For example, the periods from late 1976 through mid 1977 and from 1983 through mid 1985 saw little intervention despite the fact that the exchange rate moved substantially; hardly any intervention took place when the yen depreciated by nearly 7 percent during the second quarter of 1981 or when it appreciated by 10 percent during the fourth quarter of 1990. In the latter part of 1985, when the yen appreciated by as much as 20 percent, Japanese authorities *sold* 2 billion dollars in order to support the dollar's decline. This occurred against the background of a concerted effort among the Group of Five (G5) countries to effect an orderly downward adjustment of the dollar against other major currencies (the Plaza Agreement). In March 1986, however, Japanese authorities reverted to the LATW strategy when the yen crossed the then post-Bretton Woods record of

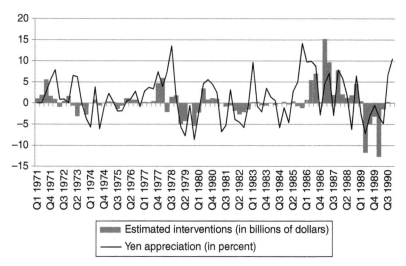

Figure 4.4. Yen's quarterly average changes against US dollar and estimated foreign exchange market intervention in Japan, Q1 1971–Q4 1990[a] (in percent; in billions of US dollars)

[a] A positive number indicates the yen's appreciation or purchases of dollars; estimated from changes in the balance of foreign exchange reserves and the US Treasury bill rate

Sources: IMF, *International Financial Statistics*; author's estimates

¥178 (Cargill et al. 1997). They purchased an estimated 12.5 billion dollars over two quarters.

A number of empirical studies confirm that Japan's official intervention during this period was largely of the LATW type. Green (1990), for example, estimates the intervention reaction function of the Japanese authorities by using monthly data for March 1973–October 1988, with a change in official reserves (adjusted for an estimated interest income) on the left-hand side. The author finds that intervention responded symmetrically to depreciation and appreciation for the entire period as well as for any of the subperiods (similar conclusions were reached by Quirk (1977) for March 1973–October 1976). Descriptively, 83.0 percent of the monthly foreign exchange reserve changes were of the LATW type, with 82.6 percent for yen depreciation and 83.3 percent for yen appreciation.

Takagi (1991) formally tested whether intervention was symmetric with respect to appreciation and depreciation. Using quarterly data for Q1 1973–Q2 1989, the author finds that intervention behavior was period-specific. While LATW behavior was confirmed for the entire period only for yen appreciation, if the sample was divided, intervention was found biased toward depreciation for Q3 1978–Q3 1985 and toward appreciation for Q4 1985–Q2 1989. The overall bias probably reflects the fact that the yen experienced a net appreciation over the entire period. The apparent asymmetry found across the subsamples can be interpreted in terms of the different environments under which monetary authorities were operating. During Q3 1978–Q3 1985, the yen was generally depreciating, while it was largely appreciating during Q4 1985–Q2 1989. We must thus conclude that official intervention was largely symmetric, reflecting the desire not only to minimize exchange rate volatility but also to avoid complicating international trade and macroeconomic policy negotiations.

4.2.3. Fiscal Policy

Fiscal policy was used more modestly than monetary policy or intervention, even though relative fiscal positions were an important determinant of the bilateral current account imbalance between Japan and the United States. Noland (1989a), for example, estimates a vector autoregressive (VAR) model of the two countries for the period Q1 1970–Q4 1987 to suggest that if Japan had increased the government budget deficit by 2 percentage points of GNP from 1988 through 1991, its bilateral current account surplus with the United States would have fallen by 21 percent. Fiscal policy was used rather actively during the 1970s, as the Japanese Government resorted to Keynesian-type policy when faced with a slowdown in economic growth. In contravention of the Fiscal Law, deficit-financing bonds were issued for the first time in 1975.[6] In 1976, the government announced a plan to eliminate the issuance of deficit-financing bonds by 1980, but the general government deficit kept increasing through the rest of the decade. As it became clear that the goal would not be achieved, in 1979, the fiscal consolidation target was pushed back to FY 1984.

Fiscal consolidation began in earnest in 1983, when the government announced a revised plan to eliminate the issuance of deficit-financing bonds by FY 1990. From then on, the deficit began to decline as a share of GNP, and the goal was eventually reached by freezing the nominal value of discretionary expenditures and maintaining the existing income tax brackets in nominal terms. These developments meant that fiscal policy had little room to maneuver after 1976 (when the first fiscal consolidation plan was announced) and especially after 1983 when determined fiscal consolidation efforts began. Asako and Ito (1991) show that, even though Japan agreed at the Group of Seven (G7) Summit in 1978 to become a "locomotive" for the rest of the world by providing a major fiscal stimulus, the budget was only slightly larger in 1978 than in 1977, and the rate of budgetary growth actually dropped sharply

---

[6] The Fiscal Law authorizes the issuance of what it calls construction bonds only, the proceeds from which are in principle used to finance the building of infrastructure or for capital subscriptions. Government bonds, issued for noncapital spending under a special Diet authorization annually, are called deficit-financing bonds.

in 1979. A number of fiscal stimulus measures were announced in response to exchange rate and current account developments (see Table 4.1), but many of them were largely cosmetic actions with limited impact.

4.2.4. Exchange and Capital Controls

Japan's current account was almost entirely free of restrictions during the period under consideration (see Section 2.7.3 in Chapter 2), so there was little scope for using exchange controls, but authorities did attempt to control disguised capital flows by limiting the leads and lags in trade payments. For example, they imposed a limit on prepayments for Japanese exports in August 1971 to contain appreciation pressure and lifted it in January 1972 when the pressure abated; they used a similar measure from February 1972 to May 1979 in order to manage exchange market pressure. The only remaining exchange restriction, permitted subject to approval from the International Monetary Fund (IMF), was the maximum amount of foreign exchange Japanese tourists could take out of the country. Authorities raised or lowered the limit, depending on the direction of exchange market pressure. The limit was altogether eliminated on 1 April 1978 during the middle of a major appreciation cycle for the yen.

Use of capital controls was more systematic. From 1971 to 1980, each appreciation cycle saw a tightening (relaxing) of controls on inflows (outflows), and each depreciation cycle saw a reversal of this. All this changed in December 1980 with the new Foreign Exchange Law, which established the principle that capital transactions were freely permitted unless explicitly prohibited. Although capital controls remained in the form of prudential regulations for financial institutions and institutional investors, these were also eased from that time on. The depreciation of the yen in the early 1980s coincided with a progressive easing of regulations on foreign investment by institutional investors, who took the opportunity to diversify their portfolios (see Section 5.1 in Chapter 5).

Other administrative measures adopted during the period include the placement of official reserves with private banks in 1971 to reduce short-term external borrowing, to facilitate the provision of forward cover (which no private counterparty was willing to offer), and to slow the growth of reserves. In 1973, faced with depreciation pressure, authorities scaled down the program of lending foreign exchange for import financing. Faced with appreciation pressure in 1978, on the other hand, they encouraged banks to shift from dollar to yen financing of imports by offering to discount import settlement bills outside the regular ceilings. The low-cost yen import financing scheme was abolished in 1979 during the middle of a depreciation cycle. When the yen was seen to have depreciated too far in March 1982, authorities "requested" securities companies to refrain temporarily from selling zero-coupon bonds to residents while tightening reporting requirements for the holders of such securities, with the pretext of limiting income tax avoidance. Under an open capital account, authorities had few options left except for moral suasion and reporting requirements.

4.2.5. Trade Measures

Because exchange rate pressure was often related to current account developments, authorities also used trade measures to directly influence exports and imports. In 1972, in connection with a supplementary budget, they announced an import promotion scheme as well as a voluntary export restraint (VER) plan in order to contain appreciation pressure on the yen. In April 1978, again to limit upward pressure on the yen, they issued administrative guidance to curtail the growth of exports and began to stockpile essential imported commodities; this was followed, in August, by a program of emergency imports. A number of import promotion schemes were adopted throughout the 1980s, including in January 1982, July 1985, and May 1987. Because trade frictions were perennial issues, trade measures were constantly employed. In this sense, they were not exchange rate policy measures per se. Sharp appreciation of the yen often triggered an introduction or intensification of measures but, unlike bona fide exchange rate policy measures, many of the import measures were never rescinded once introduced (though some, like stockpiling of imports, were obviously one-shot measures).

Japan was constantly in negotiation with the United States (as well as Europe) on trade issues. The focus was initially on the penetration of Japanese products in the United States. Japan agreed to multi-year VERs on steel (from 1969), color television sets (from 1977), and automobiles (from 1981). The focus of trade talks shifted to the penetration of American goods in the Japanese market. Tariffs and quotas were first targeted, followed by nontariff barriers, although recent research establishes that use of such measures was no more pervasive in Japan than in the United States (Clark 1994). US negotiators then began to look at impediments in specific market segments of strategic importance, such as telecommunications, medical equipment and pharmaceuticals, electronics, and forest products, under the so-called Market Oriented Sector Selective (MOSS) talks that started in early 1985. The Structural Impediments Initiative (SII), from 1989 to 1990, focused on removing Japan's structural impediments to foreign imports, including saving and investment patterns, land policy, the distribution system, exclusionary business practices, *keiretsu* (corporate group) relationships, and pricing mechanisms (Abe 2013).

4.3. THE CURRENCY CRISES

4.3.1. Collapse of the Bretton Woods System: 1971

Japan's widening payments surplus became a focus of international attention in early 1969, and the call for Japan to revalue its currency became louder. When the deutsche mark was revalued in the fall, rumors of a similar action for the yen circulated. The Japanese business establishment, however, argued that a yen revaluation would be "suicidal" because it would weaken the competitiveness of Japan and damage the small to medium-size enterprises in the import-competing sector (Nihon Keizai Shimbunsha 1969). Japanese authorities were opposed to any thought of revaluation, believing that Japan's strong external payments position was a mirage based on import restrictions and capital controls (Chōgin Sangyō Kenkyūkai 1970). As the current account surplus increased, the government limited the rise in official reserves by lending foreign exchange to domestic banks, allowing them to pay off their short-term external liabilities.[7]

From 1970 to 1971, the Japanese and US economies were in different cyclical positions, calling for divergent macroeconomic policies (see Table 4.2). Japan's cyclical peak had been reached in late 1969 and, with a tighter policy stance, the economy was slowing (though still growing at nearly 10 percent in 1970). Consumer price inflation, hovering at 5.5 percent in 1968–9, had climbed to 7.6 percent. In contrast, the US economy was in recession, and US authorities were easing fiscal and monetary policies. As the yen came under appreciation pressure, Japanese authorities were therefore unwilling to expand macroeconomic policies under these circumstances. Though the obvious macroeconomic policy course at this point would have been to revalue the yen (Cargill et al. 1997), the Japanese Government was not intellectually open to considering revaluing or floating the yen.[8] In fact, the mere mention of greater flexibility remained taboo in the press (Hamada and Patrick 1988).

In early May 1971, a report by major German economic research institutes recommending a floating or a revaluation of the mark as the best solution to the policy dilemma the country faced was greeted sympathetically by certain high-ranking German officials. The market seized on this apparent shift of policy, and speculative funds flooded into West Germany. On 5 May, the Bundesbank withdrew from the market, followed immediately by the central

---

[7] As a result, the short-term external position of the banking sector shifted from a net debtor position of $1.2 billion at the end of March 1968 to a net creditor position of $400 million at the end of March 1970 (Chōgin Sangyō Kenkyūkai 1970).

[8] According to Houthakker (1978), Japan was the only country that turned down a US invitation to participate in bilateral discussions on exchange rate flexibility. In the IMF debate on reforming the international monetary system, Japan consistently opposed any proposals to make exchange rates more flexible (Odell 1982).

Table 4.2. Selected macroeconomic indicators in Japan and United States, 1970–5

		1970	1971	1972	1973	1974	1975
Year-on-year growth in real gross national product (in percent)	Japan	9.86	4.69	8.97	8.82	−1.24	2.42
	United States	−0.19	3.39	5.66	5.77	−0.63	−1.18
Current account balance (in billions of US dollars; percent of gross domestic product in parentheses)	Japan	2.00 (0.98)	5.81 (2.52)	6.67 (2.19)	−0.12 (−0.03)	−4.72 (−1.03)	−0.69 (−0.14)
	United States	2.32 (0.24)	−1.45 (−0.14)	−5.78 (−0.49)	7.07 (0.54)	2.1 (0.15)	18.32 (1.20)
Government budget deficit (in percent of gross domestic product)	Japan	−0.44	−0.22	−1.58	−1.62	−1.34	−4.76
	United States	−1.15	−2.32	−1.48	−0.61	−0.77	−4.92
Year-on-year growth in government expenditure (in percent)	Japan	21.15	8.13	14.69	28.71	17.23	6.74
	United States	5.41	6.72	7.75	6.84	12.46	11.77
Year-on-year rate of consumer price inflation (in percent)	Japan	7.63	6.15	4.45	11.73	24.43	11.81
	United States	5.84	4.25	3.46	6.10	10.95	9.20
Discount rate (in percent; end of year)	Japan	6.00	4.75	4.25	9.00	9.00	6.50
	United States	5.50	4.50	4.50	7.50	7.75	6.00
Year-on-year growth in broad money (in percent)	Japan	16.89	24.27	24.69	16.83	11.51	14.46
	United States	5.94	10.48	10.13	5.18	4.64	10.20

Source: IMF, *International Financial Statistics*

banks of Austria, Belgium, the Netherlands, and Switzerland. Over the weekend, the Swiss franc and the Austrian schilling were revalued by 7.07 percent and 5.05 percent, respectively, while the deutsche mark and the Dutch guilder began to float. The Belgian market was reopened based on previous intervention limits but with further separation of the official and financial franc markets (FRBNY, October 1971). This pushed the yen close to the upper limit of ¥357.30 to the dollar, where it would remain through the end of the Bretton Woods era.

With expectations of a yen revaluation, leads and lags resulted in a large influx of funds to Japan; in particular, there were sizable yen prepayments for ships under construction in Japanese yards. From March to August 1971, Japanese authorities tightened controls on capital inflows and eased monetary policy. On 4 June, moreover, the government adopted an "Eight-Point Program for Avoiding Yen Revaluation." The package included: (1) reduction in the number of import quotas; (2) preferential tariffs for imports from developing countries; (3) additional general tariff reductions; (4) liberalization of capital outflows; (5) reduction of nontariff trade barriers; (6) increased aid to developing countries; (7) abolishment of preferential financing of exports and of special tax benefits for exporters; and (8) monetary and fiscal policies designed to stimulate the domestic economy (Odell 1982). Authorities also began to place dollar deposits with foreign exchange banks to enable them to purchase export bills (such deposits would amount to $1.2 billion by early October), and additional deposits were subsequently placed to facilitate the provision of forward cover for small and medium-sized enterprises (FRBNY, October 1971). The MOF hastily prepared the Eight-Point Program with political support but little prior consultation with other agencies responsible for some of the measures, so implementation efforts met stiff resistance. The program was never fully implemented, at least in time to avert the revaluation of the yen—the very purpose for which it was intended (Angel 1991).

On 6 August 1971, a US Congressional report asserting that the dollar had become overvalued called for corrective action through general exchange rate realignment. On the same day, the US Treasury reported a loss of gold and other reserve assets totaling more than $1 billion. Over the following week, the flight from the dollar accelerated sharply. It was under these circumstances that on Sunday, 15 August, President Richard Nixon, with no prior consultation with major trading partners, unilaterally announced the suspension of gold convertibility for the dollar, along with a ninety-day freeze on wages and prices, tax measures to stimulate production and employment, and a 10-percent temporary surcharge on dutiable imports.[9] This led major

---

[9] With no prior bargaining with or even warning to foreign governments, this was a unilateral campaign to coerce major foreign governments into revaluing their currencies (Odell 1982). Many senior officials in the Nixon administration felt that, by this decision, "they were freeing America from the bondage of the dollar commitment to uphold the Bretton Woods system," thereby creating "more room in domestic policy to deal with recession" (Gowa 1983).

European governments to close their foreign exchange markets. Failing to develop a joint policy response, however, these governments reopened the markets on Monday, 23 August, with all but France suspending commitments to defend the previous upper limits for their currencies.[10]

The announcement of 15 August (on the morning of 16 August, Japan time) precipitated a heavy sale of dollars in the Tokyo market, which was already open for trading. Even though other major markets closed the morning of 16 August, the Tokyo market was kept open for trading. Nonresidents had been prohibited from purchasing short-term government securities since 15 March 1971 and unlisted bonds since 17 May, and authorities believed that these and other capital controls in place were sufficient to prevent speculative capital inflows (Inuta 2000; Volcker and Gyohten 1992). On 19 August, they introduced additional restrictions on foreign exchange transactions, including: (1) a request for foreign exchange banks to comply strictly with yen conversion limits; (2) a directive for foreign exchange banks to maintain the balance of free-yen deposits (FYDs), borrowing from foreign banks, and other foreign currency liabilities within the 18 August balance; and (3) an on-site inspection, at foreign exchange banks and trading companies, to verify advanced export receipts against documents (see Table 4.3). Restrictions were so intense that banks could no longer hedge their dollar purchases and suspended publishing forward rates from 19 August to 29 October (Fukao 2003). Even so, speculation intensified when the European markets reopened on 23 August. From 26 August, the BOJ reportedly encouraged banks to reduce their foreign exchange risk in the event of a yen revaluation. On Friday, 27 August, a total of $1.20 billion was sold in the Tokyo market, of which monetary authorities are reported to have purchased $1.19 billion; this made Japan the world's largest holder of foreign exchange reserves, surpassing the United States. Trading was allowed to continue for a short period after the market closed, but the scheduled Saturday trading was canceled (Angel 1991).

The Japanese Government announced on the evening of 27 August that, beginning the following day, it would "temporarily" suspend the 1-percent margins around the IMF parity stipulated by the IMF Articles of Agreement and implement a package of "yen recession countermeasures" to offset the adverse real effect of revaluation, mostly through expansionary fiscal policy.[11] But the float would be tightly managed. On 28 August 1971, authorities reiterated the directive of 19 August on FYDs, stating that the balance should be kept within the 27 August balance; on 31 August, they subjected the

---

[10] Such continuing intervention by the Bank of France was confined to a segregated market for commercial transactions, while all other transactions were diverted to a financial franc market that was allowed to find its own level (FRBNY, October 1971).

[11] The finance minister and the BOJ governor met on 25 August to agree to float the yen from Monday, 30 August, with a target rate of ¥335. The massive sale of dollars on Friday, however, necessitated the suspension of trading on Saturday (MOF 1992).

Table 4.3. Selected exchange and capital control measures in Japan, August 1971–January 1972

	Exchange controls	Capital controls	Relaxation
19 August	On-site inspection of advanced export receipts begins for foreign exchange banks and trading companies (to verify compliance with one-year limit, except for ships and plants for which limit was three years)		n.a.
		Foreign exchange banks requested to comply with yen conversion limits	n.a.
28 August		Foreign exchange banks instructed to maintain balance of short-term foreign liabilities within 18 August balance	Abolished (21 December 1971)
		As enhancement of 19 August regulation, foreign exchange banks requested to maintain balance of nonresident free-yen deposits (FYDs) within 27 August balance	Abolished (6 January 1972)
31 August	Foreign exchange banks prohibited in principle from converting advanced export receipts into yen (amount less than $10,000 remained freely allowed)		Abolished (6 January 1972)
		Securities companies instructed to maintain balance held in special investment accounts for nonresident investors within peak balance in August	Abolished (6 January 1972)
7 September		Regulations on yen conversion limits, short-term foreign liability balances, and FYD balances given legal status	n.a.
		Yen conversion limits enforced on daily basis	Changed back to monthly basis (21 December 1971)

Sources: BOJ (1988); Inuta (2000)

exchange of advanced export receipts for yen above the $10,000 limit to approval and required securities companies to maintain the balance of non-resident securities investment accounts within the maximum daily balance observed in August 1971 (both effective from 1 September).[12] With exchange and capital controls in place, trading in Japanese yen dropped to nominal levels in New York, and in early September the yen was suspended from official trading in Frankfurt (FRBNY, October 1971). The Japanese business community began to complain about the stricture of the exchange controls. Japanese authorities intervened in the foreign exchange market on a substantial scale, which Washington criticized as "dirty floating" (Strange 1976). Still, the yen managed to edge upward to ¥325 per dollar in October.

Reflecting the heavy intervention to defend the peg, the balance of foreign exchange reserves rose during August by $4.6 billion, an amount equal to Japan's entire reserve stock before 1971 and exceeding the amount of recorded net capital inflows (see Figure 4.5 for quarterly figures). Two types of capital inflows were mainly responsible. First, until the end of the month, advanced foreign exchange receipts for Japanese exporters were freely allowed for up to a year before customs clearance. A large inflow of capital through advanced export receipts had already begun in May. According to Inuta (2000), from 17 to 30 August, as much as $1.5 billion of funds came into the country through

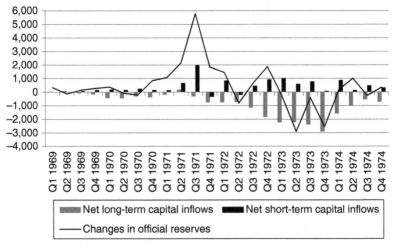

Figure 4.5. Capital flows and changes in official reserves in Japan, Q1 1969–Q4 1974 (in millions of US dollars)

Source: MOF, *Fiscal and Monetary Statistics Monthly*

---

[12] From May 1964, six major securities companies had been authorized to maintain special investment accounts on behalf of nonresident investors to facilitate their securities investment in Japan (Inuta 2000).

this channel. On 30 September 1971, a Diet testimony by a senior MOF official revealed that some of these transactions had been based on fictitious contracts (Angel 1991). Second, authorized foreign exchange banks typically extended export finance by borrowing from the BOJ against export bills as collateral. Finding it difficult to hedge their long positions in the forward market, especially beginning in July, they attempted to sell dollars in the spot foreign exchange market; it was reported that some even risked violating the yen conversion limits by holding a short position in dollars (Inuta 2000).

The last-ditch effort to defend the peg cost the Japanese Government a capital loss on the foreign exchange reserves, which became a target of considerable criticism, including at the Diet (Odell 1982). In coming to a decision to keep the market open, the MOF was aware of the foreign currency exposure of Japanese banks and firms, particularly the large trading companies. Some in the private sector had been warning since 1970 that the balance sheet impact of a yen revaluation would adversely affect shipbuilders and trading companies, given the balance of dollar-denominated export credits (e.g., Chōgin Sangyō Kenkyūkai 1970). Authorities were also aware that they had been complicit by repeatedly assuring the private sector that the fixed exchange rate would be defended. Authorities had even persuaded banks to take dollar assets to help defend the dollar. After a heated internal debate within the MOF, those who argued for keeping the market open prevailed (Volcker and Gyohten 1992).[13]

Both Komiya and Suda (1983) and Angel (1991) characterize the decision to keep the Tokyo market open as a colossal failure in Japan's economic policy-making, but the counterfactual should carefully be considered. Roughly, $4.6 billion multiplied by ¥52 (the Smithsonian revaluation of the yen against the US dollar)—¥260 billion—represented the government's assumption of exchange rate risk from the private sector. What Japan did in 1971 was the opposite of what Brazil would do in 1998 by maintaining a peg that was widely perceived to be unsustainable in order to unwind the dollar liabilities of the private sector (IEO 2003). An important consideration was that the adverse balance sheet effect of any yen revaluation would be concentrated in the relatively small number of banks and trading companies that held most of the dollar assets. Yet, the overall amount—about 0.3 percent of GNP and 3.0 percent of Japan's total exports—was probably small enough to be absorbed without much difficulty. In the event, the private sector was overcompensated. Authorities later learned that, after 15 August, banks and trading companies had borrowed dollars abroad and sold them in Tokyo to make arbitrage profits (Volcker and Gyohten 1992).

---

[13] Some critics charged that this had been done to help secure their post-retirement jobs with banks.

4.3.2. The Smithsonian Agreement: 1971

The nature of the problem called for a smaller group of countries to negotiate a solution outside the mechanism provided by the IMF. The Group of Ten (G10) thus became the primary forum in which a response to the currency crisis was to be discussed. The first G10 deputies' meeting was held as early as 3–4 September 1971 in order to pave the way for a ministerial meeting scheduled in London later that month.[14] But little progress could be made as long as the US Government was adamantly opposed to a devaluation of the dollar against gold. Within the United States, however, criticism of the Nixon strategy of unilateral action and refusal to negotiate began to mount from Congress, the press, and professional economists. By the end of November, negotiations over the preceding weeks had narrowed the differences of view sufficiently to convene another ministerial meeting. Within Japan, the business community was pressing the government to end the float; faced with the political reality, the government is said to have raised the maximum revaluation it was willing to accept from 9 percent in mid October to 15–18 percent (Strange 1976).[15]

The G10 finance ministers and central bank governors convened at the Smithsonian Institution in Washington on 17–18 December 1971. The meeting followed a joint conference of G10 deputies and the IMF Executive Board on 16 December, which was designed to involve non-G10 countries in a major reform of the international monetary system before any final decisions were reached. At the Smithsonian meeting it was agreed, among other things, that the dollar would be devalued by 8.57 percent against gold (from $35 to $38 per ounce) and that the yen would be revalued by 16.88 percent against the US dollar (to ¥308 per dollar).[16] This represented a 7.66 percent revaluation in terms of the yen's par value and a revaluation of about 12.5 percent on a trade-weighted basis (Krause and Sekiguchi 1976).

The Smithsonian Agreement, as endorsed by the IMF Executive Board, allowed countries to declare central rates (instead of parities), which they could change without IMF approval. Most industrial countries, including Japan, chose to use the central rates; the yen was allowed to fluctuate within

[14] A detailed account of currency diplomacy from August to December 1971 is provided in Solomon (1977), Chapter 12.

[15] US Treasury Secretary John Connally, however, was demanding that Japan revalue the yen against the dollar by 25 percent (Odell 1982).

[16] According to a member of the Japanese delegation, Japan initially had ¥315–20 to a dollar in mind (Kashiwagi 1972). At the Smithsonian, the US side initially demanded a revaluation of 18 percent, while the Japanese side argued for less than 17 percent. Finance Minister Mikio Mizuta then stated that 17 percent was an ominous number for a Japanese finance minister in light of what had happened in 1930. Finance Minister Junnosuke Inoue, who restored the gold standard at the old parity by revaluing the yen by 17 percent, was later assassinated (Volcker and Gyohten 1992).

2.25 percent on either side of the central rate, namely between ¥314.93 and ¥301.07 per US dollar.[17] On Monday, 20 December, Japanese authorities kept the Tokyo exchange market closed while abolishing some of the measures introduced earlier to block the inflow of funds, such as reverting yen conversion limits back to a monthly basis and lifting the regulation on the balance of short-term foreign liabilities (see Table 4.3). When the market reopened on 21 December 1971, the spot rate was quoted just above the new floor (¥314), an appreciation of about 2 percent from the last quote on Saturday, 18 December (¥320), with a moderate outflow of capital developing. In late December, the BOJ lowered the discount rate by 0.5 percentage points to 4.75 percent in order to soften the domestic impact of the yen's revaluation and to help stimulate the economy. Judging that stability had returned to the foreign exchange market, beginning 6 January 1972, authorities eliminated regulations on advanced export receipts and nonresident securities investment accounts (see Table 4.3). With these measures, all the inflow control measures that had been introduced after March 1971 were terminated.

4.3.3. Demise of the Smithsonian Agreement: 1973

A speculative pressure hit again in late January. The yen, starting from close to the upper limit (¥314.80 per dollar) in early 1972, edged closer to the lower limit (¥301.07) by 24 February (see Figure 4.6). In response, effective 25 February 1972, authorities restored the $10,000 limit on advanced export receipts. Effective 1 March, they tightened the application of yen conversion limits for resident foreign banks, making them similar to those for domestic institutions.[18] The MOF began to deposit official reserves with Japanese banks amounting to $200 million in February and another $100 million in March to reduce borrowing from abroad. Depositing foreign exchange reserves with banks to facilitate the provision of export cover had been initiated in June 1971, and these new deposits raised the total amount transferred out of the official reserves to $1.5 billion (FRBNY, March 1972).

Japanese authorities, perceiving the domestic economy to be in recession (though growing at the annual rate of 4 percent), became concerned that the higher yen would postpone the recovery. On 20 May 1972, they announced a seven-point program of "international economic countermeasures," consisting of: (1) expansionary macroeconomic policies, including the front loading

---

[17] The margin of 2.25 percent emerged as a compromise between 1 percent proposed by France and 3 percent proposed by the United States (Kashiwagi 1972).

[18] In view of their limited domestic deposit base, resident foreign banks had been receiving preferential treatment. In exchange for accepting tighter yen conversion limits, they were given access to the call and bill-discount markets on the same terms as domestic banks (Inuta 2000).

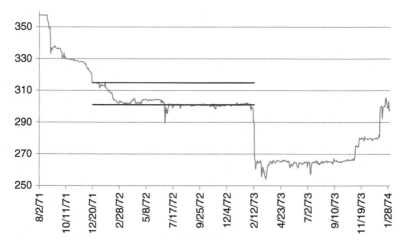

Figure 4.6. Yen–dollar exchange rate, 2 August 1971–31 January 1974[a] (yen per US dollar)

[a] Solid lines represent the upper and lower magins of the Smithsonian central rate for the yen.
Source: Datastream (London closing)

of public works spending and a further cut in lending rates; (2) measures to increase imports, including through the enlargement of quotas; (3) measures to restrain exports; (4) promotion of capital outflows through liberalization of restrictions on Japanese purchases of foreign equities and facilitation of yen bond issuance by international organizations and foreign governments; (5) depositing of official reserves with foreign exchange banks to help repay foreign liabilities and with the Export–Import Bank of Japan (Eximbank) to encourage outward foreign direct investment (FDI) in the natural resource sector; (6) provision of financial support to international organizations, as well as greater foreign aid to developing countries; and (7) additional spending to build social capital and promote social security.

Despite substantial appreciation of the yen, Japan's current account surplus widened from 1971 to 1972 while the US trade and capital account balances deteriorated. The United States experienced a speculative capital outflow, but the first major currency that came under pressure was the pound sterling. At the Smithsonian meeting, sterling had maintained its gold parity, which meant that it was revalued against the US dollar by 8.57 percent (equivalent to the size of the dollar's devaluation against gold).[19] The United Kingdom's current account balance, though in surplus, began to deteriorate against renewed inflationary pressure. As the market perceived British authorities as unwilling to tighten monetary policy to defend the exchange rate, a speculative attack on

[19] The pound, which had been priced at $2.40 since 1967, was revalued to $2.60 at the Smithsonian.

the currency ensued. The country lost a third of its official reserves within a week and, on Friday, 23 June 1972, allowed the pound to float. Experiencing massive capital inflows, the Tokyo market closed for trading from the next day.

When the Tokyo market reopened on 29 June 1972, the yen had appreciated to the lower limit of the Smithsonian band, forcing Japanese authorities to take a set of additional measures (see Table 4.4). In particular, they lowered the

Table 4.4. Selected exchange and capital control measures in Japan, 1972

	Exchange controls	Capital controls	Relaxation
25 February	Advanced export receipts beyond $10,000 subject to approval		n.a.
28 February		Purchases of listed foreign securities liberalized for trust banks	n.a.
8 May	Foreign exchange surrender requirements abolished		n.a.
22 May		Secondary purchases of foreign securities permitted for insurance companies	n.a.
1 June		Marginal reserve requirement of 25 percent introduced on balance of free-yen deposits (FYDs) beyond actual 21 April–20 May balance	Reduced to 10 percent (10 December 1973) and further to zero (September 1974)
29 June		Marginal reserve requirement on FYDs raised 50 percent	Reduced to 10 percent (10 December 1973) and further to zero (September 1974)
		Yen conversion prohibited from special securities investment accounts for nonresidents	Abolished (17 January 1974)
	Freely allowable limit for advanced export receipts reduced to $5,000		Raised to $10,000 (24 November 1973) and further to $100,000 (7 January 1974) and $500,000 (30 July 1974). Abolished 15 May 1979

(continued)

Table 4.4. Continued

	Exchange controls	Capital controls	Relaxation
21 October		Purchases by nonresidents of stocks and bonds permitted only when made through securities companies or foreign exchange banks as agents; no security company or bank acting as agent for nonresident investors allowed in principle to increase net investment position	Abolished for stocks (6 November 1973) and for bonds and investment trust beneficiary certificates, except for short-term government bills and unlisted bonds with remaining maturities of less than one year (1 December 1973)
		Medium to long-term overseas lending by foreign exchange banks subject to item-by-item approval	n.a.
23 October	Export of used ships subject to BOJ approval if they were to be chartered back for use by resident shipping companies		Abolished (24 November 1973)
17 November		Purchases of foreign securities by individual investors liberalized when made through resident securities companies	n.a.
24 November	Foreign exchange limit (of $3,000) for Japanese tourists abolished; foreign transfer limit raised from $1,000 to $3,000 per remittance		n.a.

Sources: BOJ (1988); Inuta (2000)

freely allowable limit for advanced export receipts from $10,000 to $5,000, and raised the marginal reserve requirement on FYDs from 25 to 50 percent (25 percent had been set on 1 June 1972 for any amount beyond the average 21 April–20 May 1972 balance). In addition, authorities divided nonresident special securities investment accounts into yen-denominated and (newly created) foreign currency-denominated components and limited the yen component to the settlement of securities transactions that had already been executed; new foreign exchange funds would be kept in foreign currency-denominated accounts (Inuta 2000). This effectively suspended new purchases by nonresidents of Japanese securities through this channel.[20] Despite these measures, the yen stayed close to the floor of the Smithsonian band.

As Japan's official reserves rose steadily, market participants became increasingly persuaded that a further upward adjustment of the yen was unavoidable. To slow the growth of reserves, the MOF continued its program of depositing dollars with foreign exchange banks to enable them to repay short-term dollar liabilities. Taken together, in September and October, a further $600 million was deposited, followed by another $800 million in November and December. But the meeting between the Japanese finance minister and the US treasury secretary on 18 October 1972 created speculation about an impending revaluation of the yen. In response, on 20 October, the government announced a set of additional measures, including programs of export restraint and import promotion, a limit on the acquisition by nonresidents of Japanese securities,[21] a program of official capital outflows through the Eximbank and the Overseas Economic Cooperation Fund (OECF), and a supplementary budget designed to shift resources out of export production and into public goods and services. It was under this program that authorities substantially eased remaining exchange controls over the coming months, such as the amount of foreign exchange that could be taken out of the country by residents traveling abroad as well as the amount of remittances abroad by individuals (see Table 4.4).

When the adverse US trade deficit figure for 1972 was released in early 1973, major currencies were subjected to an intense speculative pressure.[22] On 20 January 1973, Italy introduced a two-tier market for the lira. On 1 February, the deutsche mark hit the ceiling, as did the yen. Japanese authorities reportedly sold $1.1 billion equivalent of yen through 9 February (FRBNY, March 1973) but, finding it impossible any longer to support the Smithsonian rate, closed the Tokyo market for trading on Saturday, 10 February 1973. While intensive international negotiations got under way,[23] it was announced that

[20] This regulation was tightened further on 6 October 1972 by limiting the length of time yen funds could be kept in special investment accounts to one month.

[21] Nonresidents were allowed to purchase Japanese securities only through securities companies or authorized foreign exchange banks acting as their agents—and in principle only up to the amount of the liquidation of their existing investment positions.

[22] Solomon (1977), Chapter 13, provides a detailed account of the crumbling of the Smithsonian Agreement, written from the US side.

[23] The change in leadership of the US Treasury explains the departure of American monetary diplomacy from unilateralism. In May 1972, Treasury Secretary Connally had resigned and was replaced by George Shultz, who brought back an inclination toward multilateral compromise rather than unilateral coercive diplomacy, along with a salient belief in freely floating exchange rates (Odell 1982).

the Japanese and European markets would be closed on the following Monday and Tuesday.

On the evening of Monday, 12 February (in the early afternoon of 13 February, Japan time), US Treasury Secretary George Shultz announced that the dollar would be devalued by 10 percent against gold and that, in addition to those currencies already floating, it was understood that the Japanese yen would be allowed to float temporarily. Prior to this announcement, the US Government had consulted with the Japanese counterpart, proposing that Japan should revalue the yen by another 10 percent as the United States was prepared to devalue the dollar by 10 percent.[24] Japan refused but, with the concurrence of the United States, decided to allow the yen to float (Odell 1982). When the Tokyo market opened on 14 February, trading began at ¥271.2, but heavy demand drove up the yen by 17 percent above the Smithsonian rate; it was trading at ¥265.5 on 15 February. Activity then subsided, and the yen edged lower through the end of February.

When heavy pressure against the dollar reemerged, Japanese authorities, acting in concert with European counterparts, closed the Tokyo market indefinitely beginning on Friday, 2 March. On 5 March 1973, they temporarily tightened controls on purchases by nonresidents of Japanese equities, for which an exception to the 21 October 1972 control had been allowed.[25] Following the G10 communiqué of 16 March,[26] normal trading in yen resumed on 19 March, but a strong reversal of earlier speculation in favor of the yen started to emerge. By late March 1973, the dollar had strengthened in response to a variety of factors, including the unwinding of the leads and lags built up during the previous months, the impact of the export-restraint measures instituted in 1972, and the strong import demand arising from economic expansion and a higher yen (FRBNY, September 1973). Long-term capital outflows swelled as Japanese firms increased their direct investment abroad.

---

[24] The second proposal received from the US Government on 11 February was to revalue the yen to ¥250 per dollar. In the morning of 13 February (Japan time), Japan conceded to revalue the yen up to ¥264 but the US Government considered anything above ¥257 as unacceptable. Japan, seeing that the gap of seven yen could not be closed, decided to float the yen. See MOF (1992).

[25] The control on the acquisition of equities was lifted on 6 November 1973; the control on the acquisition of bonds and beneficiary certificates was lifted on 1 December 1973, except for short-term government bills and unlisted bonds with remaining maturities of less than one year.

[26] Five days earlier, on 11 March, six member countries of the European Communities (EC) had agreed to maintain fixed exchange rates among their currencies within a 2.25 percent band, which would float as a bloc against the dollar. At this time, the deutsche mark was revalued by 3 percent. Most countries participating in this arrangement, which came to be known as the Snake, tightened existing exchange controls (FRBNY, July 1973).

4.4. THE OIL CRISES

Japan experienced an oil crisis twice during the period under consideration, in 1973–4 and 1979–80, each time as a consequence of a sharp price increase in imported oil. On both occasions, the yen depreciated substantially while the current account deteriorated and turned to deficit.

4.4.1. The 1973–4 Crisis

Once the yen had appreciated sufficiently in 1973, the currency faced a reversal of short-term speculative capital inflows during the rest of the year. The year as a whole saw a net decline in the balance of private external liabilities as well as a sharp pickup in the balance of private external assets— which, combined, amounted to a net private capital outflow of more than $5 billion (see Figure 4.7). The stance of exchange rate policy shifted from preventing the yen from appreciating to supporting the yen, with heavy dollar sales at the initial level of ¥265 (see Figure 4.6). Komiya and Suda (1983) estimate the size of intervention from March to September 1973 to be as much as 50 percent of total trading volume in Tokyo. As a consequence, the balance of official foreign exchange reserves declined by more than $4 billion.

The yen was clearly overvalued at ¥265 per dollar, but authorities preferred a stable exchange rate. Ito (2009) explains that the government managed the exchange rate tightly in the hope of returning to a fixed exchange rate at an appropriate time and fending off foreign criticism by running down the

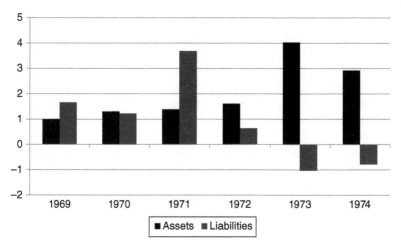

Figure 4.7. Private capital flows in Japan, 1969–74 (in billions of US dollars)
Source: MOF, *Fiscal and Monetary Statistics Monthly*

balance of foreign exchange reserves. Also, the rate of ¥265 was close to the upper limit of the Japan–US "non-agreement" of 13 February 1973 in which Japan expressed its willingness to revalue the yen to ¥264 (MOF 1992).[27] The policy of massive intervention to peg the yen was misguided, however, as it involved selling at ¥265 the dollars acquired earlier at ¥301–57. Komiya and Suda (1983) estimate the capital loss incurred by the Japanese Government at several hundred billion yen. Given the extensive capital controls preventing covered interest arbitrage, moreover, a stable spot rate meant widely fluctuating forward rates.

By this time, the government's earlier attempt to mitigate the adverse impact of the higher yen had led to substantial monetary easing. Fiscal policy had also been eased substantially in 1972 and 1973, driven by Prime Minister Kakukei Tanaka's grand scheme to "Reconstruct the Japanese Archipelago" through large public works projects. The government had willingly accommodated the emerging inflationary pressure as a way to keep the nominal peg while allowing the yen to appreciate in real terms. In retrospect, macroeconomic policies were kept excessive for too long, given that the economy had already recovered by mid 1972 from the slowdown that turned out to be mild; any adverse impact on investment and exports was offset by the rapid growth of world income, which rose by a cumulative 12 percent from 1971 to 1973 (Eichengreen and Hatase 2005). The BOJ became aware of the need to tighten monetary policy but was powerless to resist the political pressure (Hamada and Hayashi 1985; Shirakawa 2008). The built-up inflationary pressure erupted in 1973, with double-digit inflation emerging during the second quarter.

It was under these circumstances that, in October 1973, the world economy was hit by a cutback of oil supplies by Middle Eastern countries. Monthly inflation in Japan shot up to nearly 90 percent (annualized) in December 1973 in terms of the wholesale price index and more than 50 percent (annualized) in January 1974 for the consumer price index. Inflation remained elevated throughout 1974 (see Figure 4.8), rekindling memories of the postwar inflation (Cargill et al. 1997). The oil shock intensified selling pressure on the yen as the market recognized that Japan was far more dependent on imported oil than the United States. Heavy sales of yen started on 29 October 1973. In November, Japanese authorities raised the target exchange rate in three steps, by ¥5 at a time, from ¥265 to ¥270 on 1 November, then to ¥275 on 2 November, and finally to ¥280 on 13 November (MOF 1992). Intervention to support the yen was heavy, reportedly amounting to $2.44 billion in November and $1.45 billion in December. To contain domestic inflation, in December, authorities tightened monetary policy further, continuing the

---

[27] But the US side refused to accept anything above ¥257.

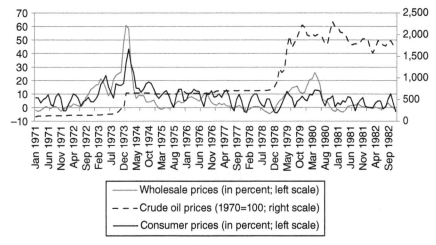

Figure 4.8. Wholesale, consumer, and crude oil prices in Japan, January 1969–December 1982 (annualized monthly percentage change; US dollars per barrel, 1970=100)
Source: IMF, *International Financial Statistics*

policy they had initiated in the spring; they also cut back on the budgeted increase in government expenditures.

From November 1973 to January 1974, Japanese authorities shifted the direction of capital controls. On 6 November 1973, they lifted the restriction (in place since 5 March 1973) on purchases by nonresidents of Japanese equities; likewise, on 1 December 1973, they lifted the restriction (in place since 21 October 1972) on purchases by nonresidents of bonds and beneficiary certificates, except for short-term government securities and unlisted bonds with remaining maturities of less than one year.[28] Beginning 13 November 1973, authorities subjected purchases by residents of short-term foreign securities (with maturities of less than six months) to approval requirements. Effective 15 November, they excluded certain FYD inflows from the application of yen conversion limits and, on 17 December, removed all FYDs (except for internal head office–branch accounts) from conversion limits, while they cut the marginal reserve requirement from 50 to 10 percent on 10 December. On 24 November, authorities raised the freely allowable limit for advanced export receipts from $5,000 back to $10,000.[29] On 7 January 1974, they authorized certain firms in key industrial sectors, such as electric power and gas, to obtain "impact loans" from abroad (Inuta 2000).[30]

---

[28] This exception would be eliminated altogether on 26 August 1974.
[29] The limit was raised to $100,000 on 7 January 1974 and further to $500,000 on 30 July 1974. It was altogether eliminated on 15 May 1979.
[30] The term *impact loans* refers to general-purpose foreign currency loans, in contrast to *project loans*.

Despite these measures, the doubling of the price of Persian Gulf oil announced in late December set off an even greater wave of selling pressure against the yen. The forward rate reached ¥302 for three-month contracts and ¥308 for six-month contracts (MOF 1992). On 7 January 1974, Japanese authorities suspended support of the ¥280 level, and the yen moved closer to pre-float levels. In the wake of a French decision to move the franc out of the European Snake on Saturday, 19 January 1974, Japanese authorities closed the Tokyo market for two days (21–2 January). When the market reopened on Wednesday, 23 January, authorities raised the target exchange rate to ¥300 while sporadically selling dollars (Komiya and Suda 1983; Quirk 1977). Following consultations between Japanese and US authorities, the Federal Reserve Bank of New York intervened to sell 4.3 million dollars on behalf of the US Treasury (FRBNY, March 1974).

With the quadrupling of oil prices, Japan's current account turned into deep deficit in early 1974. In January, authorities placed restrictions on the acquisition of short-term foreign securities by Japanese institutional investors in order to discourage outflows. Faced with continued selling pressure against the yen, on 5 August and again on 26 August, they raised yen conversion limits for foreign banks to encourage inflows. On 26 August 1974, they fully liberalized purchases of short-term Japanese government securities (as well as unlisted bonds with remaining maturities of less than one year) by nonresidents. On 11 September, reserve requirements on FYDs were effectively terminated, with the marginal reserve requirement of 10 percent reduced to zero. On 15 November, authorities stated that they would approve, on a case-by-case basis, requests by nonfinancial firms to raise funds by issuing foreign currency bonds abroad for use in Japan (Inuta 2000).

The difficulty experienced by Japan in financing the current account deficit from July to September 1974 was called the "August crisis." With tightening credit conditions, Japanese banks faced a premium of 0.25–0.5 percent in the Eurodollar markets. To alleviate the situation, in August, the Japanese Government secretly borrowed $1 billion from Saudi Arabia, with an installment of $500 million each received in September and October. According to a press report, the loan was for five years and borrowed by the Bank of Tokyo with a government guarantee at 10.5 percent. Komiya and Suda (1983) argue that the loan was unnecessary because (1) the proceeds were received after the crisis of August was over and (2) the balance of foreign exchange reserves without the loan would have only been $11.8 billion instead of $12.8 billion at its lowest point in December 1975.[31] Even so, rumors of financial assistance from Saudi

---

[31] Neither were the terms favourable to Japan. The interest rate of 10.5 percent, which was close to the highest short-term rate observed in the summer of 1974, was too high for a five-year loan.

Arabia sparked active bidding for the yen in mid September (Kuroda 2003; FRBNY, March 1975; Volcker and Gyohten 1992).

From 1974 to 1975, Japan experienced its worst recession since the end of World War II. Output had actually dropped, and the rate of unemployment edged up steadily from 1.2 percent in January 1974 to exceed 2 percent in late 1975. Although upward pressure on wholesale prices had abated, consumer prices continued to rise rapidly, leading monetary authorities to maintain the highly restrictive monetary policy. Japan's trade balance, after a $2.7 billion first-half deficit, swung decisively into surplus by the late summer of 1974. As the rise in consumer prices slackened further to an annual rate of only about 6 percent in the first quarter of 1975 and wholesale prices remained steady, the government was prepared to shift to a cautiously expansionary policy to support an incipient recovery.

From March to early August 1975, authorities virtually stayed away from the market, allowing the exchange rate to fluctuate between ¥290 and ¥298 per dollar (Komiya and Suda 1983). As the yen began to strengthen in early 1975, authorities eased controls on capital outflows. The active use of capital controls had been criticized as creating unnecessary unpredictability in economic decision-making. It was against this background that authorities focused this time on easing outflows without tightening inflows (Inuta 2000). Effective 10 June 1975, they eased the restriction on foreign securities investment by resident nonbank financial firms (in place since 7 January 1974),[32] except for foreign securities with remaining maturities of less than one year.[33] Moreover, they resumed the program of allowing foreign public entities to raise bonds in the Tokyo market (suspended since late 1973), with Finland and New Zealand raising ¥10 billion each in May and November 1975, respectively. From early August to the end of 1975, authorities followed what could be characterized as a crawling peg, engineering an orderly depreciation of the yen from ¥298 to ¥303 per dollar in several steps; then, from December, they defended the rate of ¥305–7. In January 1976, they switched from dollar sales to dollar purchases, as appreciation pressure emerged on the yen.

Japan's post-oil crisis stagflation was the worst among the member countries of the Organization for Economic Cooperation and Development (OECD). Komiya and Yasui (1984) argue that the wage–price spiral was broken thanks to Japan's flexible labor market institutions, which limited the increase in nominal wages in 1976. From this, Japanese policymakers learned a great lesson, namely, the inflationary consequences of sacrificing domestic stability for external objectives. Easy monetary policy was kept too long to defend the peg, when domestic considerations dictated a tighter macroeconomic policy. Hamada and Hayashi (1985) argue that this shared interpretation of the

---

[32] This measure became applicable to banks on 9 March 1977.
[33] The exception was removed on 27 June 1977.

experience gave the BOJ greater de facto autonomy to pursue price stability oriented monetary policy. In 1975, the BOJ began to follow a "money-focused" monetary policy by aiming to control broad money—M2 plus certificates of deposit (CDs)—over the medium term; in 1978, it formalized the framework by beginning to announce publicly the forecast of M2+CDs for the subsequent quarter. The medium-term focus on the broad monetary aggregate, however, allowed the central bank to continue to pay attention to other factors, including the exchange rate, in its conduct of monetary policy.

4.4.2. The 1979–80 Crisis

A worsening political situation in Iran and the suspension of Iranian oil exports in December 1978 led to a scramble for spot crude oil around the world and prompted members of the Organization of the Petroleum Exporting Countries (OPEC) to jack up their prices. As a result, the spot price of crude oil rose from less than $13 to $36 per barrel between October 1978 and mid June 1979 (see Figure 4.8). Sentiment turned against the currencies of countries heavily dependent on imported oil. Japan's current account surplus had already been shrinking, given the sharp appreciation of the yen and expansion of the Japanese economy during the preceding years. Coming on top of these developments, the increase in crude oil prices swung Japan's current account balance into a large deficit in 1979 and 1980. With the Japanese economy decelerating, confidence in the yen waned and, in late 1978, the currency began a sustained depreciation against the US dollar. Intervention reversed its earlier pattern with large sales of dollars in 1979, which were reportedly massive from March to May and from October to November. This stance continued until April 1980 (Komiya and Suda 1983; Ohta 1982).

Concurrent with foreign exchange market intervention to support the yen, authorities liberalized controls on capital inflows to arrest the decline of the yen. On 15 May 1979, they fully liberalized advanced export receipts by removing the limit of $500,000 (in place since July 1974). Limitations on nonresident purchases of yen bonds were progressively eliminated, the marginal reserve requirement on FYDs was phased out (see Table 3.5 in Chapter 3), and the period for converting the proceeds of nonresident issues of yen-denominated bonds was lengthened. As the yen rose beyond the ¥250 mark on 27 November 1979, authorities required banks to report foreign exchange transactions on a daily basis and trading companies to report export and import contracts on a monthly basis. The other yen-support measures announced during 1979 included relaxation of open spot position controls for foreign exchange banks, tightening and then prohibition in principle of medium- to long-term external lending, progressive easing of terms for impact loans, and suspension of the import settlement scheme providing Japanese banks with low-cost yen financing.

The sharp depreciation of the yen magnified the inflationary consequence of rapidly rising commodity prices (see Figure 4.8). With these concerns in mind, on 17 April 1979, the BOJ raised the discount rate by 0.75 percentage points to 4.25 percent. Selling pressure on the yen continued, with the yen falling to ¥225.25. On 24 July 1979, the BOJ raised the discount rate by another 1 percent to 5.25 percent. Despite the monetary tightening at home, the upward trend in interest rates abroad (especially after the 6 October 1979 actions by the US Federal Reserve)[34] led to a heavy outflow of capital. The BOJ raised the discount rate by another 1 percent on 2 November and again on 19 February 1980. To counter domestic inflationary pressure, the government also substantially slashed the scheduled public works expenditures for the January–March 1980 quarter. Inflation would peak in April 1980, with wholesale and consumer price inflation reaching the annualized rates of 37 and 22 percent, respectively.

When the weakening of the yen saw no sign of abating, in the late evening of Sunday, 2 March 1980, Finance Minister Nobuo Takeshita called an emergency press conference to announce a package of measures, including: (1) coordinated intervention with the authorities of the United States, Germany, and Switzerland;[35] (2) allowing foreign currency funds to be brought in from foreign branches if they were to remain in Japan for three to twelve months; (3) liberalization of interest rates on deposits held by foreign governments and international organizations; (4) easing of conditions on the private placement of yen-denominated bonds with nonresidents; and (5) authorization for Japanese banks to extend medium- to long-term impact loans to domestic customers (which had previously been exclusively allowed for resident foreign banks). Later in the month, the BOJ abolished its 1970 arrangement with banks providing for yen–dollar swap facilities to finance imports, thereby rescinding the last of the major import promotion schemes. The authorization of higher ceilings for the issuance of yen-denominated CDs increased the scope for short-term capital inflows.

These measures were reinforced by a broad anti-inflation program, introduced on 19 March 1980. The BOJ raised the discount rate by another 1.75 percentage points to 9 percent, subsequently increased reserve requirements, and tightened window guidance limits on bank lending. Public works expenditures, already trimmed back, were postponed. In the meantime, with a lower

---

[34] On 6 October 1979, the Federal Reserve announced a series of complementary actions to ensure better control over the expansion of money and credit, including an increase in the discount rate of one percentage point to 12 percent and the imposition of an 8 percent marginal reserve requirement on increases in managed liabilities.

[35] Following up on this agreement, the Federal Reserve bought a total of $216.8 million equivalent of yen for its own account in New York (FRBNY, Summer 1980).

yen and weaker domestic demand, a sharp increase in net exports was showing through in Japan's trade figures, and the overall trade and current-account deficits were beginning to level off. By the third quarter of 1980, Japan was experiencing a dramatic turnaround in its balance of payments. This shift occurred initially in the capital account, where heavy inflows first into the banking sector and later into stocks and bonds had provided more than adequate financing for a current account deficit still running at $20 billion annual rate through the first half of the year. On the strength of these favorable developments, the yen began to appreciate in the middle of 1980.

The sharp recovery of the yen, together with the improved balance-of-payments performance, touched off a debate within Japan on whether or not to lower domestic interest rates. In the summer of 1980, the BOJ resisted pressure to ease monetary policy, although the pace of economic expansion had slowed and industrial production registered a decline. Governor Haruo Mayekawa stressed that an easing of monetary policy was premature in light of continuing inflationary pressure. It was only in late August that the BOJ cautiously shifted to an easier policy stance. In contrast to its earlier experience with the first oil crisis, Japan's damage from the second oil crisis turned out to be the smallest among OECD countries. Hamada and Hayashi (1985) assessed Japan's monetary management after the second oil crisis as among the most successful in any industrial country.

4.5. INTERNATIONAL POLICY COORDINATION

The mid 1970s to the late 1980s was a period in which major industrial countries experimented with macroeconomic policy coordination as the Group of Five or Seven (G5 or G7). Japan, as the world's second largest economy, was an important participant in these policy coordination efforts. While the G5/G7 process did not always involve explicit exchange rate coordination (the United States generally took a benign neglect policy toward the dollar from early 1981 to early 1985), the statements of agreement often made exchange rate-related references.[36] Exchange rate and current account developments were behind many of the important agreements reached, especially the Bonn Agreement of 1978, the Plaza Agreement of 1985, and the Louvre Accord of 1987.

---

[36] Fratzscher (2009), in an event study for 1975–2008, finds that G7 statements by and large moved the yen–dollar and deutsche mark (euro)–dollar exchange rates in the intended direction, especially over the short term of up to a few months.

4.5.1. The Bonn Agreement: 1978

The sharp appreciation of the yen from 1976 occurred against the background of Japan's rising current account surplus and the interest rate differentials favoring yen-denominated instruments (see Table 4.5). This was a period of global economic expansion, but the Japanese economy was cyclically behind the US economy. All through this period of yen strength, Japan's large and widening trade surplus (especially vis-à-vis the United States) loomed large as an international political issue. It was a topic of discussion at the G7 Economic Summit of June 1976 held in San Juan, Puerto Rico. The US Government repeatedly pressed Japan and other surplus countries for strong action to bring their external accounts into balance, including through more rapid expansion of their economies, opening up of their domestic markets to foreign compe-tition, and exchange rate appreciation.

Intervention to limit the yen's appreciation was initially heavy (Bergsten 1982) but was scaled down following the G7 meeting of June 1976. Japanese authorities even refrained from intervention altogether when the yen rose sharply at the beginning of 1977. Intent on depreciating the dollar, US officials started to "talk down" the dollar; helped by an easy monetary policy, the dollar continued to slide through 1978 (Frankel 1990). As the yen began to strength-en further, Japanese authorities resumed intervention to purchase dollars, and the scale of intervention became large in late 1977 and early 1978. Green (1990) calls this the first episode, since the floating of the yen, of prolonged and intensive intervention in the market. Komiya and Suda (1983) estimate the volume of intervention in November 1977 and in March 1978 to be about 32 and 44 percent, respectively, of total trading volume in Tokyo. Authorities,

Table 4.5. Selected macroeconomic indicators in Japan and United States, 1976–9

		1976	1977	1978	1979
Year-on-year growth in gross	Japan	5.31	5.31	5.12	5.23
national product (in percent)	United States	5.41	5.50	5.03	2.84
Year-on-year consumer price	Japan	9.33	8.03	3.83	3.58
inflation (in percent)	United States	5.82	6.51	7.61	11.24
Budget deficit (in percent	Japan	−1.98	−6.19	−6.61	−5.38
of gross domestic product)	United States	−3.33	−2.69	−2.07	−1.18
Current account balance	Japan	3.74 (0.67)	10.93 (1.59)	17.52 (1.82)	−8.75 (−0.88)
(in billions of US dollars; percent of gross domestic product in parentheses)	United States	4.37 (0.26)	−14.06 (−0.74)	−14.81 (-0.69)	−0.48 (−0.02)

Source: IMF, *International Financial Statistics*

however, abruptly ceased to intervene in the market, following the largest
dollar-purchase operation since the beginning of the floating on 28 March
1978, estimated to be $800 million (Komiya and Suda 1983). Afterwards, they
only intervened on a small scale on a few occasions through the end of
October (there was no intervention in April and May), allowing the yen to
appreciate sharply. Authorities eased monetary policy to stimulate domestic
demand, but they could only proceed cautiously in view of the still elevated
rate of inflation (see Table 4.5).

From 1977 to 1978, Japanese authorities took steps to encourage capital
outflows and discourage inflows (see Table 4.6). In June 1977, they eased
restrictions on the acquisition of foreign securities by resident investors by
expanding the scope of eligible securities. In November, they announced that
they would temporarily suspend the public auction of short-term government
financing bills in order to prevent nonresidents from purchasing them (effective from 21 November). On 22 November, they reinstated the marginal
reserve requirement (which had been reduced to zero in September 1974) at
50 percent; on 18 March 1978, the requirement was raised to 100 percent.
Beginning on 16 March 1978, authorities virtually prohibited purchases by
nonresidents of yen-denominated bonds with remaining maturities of more
than five years and one month. In April, moreover, authorities restrained

Table 4.6. Selected capital control measures in Japan, 1977–8

	Control measures	Relaxation
27 May 1977	Short-term external lending by Japanese banks liberalized	n.a.
27 June 1977	Restrictions on purchases by residents of short-term foreign currency bonds removed; scope of eligible securities expanded	n.a.
21 November 1977	Public auction of short-term government bills suspended, both for residents and nonresidents	Abolished (20 March 1978)
22 November 1977	Marginal reserve requirement on balance of free-yen deposits (FYDs) reinstated at 50 percent above average October balance	n.a.
16 March 1978	Purchases by nonresidents of yen-denominated bonds with remaining maturities of less than five years and one month prohibited	Maturity limit reduced to one year and one month (23 January 1979) and then abolished (24 February 1979)
18 March 1978	Marginal reserve requirement on FYDs raised to 100 percent (beyond average February balance)	Reduced back to 50 percent (17 January 1979) and then eliminated (10 February 1979)

Sources: BOJ (1988); Inuta (2000).

some exports through administrative guidance, increased imports through commodity stockpiling, and encouraged a shift from dollar to yen financing by offering to refinance import settlement bills for banks outside their regular rediscount ceilings.

Increasingly, there was a view within the US Government that exchange rate adjustment alone would be insufficient to bring about the desired trade balance adjustment. By early 1977, the so-called "locomotive" theory had won broad endorsement in the policymaking community, with the influence of Keynesian-leaning economists close to President Jimmy Carter (Putnam and Bayne 1984). The Japanese MOF was unconvinced of the validity of the Keynesian logic, but there were also voices for fiscal expansion within the Japanese establishment, notably the Ministry of International Trade and Industry (MITI) and the business community. Following the G7 Summit held in London on 7–8 May, during which Japan committed to 6.7 percent growth for the following year, the domestic political balance was tipped in favor of expansionary fiscal policy (Destler and Mitsuyu 1982). Prime Minister Takeo Fukuda thus announced a supplementary budget for the last three months of FY 1977 (January–March 1978) and an expansionary budget for FY 1978.

Following up on the London Summit of the previous year, international policy coordination intensified during the summer of 1978. At the G7 Summit held in Bonn on 16–17 July, the United States used the locomotive theory to press Japan (and West Germany) to pull the world economy though substantial easing of macroeconomic policies. Japan had already agreed to do so bilaterally with the United States before the meeting (Scammell 1980), but the prime minister succumbed to US pressure to allow the communiqué to state that, in August or September, the Japanese Government would consider additional measures if necessary to achieve the ambitious growth target of 7 percent and that the government would import more and would aim to keep the volume of exports for FY 1978 at or below the previous year's level. As the government delivered most of the promised fiscal measures, Japan's already large budget deficits remained high, if not grew larger, during 1978–9 (see Table 4.5).

The timing of the Bonn Agreement was unfortunate. Shortly after the Bonn meeting, adverse trade figures for the United States and large surpluses for Japan and West Germany came to light. Heavy speculative pressure on the dollar ensued. As the dollar fell closer to ¥180, on 16 August 1978, President Carter expressed deep concern over the dollar's continued decline and initiated discussions with Japanese authorities on means of hastening the adjustment process. In late August, the Japanese Government introduced a ¥2.5 trillion supplementary budget, which included an additional stimulus, mainly through public works projects and the liberal extension of housing credit; it also took steps to increase emergency imports and foreign aid. The volume of

Japanese exports in 1978 declined by 2 percent from the previous year, while the volume of imports increased by 10 percent (Putnam and Bayne 1984). Yet, Japan fell far short of the 7 percent growth commitment (see Table 4.5).

After consulting with Japan and other major trading partners in late October (Volcker and Gyohten 1992), on 1 November 1978, President Carter announced a package of measures to correct "the excessive decline of the dollar," including a pledge to intervene in the foreign exchange market on a massive scale if necessary. Carter stated that these measures had been developed and would be implemented in close cooperation with major governments and central banks abroad. Across the Pacific, coinciding with this announcement, the governor of the BOJ held a press conference at the unusual hour of 11 pm to state his intention to engage in dollar-purchase operations. The yen fell dramatically and moved beyond the ¥200 mark by early 1979. Japanese authorities took the opportunity to dismantle some of the barriers to capital inflows, cutting in half the marginal reserve requirement on FYDs and relaxing restrictions on nonresident purchases of Japanese securities.

4.5.2. The Plaza Agreement: 1985

In the early 1980s, the yen remained under selling pressure, against the background of price stability, a widening current account surplus, and interest rate differentials favoring dollar instruments. The yen's weakness was aided by the liberalization of foreign investment by institutional investors and the US policy of "benign neglect" toward the dollar.[37] Easing of macroeconomic policies could only be cautious, given the stated goal of fiscal consolidation and the fear that substantial monetary easing might precipitate the yen's further depreciation. In the meantime, Japan's large current account surplus was inviting criticism from abroad. The US manufacturing sector in particular was pressuring the administration and Congress for relief from the adverse competitive effects of the strong dollar; Congress began to consider a range of protectionist legislation (Bordo et al. 2010; Frankel 1984).

It was under such pressure that a gradual shift took place in the benign neglect policy of US authorities. The shift was complete at the beginning of 1985, when Donald Regan and Beryl Sprinkel left the Treasury and were succeeded by James A. Baker III and Richard G. Darman. The new Baker treasury devised a new strategy to combat the rise of protectionism in the US

---

[37] In mid April 1981, the US Treasury announced that, after study and consultation with officials of the Federal Reserve, US authorities had adopted a minimal intervention approach and would now intervene only when necessary to counter conditions of disorder in the exchange market. In the prevailing market atmosphere, many participants interpreted this change in approach as removing a constraint on the dollar's rise (FRBNY, Summer 1981).

Congress and to maintain global economic growth by stimulating domestic demand in Japan and West Germany (Funabashi 1988). In a dramatic change of attitude, on 17 January 1985, the US Government met with the other G5 countries in London to agree on coordinated intervention in the foreign exchange market. On several occasions from late January to early March, US authorities sold dollars against yen and deutsche marks (FRBNY, Autumn 1985). Around this time, the dollar began to depreciate against the yen and other major currencies.

In June 1985, US authorities approached their Japanese counterparts for a possible realignment of the yen against the dollar, after which they worked on the Europeans. Broad agreement for a realignment of G5 currencies was reached by the end of August (Funabashi 1988). The new Baker strategy suited the wishes of Japanese authorities, who sought to deflect pressure for fiscal stimulus. German authorities also readily embraced the idea because they had feared that a freefall of the dollar might create tension within the European Monetary System (EMS); they too saw in the realignment approach a means of deflecting foreign pressure away from the "locomotive" approach of the late 1970s. The G5 governments met over the weekend of 21–2 September 1985 at the Plaza Hotel in New York City to announce what has become known as the Plaza Agreement. The communiqué, dated 22 September, in part read: "[The ministers and governors] believe that . . . some further orderly appreciation of the main non-dollar currencies against the dollar is desirable. They stand ready to cooperate more closely to encourage this when to do so would be helpful."

Funabashi (1988) gives a blow-by-blow account of the negotiations that took place before, during, and after the Plaza meeting. According to this account, the United States proposed a range of 10–12 percent for realignment of the yen–dollar exchange rate, which meant a drop to ¥214–18 from the prevailing rate of ¥240, but the Japanese side was willing to see the yen as high as ¥200. The parties purportedly agreed that they would intervene in the foreign exchange market over a six-week period, with the total amount of intervention set at $18 billion—the United States and Japan would each assume 30 percent of the financial burden. The author further states that Japan agreed to stimulate domestic demand by increasing private consumption and investment; Japan's fiscal policy would provide a positive growth environment for the private sector while cutting the budget deficit.

The Plaza Agreement was spectacularly successful in causing the yen (and the deutsche mark) to appreciate sharply against the US dollar (see Figure 4.9). With Tokyo closed for a holiday, the first intervention took place in Europe. By the time the Japanese market opened on Tuesday, 24 September, the currency had already appreciated by more than 10 yen to a dollar. However, there was strong dollar demand from corporations and investors, which spurred the largest turnover on record for spot dollar–yen trading. Japanese

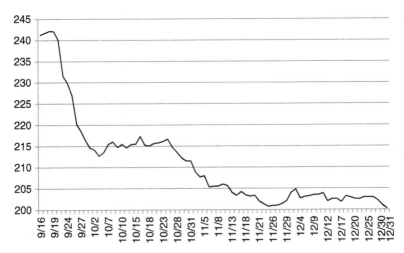

Figure 4.9. Yen–dollar exchange rate, 16 September–31 December 1985 (yen per US dollar)

Source: Datastream (London closing)

authorities intervened heavily (reportedly by selling 1.3 billion dollars), but the yen actually depreciated slightly during the course of the day. It was on the following day that the yen began to appreciate, a trend that continued until it reached ¥212 per dollar in early October. US authorities sold 262 million dollars against the yen during the last week of September and the first week of October (FRBNY, Winter 1985–6).

The effects of the Plaza Agreement appeared to wear off by early October. On 16 October, the dollar staged its strongest rebound, even though Japan on the previous day (15 October) had announced a stimulus package. On 24 October, the BOJ allowed short-term interest rates to jump from 5.6 to 6.3 percent. While market participants saw this as evidence of the willingness of Japanese authorities to boost the yen, they questioned if it was consistent with Japan's need to boost domestic demand (FRBNY, Winter 1985–6). The truth is that neither the MOF nor the US authorities had been consulted (that is why the action did not involve a change in the discount rate, which would have required government approval). Reportedly, Federal Reserve Chairman Paul Volcker, fearful that a higher interest rate would hamper Japanese growth, conveyed to the BOJ that the action was "unnecessary and unwise."[38] Even so, the yen's appreciation resumed on the following day. Because most of the yen's appreciation during this period occurred during Tokyo trading, Ito (1987) argues that the perceived change in Japanese monetary policy was the likely driving force.

[38] Funabashi (1988) concludes that this incident illustrated the "unpreparedness and unwillingness among the central bankers to coordinate monetary policy."

At the end of the purportedly agreed six-week period, the dollar was some 13 percent down. The initial goal of 10 to 12 percent realignment had been accomplished without the $18 billion "war chest" having been exhausted (Funabashi 1988).[39] Concerned about the adverse impact of the ever-higher yen, the MITI announced an emergency package of financial relief, which included ¥100 billion ($487.8 million at ¥205 per dollar) of low-interest loans to small and medium-sized exporters, to be offered from December 1985 to March 1986 through quasi-governmental financial institutions. The Reagan administration and the US Congress quickly protested this as "unfair government subsidies" in violation of General Agreement on Tariffs and Trade (GATT) rules. The MITI was compelled to administer relief funds solely toward restructuring the export-led industries into domestic demand-oriented businesses (Funabashi 1988).

A sense of crisis and a perceived need for radical change prompted Prime Minister Yasuhiro Nakasone to commission, at the end of October 1985, a seventeen-member, blue-ribbon "Advisory Group on Economic Structural Adjustment for International Harmony," headed by Haruo Mayekawa (former BOJ governor), to propose how Japan should conduct its economic management over the medium term. The group's report to the prime minister was released on 7 April 1986, setting a reduction of Japan's large current account surplus (which was 3.6 percent of GNP in 1985) as the medium-term goal, not only for Japan's own sake but also for the "harmonious growth of the world economy." To achieve this, the Mayekawa Report called for a fundamental restructuring of the Japanese economy away from export dependence toward domestic demand-driven growth through deregulation, public investment, and tax measures.[40] This proposal, along with its sequel a year later, became the intellectual basis for the fiscal packages that would be implemented over the coming years.[41]

Because there was little immediate change in the trade imbalance, US authorities were willing to see a further decline of the dollar, while Japan

---

[39] The United States sold 483 million dollars against the yen during the six weeks following the Plaza Agreement.

[40] The proposed measures included: (1) imports would be increased, especially of finished products and from developing countries, through improved market access and strict enforcement of penalties against anticompetitive practices; (2) private consumption would be increased through an income tax cut and shorter working hours; (3) private-sector activity would be stimulated through deregulation; (4) the quality of life would be improved through increased public investment in social capital by local governments; and (5) both inward and outward FDI would be promoted. Grimes (2001) argues that the report "faithfully" reflected the MOF's fiscal conservatism through its influence on the former bureaucrats on the committee.

[41] Following the release of the Mayekawa Report, in August 1986, the prime minister instructed the Economic Council to prepare specific measures to shift the structure of the Japanese economy from export-driven to domestic demand-driven. Haruo Mayekawa was asked to chair the working group charged with this task. The report of the working group, known as the new Mayekawa Report, was released in April 1987.

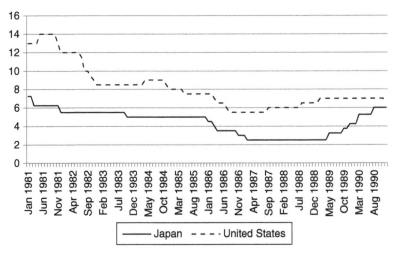

Figure 4.10. Official discount rates in Japan and United States, 1981–90 (in percent)
Source: BOJ, *Economic Statistics Monthly*

and West Germany saw no need for further adjustment. Japan in particular was becoming increasingly concerned about the contractionary impact of the sharp yen appreciation. At a January 1986 G5 meeting in London, Japan pushed for coordinated interest rate cuts as a means of stimulating domestic demand without disrupting the existing configuration of exchange rates. The idea suited Secretary Baker, who saw a need to ease the payment burden on indebted developing countries (Funabashi 1988). As a result, major central banks, including the BOJ, cut discount rates from the end of January through April (see Figure 4.10). After failing to secure US commitment to exchange rate stability at the highest political level,[42] on 4–5 May 1986, Japan reluctantly agreed at the Tokyo G7 Summit to the "indicator" approach advocated by the United States, which non-US participants saw as a backdoor way to boost domestic demand in Japan and West Germany.[43] After the summit, Toyoo Gyohten, vice minister from June 1986 to July 1989, recalls being instructed by Prime Minister Nakasone to intervene in the market to restore the ¥170 per

---

[42] On 8 April, Finance Minister Noboru Takeshita met with Secretary Baker. This was followed by a meeting on 13 April at Camp David between Prime Minister Nakasone and President Ronald Reagan. To Nakasone's request for cooperation in stabilizing the exchange rate, Reagan reportedly replied that it should be left to market forces (Funabashi 1988).

[43] The Tokyo Declaration proposed: (1) formation of a group of G7 finance ministers that would meet frequently between summits and (2) use of objective indicators—including the exchange rate—to assess the economic performance of the participants. The idea was for the countries to agree in each meeting on a set of quantitative predictions or goals for each of the indicator variables and to "make their best efforts to reach an understanding on appropriate remedial measures whenever there are significant deviations from an intended course." To the relief of Japanese officials, the indicator approach never came to much (Grimes 2001).

dollar mark (from the prevailing rate of around ¥165) before the 6 July national elections. The effort was not successful, but the ruling Liberal Democratic Party (LDP) won a landslide victory in any case (Volcker and Gyohten 1992).

To counter the yen's appreciation, Japanese authorities relaxed prudential regulations on purchases of foreign securities by institutional investors (see Section 5.1 in Chapter 5). For example, in April 1986, they raised the limit that restricted monthly purchases by life insurance companies from 20 percent of new investments to 40 percent; the limit was then abolished entirely in August 1986, when similar flow restrictions were suspended for other types of institutional investors. Stock restrictions were also relaxed. In March and April 1986, authorities raised the ceiling on foreign securities investments by insurance companies and trust banks (for pension trust accounts) from 10 to 25 percent of total assets; the ceiling was further raised to 30 percent in August 1986. Trust banks were authorized to invest in foreign bonds (for loan trust accounts) for as much as to 1 percent of total assets in February 1986 and up to 3 percent in June 1986 (and further to 5 percent in February 1989).

Why did the Plaza strategy work so well in apparently causing the yen to appreciate? Observing that the initial appreciation of the yen almost entirely occurred during New York trading, Ito (1987) argues that the announcement effect of the G5 process was the critical factor, especially the reversal of the US benign neglect policy. Klein et al. (1991) show in an event study framework that, while the exchange rates did not respond to unexpected movements in the US trade balance during January 1980–August 1985, they displayed a strong contemporaneous response during September 1985–April 1988. This may mean that market participants perceived that, under the Plaza regime, G5 authorities would change macroeconomic policies in a coordinated manner when there were unexpected trade balance movements.

Importantly, the Plaza realignment was consistent with economic fundamentals. The yen's appreciation had already started in early 1985 as the Federal Reserve eased monetary policy. This and subsequent exchange rate adjustment was likely in the direction of correcting the large misalignment. Yoshikawa (1990) estimates a model of the long-run equilibrium exchange rate for the yen in terms of labor and natural-resource inputs in Japan's production function (relative to the United States) to see how the real exchange rate would have responded to wage, price, and technological developments during 1973–87. His estimates suggest that, in 1985, the yen (at ¥239) was overvalued by more than 50 percent relative to the long-run equilibrium rate (at ¥157). The yen subsequently received a boost from a favorable shift in Japan's terms of trade, with the beginning of a sharp decline in oil prices in December 1985. Chinn (1997), by estimating the quarterly real yen–dollar exchange rate in terms of relative productivity and fiscal positions between Japan and the United States for 1974–95, finds that the oil price was a significant determinant. The appreciation of the yen from 1985 to 1987 could have been a reversion to its long-run real equilibrium level.

4.5.3. The Louvre Accord: 1987

Japan was desperate for exchange rate stability, but any US offer was contingent upon Japan agreeing to expand domestic demand. In September and again in October 1986, Japanese Finance Minister Kiichi Miyazawa flew to the United States to meet with Secretary Baker. The Baker–Miyazawa Accord of 31 October 1986 included a number of Japanese commitments to expand fiscal policy[44] and to lower the discount rate from 3.5 to 3 percent. The communiqué in particular stated that the two ministers had "expressed their mutual understanding that with the actions and commitments mentioned above, the exchange rate realignment achieved between the yen and the dollar since the Plaza Agreement is now broadly consistent with the present underlying fundamentals." In December 1986, the Japanese Government adopted a budget for FY 1987 that did appear to provide the degree of fiscal support agreed upon (see Figure 4.11). Frankel (1990) calls the Baker–Miyazawa Accord a "dry run" for the forthcoming Louvre Accord of February 1987.

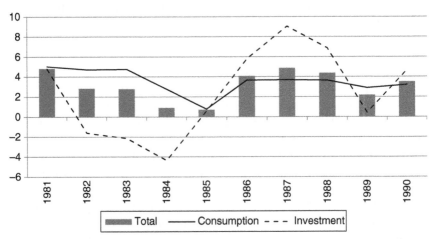

Figure 4.11. Year-on-year growth in components of government expenditures in Japan, 1981–90 (in percent)

Source: Cabinet Office

[44] The Japanese Government agreed to submit a supplementary budget to the Diet to provide "a substantial stimulus" to the Japanese economy and to implement as soon as possible a tax reform plan including reductions in the marginal tax rates for personal and corporate income to stimulate investment and business activity.

In early 1987, the yen came under renewed upward pressure[45] as US authorities began to talk down the dollar. In near desperation, Miyazawa rushed to a snow-covered Washington on 21 January 1987 to reaffirm the October 1986 communiqué. On 28 January 1987, US authorities intervened to sell $50 million equivalent of Japanese yen, the first "reverse" intervention to defend the floor of the dollar since the Plaza meeting (Bordo et al. 2010; Funabashi 1988). Miyazawa, a fiscal expansionist by persuasion, exploited Baker's offer of currency stability for a fiscal stimulus against strong resistance from within the MOF (Funabashi 1988; Grimes 2001). By the spring of 1987, the combined pressures of the MITI and the Ministry of Foreign Affairs had succeeded in overcoming the MOF's resistance, and Prime Minister Nakasone accommodated Miyazawa's expansionist policy in a supplementary budget. Monetary policy was eased again, with a discount rate cut on 20 February 1987.

On 22 February 1987, following meetings held at the Louvre, the Group of Six (G6) leaders stated that, given the economic policy commitments they were making, their currencies were now "within ranges broadly consistent with underlying economic fundamentals." The communiqué further stated: "Further substantial exchange rate shifts . . . could damage growth and adjustment prospects."[46] In the announcement, in exchange for the US promise to resist protectionism and substantially reduce the budget deficit for FY 1988, Japan agreed to provide an additional stimulus (at the end of May, the government announced an "emergency economic measures" totaling over ¥6 trillion in fiscal measures, a cut in the discount rate to 2.5 percent, and structural reforms as outlined by the new Mayekawa Report to expand domestic demand). Following the Louvre Accord, the dollar strengthened but started to weaken again in mid March, with an announcement that the United States would impose sanctions on selected Japanese products following a dispute over semiconductor products. On 23 March, the yen moved below the ¥150 mark, defended as a political imperative for Japanese authorities. The authorities bought dollars in record amounts, while US counterparts made daily purchases of dollars against yen from 23 March to 6 April, amounting to more than $3 billion (FRBNY, Spring 1987).

Operational details of the Louvre Accord were not disclosed, but some claim that the G6 governments established a target zone for the yen–dollar and deutsche mark–dollar exchange rates. Funabashi (1988), based on interviews with senior G5 policymakers, suggests that the central rate for the yen was set at ¥153.5, with a margin of 5 percent on either side (see Figure 4.12).

---

[45] On 19 January the dollar dropped to a post-World War II low of ¥149.98.

[46] Although the Louvre meeting had been planned for Sunday, 22 February 1987, as a meeting of the G7, the principal deals were made by the G5 ministers and central bank governors who met on Saturday, 21 February. Italy boycotted the meeting because it opposed the continued existence of the G5 as a separate entity.

Figure 4.12. Yen–dollar exchange rate, 23 February–16 October 1987

Source: Nihon Keizai Shinbun; Funabashi (1988)

The margin of 2.5 percent was designated as a first line of defense for mutual intervention on a voluntary basis; at 5 percent, consultation on policy adjustment became obligatory; and intervention efforts were to intensify as the exchange rate moved from 2.5 to 5 percent. The participants agreed to intervene until the following G5 meeting planned for early April, with a total amount of $4 billion roughly equally divided among the United States, Japan, and Europe. Bordo et al. (2010), however, argue that any obligations the countries assumed were vague and open to interpretation. According to a participant's account, the expression in the original draft worked out by the deputies, "seek to maintain exchange rates within agreed ranges until the next meeting in early April," was changed at the Louvre to "seek to maintain exchange rates around current levels for the time being" (Volcker and Gyohten 1992).

The advantage of having kept the operational details of any agreement secret was proved when the dollar broke out of the lower end of the presumed range. In a G5 meeting held in Washington on 7 April 1987, Miyazawa was reportedly forced to accept Secretary Baker's proposal to rebase at the previous day's closing rate of ¥146 to a dollar, with 5 percent margins (¥139.04–53.30). The countries also reportedly agreed to intervene until the augmented "war chest" of $15 billion was empty; the revised target range would be in place until 18 October 1987 (Funabashi 1988; Frankel 1990). At this meeting, Miyazawa made a commitment to implement a fiscal package of ¥5 trillion (which would be raised to ¥6 trillion at the Venice Summit in late May). The US dollar continued to move downward, however, despite the G5 monetary authorities' coordinated intervention.[47] During the last week of April, the dollar came under strong selling pressure as the Japanese Diet appeared unlikely to pass the expansionary budget and Japan–US trade negotiations faltered. In early May, Japanese and US authorities intervened to purchase dollars on a massive scale.

Press reports suggest that Japanese authorities intervened on thirty-seven days (out of 169 days) between 22 February and 18 October 1987. Lewis (1995a) shows that the intensity of intervention increased as the exchange rate deviated more from the presumed central rate. Esaka (2000), based on the methodology proposed by Lewis (1995a), assigns the numbers 0, −1, and +1, respectively, to no intervention, dollar-selling intervention, and dollar-purchasing intervention (based on information obtained from Japanese press reports) and estimates a multinominal logit model of intervention under the Louvre Accord. His key finding is that, between 23 February and 18 October, the probability of dollar-purchasing intervention became equal to the probability of dollar-selling intervention at ¥151.91 to the dollar, while the probability of intervention was minimized at ¥150.08.[48] These estimates give broad empirical support to the existence of a target zone, as does the fact that the yen–dollar exchange rate almost perfectly stayed within the presumed target ranges over the period (see Figure 4.12). However, the estimated expected rate of devaluation was significantly negative during most of the Louvre period, suggesting that the target zone for the yen was not credible if it indeed existed.

To promote exchange rate stability, Japanese authorities continued to relax prudential regulations on the foreign investment activities of institutional investors. In April 1987, the MOF's Trust Fund Bureau was authorized to invest in foreign securities for the first time, up to 10 percent of total assets. In June 1987, the ceiling for the Postal Life Insurance System was increased from 10 to 20 percent of total assets. For all intents and purposes, Japan had a fully open capital account by this time, with any remaining prudential regulations no longer binding on the behavior of institutional investors (Fukao and Okina 1989). Capital controls—prudential or otherwise—ceased to exist as an instrument of exchange rate policy. In May 1987, when the yen–dollar exchange rate hit the presumed floor under the Louvre Accord, the only thing the MOF could do was to "urge" financial institutions to refrain from speculative dollar sales and to require them to report their foreign exchange positions more frequently. Koo (1993) calls this a "harassment" of foreign exchange banks by requiring every conceivable kind of data on their foreign exchange dealings.

---

[47] According to Funabashi (1988), the scale after the Louvre meeting exceeded the agreed amount, while the scale of intervention following the Plaza meeting had been less than half the agreed amount.

[48] The implied target levels were ¥149 and ¥148 to the dollar, respectively, for 7 April–18 October. Lewis (1995a), using a similar methodology, finds that the implied target level for the yen (corresponding to the second measure) was ¥150.4 to the dollar for the entire period.

The Louvre regime ended with the crash of world stock markets on 19 October 1987, which highlighted the potential for conflict between monetary policy and intervention. To avert a financial crisis, the Federal Reserve eased monetary policy aggressively. Although the US authorities sold yen to stem the dollar's fall, from late October to early November, with heightened concerns about a possible recession, public support for exchange rate stabilization began to wane. Market participants remained unconvinced that decisive action would be taken to halt the dollar's decline. The dollar depreciated from ¥140 in October to ¥120 in December. When the G7 countries in a "Telephone Accord" or "Christmas Communiqué" proclaimed on 23 December that the dollar had fallen far enough and affirmed the desirability of exchange rate stability, the markets no longer believed the credibility of G5/G7 policy coordination.[49] The Louvre Accord would become irrelevant in any case because the yen stabilized during 1988 and in 1989 started a sustained depreciation against the US dollar.

4.6. ECONOMIC CONSEQUENCES OF THE HIGHER YEN

4.6.1. Sluggish External Adjustment

From early 1985 to late 1988, the yen more than doubled in nominal value against the US dollar. The yen's real effective appreciation was smaller, however, reflecting the fact that Japan had lower inflation than the United States and that the dollar had also depreciated against most other major currencies. Even so, the yen's real effective exchange rate (the IMF index) appreciated by 37 percent from 1985 to 1988. In line with the exchange rate adjustment, Japan's current account surplus declined from 3.7 percent of GNP in 1985 to 2.6 percent in 1988 and further down to 1.1 percent in 1990; in terms of yen, the surplus declined from ¥11.5 trillion to ¥10.2 trillion and then to ¥5.2 trillion over the same period (see Table 4.7). In terms of US dollars, however, the surplus rose from $49.2 billion in 1985 to $87.0 billion in 1987 before beginning to show a marginal decline in 1988. Japan's large bilateral trade surplus with the United States, a principal metric the Plaza strategy attempted to address, became larger, rising from $39.5 billion in 1985 to $52.1 billion in 1987 before declining to $47.6 billion in 1988.

---

[49] The G7 countries dared not call a meeting for fear that if it failed to produce anything tangible, the market might collapse again (Volcker and Gyohten 1992).

Table 4.7. Japan's external adjustment, 1985–90

	1985	1986	1987	1988	1989	1990
(1) Current account balance (in billions of dollars)	49.2	85.8	87.0	79.6	57.2	35.8
(2) Current account balance (in trillions of yen)	11.52	14.18	12.54	10.19	7.85	5.20
(3) Current account balance (in percent of gross national product)	3.7	4.4	3.3	2.6	1.9	1.1
(4) Bilateral trade balance with United States (in billions of dollars)	39.5	51.4	52.1	47.6	45.0	37.9
(5) Exports to United States (in billions of dollars)	65.3	80.5	83.6	89.6	93.2	90.3
(6) Imports from United States (in billions of dollars)	25.8	29.1	31.5	42.0	48.2	52.4
(7) Bilateral trade balance with United States (in billions of dollars)	9.37	8.65	7.57	6.10	6.18	5.47
(8) Exports to United States (in trillions of yen)[a]	15.49	13.54	12.14	11.48	12.81	13.03
(9) Imports from United States (in billions of dollars)[a]	6.12	4.89	4.57	5.38	6.62	7.56
(10) Change in export prices (in percent; year-on-year)	−1.4	−15.1	−5.0	−2.3	4.4	2.1
(11) Change in import prices (in percent; year-on-year)	−2.4	−35.8	−8.2	−4.6	7.5	8.7
(12) Exports to United States in 1985 prices (in trillions of yen)[b]	15.49	15.95	15.06	14.57	15.57	15.51
(13) Imports from United States in 1985 prices (in trillions of yen)[b]	6.12	7.63	7.76	9.57	10.96	11.51

[a] Estimated from dollar figures using annual average exchange rates
[b] Estimated from (10) and (11) using export and import price indices
Sources: MOF, *Fiscal and Monetary Statistics Monthly* for (1)–(7); IMF, *International Financial Statistics* for (10) and (11); author's estimates for (8), (9), (12), and (13)

Japan's stubbornly large current account surplus, especially when expressed in nominal US dollars, began to be debated in the academic and policymaking communities (Hickok 1989; Meade 1988). The perverseness of immediate adjustment was explained as a conventional J-curve phenomenon: given the slow short-run quantity adjustment, an appreciation of the yen caused the dollar value of exports to rise while the dollar value of imports remained relatively stable.[50] Such a valuation effect of the exchange rate change was

---

[50] The J-curve effect may not have existed for Japan–US trade. Hsing (2005) estimates a vector error correction (VEC) model of Japan's aggregate export–import ratio (or bilateral export–import ratio with the United States), the real effective exchange rate (the real yen–dollar exchange rate), domestic industrial production, and world (US) industrial production for

magnified by the substantial starting surplus in Japan's favor. The country also benefited from declining world commodity prices, especially given the composition of trade where imports were dominated by raw materials. For example, Japan's oil bill fell from ¥9.7 trillion in 1985 to ¥3.3 trillion in 1988.

The slow external adjustment reflected the historically low exchange rate elasticities of Japan's imports and exports. For example, Noland (1989b) finds the long-run relative price elasticities during Q1 1970–Q4 1985 to be 0.41 for exports (with four quarterly lags) and 0.67 for imports (with nine quarterly lags); the income elasticities, on the other hand, were greater than unity for both exports and imports. For Japan–US trade, Breuer and Clements (2003) estimate the average elasticities of Japanese imports from the United States and Japanese exports to the United States during January 1978–November 1996 to be 0.4 and 0.3, respectively, suggesting that a 10 percent real depreciation of the dollar would only cause imports to increase by 4 percent and exports to decline by 3 percent. The limited role of the real exchange rate as a determinant of Japan's bilateral exports is also noted by Bahmani-Oskooee and Goswami (2004), with respect to several other major trading partners during 1973–98.

4.6.2. The Savings–Investment Balance

As Japan continued to register a surplus year after year, the academic and policy debate increasingly shifted to questioning the validity of the elasticity approach to the balance of payments. The intellectual alternative to the elasticity approach had been the absorption approach of Alexander (1952), but what emerged to take its place as the principal macroeconomic paradigm was the savings–investment (SI) balance approach. Devoid of the Keynesian flavor of the absorption approach, the SI approach is solely based on the simple accounting identity relating the current account balance to the difference between domestic savings and investment. The SI balance approach was used to explain why Japan's current account surplus was so persistent despite significant yen appreciation.

Some noted that Japan's current account surplus was a structural one, associated with a deceleration of growth in the early 1970s that reduced the demand for funds by the corporate sector (Sato 1988). Combined with a relatively high household savings rate, this meant that the private sector

Q1 1980–Q1 2001. The estimated impulse response functions show that the J-curve effect was found only for the aggregate export–import ratio and not for the bilateral export–import ratio with the United States. Likewise, Meade (1988) observes that any J-curve effect was small for US trade. Bahmani-Oskooee and Hegerty (2009) identify a J-curve effect only in four industrial sectors (out of more than a hundred sectors examined) during 1973–2006.

started to generate large net savings. The current account surplus remained relatively small as long as the private net savings were offset by a large public sector deficit. But the government in the late 1970s initiated fiscal consolidation efforts, which caused the public sector deficit to decline from more than 4 percent of GNP to about 1 percent in the mid 1980s. The 5-percentage-point rise in Japan's savings rate, from 1984 to 1988, mostly reflected the shift in the public sector balance (Hayashi 1992).

It is not a simple matter to predict how a particular exchange rate change would affect the SI balance. Turner (1988) estimates the real exchange rate sensitivities of components of Japan's SI balance. His analysis shows that, from 1979 to 1984, the yen depreciation explained about a third of the increase in Japan's current account surplus; the reduction in the fiscal deficit explained about half. The upshot of this analysis is that exchange rate adjustment is of limited effectiveness in bringing about current account adjustment when it is not accompanied by a fundamental change in the economy's saving and investment behavior.

4.6.3. Exchange Rate Pass-through

Some challenged the elasticity approach, not necessarily for its intrinsic usefulness, but for the assumptions it makes about the link between a change in the exchange rate and a change in import and export prices. It was observed that Japanese export prices declined every year from 1985 to 1988, while import prices did not appear to fall as much as the yen appreciated (discounting the decline in world commodity prices) (see Table 4.7). This implies that the domestic prices of Japanese imports in Japan's export markets did not rise as much as the yen's appreciation, which in turn implies that Japanese exporters cut profit margins in order to stabilize local prices. On the import side, Otani et al. (2003), based on monthly data for January 1978–December 1989, find that the import prices for eight categories of goods changed on average 20 percent less in response to a change in the exchange rate, although the long-run elasticity was greater than unity.

Mann (1986) was among the first to recognize that the pass-through of the dollar's appreciation onto import prices was smaller in the early 1980s than had been observed previously, concluding that exporters had increased profit margins. Beginning in 1985, these margins allowed the same exporters to limit raising import prices in the US market when the dollar began to depreciate. Moffett (1989) likewise observes that the degree of exchange rate pass-through declined in the US import market in the 1980s, although part of this could be due to a concurrent fall in production costs associated with technological innovation and declining commodity prices (Meade 1988). In the Japanese import market, Otani et al. (2003) use rolling regression to show that the degree of exchange rate pass-through saw a steady trend decline beginning in the early 1980s (and the decline would accelerate in the 1990s).

Two reasons were offered to explain the imperfect pass-through of exchange rate changes onto export or import prices. First, Krugman (1987) and Baldwin (1988) proposed the concept of *hysteresis*, which is based on the notion that exchange rate changes are a stochastic process and that trade involves sunk costs. This means that traders who are contemplating responding to the latest movement in the exchange rate may wait to see if the change is permanent or sufficiently large before taking action. In particular, Japanese exporting firms had set up marketing networks in foreign markets during the period of yen weakness. According to hysteresis, such fixed investments could not be reversed quickly just because the yen had started to appreciate. The exporters instead suppressed a rise in export prices (import prices in the destination market) by reducing profit margins while assessing whether the higher value of the yen was permanent or transitory.

Dixit (1994), in explaining how Japan's sustained current account surplus was consistent with hysteresis, argues that the exchange rate in 1985 was far out of line with its long-run equilibrium level. This meant that the exchange rate needed not only to return to the equilibrium level but also to move sufficiently beyond that level to trigger an initial response from the traders. Even so, hysteresis (if it operated at all) appears to have weakened after mid 1986, when some Japanese firms began to retreat from the foreign markets or to move their production sites abroad. From 1985 to 1990, for example, Japan's outward FDI in manufacturing rose from $2.3 billion to $15.0 billion; for North America alone, the increase was from $1.2 billion to $6.8 billion. Local production of automobiles in North America increased from 254,000 units in 1985 to 1.6 million units in 1990, while the export of automobiles declined from 2.6 million units to 1.9 million units (Wakasugi 1994).

Second, more generally, the divergence between domestic and export prices was explained as reflecting the pricing-to-market (PTM) behavior of exporting firms under monopolistic competition. These firms, in order to maximize profits, attempt to charge different prices across segmented markets. Giovannini (1988) was among the first to show that Japan's export prices deviated substantially from the domestic prices for the same goods and that the differences between the two were systematically influenced by exchange rate changes. Marston (1990) estimates what he calls PTM elasticity (how the difference between domestic and export prices responds to a change in the real exchange rate) for Japanese manufacturing firms during the 1980s and finds that the elasticity was almost always positive (when the yen appreciates, domestic prices of exports decline), statistically significant, and symmetric with respect to depreciation and appreciation.

In identifying the determinants of PTM behavior, Shinjo (1993) looks at about a hundred commodity groups to find that such behavior was more pronounced for firms with greater oligopolistic power in the Japanese market but less pronounced for firms with a larger export share (hence, the domestic revenue base was smaller). The author further notes that PTM behavior, evident from 1985 to 1986, began to diminish in 1987. Ohno (1989), comparing the pass-through behavior of US and Japanese firms in a number of disaggregated industries from the late 1970s to the early 1980s, finds that the pass-through coefficient was higher for US firms (0.95, insignificantly different from unity) than for Japanese firms (less than 0.80, significantly different from unity). Knetter (1993) observes that PTM behavior was industry specific and that, from 1973 to 1987, Japanese, British, and German firms displayed similar export pricing behavior to stabilize local prices across destination markets. On the other hand, US firms did not display the same behavior, likely reflecting their different pattern of industrial specialization.[51]

4.6.4. Domestic and Foreign Price Differentials

Imperfect pass-through in the context of yen appreciation means that the border prices of imported goods in Japan were lower than the downstream prices of the same or competing domestic goods. This could work to limit the increase in the volume of imports, but it also could represent, not necessarily the PTM behavior of foreign producers, but more importantly the presence of market imperfections in the distribution sector. According to Nishimura (1993), markup over cost in the distribution sector was comparable between Japan (in 1985) and the United States (in 1982). On the other hand, Baba (1995) observes that pricing above marginal cost was generally higher in the wholesale and retail sectors than in the manufacturing sector during 1972–92. Regardless, in 1989, the US trade representative identified the Japanese distribution system as a structural impediment to the sale of American goods in Japan.

Empirical studies show that the response of domestic prices in Japan to a decline in import prices was particularly slow. Sazanami et al. (1997), based on monthly data for a large number of disaggregated categories of goods, observe that the difference between external and domestic prices widened considerably during 1985–95, while import prices did not decline as much as the extent of currency appreciation, and wholesale prices did not decline as much as the import prices. Olive (2004), based on the pooled annual data of twenty-four

---

[51] The rate by which export prices were reduced in response to a currency appreciation was 48 percent for Japanese firms, 36 percent for British and German firms, and 0 for US firms.

disaggregated categories of goods for ten major countries during 1970–91, finds that Japan was the only country for which the elasticity was statistically not significant.[52] Otani et al. (2003) note that the import pass-through ratio had been declining in Japan, which they attribute to the globalization of Japanese firms (which increased the share in total imports of reimports from Japanese-affiliated firms abroad) and the greater penetration of foreign products in the Japanese market (which increased competition).

In 1991, the Japanese MITI and the US Department of Commerce conducted a joint survey to determine that about two-thirds of the products sold in Japan were more expensive than in the United States. Maki (1998) estimates the constant-utility price indices for Tokyo, New York, London, Paris, and Berlin to find that in 1993 overall prices in Tokyo were higher by 30–40 percent. Noland's (1995) regression analysis finds that nontariff barriers and commercial practices (associated with corporate groups) were the significant determinants of the domestic–foreign price differential for a large number of products in 1989 and 1991. Sazanami et al. (1997) likewise attribute the downward rigidity of domestic prices to government regulations and business practices. It was this perception—domestic prices needed to come down—that delayed the monetary policy response to the first signs of deflation in the 1990s (Bernanke and Gertler 1999), since the public initially considered the fall in prices to be a natural, downward adjustment of high prices.

4.6.5. Structural Changes in the Japanese Economy

The second half of the 1980s saw the beginning of a substantial transformation of the Japanese economy. The sharp yen appreciation initially depressed economic activity but, in 1987, the economy started to recover quickly. Though weakened export demand reduced manufacturing production, the wealth effect of the appreciation strengthened domestic demand, which helped shift industrial structure from export-oriented to domestic demand-driven. As the growth of demand in the nonmanufacturing sector outpaced the growth of demand in the manufacturing sector, nonmanufacturing industries expanded. Along with expanding domestic demand, imports grew beginning in the second quarter of 1986, thereby contributing to growth in real world trade (Das 1993).

From the second half of 1987, manufacturing production also started to show a rapid recovery, aided by monetary and fiscal expansion and cost-saving

---

[52] The slow response of domestic prices to import prices was observed in eight other countries, but the elasticity was statistically significant (though numerically small). Australia had an estimated elasticity that was both negative and statistically significant, that is, domestic prices were found to *rise* when import prices declined.

efforts. The export sector had shifted to high-tech and high-value-added goods, and trade structure changed from vertical to horizontal. The rationalization of the manufacturing sector was so thorough that many Japanese firms became competitive at ¥110–20 to the dollar. Low-tech products and semi-processed goods were abandoned. The import of manufactured goods doubled in volume terms between 1985 and 1989 and increased 2.6 times in dollar terms. In 1989, the ratio of manufactured imports to total imports exceeded 50 percent for the first time. Japan became a large importer of durable and nondurable consumer goods and intermediate manufactured products (Das 1993).

4.6.6. Asset Price Inflation

Many experts broadly agree that monetary policy was kept too easy for too long following the post-Plaza appreciation of the yen (Kuroda 2003; Okina 2011; Shirakawa 2008). Real economic growth did fall propitiously from 1985 to 1986, but what was called the *endaka* (high-yen) recession of 1986 proved short-lived (see Table 4.8). By the second quarter of 1987, real GNP was growing at the annual rate of more than 8 percent. Even so, expansionary policies were retained. Because wholesale price inflation was in the negative range and consumer price inflation was hovering near zero through early 1989, there was little recognition that the economy was overheating (Cargill et al. 1997). The discount rate had been cut in November 1986 from 3.5 to 3.0 percent and further in February 1987 to 2.5 percent, the lowest in the post-World War II period. Easy monetary policy was maintained until May 1989, when the BOJ finally shifted to tightening monetary policy.

Signs of asset price inflation emerged, with a rapid increase in money and credit (see Table 4.8). The prices of assets, ranging from stocks and land to paintings and country club memberships, doubled and then tripled within a few years. The Nikkei stock average increased from around 13,000 in December 1985 to around 39,000 in December 1989. The price index for commercial land in six metropolitan areas tripled between March 1986 and March 1990 (Cargill et al. 1997). The BOJ was alarmed by these developments, but it received little political support to tighten monetary policy. Shirakawa (2008) argues that the policy delay reflected not only the overall condition of price stability but also the Japanese Government's reluctance to weaken domestic demand and thereby to widen the current account surplus. As the world's largest creditor nation, moreover, Japan was reluctant to disturb the spirit of international policy coordination then prevailing by raising interest rates when the rest of the world was easing monetary policy. The international community was opposed to unilateral action by Japan to tighten monetary policy (see also Okina 2011).

Table 4.8. Japan's real, monetary, and price developments, 1985–90 (in percent)

	1985	1986	1987	1988	1989	1990
(1) Real gross domestic product growth, year-on-year	6.2	2.9	4.0	7.3	5.3	5.6
(2) Growth in industrial production, year-on-year	3.7	−0.2	3.4	9.6	5.9	4.0
(3) Discount rate (end-year)	5.0	3.0	2.5	2.5	4.25	6.0
(4) Growth in narrow money (M1) (December; year-on-year)	4.6	8.4	6.8	10.3	−2.0	6.2
(5) Growth in broad money (M2+CDs) (December; year-on-year)	9.3	8.2	11.5	10.4	10.6	8.5
(6) Consumer prices (year-on-year)	2.0	0.6	0.1	0.7	2.3	3.0
(7) Wholesale prices (year-on-year)	−0.8	−4.7	−3.1	−0.5	1.9	1.5
(8) Nikkei stock price average (end-year; year-on-year)	13.4	43.8	14.6	39.9	29.0	−38.7
(9) Tokyo Stock exchange price index (TOPIX) (end-year; year-on-year)	14.6	49.2	10.4	36.6	22.2	−39.8
(10) Land prices in three metropolitan areas (year-on-year)	2.9	7.1	34.4	22.4	13.9	21.5
(11) Land prices in other areas (year-on-year)	1.7	1.3	1.3	2.3	5.0	10.9

Sources: IMF, *International Financial Statistics* for (1)–(7); Bloomberg for (8) and (9); Japan Bureau of Statistics for (10) and (11)

Japan's asset price inflation proceeded against the background of easy monetary policy and aggressive bank lending to the real estate sector. Hoshi (2001) argues that the banks' aggressive behavior originated in the partially deregulated environment, where banks had lost major corporate customers to the capital markets while households had little alternative to continuing to accumulate financial wealth as bank deposits (see Sections 5.3 and 5.4.2 in Chapter 5). A close look at data, however, reveals that land prices did not rise uniformly across the country; land prices in the commercial districts of Tokyo had already started rising precipitously in 1985. In fact, land prices outside the three major metropolitan areas hardly experienced a rise (see Table 4.8); land prices in Osaka and Nagoya rose less and with a considerable time lag relative to Tokyo, where the initial increase was triggered by increased demand for commercial property associated with Tokyo's growing role as a financial center (Ito and Iwaisako 1996). These observations seem to suggest that land price inflation was at least initially a real phenomenon.

As land prices rose, the collateral value of land held by firms increased, leading to an increase in stock prices as well (Ito and Iwaisako 1996). Following the crash in world stock prices on 19 October 1987, the decline in Japanese stock prices was a modest 12.8 percent; prices recovered to the pre-crash level by the spring of 1988. From Black Monday to the end of 1989, the Nikkei stock average increased by 70 percent. Easy monetary policy provided a supportive environment, but the direct effect of monetary policy on asset prices could not have been large. In order for low interest rates to cause asset prices to rise by the magnitude observed, there must have been expectations that the low interest rates would remain at that level permanently (Ueda 1990). Nor were there changes in economic fundamentals that corresponded to the magnitude of the rise in asset prices. Thus, neither easy monetary policy nor economic growth fully explains the asset price inflation.

Even so, in retrospect, Japanese monetary authorities can be said to have sacrificed domestic stability in pursuit of external objectives. Bernanke and Gertler (1999) argue that Japanese monetary policy was too tight from 1985 to 1988, when it became too easy. In their view, if the BOJ had increased the call rate to 8 percent in 1988 and higher in 1989, the outcome might have been better. Okina (2011) concludes that the failure to put the brakes on the escalation of the asset bubble was the biggest monetary policy error of the post-Plaza period. But this was not the central bank's technical mistake as much as a failure of the broader economic policy set by the government in an environment of international policy coordination. From the end of August 1987 to Black Monday in October, the BOJ did guide the overnight call rate to a higher range while keeping the discount rate at 2.5 percent. This was the most the central bank could do when it had no operational independence from government oversight (Shirakawa 2008; also Grimes 2001).

5

Internationalizing the Yen: 1981–2003

5.1. INTRODUCTION

From the early 1980s, Japanese authorities sought to "internationalize" the yen, that is, to promote greater use of the yen in international transactions. Although yen internationalization efforts began under pressure from a foreign government, it soon became Japan's stated policy. Yen internationalization presupposes, in a world of competing international currencies, a highly open capital account and a well-developed domestic financial system that offers a variety of instruments. The efforts increasingly involved developing yen-denominated markets and instruments, and dismantling restrictions inhibiting the freedom of foreign agents to use them. Yen internationalization thus took on the character of domestic financial reforms, as the capital account only had residual controls to begin with. In 2003, after failing to observe tangible results, the government shifted its focus to making Tokyo a major international financial center; subsequently, the government assumed an essentially laissez-faire attitude toward yen or capital market internationalization.

This chapter reviews Japan's experience with yen internationalization from 1981 to 2003, a period that substantially overlaps with those covered by the preceding and succeeding chapters of this volume. The period began with a sustained weakness of the yen, which US authorities somehow attributed to its lack of attractiveness as an international currency. Though this perception—right or wrong—was the initial impetus for yen internationalization, the efforts were sustained after the yen began to appreciate sharply in 1985, and even as the bubble economy of the late 1980s was followed in the 1990s by a prolonged period of deflation and slow economic growth, suggesting that different motives were at play at different points in time. The rest of the chapter attempts to provide a glimpse into these motives, though it does not attempt a detailed discussion of the changing background, which is left to the preceding and succeeding chapters. A narrower focus is placed on the sequence of specific measures to promote greater international use of the yen.

From the point of view of exchange rate policy, yen internationalization was a continuation of the process of capital account liberalization that had started

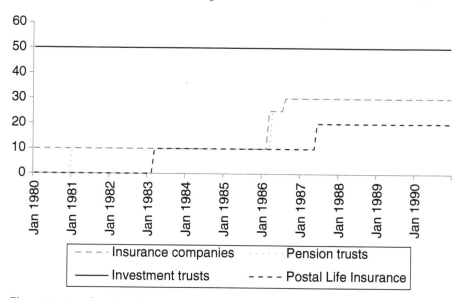

Figure 5.1. Prudential ceilings on stock of foreign investments held by major institutional investors in Japan, January 1980–December 1990 (in percent of total assets)
Source: Fukao (1990), Supplement B

two or more decades earlier. Though the revised Foreign Exchange and Foreign Trade Control Law of December 1980 gave nonfinancial institutions and individuals virtual freedom to acquire foreign financial assets, this was subject to the condition that they made all foreign exchange transactions through authorized foreign exchange banks[1] and portfolio investments through designated securities companies. Prudential regulations remained on the maximum amount of foreign assets institutional investors could hold in relation to total assets, severely limiting the ability of residents to diversify risks internationally. The early 1980s saw a progressive easing of these limits. For example, authorities allowed pension trusts to invest in foreign assets in January 1981, initially up to 10 percent of total assets; they allowed the Postal Life Insurance System to acquire foreign assets in May 1983, also initially up to 10 percent of total assets (see Figure 5.1). And virtually all remaining residual restrictions on cross-border capital flows were eliminated in April 1998, with the enactment of an entirely new Foreign Exchange and Foreign Trade Law, including the system of authorized foreign exchange banks.

The accelerated pace of easing the freedom of institutional investors to purchase foreign securities in the early 1980s became an important context to

---

[1] As a corollary of this provision, nonfinancial institutions and individuals were not allowed to hold bank deposits in foreign countries beyond certain amounts without prior approval. They were instead authorized to hold foreign currency deposits with domestic financial institutions without limit.

the yen's sustained weakness. These measures, coupled with large interest rate differentials favoring dollar-denominated securities, led to a massive acquisition of foreign assets by institutional investors, from ¥1.2 trillion at the end of 1980 to ¥11.7 trillion at the end of 1985 (see Figure 5.2).[2] It was against this background that US authorities began to push for yen internationalization. Japanese authorities introduced temporary measures to moderate the pace of foreign asset acquisition by institutional investors (Fukao 1990).[3] But the free-market paradigm of the US agenda, by pushing Japanese authorities to weaken their regulatory authority, made it difficult to invoke moral suasion to restrain Japanese investors from buying assets abroad, given the strong pent-up demand for foreign securities for diversification purposes.[4] In 1984, authorities were

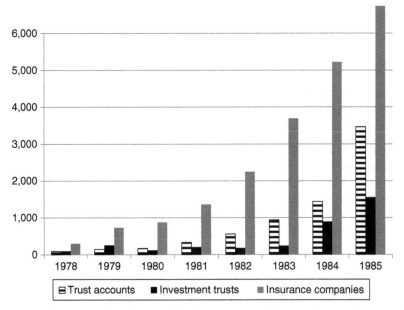

Figure 5.2. Balances of foreign portfolio investments held by institutional investors in Japan, 1978–85[a] (end of year; in billions of yen)

[a] Insurance companies include the Postal Life Insurance System
Source: BOJ, *Economic Statistics Monthly*

---

[2] The balance of foreign assets held by banks and other depository institutions increased from ¥1.5 trillion to ¥9.6 trillion over the corresponding period. Depository institutions, however, were not significant net investors in foreign assets because their open foreign exchange positions were subject to control by supervisory authorities.

[3] In April 1982, life and non-life insurance companies were requested "voluntarily" to limit net purchases of foreign bonds to 10 percent of the net increase in total assets. Likewise, the Postal Life Insurance System (in May 1983) and pension trusts (in November 1983) were requested to comply with similar "voluntary" restraints. These "flow" restraints were totally eliminated in August 1986 for all classes of institutional investors.

[4] High-yielding foreign assets were so popular that, by 1984, they had reached the prudential limit of insurance companies (Koo 1993).

compelled to adopt additional measures to liberalize capital outflows under agreement with the United States, despite the potentially adverse impact on the exchange rate. Japan's financial opening stayed on course.

The rest of the chapter discusses how, under the rubric of yen internationalization, this momentum for capital account and financial liberalization was sustained from this time on. It begins by tracing the origins of yen internationalization to the unprecedented weakness of the yen in the early 1980s and the Japan–US economic diplomacy that ensued. The chapter then reviews Japan's early attempts to liberalize the financial system from the late 1970s and its cautious approach to financial liberalization after 1984. This is followed by a review of steps the Japanese Government took to internationalize the yen from 1984 to 2003, including those designed to liberalize Euroyen transactions, reforms of the government debt market, and the financial "big bang" of 1998–2001, which essentially exhausted what government policy could do. The chapter concludes by assessing the economic impact of yen internationalization efforts.

5.2. THE ORIGINS OF YEN INTERNATIONALIZATION

5.2.1. Unprecedented Dollar Strength: 1980–3

The origins of yen internationalization can be traced directly to the pressure exerted during 1983–4 by US authorities, who suspected that the unprecedented weakness of the yen somehow reflected its unattractiveness as an international currency. According to this logic, the solution to the yen's weakness was to increase international use of the yen, inter alia, by deregulating the Japanese financial and capital markets and thereby making Japan a more attractive place for foreign investment. Financial liberalization was already in progress at that time, albeit in a piecemeal fashion. Yen internationalization had also been on the policy agenda of the Ministry of Finance (MOF) for some time. But it was pressure from the US Government that determined the timing of the MOF's systematic efforts to internationalize the yen and dictated the pace and scope of financial market reforms subsequent to the 1984 landmark agreement.

Sustained appreciation of the US dollar in the early 1980s occurred against the background of three factors. First, following the October 1979 arrival of Paul Volcker as chairman, the Federal Reserve began to tighten money and credit conditions substantially while deregulating interest rates. As a result, US short-term money market rates surged from 10 to 17 percent in late 1980, causing interest rate differentials to move in the dollar's favor. Second, the new Reagan administration pursued an increasingly expansionary fiscal policy. Because fiscal expansion coincided with monetary tightening, the US dollar saw a renewed strengthening after 1983. Third, during 1981–4, the Reagan administration adopted a "benign neglect" policy toward the exchange rate (Bergsten 1981). The US Government generally refrained from intervention, believing that the determination of exchange rates should be left to market forces. Between 20 April 1981 and 29 March 1985, a period consisting of 1,030 business days, the United States intervened only on eleven days against the Japanese yen (Bordo et al. 2010).[5]

Compounding the impact of "Reaganomics" was the divergent policy mix of Japan. First, Japanese authorities were intent on reducing the budget deficit, which had reached 5.5 percent of gross national product (GNP) in 1978. From 1981 to 1984, the growth of government spending was kept under control, with negative growth for investment. Between 1980 and 1984, the structural budget deficit was cut by an estimated 2.8 percent of GNP (Frankel 1984). In Japan and West Germany, it became the received wisdom that the 1978 coordinated push for fiscal expansion had been ill-advised and that the era for active demand management had come to an end (Putnam and Bayne 1984). Second, monetary policy in Japan was progressively eased from mid 1980 as growth decelerated, although it was kept tighter than warranted to limit the yen's depreciation (Hamada and Hayashi 1985). The policy divergence between the two countries pushed the dollar to appreciate, especially when the prudential ceilings on the balance of foreign investments by institutional investors were being raised in Japan. For the most part, the depreciation of the yen reflected the large outflows of capital, which overshadowed the country's equally large current account surplus (see Figure 5.3).

The conflict between external and domestic objectives came to the fore during 1981–2, when the yen declined in value from ¥205 to ¥260 per dollar. With inflation running at around 3 percent, domestic considerations argued in favor of monetary easing, while it was feared that a cut in the discount rate would further weaken the yen and aggravate trade frictions. Under these circumstances, the Bank of Japan (BOJ) allowed the call rate to drift upward in late March 1982 from 6.5 to 7.1 percent despite signs of weakening economic activity.[6] At the same time, on 3 March 1982, authorities requested that Japanese securities companies refrain "voluntarily" from selling zero-coupon bonds and announced their intention to establish reporting requirements for holders of these securities ostensibly to limit income tax avoidance (this restriction was partially withdrawn on 1 February 1983). Although the high interest rate policy was soon rescinded, concern over possible foreign

---

[5] The March 1981 shooting and wounding of President Ronald Reagan was virtually the only occasion between 1981 and 1984 when US authorities decisively intervened in the market (Frankel 1990).

[6] Japan's fourth quarter 1981 GNP had shown the first quarterly decline in nearly seven years. The high interest rate policy was eased in late August and terminated in late November (Komiya and Suda 1983).

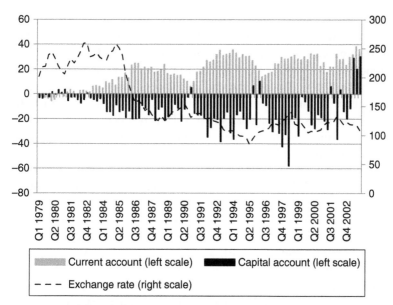

Figure 5.3. Yen–dollar exchange rate and Japan's balance of payments, Q1 1979–Q4 2002 (yen per dollar; in billions of US dollars)

Sources: IMF, *International Financial Statistics*; MOF, *Fiscal and Monetary Statistics Monthly*

exchange impact held authorities back from easing monetary policy. Even though interest rates were declining in other major countries and economic growth was slowing down, the BOJ delayed a half-point reduction in the discount rate until October 1983 (Komiya and Suda 1983; also Green 1990).

5.2.2. The Yen/Dollar Committee of 1983–4

By fall 1983, the large and widening trade imbalance between Japan and the United States was becoming a source of serious bilateral contention, with some observers claiming that a weak yen was the principal contributing factor. Bergsten (1981) called this the third episode of major economic conflict between the two countries since 1970 (with the other two episodes having been in 1970–1 and 1977–8). The US bilateral deficit with Japan reached a record $19.3 billion in 1983, and there was every indication that, in 1984, it would go much higher. The US business community, with Caterpillar chairman Lee L. Morgan as spokesman, urged the US Government to depart from the policy of benign neglect toward the exchange rate and suggested a list of measures Japan should be encouraged to take to raise the value of the yen. An extended list of measures—including yen internationalization and domestic financial market opening—was drawn up in early October, and the matter was given high priority when President Ronald Reagan made a state visit to Japan in November 1983 (Frankel 1984). To lay the ground work, Finance Minister Noboru Takeshita and Treasury Secretary Donald Regan met secretly in Honolulu in September and agreed to boost the attractiveness of the yen (Rosenbluth 1989). Toward the end of October, the Japanese Government announced a "Comprehensive Economic Plan," which, among others things, included measures to (1) abolish the so-called "real demand rule" (whereby a forward exchange contract needed to correspond to a bona fide transaction) and (2) establish a yen bankers' acceptance (BA) market.

At the conclusion of President Reagan's visit to Tokyo, on 10 November, Finance Minister Takeshita and Treasury Secretary Regan issued a joint press statement announcing Japan's agreement to liberalize the domestic financial and capital markets, internationalize the yen, and allow the yen to more fully reflect its underlying strength. The announcement also noted that the MOF and the Treasury would establish a joint ad hoc "Working Group on Yen/ Dollar Exchange Rate Issues" (henceforth Yen/Dollar Committee). The US position, based on what Frankel (1984) calls "questionable economic logic," held that the yen was undervalued because (1) Japan was not attractive to international investors and (2) the currency was not attractive to international users. Japanese authorities did not necessarily agree with such an assessment but went along because the alternatives (such as further trade concessions) were far worse. The group, co-chaired by Vice Finance Minister Tomomitsu Oba and Under Secretary Baryl W. Sprinkel, would monitor progress in implementing the agreed-upon measures and develop additional steps.

The US position was not only to internationalize the yen and open up Tokyo's financial and capital markets (in hopes of appreciating the currency over the medium term) but also to allow US financial firms greater business opportunities in the expanding Japanese market. In substance, the Japanese position differed little. Around the same time, the Japanese Government's policy agenda was already beginning to include yen internationalization and financial liberalization. In October 1983, for example, the MOF had proposed "the internationalization of the yen and the liberalization of financial and capital markets" as future policy objectives. The Japanese, however, preferred a much slower pace of reform than the Americans were willing to accept. The committee became a forum in which the two sides were to discuss the content and pace of financial market reforms Japan would undertake to open its markets and to internationalize the yen.

Although the discussions proceeded at the technical level, the work had a strong political dimension. In the first place, the creation of the committee itself was conceived at the highest political level, between Prime Minister Yasuhiro Nakasone and President Reagan. On more than one occasion, the prime minister is said to have intervened to push reluctant MOF officials forward in reaching agreement with the American side. There were two contentious issues (Takita 2006). First, the Japanese side wanted to publish a report for domestic consumption before the committee report, while the American side wanted the exact opposite. Second, debate within the MOF concerned the sequencing of domestic financial liberalization and yen internationalization (i.e., liberalization of Euroyen transactions). The MOF wanted to liberalize domestic markets before internationalizing the currency but yielded to US pressure by allowing both to proceed simultaneously.[7]

The Yen/Dollar Committee met six times from February to May 1984 and released its report on 30 May (29 May, US time), covering (1) removal of Japanese barriers against the inflow and outflow of capital, (2) international-ization of the yen, (3) more favorable treatment of US banks and other financial firms wishing to conduct business in Japan, and (4) deregulation of domestic Japanese financial and capital markets, allowing more interest rates to be market-determined. The MOF, however, did everything possible to avoid the appearance of being forced to open the Japanese markets; it concurrently prepared a report for domestic consumption on financial liberalization and yen internationalization. The report, entitled "The Present Status and Outlook on Financial Liberalization and Yen Internationalization," was released to the public at the same time as the Yen/Dollar Committee Report.

The Yen/Dollar Committee Report in part stated:

> The yen's internationalization will basically proceed as a natural evolution through the choice of market participants. Thus, what is needed are policy initiatives to remove a barrier and to provide an environment enabling market participants to select the yen whenever they wish. More concretely, the yen's internationalization calls for the liberalization of Japan's domestic financial and capital markets as well as permitting the use of the yen in the Euro market. (p. 25)

There were differences of views between Japan and the United States on the role of the Euro market. The US Treasury took the position that "the estab-lishment of a completely free Euroyen market [was] the cornerstone of progress toward the internationalization of the yen," while the MOF cautioned that "a too rapid establishment of a free Euroyen market [might] have adverse effects on Japanese fiscal and monetary policies, exchange rates, and Japan's domestic financial systems." Both governments, however, agreed that "devel-opment of a Euroyen market would represent a significant contribution to the Japanese and world economies."[8]

---

[7] The literature on the so-called order of economic liberalization (e.g., McKinnon 1982) generally suggests that, to be non-distortionary, capital account liberalization should follow financial liberalization. This principle was violated in the case of Japan as the two proceeded almost simultaneously—or one can even argue that the former preceded the latter.

[8] Japanese Ministry of Finance–US Department of the Treasury Working Group, 1984, "Report on Yen/Dollar Exchange Rate Issues," p. 25.

During the course of 1984, concurrent with or subsequent to the work of the committee, a number of market-opening and liberalization measures were announced or implemented. These measures included elimination of the real demand rule in April, relaxation of the conditions for Euroyen issues by residents in April, abolishment of nonprudential limits on external yen lending by Japanese banks in April, authorization for Japanese banks to sell in Japan foreign commercial paper (CP) and certificates of deposit (CDs) in April, complete abolishment of yen conversion limits in June, and relaxation of conditions for Euroyen issues by nonresidents in December. Foreign private borrowers rushed to take advantage of the newly opened Euroyen market, effective 1 December 1984. This helped further weaken the yen because these issues were purchased by Japanese residents (FRBNY, Spring 1985).

Because Euroyen transactions were among the transactions that required approval under the revised Foreign Exchange Law, and given the US position underscoring the critical role the Euroyen market could play in the yen's internationalization, authorities naturally focused on this market segment during subsequent years. Additional measures agreed on or proposed by the Yen/Dollar Committee Report would be implemented over the longer term, including liberalization of yen-denominated external lending, relaxation of eligibility requirements for nonresident firms to issue yen-denominated (Samurai) bonds in Japan and their terms, development of a short-term government bond market, establishment of a yen-denominated BA market, and deregulation of interest rates on deposits, starting with larger denomination deposits, "as expeditiously as circumstances warrant without causing market instability."[9] These and other post-1984 measures will be discussed in a later section of this chapter (see Section 5.4.1).

5.2.3. Currency Internationalization

An international currency is expected to serve one or more of the three functions of money outside the issuing country: (1) as a medium of exchange; (2) as a unit of account; and (3) as a store of value (Tavlas and Ozeki 1992). Of the six potential subfunctions (one set each for private and public users, see Table 5.1), Japanese authorities focused on the role of the yen as invoice currency, investment currency, and reserve currency (the third, fifth, and sixth roles, respectively, in the table). Specifically, authorities defined internationalization of the yen as "the expanding role of the yen in the international monetary system and the growing weight of the yen in current account transactions, capital account transactions, and foreign exchange reserves"

[9] Japanese Ministry of Finance–US Department of the Treasury Working Group, 1984, "Report on Yen/Dollar Exchange Rate Issues," p. 14.

Table 5.1. Monetary functions of international currency

Domestic currency equivalents	Private use	Public use
Medium of exchange	(1) vehicle currency (in foreign exchange transactions)	(2) intervention currency
Unit of account	(3) contract or invoice currency (in international trade)	(4) reference currency (as in exchange rate peg)
Store of value	(5) investment currency (in capital account transactions)	(6) reserve currency (held as foreign exchange reserves)

(see MOF 1999a). They had no ambition to make the yen a vehicle currency or promote greater use of the yen as a reference currency for exchange rate policy or, as a corollary, an intervention currency.

This narrower focus of yen internationalization efforts reflected the recognition that the choice of vehicle currency in foreign exchange transactions is characterized by network externalities, which tend to favor the incumbent.[10] Once a currency is established as a vehicle, concentration of trading further solidifies its position by reducing transactions costs (Black 1991). Although multiple equilibria could include one in which the dollar is supplemented by one or more subsidiary currencies, a large and sustained shock would be required to upset the status of the dollar as the world's foremost vehicle currency (Hartmann 1998). Japan's share in bilateral trade with any country was not so dominant that one could expect the yen to be a reference currency for exchange rate policy. A non-vehicle, non-reference currency could not be expected to become an intervention currency. On the other hand, the choice of investment currency is characterized by diversification considerations, so authorities saw scope for promoting greater international use of the yen by increasing its usability in that function.

The Japanese Government was initially cautious about yen internationalization. Until 1964, Japan restricted use of the yen by residents even for current international transactions, although it had earlier in 1960 established external current account convertibility for the yen (see Chapter 2, especially Section 2.7.3). Subsequently, the government circumspectly eased remaining exchange and capital controls, including abolishment in May 1972 of surrender requirements and progressive liberalization of foreign direct investment (FDI) from the late 1960s to the mid 1970s (see Section 3.5.2 in Chapter 3). It was only in 1980 that the revised Foreign Exchange Law formally allowed all

---

[10] Some have applied the term *vehicle currency* when a third currency is employed as a contracting currency for trade between exporter and importer (Magee and Rao 1980). This is not the sense in which the term is used here.

external transactions in principle to be conducted freely, but this did not mean that the authorities encouraged international use of the yen. In a world of competing currencies, capital account restrictions and underdevelopment of domestic financial markets would limit a currency's potential to be used widely outside the issuing country.

The policy of limiting international use of the yen meant that Japan's share of external receipts and payments (including long-term capital transactions) denominated in yen was small. In 1960, the share was 0.3 and 0.5 percent, respectively, for all external receipts and payments; it rose only to about 2.5 percent for both in 1968.[11] In 1970, the share of Japanese trade invoiced in yen was 0.9 percent for exports and 0.3 percent for imports, although the share rose to 29.4 and 2.4 percent, respectively, in 1980. When yen internationalization became official policy, the authorities stated that the limited use of the yen in international transactions was not "commensurate with the share of the Japanese economy in the world and Japan's status as the world's largest net creditor nation" (MOF 1999a). The small share of yen invoicing in Japanese exports was considered to be an anomaly in view of Grassman's Law, which states that, among industrial countries, the majority of contracts for trade in manufactured goods are typically invoiced in exporters' currency (Grassman 1973).[12]

Two theories have been advanced to explain Grassman's Law. First, Rao and Magee (1980) argue that, in equilibrium, the currency of denomination for international trade contracts should be irrelevant because prices would be negotiated between exporter and importer to equate the expected value in one currency to the expected value in another, adjusted for the market price of exchange rate risk; the party who accepts foreign currency invoicing would be compensated for taking the risk. In this view, Grassman's Law, based on data from a small number of countries, is spurious—two-thirds is not statistically different from one-half or a random distribution (see also Magee and Rao 1980). Second, Bilson (1983) argues that both exporter and importer should prefer invoicing in the exporter's currency because importers can raise the domestic price of imports if an unexpected devaluation occurs, whereas exporters cannot cut the price of contractually set wage and interest payments in response to a revaluation-induced decline in the home currency price of exports.

In the case of Japanese trade, two special factors need to be noted. First, Japanese imports are predominantly raw materials and primary commodities,

---

[11] MOF (1992), Table 2-11, p. 46.

[12] According to Page (1981), Finland, Ireland, and Italy were also exceptions to Grassman's Law: the domestic currency shares of exports and imports were, respectively, 2.4 and 2.7 percent for Finland (1977), 31.3 and 9.1 percent for Italy (1976), and 23.5 and 26.9 percent for Ireland (1981). The author reports comparable figures for Japan (1980) as 32.7 and 2.0 percent.

homogeneous goods for which information costs explain the worldwide use of the US dollar as a numeraire. Second, a large share of Japanese trade takes place with the United States, whose currency is the dominant global vehicle currency. In fact, in 1987 (the first year for which the geographical breakdown of currency contracting shares is available), yen contracting in Japanese exports was as high as 44.0 percent of total for the European Communities (EC) and 41.1 percent for Southeast Asia, whereas the share was only 15.0 percent for the United States (Sato 1999). If we discount the small share of yen invoicing in exports to the United States, Japan's overall share of more than 40 percent in the early 1980s was not far out of line with what Rao and Magee's irrelevance proposition would have predicted.

In pursuing the policy of yen internationalization, the Japanese Government stated that internationalizing the yen would be beneficial to the country by (1) reducing exchange rate risk for Japanese firms, (2) strengthening the international competitiveness of Japanese financial institutions, and (3) facilitating the development of Japanese markets as an international financial center. Regional and international benefits were also claimed, such as: (1) greater use of the yen in Asia would lead to greater stability of exports from Asian countries and contribute to their economic stability; and (2) greater use of the yen internationally, supplementing the US dollar, would contribute to a more stable international monetary system as well as greater risk diversification for investors and central banks worldwide. But, whatever the benefits, the initial push for yen internationalization did not come from within Japan, but from the US Government.

5.3. EARLY ATTEMPTS AT FINANCIAL LIBERALIZATION

The literature generally suggests two principal prerequisites for international use of a nation's currency (Tavlas and Ozeki 1992). The first is confidence in the political stability of the issuing country and in the relative stability of the purchasing power of its currency. The second is availability of markets for financial instruments denominated in that currency that are sufficiently broad, deep, liquid, and free of controls. Liquid, short-term markets are especially important because they allow nonresidents to move funds in, briefly park them, and move them out (Garber 1996). Japan had largely met the first of these conditions by the time yen internationalization efforts began in earnest. Domestic financial liberalization had also been in progress for some time, in creating domestic financial markets in an otherwise bank-dominated system. The process, initially triggered by expansion of the secondary market in government bonds, was given continuous impetus by the removal of one set of regulatory restrictions undermining the effectiveness of another extant set of regulations.

Financial liberalization, however, proceeded slowly and cautiously, focused mostly on government and corporate bond markets, which were subject to market forces outside government control. Reforms were meticulously supervised by the MOF to avoid disturbing the so-called convey system, which segmented the financial sector by type of institution (e.g., between banks and securities companies; between long-term and short-term finance; non-life and life insurance; commercial banks and trust banks) and implicitly guaranteed that no financial firm would be allowed to fail.[13] Only after the Yen/Dollar Agreement of 1984 would interest rates on deposits be liberalized,[14] and only during 1991–3 would the segmentation of the financial sector be broken down by allowing limited cross-entry through subsidiaries.

5.3.1. Emergence of a Government Bond Market

The virtual absence of a government bond market during the early post-World War II period reflected the Fiscal Law of 1947, which, in light of rampant inflation caused by deficit spending, stipulated that the government could issue bonds only for long-term investment (or "construction") except under special authorization (Clause 4) and that it could not directly place them with the central bank (Clause 5). Because the central government virtually refrained from issuing bonds,[15] there was only a small primary market for nongovernment bonds, including corporate bonds issued by public utilities and debentures issued by long-term credit banks partly as compensation for restrictions on branching and other deposit-taking activities.

In January 1966, the deterioration of Japan's fiscal position caused by the recession forced the government to begin issuing "construction" bonds. Yet, a wholesale development of the secondary market in government bonds did not take place at that time for two reasons. First, the MOF devised a system under which new issues of government bonds were subscribed by underwriting syndicates of financial institutions below secondary yields, with the restriction

---

[13] Horne (1985) provides a political analysis of the interaction of different actors, the Liberal Democratic Party, the bureaucracy, and regulated financial institutions, in the process of financial liberalization from the late 1970s to the early 1980s.

[14] Rosenbluth (1989) notes that international political pressure was only one of many factors driving financial liberalization in Japan; it was conspicuously absent in many of the regulatory changes. American demands to open financial markets were successful when domestic interests were already moving in that direction—when the domestic financial industry no longer benefited from the old rules.

[15] The government did issue, in addition to short-term financing bills for cash management purposes, a small number of special authorization bonds for compensation of the war dead and for subscription to international organizations.

that the purchased bonds could not be sold in the secondary market. Banks were willing to subscribe to new bond issues only because of the implicit guarantee that bonds in their portfolios would be purchased by the BOJ after one year[16] and because initial holding period returns, which included the commissions they earned, were closer to market terms. Second, syndicate-member securities companies were under administrative guidance to maintain secondary yields in organized exchanges as close as possible to primary yields.[17]

All of this changed in the mid 1970s, when a fundamental shift took place in the flow of funds between the corporate and public sectors. This facilitated development of two major open markets. First, the *gensaki* market—the market for bond trading with repurchase agreements—became a major short-term money market after 1974 when the first oil shock coincided with a permanent deceleration in the growth of corporate investment, resulting in an improvement in the corporate sector's cash position. The *gensaki* market had emerged earlier with the expansion of over-the-counter (OTC) bond trading when an increase in secondary trading necessitated an outlet for short-term inventory financing. As a substantial volume of short-term funds shifted out of the regulated bank deposit market, the government recognized the *gensaki* market and instituted prudential guidelines in 1976.

Second, the secondary market for government bonds became a major open market in the latter part of the 1970s (BOJ 1982, 1986). This occurred as the slowdown in economic growth caused a sharp deterioration of the government's fiscal position and necessitated large, continuous issues of government bonds (see Figure 5.4). The balance of government bonds, at a mere ¥10 trillion at the end of 1974, rose to ¥71 trillion in 1980 and exceeded ¥133 trillion in 1985. In order to facilitate the placement of ever-increasing debt, the MOF began to offer instruments with a variety of maturities, such as five-year discount bonds (January 1977) and coupon-bearing bonds with shorter maturities of two to four years (designated as medium-term bonds) at market terms (June 1978).[18] The increased amount of government bonds in bank portfolios led not only to suspension of the BOJ's guaranteed full repurchase but also to deterioration in the liquidity position of syndicate-member banks.

---

[16] At the end of March 1971, syndicate-member banks held only about 20 percent of the long-term government bonds they had purchased during the first five fiscal years (through March 1970). Purchases of bank-held bonds were made not only by the BOJ but also by the MOF's Trust Fund Bureau for the investment of government-intermediated funds.

[17] There were no restrictions on secondary sales of a small number of government bonds held by individual investors and life insurance companies (Kuroda 1982).

[18] From 1968 until 1977, the MOF issued only ten-year government bonds (designated as long-term bonds). From January 1966 until January 1968, the maturity of long-term government bonds was seven years. Beginning in February 1983, fifteen-year bonds with variable interest rates were issued mainly to trust banks; and in September 1983, twenty-year bonds with fixed interest rates began to be issued to life insurance companies and, from October 1986, to an underwriting syndicate of financial institutions.

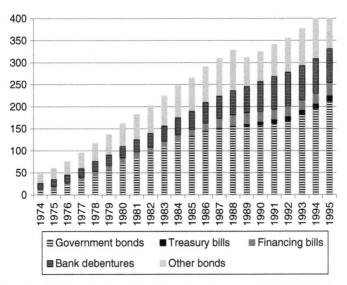

Figure 5.4. Outstanding stocks of bonds in Japan by type, 1974–95 (end of year; in trillions of yen)

Source: BOJ, *Economic Statistics Monthly*

This created pressure for further easing of restrictions in the government bond market (see Table 5.2).

In April 1977, syndicate-member banks were allowed to sell government bonds in the secondary market after the minimum holding period of one year; at around the same time, the price support measures applied to syndicate-member securities companies were lifted. The minimum holding period for syndicate-member banks was reduced to about seven to nine months (depending on the month of issue) in May 1980, about a hundred days in April 1981, and forty days in January 1985.[19] In April 1983, banks were allowed to sell over the counter newly issued long-term government bonds and, in October 1983, to sell newly issued medium-term government bonds. In June 1984, they were further authorized to deal in secondary trading for public-sector bonds. The volume of OTC trading in government bonds, which had been miniscule before 1977, increased to ¥68 trillion per year in 1978 and exploded to ¥1.3 quadrillion in 1985 and ¥5.4 quadrillion in 1987 before declining somewhat (see Figure 5.5).[20] Liberalization of the government bond market was virtually complete by the mid 1980s.

---

[19] The forty-day holding period applied only to the dealing account. Effective April 1986, the minimum holding period was shortened to ten days for the dealing account and forty days for the investment account.

[20] Part of this rapid expansion was caused by the commencement of futures trading in October 1985.

Table 5.2. Liberalization measures introduced in Japanese government bond market, 1977–86

Month of action	Measures taken
January 1977	Five-year discount bonds issued
April 1977	Secondary sales of special-authorization ("deficit") bonds by banks authorized after minimum holding period of one year
October 1977	Secondary sales of construction bonds by banks authorized after minimum holding period of one year
June 1978	Three-year bonds issued at market rates
May 1979	Two-year bonds issued at market rates
May 1980	Secondary sales of bonds by banks authorized following commencement of trading in organized securities exchanges (i.e., about seven to nine months after subscription)
June 1980	Four-year bonds issued at market rates
April 1981	Secondary sales of bonds by banks authorized following first business day in fourth month after subscription (i.e., about 100 days)
February 1983	Fifteen-year bonds with variable interest rates issued
April 1983	Over-the-counter (OTC) sales of newly issued long-term (ten-year) bonds by banks authorized
September 1983	Twenty-year bonds with fixed interest rates issued
October 1983	OTC sales of newly issued medium-term (two- to five-year) bonds by banks authorized
June 1984	Bank dealing in bonds with remaining maturities of less than two years authorized
June 1985	Banks authorized to use interdealer brokerage services provided by Nihon Sōgo Shōken
June 1985	Bank dealing in bonds fully liberalized
June 1985	Secondary sales of bonds by banks authorized following first business day in second calendar month after subscription (i.e., about forty days) for dealing account only
October 1985	Bond futures market established
February 1986	Six-month bonds (Treasury bills) issued at market rates with minimum denomination of ¥100 million
April 1986	Secondary sales of bonds by banks authorized following first business day in first calendar month after subscription (i.e., about ten days) for dealing account; following first business day in second calendar month after subscription (i.e., about forty days) for investment account

5.3.2. The Expanding Money Market

Along with these and other developments in the government bond market, authorities implemented a series of measures in the open money market and in the interbank market to introduce new instruments and diversify maturities. Most notably, new market segments were created beginning in 1979 (see Table 5.3).

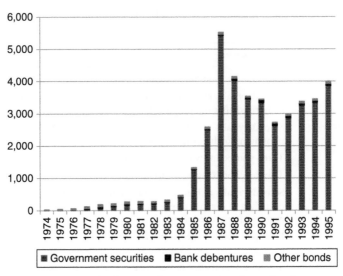

Figure 5.5. Trading in Tokyo's over-the-counter bond market by type of bond, 1974–95 (in trillions of yen)

Source: BOJ, *Economic Statistics Monthly*

Table 5.3. Liberalization measures introduced in Japanese money market, 1978–85

Month of action	Measures taken
June 1978	Flexible pricing introduced in call market; resale of bills before maturity at free rates permitted in bill-discount market
October 1978	New seven-day instruments with free rates introduced in call market
November 1978	New one-month instruments with free rates introduced in bill-discount market; posted rates abolished for three- and one-month instruments in bill-discount market
April 1979	Posted rates abolished in call market; two- to six-day instruments introduced in call market
May 1979	Negotiable certificates of deposit (CDs) with maturities of three to six months and minimum denomination of ¥500 million introduced up to 10 percent of issuing banks' net worth
October 1979	Posted rates abolished in bill-discount market
April 1980	Ceiling for CDs raised to 50 percent of net worth
November 1980	Simultaneous borrowing in call market and investing in bill-discount market authorized for regional and trust banks
April 1982	Simultaneous borrowing in bill-discount market and investing in call market authorized for city banks; money brokers authorized to deal in bill-discount market
February 1983	Ceiling for CDs raised to 75 percent of net worth
January 1984	Minimum denomination for CDs reduced to ¥300 million
March 1985	Simultaneous borrowing and investing in bill-discount market authorized; money market certificates (MMCs) with maturities of one to six months and minimum denomination of ¥50 million introduced

April 1985	Ceiling for CDs raised to 100 percent of net worth; minimum denomination reduced to ¥100 million; and minimum maturity reduced to one month
June 1985	Five- and six-month instruments introduced in bill-discount market; yen-denominated bankers' acceptance (BA) market established with minimum denomination of ¥100 million and maturities of one to six months
July 1985	Unsecured call loans authorized
August 1985	Two- and three-week instruments (secured) introduced in call market
September 1985	Two- and three-week instruments (unsecured) introduced in call market
October 1985	Ceiling for CDs raised to 150 percent of net worth
December 1985	Mutual savings and loans banks authorized to raise funds in bill-discount market
February 1986	Public auction of Treasury bills (TBs) begins
April 1986	Ceiling for CDs raised to 200 percent of net worth; maximum maturity of CDs and MMCs increased to twelve months
September 1986	Minimum denomination of MMCs reduced to ¥30 million; ceiling for CDs raised to 250 percent of net worth
April 1987	Minimum denomination of MMCs reduced to ¥20 million; maximum maturity of MMCs increased to two years
April 1987	Ceiling for CDs raised to 300 percent of net worth; ceiling for foreign banks abolished
October 1987	Minimum denomination of MMCs reduced to ¥10 million
October 1987	Ceiling for CDs abolished for all banks
November 1987	Market for commercial paper (CP) created, with minimum face value of ¥100 million

First, banks were authorized to issue negotiable CDs in May 1979 when a large amount of funds had moved out of the regulated deposit market into the secondary government bond market; authorities progressively eased the issuing conditions for CDs over 1981–5, in accordance with commitments made in the Yen/Dollar Agreement. Second, authorities created a market for yen-denominated BAs in June 1985, in part to promote yen invoicing in international trade. Although creation of a BA market had been discussed within the Japanese Government since 1983, this was also implemented as part of the commitments agreed upon under the Yen/Dollar Committee. However, the market never took off, suggesting that there was no demand for an alternative mechanism for trade financing.[21]

---

[21] Cumbersome registration procedures and progressive stamp duty were said to be factors that diminished the attractiveness of BAs as a means of trade financing. The failure of the BA market to develop in turn was an indication that the existing trade financing method worked quite well and that a government-directed "liberalization" measure does not work when there is no private demand for it (Royama 1986).

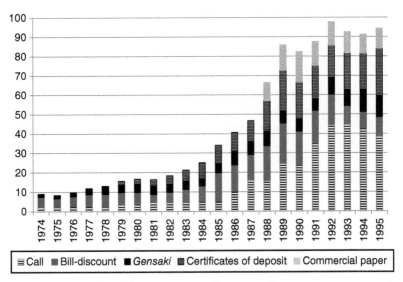

Figure 5.6. Outstanding balances in Japan's major short-term money markets, 1974–95 (end of year; in trillions of yen)

Source: BOJ, *Economic Statistics Monthly*

Third, in February 1986, the government began to issue Treasury bills (TBs) through public auction. TBs are short-term government bonds designed to increase the flexibility of the government as it tried to refinance a large quantity of maturing debt (TBs are included as part of government securities in Figure 5.5). Finally, a market for CP was launched in November 1987, when nonresident Euroyen CP was also authorized (see Section 5.4). Initially, there was a minimum face value of ¥100 million, and maturities had to be between one and six months. Authorities subsequently relaxed the eligibility require-ments for issuing firms (which increased the number from about 200 initially to more than 500) as well as the maturity restrictions. As a result of these and other measures, the size of the short-term money market expanded rapidly: the value of outstanding balances in the five major markets (excluding the TB market, which is included in the bond market for statistical purposes) increased from ¥12 trillion in 1977 to ¥34 trillion in 1985, and further to ¥66 trillion in 1988 and ¥86 trillion in 1989 (see Figure 5.6).

5.3.3. Lifting Barriers to Market Access

An important aspect of financial liberalization was the removal of various restrictions on pricing and market access. In the convoy system, the activities of different types of institutions were carefully prescribed, with access to certain markets limited to specific types of institutions. As an initial step to remove these barriers, authorities in the late 1970s progressively relaxed city banks' access to the *gensaki* market, a market that had previously been open only to securities companies; in the early 1980s, they in turn relaxed securities companies' access to the call market (see Table 5.4). Pricing practices and maturities were also deregulated. In 1978–9, the BOJ abolished the so-called "posted rate system"—under which interest rates were "posted" once a day by the lead money broker in implicit consultation with the central bank—and diversified the maturities of instruments by introducing seven-day and one-month bills at market rates. By implementing these measures, authorities sought to maintain the depth of the interbank market and to facilitate arbitrage with the open market, in which they initially lacked instruments to intervene directly.

Empirical studies show that, as a result of domestic financial liberalization, transactions costs declined, and greater arbitrage ensued in the Japanese financial market (Takagi 1987, 1988a). Because Euroyen transactions were progressively eased at the same time (see Section 5.4), moreover, a high degree of interest rate arbitrage between external and domestic markets emerged. The complete lifting of yen conversion limits in June 1984 was especially critical in this respect because it meant eliminating the limit on the volume of arbitrage funds (before June 1984, interbank interest rates had tended to remain somewhat above the corresponding Euroyen interest rates). The absolute monthly average deviation between the two-month Euroyen deposit rate

Table 5.4. Measures to promote inter-market arbitrage in Japan

Month of action	Measures taken
October 1978	City banks authorized to borrow up to ¥20 billion in *gensaki* market
January 1979	Stepwise easing of ceiling on *gensaki* borrowing by city banks begins
April 1980	Ceiling on *gensaki* borrowing by city banks raised to ¥150 billion (stepwise easing completed)
November 1980	Four largest securities companies authorized, for first time since 1965, to borrow in call market up to ¥10 billion
April 1981	City banks authorized to invest in *gensaki* market for first time
December 1982	Borrowing in call market authorized for eight additional securities companies up to ¥5 billion each
December 1982	Ceiling on borrowing in call market by four largest securities companies raised to ¥30 billion
January 1982	Two additional securities companies permitted to borrow in call market
May 1985	Securities companies authorized to lend in interbank market
June 1985	Securities companies authorized to deal in secondary bank certificates of deposits (CDs)
April 1986	Securities companies authorized to deal in yen bankers' acceptances (BAs)

and the two-month bill-discount rate, for example, fell from 0.32 percent during January 1981–May 1984 to 0.18 percent during June 1984–December 1985. Likewise, the yield on one-year bank debentures converged with the one-year Euroyen deposit rate in the latter part of the 1980s (Takagi 1988b).

5.4. YEN INTERNATIONALIZATION EFFORTS

5.4.1. Post-Yen/Dollar Committee Reforms

The government's stance toward yen internationalization is said to have been neutral during the deliberations of the Yen/Dollar Committee (MOF 1995: p. 41). The stance became explicitly positive only during the work of the Council on Foreign Exchange and Other Transactions (henceforth referred to as the Foreign Exchange Council), an advisory body to the minister of finance. The council's report, issued in March 1985, put forth the idea that the yen's internationalization should be actively promoted and suggested the following as necessary steps: (1) domestic financial liberalization as a means of providing attractive yen instruments to nonresidents; (2) liberalization of Euroyen transactions; and (3) internationalization of Tokyo as a major financial center.

The liberalization of Euroyen transactions received special emphasis in the Yen/Dollar Committee Report (see Table 5.5 for details). Specifically, measures suggested by the report (and implemented over subsequent years) included: (1) issuing terms for Euroyen bonds be eased and withholding tax be abolished for nonresidents (implemented in April 1985); (2) medium- to long-term Euroyen lending be permitted for Japanese banks (April 1985 for nonresidents; May 1989 for residents); and (3) the maturity of Euroyen CDs be extended from less than six months to one year (April 1986) and then to two years (April 1989). In addition, as a measure to internationalize the Tokyo markets, the Tokyo Stock Exchange extended membership to foreign securities companies in December 1985. In 1986, the revised Foreign Exchange Law was modified to allow the establishment of offshore accounts, leading to the launch of an offshore market in December (see Table 5.6). As Euroyen transactions were relaxed, pressure increased to liberalize domestic financial transactions.

Additional government reports were prepared over subsequent years and repeated the same theme with variations. For example, the June 1987 report stressed the need to improve the attractiveness of instruments traded in the short-term government debt markets. The outcome of these efforts went beyond the progressive liberalization of Euroyen transactions. Different segments of domestic financial and capital markets were developed over time,

Table 5.5. Selected measures to liberalize Euroyen transactions, 1984–98

Month of action	Measures taken
April 1984	Issuing guidelines established for resident Euroyen bonds
June 1984	Short-term Euroyen loans to residents authorized (subject to notification)
December 1984	Foreign securities companies allowed to become lead manager of Euroyen bonds; issuing of Euroyen certificates of deposit (CDs) authorized with maturity of up to six months; issuing of Euroyen bonds authorized for nonresidents
April 1985	Withholding tax on resident Euroyen bonds abolished; medium to long-term Euroyen loans to nonresidents liberalized; issuing guidelines relaxed for nonresident Euroyen bonds (rating of AA or above)
May 1985	Short-term Euroyen loans to residents liberalized
April 1986	Issuing guidelines further relaxed for nonresident Euroyen bonds (eligibility solely based on credit rating); minimum repatriation period for resident and nonresident Euroyen bonds shortened from 180 days to 90 days; maturity of Euroyen CDs lengthened to one year
July 1987	Issuing guidelines relaxed for resident Euroyen bonds (credit rating introduced)
November 1987	Nonresident Euroyen commercial paper (CP) authorized
April 1988	Maturity of Euroyen CDs lengthened to two years
May 1989	Medium to long-term Euroyen loans to residents liberalized
June 1989	Further relaxation of eligibility criteria for nonresident Euroyen bonds (credit rating no longer required)
June 1989	Nonresident Euroyen bonds with maturities of less than four months authorized
July 1993	Eligibility criteria for nonresident Euroyen bonds abolished
January 1994	Minimum repatriation period for sovereign Euroyen bonds abolished
April 1995	Procedures for approval and notification made flexible for nonresident Euroyen bonds
August 1995	Minimum repatriation period abolished for nonresident Euroyen bonds
January 1996	Eligibility criteria for resident Euroyen bonds abolished
April 1996	Minimum repatriation period for resident Euroyen bonds shortened from ninety to forty days
April 1996	Issuing rules for Euroyen CP abolished (virtual elimination of all restrictions on bringing proceeds back into domestic market)
April 1998	Minimum repatriation period for resident Euroyen bonds abolished

Source: Ministry of Finance

including establishment of a yen-denominated BA market, as previously noted, and various markets for financial futures and options (see Table 5.6). Efforts to internationalize the yen during this period were part of overall efforts to liberalize domestic financial transactions and to develop domestic financial markets.

Table 5.6. Selected measures to liberalize cross-border financial transactions and to internationalize domestic market segments in Japan, 1984–96[a]

Month of action	Measures taken
April 1984	Real demand rule abolished for forward exchange transactions
June 1984	Regulation on yen conversion abolished
June 1985	Yen-denominated bankers' acceptance (BA) market established
December 1986	Tokyo offshore market established
June 1987	Trading in stock futures commences (Osaka)
September 1988	Trading in Nikkei-225 futures commences (Osaka)
April 1989	Tokyo Financial Futures Exchange established
June 1989	Trading in Nikkei-225 options commences (Osaka)
July 1989	Resident individuals authorized to hold foreign currency bank deposits abroad up to equivalent of ¥5 million without obtaining approval
July 1990	Resident corporations and individuals authorized to hold foreign currency bank deposits abroad for portfolio investment up to equivalent of ¥30 million without obtaining approval
January 1994	Eligibility criteria relaxed for resident foreign bonds and Samurai bonds
March 1994	Freely allowable limit for foreign currency deposits abroad by residents increased to ¥100 million
July 1994	Eligibility criteria relaxed for yen-denominated foreign bonds
April 1995	Procedures for approval and notification made flexible for nonresident domestic bonds
January 1996	Eligibility criteria abolished for nonresident domestic bonds
April 1996	Freely allowable limit for foreign currency deposits abroad by residents increased to ¥200 million

[a] Excludes measures related to Euroyen transactions
Source: Ministry of Finance

5.4.2. The Financial "Big Bang"

The tremendous transformation of the global financial landscape increasingly made the Foreign Exchange Law of 1980 outdated. For example, the law, while liberalizing external financial transactions, preserved the convoy system for domestic financial firms. External transactions may have been free, but they were subject to the requirement that all foreign exchange transactions be conducted through authorized foreign exchange banks. Some new financial products, such as interest rate swaps between residents and nonresidents, were subject to control. In the meantime, heavily regulated financial firms had lost incentives to innovate and become increasingly inefficient; the hollowing-out of financial services followed, with market players leaving Tokyo for New York, London, Hong Kong, or Singapore (Toya 2006). National borders within Europe were being eliminated for financial transactions, allowing large European financial institutions to emerge as global players. There was increasing awareness within Japan's establishment that the country was being left out of sweeping changes taking place in the rest of the industrial world (Sakakibara 2000).

It was against this sense of urgency that the Japanese Government unveiled in November 1996 a sweeping reform of Japan's financial system. This reform would be carried out over a three-year period, starting in April 1998, and cover the banking, securities, and insurance industries, as well as foreign exchange and accounting standards. Called the financial "big bang," a term borrowed from the deregulation of London's financial markets in the 1980s, the plan sought to make Japan's financial markets and institutions market-based ("free"), transparent and rules-based ("fair"), and consistent with internationally accepted legal, accounting, and super-visory standards ("global") (Dekle 1998). This would be brought about by removing regulatory barriers separating the activities of various types of financial firms as well as restrictions on the menu of products and services they could offer.

When these ideas were being developed within the MOF, some resisted the loss of regulatory power, which was the source of their prestige; others were concerned that full deregulation might lead to an erosion of tax revenue. It was only under the visionary leadership of the director generals of the International Finance and Securities Bureaus (Eisuke Sakakibara and Atsushi Nagano) that the bold deregulatory initiative moved forward within the bureaucracy (Sakakibara 2000). Even so, these efforts may have still failed to materialize if they had not received strong political support from the ruling Liberal Demo-cratic Party (LDP), especially Prime Minister Ryutaro Hashimoto. The prime minister, in announcing the initiative in November 2006, promoted it as his own; the big bang initiative was also made part of a larger reform package, which included a major revision of the Bank of Japan Law. Hashimoto noted that one of the purposes was to restore the status of the Tokyo market, whose share in global trading had been declining from its heyday in the 1980s (see Table 5.7).

The big bang initiative did not evolve from the informal bargaining process among actors that had characterized public policymaking in postwar Japan.

Table 5.7. Status of yen and Tokyo market in global foreign exchange trading, 1989–2004 (in percent of global total)

	1989	1992	1995	1998	2001	2004
Share of yen	13.5	11.7	12.1	10.1	11.4	10.1
Share of Tokyo	15.5	11.2	10.2	6.9	9.1	8.2

Source: Bank for International Settlements, Triennial Central Bank Survey of Foreign Exchange and Derivatives Market Activity, triennial issues, 1990–2005

When Prime Minister Hashimoto announced it two weeks after the LDP victory in the Lower House elections, it took many, including in the financial industry, by surprise. Two factors were responsible (Toya 2006). First, both the LDP and the MOF had been discredited by the financial crisis and associated corruption scandals.[22] The LDP had lost power in 1993 for the first time in nearly forty years of single-party rule. The financial crisis meant that the MOF had failed in its supervision of the convoy system; it was also an indication that the slow pace of institutional adaptation had not kept up with the pace of technological and other environmental changes. Second, because the loss of public trust threatened their survival, the LDP and the MOF sought to recoup public trust by enhancing public interest over constituents' interest. Instead of seeking perpetuation of the status quo, the LDP and the MOF saw political gains in pushing for drastic reforms the public demanded. Ownership by Hashimoto made it difficult for industry organizations to assemble a counter-coalition.

The big bang initiative had two phases. The first phase commenced with complete deregulation of foreign exchange transactions in April 1998, while the bulk of the other reforms took effect in December 1998, including comprehensive revision of the securities, banking, and insurance laws. The big bang initiative was an effort to complete the desegmentation of the financial system that had begun with the half-hearted financial reforms of 1991–3. Revision of the Bank of Japan Law was conceived as a means to gain public support for injecting public money into troubled housing loan companies (Toya 2006). Some within the political establishment believed that the bubble economy of the late 1980s had resulted from the subordination of monetary policy to the fiscal authorities. For their part, MOF officials were willing to concede a loss of influence over the central bank, as long as their authority over financial administration was not revoked. The LDP's project team proceeded from March 1996 to work on BOJ reform. In a reform paralleling the big bang, the Bank of Japan Law was revised to take effect in April 1998.[23] The Diet passed the law on 11 June 1997.

The decision to make the new Foreign Exchange Law the forerunner of the big bang reforms was a controversial one because it would give Japanese asset holders an exit option before deregulation of the domestic financial system was complete. The decision was deliberate. The architects of the reforms thereby sought to ensure that the envisioned domestic reforms would be

---

[22] The Housing Loan Affair of 1995–6 involved seven housing loan companies managed by retired MOF officials whose losses had grown larger in the face of inaction by the MOF. The Wining and Dining Scandals of 1994–6 involved a questionable relationship of incumbent MOF officials with rogue financiers. These scandals led to a public uproar not only against the MOF but also against the LDP and the banking industry, as well as to a call for an overhaul of Japan's financial system. See Toya (2006).

[23] Grimes (2001: pp. 204–7) provides an account of how the Bank of Japan Law revision was conceived and implemented.

carried through (Toya 2006; also Ito and Melvin 1999). To map out the course of action, in January 1997, the Foreign Exchange Council submitted a report to the minister of finance, calling for (1) complete liberalization of cross-border financial transactions by abolishing prior approval or notification requirements, (2) abolishment of authorized foreign exchange banks and designated securities companies in order to increase the depth of the market, and (3) abolishment in principle of approval or notification requirements for outward FDI (MOF 1997).[24]

The Diet passed the new Foreign Exchange and Foreign Trade Law in May 1997, and the law came into force on 1 April 1998 (with the word *control* removed from the title). The 1980 Foreign Exchange Law was revised to shift the legal basis of oversight from prior approval or application to ex-post reporting requirements, if any. In particular, as recommended by the 1997 Foreign Exchange Council report, prior approval or notification requirements were in principle abolished; instead, ex-post-facto reporting requirements were prescribed for transactions exceeding a stipulated amount for statistical purposes. The systems of authorized foreign exchange banks and designated securities companies were abolished.[25] As a result, nonfinancial institutions were allowed to deal directly in foreign exchange transactions without inter-mediation by authorized foreign exchange banks, and Japanese residents were freely allowed to open and maintain deposit and brokerage accounts with financial institutions located in foreign countries. The monopoly of banks in the foreign exchange business was terminated.[26]

Authorities anticipated an exodus of funds when the new Foreign Exchange Law took effect. The portfolio shift from yen to dollars (and other currencies) might have also been magnified by attempts by domestic institutions to offer better terms on their foreign currency deposits. In the event, the yen did depreciate against the dollar during the first week of April, from about ¥130 to ¥135. The yen's loss, however, was fully reversed over the following week as Japanese monetary authorities intervened in the foreign exchange market to support it.[27] Beginning in the third week of April, the yen began to depreciate again until it peaked at over ¥145 in the second week of June. It is not clear if the subsequent fall of the yen was necessarily due to the big bang reforms, however, because this period also saw plenty of bad news related to the

[24] For inward FDI, prior notification requirements had been abolished in principle in 1992, with only ex-post reporting requirements retained.

[25] At the same time, procedures were introduced whereby economic sanctions could be imposed in order to meet Japan's international obligations or for other political purposes. In 2001 and 2004, the law was further strengthened in this area, especially with regard to international terrorism and money laundering activities.

[26] Up to this point, Japanese residents had been allowed to maintain deposits with overseas banks up to ¥5 million (since July 1989), ¥30 million (since July 1990), ¥100 million (since March 1994), and ¥200 million (since April 1996). See Table 5.6.

[27] On 9–10 April 1998, they sold over 20 billion dollars for 2.8 trillion yen.

Japanese economy. The lasting impact of the financial big bang appears to lie in the workings of the foreign exchange market. Both the bid-ask spreads of dealer quotes and exchange rate volatility declined, with little impact on the volume of trading, suggesting that competition and efficiency increased in the foreign exchange market (Ito and Melvin 1999).

5.4.3. The Subcouncil on Yen Internationalization

The subsequent five years (July 1998–January 2003) saw an intensification of government efforts to internationalize the yen. The work began in July 1998, when the minister of finance requested that the Foreign Exchange Council investigate and deliberate the internationalization of the yen "from the perspective of the ongoing changes in the economic and financial conditions in Japan and abroad." Work was carried out by the Council's Subcouncil on Yen Internationalization, whose interim report was issued in November (MOF 1998). The full council's final report, issued in April 1999, was almost entirely based on the interim report of the subcouncil, except for the measures that had already been implemented (MOF 1999a).

The subcouncil recognized scope for improving the yen's usability further, especially in terms of providing risk-free, highly liquid financial products as well as a benchmark. From this standpoint, it stressed the importance of improving the market for government debt. In particular, it noted that: (1) the markets for financing bills (FBs) and TBs lacked depth; (2) the repurchase (repo) market in Japan was based on borrowing and lending of bonds with cash collateral (whereas, in the United States and Europe, the repo market was based on sale or purchase of securities with a repurchase or resale agreement); (3) the long-term government bond market was not liquid across maturities and did not allow efficient formation of a yield curve, thus limiting its usefulness as a risk-hedging device; (4) withholding tax on interest and capital gains affected cash flows and pricing and discouraged nonresidents from entering the market; and (5) the settlement system was not efficient.

To overcome these problems and help improve the operation of Japanese government debt markets, the subcouncil made the following recommendations: (1) FBs should be publicly auctioned; (2) withholding tax on capital gains for TBs and FBs should be abolished; (3) long-term government bond issues should be diversified; (4) withholding tax on interest income for nonresidents should be exempted; and (5) "delivery versus payment (DVP)" and "real time gross settlement (RTGS)" should be promoted to improve the settlement system. Decisions about some of these measures were implemented or announced even before the report of the full council was issued in April 1999, with the government making an announcement of "Measures to Facilitate the Internationalization of the Yen" in December 1998 (see Table 5.8).

Table 5.8. Selected measures taken by Japan following April 1999 report on yen internationalization

Recommendations in report	Measures taken and when
Public auction of financing bills (FBs)	Completed, April 1999
Abolish withholding tax related to public bonds	(1) Abolished for certain types of FBs and Treasury bills (TBs) issued after 1 April 1999; (2) foreign corporations exempted from withholding tax, 1 April 1999; (3) nonresidents and foreign corporations exempted from withholding tax for certain Japanese government bonds (JGBs) with interest calculated after 1 September 1999; (4) scope for tax exemption expanded for nonresidents and foreign corporations, effective April 2001
Develop repurchase (repo) market	Repo transactions based on repurchase and resale agreements introduced in April 2001
Introduce five-year interest-bearing JGBs	Introduced in February 2000
Introduce gross settlement into, and expand operating hours for, Bank of Japan Net	Completed, 4 January 2001
Establish delivery versus payments (DVP) settlement system for commercial paper (CP)	Enabling law enacted in June 2001 (with system coming into operation in March 2003)

Source: Ministry of Finance

In April 1999, authorities put in place early measures to improve the operation of Japanese government debt markets against the background of two independent considerations. First, before March 1999, almost all FBs had been purchased by the BOJ because they were issued below market terms. This allowed the MOF flexibility to manage Treasury operations without maintaining excess cash. However, authorities were concerned that central bank underwriting of FBs violated the spirit of the Fiscal Law, which prohibited the primary placement of government debt with the central bank. Second, authorities increasingly began to believe that a market for risk-free, short-term government securities should be developed in order to help internationalize the yen. In early 1999, the BOJ's Monetary Policy Board meeting under the new Bank of Japan Law agreed on the provisions governing its transactions with the government, under which the BOJ was allowed to purchase FBs on a temporary basis but the government was expected to redeem them by raising funds in the market through public auction.

At this time, Japanese authorities also decided that the maturity of FBs would be thirteen weeks; auctions were in principle to be held weekly; and FBs would no longer be underwritten by the BOJ after a transitional period of about one year. Withholding tax on capital gains was exempted for foreign corporations (followed by the exemption of withholding tax on interest income for nonresidents and foreign corporations in September 1999). Securities transactions and exchange taxes were abolished. Thirty-year Japanese government bonds (JGBs) and one-year TBs were introduced to diversify maturities. Primary placements of FBs with the central bank were entirely terminated from April 1999, except for those issued in connection with foreign exchange market interventions.

The report of the full Foreign Exchange Council, issued in April 1999, outlined remaining tasks to complete development of the infrastructure needed to increase the convenience of using the yen. These measures included: (1) development of a repo market (based on sales/purchases with repurchase/resale agreements); (2) introduction of five-year JGBs to serve as a benchmark for creating an efficient yield curve for government debt; (3) diversification of the types of JGBs, including STRIPS bonds;[28] (4) introduction of RTGS to the BOJ's clearing system (BOJ Net) by the end of FY 2000 and lengthening of operating hours; (5) achievement of DVP for the settlement of CDs and CP as early as possible (to enable full dematerialization); and (6) promotion of yen invoicing in imports to increase nonresident holding of yen. The 1999 report further noted the need to provide yen funds to nonresidents through capital transactions.

5.4.4. A Study Group on the Promotion of Yen Internationalization

By this time, all possible policy measures appear to have been exhausted. The government, however, made one more attempt in September 1999 by establishing a study group on the promotion of yen internationalization. The group, with some variations in membership, held three sessions over the subsequent four years (September 1999–June 2001, October 2001–June 2002, and September 2002–January 2003) to follow up on the April 1999 Foreign Exchange Council report's recommendations, and issued reports in June 2001 and June 2002 and a chairman's summary in January 2003. The study group's orientation became increasingly pragmatic over time as it began to focus on the specifics of how private-sector firms chose currency for international transactions.

The first report, issued in June 2001, stated that yen internationalization had changed very little (MOF 2001). It stated that the lack of progress was due to the lack of confidence in the Japanese economy and the limited need to use yen; the choice of currency was based on economic rationality. In order to further promote yen internationalization, it would be necessary to restore Japan's economy and financial system, to further open the Japanese markets, and to establish conditions necessary to improve the convenience of using the yen. The report still considered yen internationalization to be a long-term

---

[28] *STRIPS* stands for "separate trading of registered interest and principal securities."

goal, as it was supposed to contribute to greater exchange rate stability in Asia and hence to global monetary stability.

The second report, issued in June 2002, summarized the views expressed by Japanese private-sector firms engaged in cross-border transactions and attempted to explain why yen internationalization, as an outcome of market decisions, was difficult to achieve (IIMA 2002). In terms of current transactions, the report noted that the choice of invoice currency was determined by various factors, including market power, matching of product exports and material imports, international price-setting practice (as in energy products), preferences of importers and exporters, and the like; there was greater yen invoicing when Japan had market power for particular products. The report also mentioned Japanese corporate governance practices (under which minority shareholder rights were not well protected), high bank fees for converting Euroyen into yen, the absence of a sufficient number of risk investors in Japanese markets, the need to adopt international accounting standards, and the need to allow documents to be produced in English.

Finally, the chairman's summary, issued in January 2003, reiterated the possibility that yen internationalization was being slowed by Japan's prolonged stagnation and a resulting loss of confidence in the Japanese economy (MOF 2003a). The summary further recognized the role of inertia in the choice of key currency—conventions favored use of the US dollar. The summary only made broad recommendations, such as: (1) identifying and removing obstacles to yen invoicing in specific transactions; (2) providing technical support to develop the legal infrastructure in Asia needed to securitize export receivables from Japan (allowing establishment of a market for CP collateralized by export receivables); (3) developing a procedure to provide yen credits to Asian exporters through technical assistance; (4) further expanding the scope for exemption of withholding tax on capital gains for TBs and FBs held by nonresidents; and (5) allowing the offshore market to trade derivatives and JGBs. The summary had an Asia focus, suggesting the need for greater regional financial cooperation, including the development of Asian bond markets. Overall, it had few concrete measures that would be achievable in the short run.

5.5. COMPLETING THE INTERNATIONALIZATION AGENDA

5.5.1. Shifting the Focus of Internationalization

In 2003, the Japanese Government's focus shifted from internationalizing the yen to internationalizing the Japanese capital markets. A study group was set up at the MOF, with academic and private-sector participation, to consider internationalization of Japanese capital markets during March–July 2003. The chairman's summary (MOF 2003b), however, differed little from the similar summary of the preceding yen internationalization group issued in January, indicating that most of the measures perceived necessary to further internationalize the capital markets had already been implemented in the context of internationalizing the yen (see Table 5.9). Even so, the chairman's summary noted that the status of Japanese capital markets had declined as an international financial center, in terms of bond issues by nonresidents, new listing of foreign stocks, and offshore trading. The share of yen in global foreign exchange trading had also declined (see Table 5.6).

The chairman's summary saw a need to improve the intermediary role of Japanese markets in cross-border capital flows, and authorities began to see the legal, accounting, settlement, and tax systems as areas for improvement. For example, the summary noted that the administrative cost of issuing Samurai bonds (yen-denominated bonds issued in Japan by nonresidents) was high relative to Euroyen bonds and suggested that the Tokyo offshore market be used for that purpose. It also argued for creating a market for yen-denominated CP collateralized by export receivables by abolishing withholding tax on capital gains on electronic Samurai CP issued by foreign corporations. Other proposals

Table 5.9. Selected measures to internationalize Japanese capital markets, 1999–2003

Month of action	Measures taken
March 1999	Securities transactions tax abolished
April 1999	Withholding tax abolished for capital gains on Treasury bills (TBs) and financing bills (FBs)
September 1999	Income tax exempted for nonresidents on interest on certain Japanese government bonds (JGBs)
October 1999	Commissions fully deregulated in equity market
January 2001	Real time gross settlement (RTGS) introduced to current accounts at Bank of Japan and settlement of JGBs
April 2001	Repurchase (repo) transactions on resale and repurchase basis introduced
May 2001	Delivery versus payment (DVP) settlement introduced to listed stocks in Tokyo and Osaka
January 2003	Requirement of concurrent domestic exchange listing abolished for Samurai bonds
January 2003	Nonresidents allowed to participate in private placement market for Samurai bonds restricted to qualified institutional investors
January 2003	Book entry system for settlement in securities introduced
January 2003	STRIPS government bonds introduced[a]
July 2003	Securities and insurance companies allowed to participate in offshore market

[a] STRIPS stands for "separate trading of registered interest and principal securities"
Source: Ministry of Finance

included simplification of reporting requirements to promote foreign investment in Japanese capital markets, adoption of a book-entry system for the settlement of cross-border securities transactions to promote such transactions, and greater cooperation with Asian counterparts to promote the development of bond and foreign exchange markets, including eventual establishment of a settlement system in foreign exchange and securities (an "Asia Clear") and commencement of cross trading among Asia's currencies.

By this time, it was clear that any further attempt to internationalize the yen—or internationalize the Japanese capital markets for that matter—would be futile without a fundamental change in the economic might of Japan or major cooperation efforts among Asian countries to promote the role of the yen in the region. When the financial big bang of 1998–2001 did not produce the kind of results hoped for, those involved in policymaking began to advance reasons why the international status of the yen remained where it was, including: (1) raw materials (for which dollar invoicing was the norm) constituted a large share of Japan's imports; (2) the currencies of Asia tended to fluctuate more against the yen than against the US dollar, with virtually no cross trading; and (3) there was little need for yen-denominated loans because most trade was not invoiced in yen. But these were issues Japan alone could do very little to resolve.[29] It is possible that this realization—along with senior personnel changes within the MOF and a splitting of responsibilities between the MOF and the Financial Services Agency[30]—led to the apparent loss of interest in further internationalization efforts.

5.5.2. The Impact of Yen Internationalization Efforts

At the beginning of the new millennium, the international status of the yen essentially remained where it had started two decades earlier, before internationalization efforts began in earnest (see Table 5.10). The share of yen invoicing in Japanese trade did moderately rise, especially on the import side. The yen's share in import invoicing, which stood at a mere 2.4 percent in 1980, rose to more than 20 percent in the early 2000s (for export invoicing, the rise was just a few percentage points). But the share of yen in international financial transactions, including cross-border bank positions, external bond offerings and bank loans, and official foreign exchange reserves, either remained the same or declined over time after an initial increase in the

---

[29] Out of this came the argument that Japan should strengthen the yen's links to Asian currencies, including through adoption by Asian countries of a basket consisting of the dollar, the euro, and the yen (MOF 1999a).

[30] In June 1998, the financial supervisory functions had been removed from the MOF to create the Financial Supervisory Agency. The agency, by assuming the MOF's remaining planning function, was reconstituted as the Financial Services Agency in July 2000.

Table 5.10. International status of Japanese yen, 1980–2003 (in percent of total)

	Japanese trade invoicing[a]		Global cross-border bank positions[b]		Global external bond offerings[c]	Global external bank loans[c]	Global official foreign exchange reserves[d]
	Exports	Imports	Assets	Liabilities			
1980	29.4	2.4	2.1	1.8	4.9	—	4.4
1981	31.2	—	2.4	1.9	6.6	—	4.2
1982	32.2	—	2.4	1.9	5.6	3.7	4.7
1983	34.5	—	2.3	1.8	5.5	7.4	5.0
1984	33.7	—	3.1	2.2	7.1	16.3	5.8
1985	36.0	7.0	5.1	4.2	9.1	18.5	8.0
1986	36.5	9.7	7.2	5.9	10.4	16.1	7.9
1987	33.4	10.6	11.3	9.5	13.7	10.8	7.0
1988	34.3	13.3	12.3	10.1	8.4	5.6	7.1
1989	34.7	14.1	11.2	8.9	8.3	4.7	7.3
1990	37.5	14.5	10.6	8.0	13.5	1.7	8.0
1991	39.4	15.6	11.3	7.4	12.6	1.1	8.5
1992	40.1	17.0	9.8	5.9	11.2	1.4	7.5
1993	39.9	20.9	10.1	6.3	9.6	0.7	7.6
1994	39.7	19.2	11.0	6.7	13.3	0.2	7.8
1995	36.0	22.7	11.3	7.3	12.6	0.2	6.8
1996	35.2	20.6	10.2	6.9	8.6	0.2	6.0
1997	35.8	22.6	10.1	6.9	4.5	0.2	5.3
1998	36.0	21.8	10.3	7.5	—	—	6.2
1999	—	—	9.2	7.2	—	—	6.4
2000	36.1	23.5	8.4	6.6	—	—	6.1
2001	35.6	23.6	6.2	4.9	—	—	5.0
2002	36.7	25.5	5.6	4.8	—	—	4.4
2003	39.3	25.3	4.9	3.9	—	—	3.9

[a] Ministry of Finance
[b] Bank for International Settlements, *Quarterly Review*, March 2009, Table 5A (year-end values)
[c] Organization for Economic Cooperation and Development, *Financial Market Trends*, 1981–98
[d] International Monetary Fund, *Annual Report of the Executive Board*, annual issues

mid to late 1980s. For example, the share in global cross-border bank positions rose sharply in the 1980s to exceed 10 percent in the late 1980s or early 1990s before declining thereafter. Likewise, according to the International Monetary Fund (IMF)'s data on the currency breakdown of official foreign exchange reserves, the share of yen rose from 4.4 percent in 1980 to a peak of 8.5 percent in 1991 before declining to 3.9 percent in 2003 (although the balance of yen reserves held up in absolute value).[31]

---

[31] The IMF data were incomplete in terms of country and off-balance sheet coverage. Garber (1996) suggests that this may have biased the share of the yen downward. Some important Asian countries (potential holders of yen assets) were not covered in the data, and foreign monetary authorities could implicitly hold yen positions by holding dollar assets (which are more liquid) with a forward yen cover.

Recent research suggests that exchange rate management practices are the most important determinant of the pattern of official reserve holdings (Papaioannou et al. 2006). In capital transactions, the choice of investment currency depends on many factors, including the level of interest rates and market expectations about prospective exchange rate movements. In terms of current transactions, recent research highlights the relationship between the choice of invoice currency and pricing-to-market (PTM) behavior. Friberg (1998) formally shows that PTM behavior leads to invoicing in the importer's currency (since both are means of stabilizing local demand). As the destination market becomes more competitive, and the exporter's products become more substitutable for competing products from abroad, invoicing in the importer's currency becomes more prevalent (Bacchetta and van Wincoop 2005; also Bilson 1983). Sato (1999) notes that the share of yen invoicing had fallen during the 1990s in Japan's high-tech exports to Asia, likely reflecting the increased PTM behavior of exporters, whereas Fukuda and Cong (1994) had earlier found that, with limited PTM behavior in Asia, 60–75 percent of Japan's exports of automobiles and electronic products in 1991 were invoiced in yen.

The declining share of yen invoicing in Japan's exports to Asia may also reflect the formation of regional supply chains by large Japanese manufacturing firms. Ito et al. (2013), based on a 2009 survey of more than 200 Japanese exporting firms, report that yen invoicing was more prevalent when trade relationships were arm's-length, whereas US dollar or importer's currency invoicing tended to become more common in intra-firm trade (e.g., yen invoicing in 2009 for exports to the United States was 38.7 percent for local agents and 7.3 percent for subsidiaries). Moreover, the authors find that yen invoicing was less prevalent for larger firms, indicating that they engaged more in intra-firm transactions and chose not to impose foreign exchange risk on their subsidiaries; dollar invoicing was common for large firms with a global sales and production network. These considerations may to some extent explain why the yen's international use did not rise in the 1990s, according to the standard metrics of Table 5.10, as the Japanese economy became further integrated with the rest of the world.

It is not warranted, however, to draw a conclusion that Japan's currency internationalization efforts were a total failure. In the 2000s, the yen was an active borrowing currency. International investors reportedly borrowed in yen to take advantage of its low interest rates and invested the proceeds in higher yield currencies (see Hattori and Shin 2009). When Hungary, Iceland, and other European countries were hit hard by the global financial crisis of 2008, some of the household debt was said to be denominated in yen.[32] The importance of the yen in such carry-trades over the past decade, however, does not show up in a

---

[32] See, for example, C. Forelle, "The isle that rattled the world," *Wall Street Journal*, 27 December 2008; T. Mayer, "Avoiding financial collapse in the East," *Wall Street Journal*, 2 March 2009.

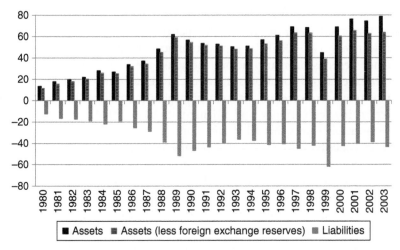

Figure 5.7. Japan's external assets and liabilities, 1980–2003 (in percent of gross domestic product)

Source: Ministry of Finance

standard metric of currency internationalization. The yen is also a highly "internationalized" currency in the sense that more than half of its trading takes place offshore: in April 2007, for example, the share of offshore trading in total global foreign exchange turnover was 67 percent for the yen, the same as the Swiss franc though lower than the US dollar (79 percent) and the euro (77 percent) (BIS 2008). But this was not what Japanese authorities had in mind when they embarked upon concerted efforts to internationalize the currency.

Japan's concerted efforts may have enhanced the necessary conditions for making the yen a major international currency of the kind that resembled the status of the deutsche mark before the launch of the euro. The lesson of 1984–2003 is that these efforts were not sufficient to make it happen against the natural forces of economics. It is possible that, as Garber (1996) argues, Japanese authorities in the end did not accept the ultimate price of full currency internationalization—giving up control over public debt management and the domestic tax base. Even so, sustained yen internationalization efforts beginning in the mid 1980s were successful in a different way: they freed up the Japanese economy from regulatory barriers inhibiting free movement of capital. The result was an accelerated financial integration of Japan with the rest of the industrial world, with the balance of cross-border assets and liabilities more than doubling over the period as a percent of gross domestic product (GDP; see Figure 5.7). Japan was now a highly financially open economy, with cross-border assets and liabilities well exceeding the size of GDP. Yen internationalization served as a banner under which parties of conflicting interests were brought together to create a highly deregulated financial system.

6

Foreign Exchange Market Intervention: 1991–2011

6.1. INTRODUCTION

When the Japanese bubble economy burst in 1991[1] economic growth decelerated and, in 1992, a prolonged period of stagnation began. From 1991 to 2011, annual growth averaged less than 1 percent, compared to more than 4 percent during the 1980s. Growth appeared to pick up in 1996 only to fall back. In 1998 severe recession set in, with negative growth in 1998 and 1999. Although annual economic growth finally exceeded 2 percent in 2004, the recovery was fragile at best. Then, the global financial crisis hit Japan hard as exports collapsed in the last quarter of 2008. This caused real gross domestic product (GDP) to contract by 1.1 and 5.5 percent, respectively, in 2008 and 2009. Even so, the Japanese yen, perceived as a safe haven currency, began an upward surge (Botman et al. 2013; De Bock and de Carvalho Filho 2013). The prolonged stagnation was compounded by sustained deflationary pressure; annual consumer price index (CPI) inflation averaged about 0.1 percent from 1991 to 2011, and producer prices actually declined by 7 percent during the period. In 2011, Japan's nominal GDP stood barely 0.3 percent above its level in 1991.

By the early 1990s, Japanese authorities had given up all direct instruments of managing the exchange rate, except for foreign exchange market intervention. Fiscal and monetary policies were still at their disposal, but aggressive easing to stimulate domestic demand and to fend off deflationary pressure quickly narrowed any remaining policy space. For example, the general government budget, which was in virtual balance in the early 1990s, deteriorated sharply (see Figure 6.1), causing the balance of gross public debt to rise from about 60 percent of GDP in 1991 to nearly 200 percent in 2011. As to monetary policy, the Bank of Japan (BOJ) cut the discount rate in several steps from 4.5 percent in December 1991 to 0.5 percent in September 1995 (see

---

[1] Stock prices peaked in December 1989 (and followed a broadly downward trend until March 2003), while real estate prices peaked in 1991.

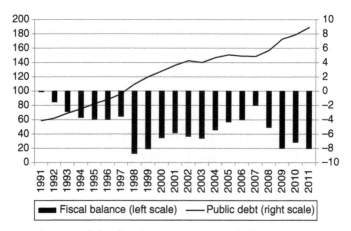

Figure 6.1. Indicators of fiscal policy in Japan, 1991–2011[a] (in percent of gross domestic product)

[a] Fiscal balance is net government lending; public debt is combined central and local government debt

Sources: International Monetary Fund, *World Economic Outlook* database, October 2013; Ministry of Finance

Figure 6.2). With no additional room left to maneuver, in February 1999, the BOJ reduced to virtually zero the overnight call rate (which, following the full deregulation of interest rates, replaced the discount rate as the main policy rate).[2] The zero interest rate policy (ZIRP) was then followed by quantitative easing monetary policy (QEMP) from March 2001 to March 2006, when the monetary base was expanded rapidly. A new round of monetary easing followed the onset of the global financial crisis in late 2008.

This chapter reviews how Japanese authorities used official foreign exchange market intervention, virtually the only remaining tool of exchange rate policy, from 1991 to 2011, a prolonged period of slow growth and deflationary pressure. Effectiveness is the chapter's overriding concern. Though details of institutional peculiarities and selected intervention episodes are presented, they are important only insofar as they have a bearing on the issue of intervention effectiveness. Fortunately, a large empirical literature has emerged on the effectiveness of Japanese intervention since the early 2000s, when the Ministry of Finance (MOF) began to disclose daily intervention data on a quarterly basis, retroactive to April 1991.[3] The chapter reviews this

---

[2] Deposit interest rates were fully deregulated in October 1994, as a result of which the BOJ in March 1995 shifted to a monetary policy operating regime based on short-term interest rates. It was further decided in January 1996 not to use the discount window as the principal tool of monetary policy. After the new Bank of Japan Law came into force in April 1998, the BOJ began to announce a target for the overnight call rate in order to fulfil accountability as an independent central bank (Shirakawa 2008; Umeda 2011).

[3] In August 2000, the MOF for the first time disclosed daily intervention data, initially covering 1 April–30 June 2000. In July 2001, it released historical data covering the period 1

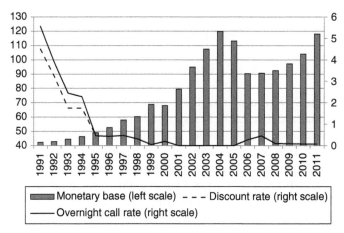

Figure 6.2. Indicators of monetary policy in Japan, 1991–2011 (in trillions of yen; percent per annum)

Source: Bank of Japan

literature to complement event-specific analyses of individual intervention episodes. In Japan, intervention decisions are made by the MOF, while the BOJ is responsible for monetary policy. Thus, the chapter also considers the issue of coordination between intervention and monetary policy (especially after the new Bank of Japan Law granted operational independence to the central bank in April 1998) because this has a particularly important bearing on the effectiveness of intervention.

   The rest of the chapter begins by providing an overview of the institutional mechanism and the main features of foreign exchange market intervention during 1991–2011, such as frequency, size, and how it was conducted, followed by an exposition of the impact of intervention on the monetary base. This sets the stage for three succeeding sections devoted to detailed analyses of major intervention episodes during three subsamples (1991–2000, 2001–4, and 2010–11), where particular attention is paid to such issues as the motives behind intervention decisions, the manner of intervention, the macroeconomic and other economic contexts, and the relationship between intervention and monetary policy. The final section reviews the empirical literature on the effectiveness of intervention in Japan and makes inferences about the channels of intervention effectiveness, concluding that each intervention episode is a unique event and therefore how and under what circumstance intervention is conducted matters for its effectiveness.

April 1991–31 March 2000, retroactively. It has since been the practice of the Japanese Government to release monthly aggregate data on a monthly basis, and daily data indicating the date, size, and currency of intervention on a quarterly basis.

6.2. AN OVERVIEW OF FOREIGN EXCHANGE
INTERVENTION IN JAPAN

6.2.1. The Legal Framework

In Japan, the government and the central bank divide responsibilities on monetary matters. The MOF is responsible for exchange rate policy, while the BOJ assumes responsibility for domestic monetary policy. The Bank of Japan Law of 1998 guarantees the central bank's independence from government oversight in its conduct of operations aimed at price and financial system stability (Cargill et al. 2000).[4] Japan is thus among the few countries—along with Canada, the United Kingdom, and the United States—in which authority to intervene rests with the government. According to a Bank for International Settlements (BIS) study, out of the twenty-two emerging market countries surveyed in December 2004, nineteen had an arrangement in which the central bank had the authority to make decisions on intervention; two out of the remaining three had a system in which the central bank and the government shared the responsibility (Moser-Boehm 2005).

Japan appears to have a particularly fragmented system in which the government seldom consults with the central bank on strategic (if not tactical) decisions related to intervention; disagreement on monetary policy was sharp between the two agencies during the early 2000s, as perceived by the public.[5] In contrast, the government and the central bank seem to work more cooperatively in other countries with a similar institutional arrangement; in the United States, for example, the Treasury and the Federal Reserve generally share the costs of intervention equally.[6] As the BOJ has no formal

---

[4] Cargill et al. (2000) discuss the background for and the nature of the 1997 revision of the Bank of Japan Law. The law was passed by the Diet in June 1997 to take effect on 1 April 1998. See also Section 5.4.2 in Chapter 5 of this volume.

[5] Part of the tension between the government and the BOJ in the early 2000s is believed to have stemmed from the central bank's desire to protect its newly acquired independence, and the public perception of such tension can be traced to the August 2000 BOJ decision to terminate ZIRP. During the 11 August Monetary Policy Board meeting in which the decision was made, the two nonvoting government representatives exercised the right granted by the 1998 Bank of Japan Law to request that a decision be postponed till the following meeting. The Policy Board unanimously rejected this request; even a member who opposed the termination of ZIRP supported the proposal to reject the government request (see Umeda 2011: pp. 82–6). Okina (2011) argues that this public display of disagreement seriously damaged the credibility of Japanese macroeconomic policymaking.

[6] In the United States, legal ambiguity exists about the respective roles of the Treasury and the Federal Reserve, but Treasury supremacy over exchange rate policy has developed through bargaining and decades of cooperation (Destler and Henning 1989). FRB (2005) states: "The Federal Reserve conducts foreign currency operations ... acting in close and continuous consultation and cooperation with the U.S. Treasury, which has overall responsibility for U.S. international financial policy." In Canada as well, the central bank is closely involved in the government's intervention decisions (Freedman 2000).

role to play in decision-making, it is inappropriate to consider official intervention in Japan as central bank intervention. Interventions are no more central bank operations than trades intermediated by a broker on behalf of clients are proprietary transactions. It is appropriate, however, to refer to the MOF and the BOJ collectively as the Japanese monetary authorities.

In this framework, the MOF—using a special account of the national budget called the Foreign Exchange Fund Special Account—intervenes in the market to purchase (or sell) dollars. To finance the costs of intervention, the MOF issues financing bills (FBs), which are short-term government notes with maturities of two months, three months, and (beginning in January 2007) six months. Although FBs have several types, almost all of them (92–9 percent during 2001–4) are associated with the Foreign Exchange Fund Special Account. Once issued, FBs are rolled over continuously as long as the underlying foreign assets remain as foreign exchange reserves. Sale of the underlying foreign assets, however, reduces the outstanding balance of FBs. Because FBs are sold to (or purchased from) the public at market rates, some have interpreted this institutional arrangement to mean that, in Japan, intervention is sterilized by design (Fatum and Hutchison 2005; Ito 2003, 2005).

This institutional feature has an important bearing on the so-called "signaling effect" of intervention. An important part of the signaling effect operates when an entity conducting intervention makes a credible commitment to a change in future monetary policy. The MOF could make such a commitment before, but not after, April 1998. Watanabe (1994) shows that a fall (rise) in the discount rate during 1973–92 and an increase (decrease) in the growth rate of money during 1976–92 were consistently preceded by purchases (sales) of foreign exchange.[7] The empirically significant influence of the exchange rate on the BOJ's monetary policy reaction function, as observed by De Andrade and Divino (2005) for 1979–94, is also consistent with what one would expect from a dependent central bank. Takagi and Okada (2013), estimating a probit model of the directional consistency between intervention and future monetary policy (the dependent variable=1 if consistent; 0 otherwise), find that the coefficient of central bank independence was negative and significant if a dummy variable was included for the period of quantitative easing (when the direction of intervention coincided with that of monetary easing). The authors thus conclude that the signaling effect of intervention diminished after April 1998.

---

[7] Okina (2011) discusses how the MOF dictated the timing and magnitude of BOJ monetary policy actions during the 1970s and 1980s.

6.2.2. The Frequency and Scale of Intervention

From April 1991 through December 2011, Japanese monetary authorities intervened in the foreign exchange market on 359 days. Nearly 99 percent of the interventions took place in the Japanese yen–US dollar market for the absolute amount of ¥84.7 trillion ($823 billion) transacted on 353 days; this amounted to ¥240 billion ($2.3 billion) per intervention day (see Table 6.1). Interventions in other market segments were rare. Authorities intervened on nineteen days in the yen–euro (or deutsche mark) market, for the total amount of ¥1.1 trillion; these all involved sales of yen and, except on two days, they were conducted simultaneously with interventions in the yen–dollar market. Only once did authorities intervene in selling dollars against deutsche

Table 6.1. Japanese foreign exchange market intervention, April 1991–December 2011[a] (amounts in billions of national currency units)

	April 1991– March 2004	First regime	Second regime[b]	Third regime[c]	April 2004– December 2011
		April 1991– May 1995	June 1995– December 2002	January 2003– March 2004	
Absolute yen amount	68,281.1	7,747.9	25,455.4	35,077.8	16,422.0
US dollar equivalents[d]	612.4	76.1	221.0	315.2	210.4
Number of intervention days (per month)	345 (2.2)	165 (3.3)	51 (0.6)	129 (8.6)	8 (0.1)
Of which, coordinated with US authorities[e]	22	18	4	0	1
Average size	197.9	47.0	499.1	271.9	2,052.8
Yen sales	63,401.7	6,974.6	21,349.3	35,077.8	16,422.0
Number of days	313	139	45	129	8
Average size	202.6	50.2	474.4	271.9	2,052.8
Yen purchases	4,879.4	773.3	4,106.1	0	0
Number of days	32	26	6	0	0
Average size	152.5	29.7	684.4	—	—
Memo: Absolute dollar amount of US interventions	8.4	6.4	2.0	—	1.0

[a] Includes only transactions involving yen against US dollars

[b] The first intervention of the month took place on 28 June, following the appointment of Eisuke Sakakibara as director general

[c] The first intervention of the month took place on 15 January, following the appointment of Zenbei Mizoguchi as vice minister

[d] Converted at monthly average exchange rates

[e] All US interventions in yen–dollar market during this period were coordinated with Japanese monetary authorities

Sources: Author's estimates based on www.mof.go.jp; Board of Governors of the Federal Reserve System, *Federal Reserve Bulletin*, monthly issues; IMF, *International Financial Statistics*

marks, for the equivalent of ¥14 billion. On six consecutive trading days in November 1997, authorities purchased rupiah against US dollars for the equivalent of ¥69 billion in support of Indonesia's crisis management program with the International Monetary Fund (IMF).

Japanese authorities intervened in the foreign exchange market rather actively from 13 May 1991 through 16 March 2004, when they all but ceased intervention. It was not until six and a half years later, on 15 September 2010, that they resumed intervention. This was followed by isolated episodes on 18 March 2011, on 4 August 2011, and on five consecutive days from 31 October to 4 November 2011, all involving sales of yen. The scale of these later operations was large, however, amounting in just eight days to nearly 20 percent of the total for the entire 1991–2011 period. The intervention that took place on 31 October 2011, at ¥8.7 trillion ($105 billion), remains the largest ever conducted by Japanese authorities on a single day (the second largest was the sale of ¥4.5 trillion on 4 August 2011). Clearly, the period following March 2004 should be considered distinct from the previous period.

Focusing on 1991–2004, Ito (2003, 2007) proposes that the period be broken down into three distinct regimes, the dividing points associated with the appointments of Eisuke Sakakibara as director general of the MOF's International Finance Bureau in June 1995 and of Zenbei Mizoguchi as vice minister of finance for international affairs in January 2003. Each regime represented a different intervention tactic. During the first regime, interventions were conducted frequently (3.3 times a month) but in small lots (¥47 billion per day); under the second regime, interventions were infrequent (0.6 times a month), but the scale was large when authorities did intervene (¥500 billion per day). This tactical change was similar to what had occurred in other advanced countries in the 1990s (Galati and Melick 2002).[8] But, under the final regime of the 1991–2004 period (i.e., January 2003–March 2004), interventions became frequent (8.6 times a month) while remaining relatively large in scale (¥272 billion per day).

Routine intervention decisions in Japan are typically made by a small group of MOF officials that includes the minister of finance, the vice minister for international affairs, the director general of the International Bureau (known as the International Finance Bureau prior to June 1998), and several other line officers. The decisions are transmitted to the trading desk at the BOJ for execution. Because the minister is typically a career politician with little professional knowledge, he often defers to the judgment of the vice minister in technical matters, although the minister or even the prime minister may

---

[8] Truman (2003) offers an interpretation of why intervention operations have become larger (and, as a consequence, less frequent): to ensure that monetary authorities inflict some damage on the traders' positions before extricating themselves from the market without admitting failure.

become personally involved when the exchange rate becomes highly politi-cized. Sakakibara (2000: p. 120) says that, when he was appointed as director general on 21 June 1995, he persuaded both the minister (Masayoshi Take-mura) and the vice minister (Takatoshi Kato) to change the tactics of inter-vention, from small and frequent smoothing operations to less frequent but more decisive ones. The same general tactic was retained (with greater inten-sity) when he became vice minister on 15 July 1997, as well as after he was succeeded in the position by Haruhiko Kuroda on 8 July 1999.[9] As a notable exception to this pattern, authorities intervened on seven days in September 2001, when the 11 September terrorist attacks on US soil caused the US dollar to depreciate from more than ¥120 toward ¥115 in ten days. On this occasion, they sold yen both for US dollars and (on three days) for euros.

The tactics changed again when Mizoguchi succeeded Kuroda as vice minister on 14 January 2003; this intervention regime is often called the "great intervention" (Taylor 2006). Faced with appreciation pressure when the economy was trapped in deflation (Mizoguchi 2004), Japanese authorities sold 35 trillion yen (about $315 billion) during the fifteen-month period, while the monetary base was allowed to expand by ¥15 trillion. Thus, the interven-tion was considered partially unsterilized and, as such, received the support of US authorities, whose position was to "help to increase the money supply in Japan" by "adopting a more tolerant position toward intervention" (Taylor 2007: p. 286).[10] Despite the determined interventions, the yen appreciated against the US dollar over the period by some 15 percent in nominal terms, from ¥120 at the end of 2002 to ¥104 at the end of March 2004.

6.2.3. The Characteristics of Intervention

Some of these interventions were coordinated with the monetary authorities of other major industrial countries. Out of the 345 days on which interventions took place in the yen–dollar market during 1991–2004, the operations were coordinated on twenty-two days with US authorities; nearly all of these interventions (eighteen) took place under the first regime, while US authorities did not enter the market at all under the last regime. Out of the twenty-two days of coordinated intervention, US authorities sold yen for dollars on eighteen days and purchased yen for dollars on four days. The single largest

---

[9] The average size of intervention when Sakakibara and Kuroda successively held the post of vice minister was 60 percent larger compared to the Kato era when Sakakibara had served as director general. In this sense, the celebrated Sakakibara regime did not strictly begin until July 1997.

[10] For this reason, the great intervention is also known in Japan as the Mizoguchi–Taylor intervention after Mizoguchi and John B. Taylor, who, as undersecretary of the US Treasury, was largely responsible for condoning the Japanese Government's intervention decisions.

intervention by US authorities was a sale of 833 million dollars on 17 June 1998, when their Japanese counterparts also intervened to sell approximately 1.6 billion dollars. Generally, US interventions were in relatively small lots, with an average size of $382 million, slightly less than the average size (about $460 million) of Japanese interventions during the first regime. The only coordinated intervention of the post-2004 period took place on 18 March 2011, when Japanese authorities were joined by their counterparts from Canada, the euro area, the United Kingdom, and the United States.

Kim and Le (2010)—by searching news reports from Reuters, the *Wall Street Journal*, the *Financial Times*, and other sources—identify that, of the 345 days of intervention during 1991–2004, intervention operations were known ("public") at the time they were conducted on 219 days, while on 126 days they were not known ("secret"). Beine and Bernal (2007), in explaining why some interventions remain unreported, stress the importance of separating the inability of the market to detect interventions from monetary authorities' desire to keep them secret. Their estimation of a logit model (with secrecy = 1) for 1991–2004 suggests that interventions were more likely to be detected if they were larger, coordinated, and clustered, while authorities preferred to intervene secretly when they were attempting to guide the exchange rate away from equilibrium. More generally, how authorities engage the market must reflect their view of what strategy would work to achieve a particular goal.

For instance, interventions under Mizoguchi were conducted almost entirely in secret, whereas under Kato, Sakakibara, and Kuroda, authorities attempted to influence the market also through communications: according to Bloomberg and Reuters, nearly 98 percent of the interventions were reported during 1996–2002, while for 2003–04 only 21 percent were detected on the same day (Beine and Bernal 2007; Beine and Lecourt 2004). Frequently, authorities used "vocal" or "oral" interventions, that is, official statements indicating the exchange rate's desired level or direction of change, a tool that has increasingly replaced actual interventions in other major industrial countries (Fratzscher 2005). Between January 2000 and August 2003, Park and Song (2008) identified 381 such interventions reported in the financial press (cf. sixty actual interventions),[11] whose frequency tended to rise when the yen appreciated against the US dollar; they also found that actual interventions typically followed several days of vocal interventions that had proven ineffective.

Reflecting the four prominent waves of sustained appreciation over the period (see Figure 6.3), Japanese authorities intervened more frequently to

---

[11] Fratzscher (2005) counts only 137 such interventions (cf. 278 actual interventions) during 1990–2003. Vocal interventions were shown to respond much less systematically to market and monetary policy developments than did actual interventions.

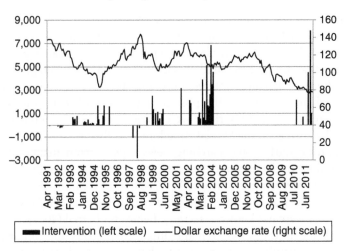

Figure 6.3. Japanese foreign exchange intervention and yen–dollar exchange rate, April 1991–December 2011 (in billions of yen; yen per US dollar)

Sources: Ministry of Finance; IMF, *International Financial Statistics*

sell yen than to buy yen: total sales were ¥79.8 trillion on 321 days, compared to total purchases of ¥4.9 trillion on thirty-two days. No yen-purchasing intervention took place under the last regime of 1991–2004 or thereafter. For the period 1990–2003, Fratzscher's (2005) logit analysis shows that Japanese intervention was biased toward weakening the yen, while US intervention showed the opposite tendency. Even so, Japanese authorities made some determined efforts to stem downward pressure on the yen when the currency, starting at a relatively depreciated level, began to edge further downward—for example, in the spring and summer of 1992 and late 1997–early 1998, in the aftermath of the Asian financial crisis when Japan was also mired in an evolving banking crisis (see Section 6.3.3). In fact, the single largest intervention of the 1991–2004 period took place on 10 April 1998, when Japanese authorities *purchased* 2.6 trillion yen (about $20 billion). During the entire period, no yen sales took place when the yen was above (more depreciated than) ¥125 to the dollar, and no yen purchases took place when the yen was below that level.

6.2.4. The Monetary Consequence of Intervention

As in any modern central banking system where monetary policy decisions are independent of government oversight, intervention is automatically sterilized in Japan given the stance of monetary policy. Otherwise, intervention would affect either the policy interest rate or the target monetary base, which is determined by the Monetary Policy Board through a transparent decision-making process when it meets once or twice a month according to a pre-announced schedule. The recent literature on Japan has given misguided emphasis to its institutional peculiarities, under which the MOF issues FBs to finance the costs of intervention. The need for a modern, independent central bank to sterilize intervention does not depend on the way the financing of intervention operations is set up. However, intervention does not need to be sterilized if it is accompanied by a simultaneous shift in the stance of monetary policy.

There are at least five channels through which a sale of yen by fiscal authorities can have a positive effect on the monetary base. First, FBs issued for intervention purposes are purchased by the BOJ in their entirety. Because auctions for FBs are held at most weekly, there is no other practical way to conduct foreign exchange market intervention in a flexible and timely manner. Before the end of FY 1998 (i.e., March 1999), the BOJ had purchased almost all primary issues of FBs because they were issued below market terms and there was thus little public demand for them (see Section 5.4.3 in Chapter 5). In April 1999, the MOF began to issue FBs on market terms and the BOJ, on its part, decided to reduce the balance of FBs in its portfolio (see Figure 6.4). But the BOJ began to build up the balance of FBs again in early 2003. When intervention is frequent, it is not practical for the BOJ expeditiously to dispose of the FBs it has purchased. Given the continuous rollover needs, the MOF usually does not repurchase the BOJ-held FBs all at once, especially if a large amount is involved.[12]

Second, outright purchases of Japanese government bonds (JGBs) are used as the principal means of expanding the monetary base and can be employed to unsterilize foreign exchange market intervention. The balance of JGBs in the BOJ's portfolio steadily rose over the period 1991–2011, from around ¥10 trillion to nearly ¥70 trillion in 2004. The balance then declined before rising again in 2010 (see Figure 6.4). In order to avoid the appearance of monetizing government debt, however, the BOJ adhered to the self-imposed rule that the balance of JGBs should remain below the outstanding balance of BOJ notes (Maeda et al. 2005). Given this constraint, the increase in the balance of currency notes was almost equally matched by an increase in BOJ holding of JGBs, so the expansion of other components of base money was supported by the acquisition of other assets, mostly discount bills (see the next paragraph).

---

[12] According to an official of the MOF's Financial Bureau, as a general rule, an auction can accommodate as much as ¥300 billion of new FB issues. This means that if there were a yen-selling intervention of ¥900 billion, it would take a minimum of three subsequent weekly auctions to unwind the position at the BOJ. Kato and Nakakita (2010) observe that it occasionally took several months for the FBs purchased by the BOJ to be redeemed when the scale of intervention was large.

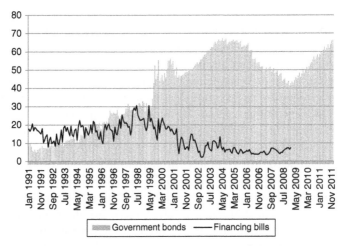

Figure 6.4. Monthly balances of financing bills (1991–2008) and government bonds (1991–2011) held by Bank of Japan[a] (in trillions of yen)

[a] The Bank of Japan ceased to publish the balance of financing bills separate from Treasury bills after February 2009 because from that month on they were issued collectively as Treasury discount bills (T-bills)
Source: Bank of Japan

Third, the BOJ can also influence the balance of base money through open market operations in other securities—typically short-term discount bills—or though short-term lending operations. To expand the monetary base on a permanent basis, the BOJ in recent years has resorted to extraordinary measures of purchasing various types of private securities. For example, the BOJ made outright purchases of stocks held by financial institutions from November 2002 to September 2004 and again from February 2009 to April 2010; and, from July 2003 to March 2006, the BOJ purchased asset-backed securities (ABS) as a time-bound measure to improve the flow of funds to small and medium-sized firms. In the aftermath of the global financial crisis, in 2009, the BOJ began outright purchases of commercial paper (CP) and asset-backed CP (ABCP) (in January) as well as corporate bonds (in February). In October 2010, the BOJ established a ¥5 trillion fund to purchase various types of assets, including CP, corporate bonds, Tokyo Stock Exchange-traded real estate investment trusts (J-REIT), and beneficiary certificates of index-linked investment trusts (the size of the fund would be raised in several steps to ¥91 trillion in October 2012).

Fourth, the BOJ can provide short-term liquidity to the government under exceptional circumstances. For example, on 26 December 2003, the MOF reached an agreement with the BOJ to sell US Treasury bills held as foreign exchange reserves. This agreement came about in a circumstance where the massive dollar-purchasing intervention of 2003 had caused the balance of FBs to reach the statutory limit set by the National Diet. Specifically, the agreement noted that this was a time-bound measure whereby the BOJ would be prepared to purchase TBs from the Foreign Exchange Fund Special Account up to ¥10 trillion until the end of March 2004; it also specified that the BOJ would resell the US Treasury bills back to the Foreign Exchange Fund Special Account within three months from purchase. In the event, the maximum of ¥6.15 trillion of short-term liquidity was provided to the MOF under this scheme, which was all unwound during the month of June 2004.

Finally, the MOF can purchase part of the new issues of FBs by using its own excess cash or funds in various government accounts. As the scale and frequency of intervention became progressively large in the early 2000s, the MOF increasingly utilized this scheme in order to prevent the clustering of large FB issues. Kato and Nakakita (2010) estimate that, in January 2004, more than ¥10 trillion of FBs was held within the national budget through inter-account cash transfers; likewise, more than ¥20 trillion of excess Treasury funds was used to purchase FBs. Yen sales financed by the Treasury's own cash or funds would directly increase the monetary base, since government deposits are transferred to the current account balances (CAB) on the liabilities side of the central bank balance sheet.

6.3. INTERVENTION TO LEAN AGAINST THE WIND: 1991–2000

6.3.1. Determinants of Intervention Decisions

The period 1991–2000 began with a perceived yen weakness, so intervention was initially in the direction of strengthening the yen. In fact, there was no yen-selling intervention for almost five years, from the end of 1988 to April 1993 (Sakakibara 2000). As the yen began to appreciate (the exchange rate edged lower from ¥125 in January to ¥110 in May 1993), the direction of intervention shifted to weakening the yen, which became progressively frequent. In 1995, authorities sold yen for dollars twenty-six times between February and May, during which time the exchange rate temporarily fell below ¥80. Although intervention became infrequent following the appointment in May 1995 of Sakakibara as director general, it occurred on five consecutive days in February 1996, apparently designed to encourage yen depreciation. In December 1997, the direction of intervention shifted again to strengthening the yen, as the currency had begun to depreciate significantly (it would cross the ¥140 mark in the summer of 1998). For the most part, the intervention of this period was of the "lean-against-the-wind (LATW)" type.

A number of empirical studies support the observation that Japanese authorities followed an LATW intervention strategy from the early 1990s through the beginning of the 2000s, whereby they purchased yen when it was "weak" and sold yen when it was "strong" (see Table 6.2). Broadly, there are two types of studies that attempt to identify the major determinants of intervention decisions. One type uses the size of the intervention, expressed in yen, as the dependent variable, while the other type employs a discrete choice variable, such as: (1) intervention versus no intervention; (2) yen-selling intervention, no intervention, or yen-purchasing intervention; or (3) large versus small intervention, in a probit or ordered probit setup. In both cases, similar explanatory variables (such as exchange rate changes and deviations from target or average exchange rates) are used, and the conclusions are also similar.

Studies differ in the identification of exchange rate variables to which intervention was seen to respond. Daily or monthly exchange rate changes are consistently found to be significant determinants of intervention, as is a deviation of the exchange rate from some "target" value. The targets frequently selected include a moving average exchange rate calculated over some period (from a month to five years) and ¥125 per dollar. In these studies, the significant explanatory power of a deviation from ¥125 reflects the fact that that yen was never sold above or purchased below ¥125. This does not mean that Japanese authorities had a particular level of exchange rate they were defending. The yen–dollar rate fluctuated considerably, often deviating away from ¥125 (or any supposed level) in either direction for a sustained period of time without monetary authorities necessarily intervening.

The tactical difference between the first and the second regime was statistically confirmed by Ito (2003), whose regression of the size of intervention over a set of explanatory variables yielded an R-squared of 0.345 under the first regime when intervention was frequent (but small) and an R-squared of 0.025 under the second when intervention was infrequent (but large). Moreover, the coefficient for the target deviation, significant under both regimes, was five times larger under the second regime. Likewise, replicating the same procedure in an ordered probit framework (sales, none, purchases), Ito and Yabu (2007) found that the distance between the two thresholds (where no intervention takes place) was much wider under the second regime than under the first, and the thresholds were tolerant more toward yen appreciation under the first regime but more toward depreciation under the second.

With respect to the influence of foreign exchange market volatility, the findings are inconclusive. Galati et al. (2005) used the second moment of the risk-neutral density (RND) of expectations extracted from currency options to show that the coefficient was positive and significant during September 1993–February 1996 and November 1997–April 2000, especially when the yen was strengthening. In contrast, Frenkel et al. (2005) used the five-day moving

	Dependent variable; methodology	Main explanatory variables	Significant major determinants[b]		
			First regime	Second regime	Third regime
1. Ito (2003)	Size of intervention; time-series	Lagged daily and monthly exchange rate changes; lagged deviation from ¥125; lagged Japan/US interventions; dummies for unilateral/ coordinated interventions	(April 1991–June 1995) Deviation from ¥125; monthly exchange rate change	(June 1995–March 2001) Deviation from ¥125; daily exchange rate change	n.a.
2. Frenkel et al. (2003)	Discrete choice variable; ordered probit (no, unilateral, coordinated interventions)	Contemporaneous deviation from ¥125; contemporaneous deviation from 25-day moving average (MA); conditional variance from GARCH (as measure of volatility); lagged intervention	(1991–2001) Deviation from ¥125; deviation from 25-day MA; lagged intervention (GARCH variance has negative, statistically significant sign)	n.a.	n.a.
3. Frenkel et al. (2004)	Discrete choice variable; ordered probit (no, small, large interventions)	Contemporaneous deviation from 25-day MA; contemporaneous deviation from ¥125; lagged intervention; lagged daily exchange rate change	(January 1991–May 1995) Deviation from ¥125; deviation from 25-day MA; lagged intervention	(January 1995–December 2001) Deviation from ¥125; daily exchange rate change; lagged intervention	n.a.
4. Ito (2005)	Size of intervention; time-series	Lagged daily exchange rate change; lagged deviations from long-term backward MA; lagged intervention; and futures positions	n.a.	n.a.	(January 2003–March 2004) Daily exchange rate change; lagged intervention; long yen futures positions
5. Galati et al. (2005)	Size of intervention; time-series	Lagged exchange rate deviation from implicit target; deviations of second to fourth moments of option prices from historical means	(September 1993– February 1996) Deviation from target; deviation of second moment from historical mean	(November 1997–April 2000) Deviation of second moment from historical mean	n.a.

(continued)

Table 6.2. Continued

	Dependent variable; methodology	Main explanatory variables	Significant major determinants[b]		
			First regime	Second regime	Third regime
6. Frenkel et al. (2005)	Discrete choice variable (probit); size of intervention (friction model—ordered probit)	5-day MA of implied volatility of foreign currency options; 5-day MA exchange rate deviation from ¥125; lagged intervention	(January 1993–December 2000) 5-day MA deviation from ¥125; lagged intervention		n.a.
7. Kearns and Rigobon (2005)[c]	Size of intervention; friction model (jointly with impact on exchange rate)	Contemporaneous exchange rate change (in one specification, 1- and 2-day-lagged exchange rate changes; 1- and 2-day-lagged interventions)	(May 1992–June 2002) Contemporaneous exchange rate change		n.a.
8. Kim and Sheen (2006)	Size of intervention; friction model	Lagged exchange rate deviation from 150-day MA; conditional volatility; unexpected positive volume change; daily changes in Japanese/US interest rates; cumulative profits from intervention; lagged intervention	(May 1991–June 1995) Deviation from MA; unexpected increase in volume; lagged intervention; daily change in Japanese interest rate (positive)	(June 1995–March 2004) Exchange rate deviation from MA; unexpected increase in volume; lagged intervention; daily change in Japanese overnight interest rate (negative); cumulative profits from interventions	
9. Hillebrand and Schnable (2006)	Discrete choice variable; probit	Lagged exchange rate change; deviation of sample average exchange rate from 1-month-lagged exchange rate; squared lagged exchange rate change, lagged dependent variable	(1991–2004) Daily exchange rate change; medium-term deviation; lagged dependent variable		

10. Ito and Yabu (2007)[d]	Discrete choice variable; ordered probit (sales, none, purchases)	Lagged daily exchange rate change; lagged monthly exchange rate change; lagged exchange rate deviations from 1-, 3-, and 5-year MAs; lagged intervention	(April 1991–June 1995) Daily and monthly exchange rate changes; deviation from 5-year MA; lagged intervention	(June 1995–December 2002) Daily and monthly exchange rate changes; deviation from 5-year MA; lagged intervention	n.a.	
11. Fatum and Hutchison (2010)	Discrete choice variable; logit (yen-selling and no interventions)	Lagged daily and monthly exchange rate changes; lagged deviation from 1-year MA; lagged intervention; macroeconomic news (positive or negative surprises) on announcement days	n.a.	(January 1999–December 2002) Daily and monthly exchange rate changes; inflation news; lagged intervention	(January 2003–December 2003) Daily and monthly exchange rate changes; lagged intervention	(January–March 2004) Economic growth news; lagged intervention
12. Chen et al. (2012)	Discrete choice variable; Tobit-GARCH (for yen sales only)	Daily exchange rate change; exchange rate deviation from 150-day MA; exchange rate deviation from 21-day MA; US intervention; interest rate differential; stock price index; lagged intervention	Exchange rate deviation from 21-day MA; exchange rate deviation from 150-day MA; US and lagged intervention	Daily exchange rate change; exchange rate deviation from 150-day MA; US and lagged intervention	Daily exchange rate change; exchange rate deviation from 150-day MA; lagged intervention	

Abbreviation: GARCH=generalized autoregressive conditional heteroskedasticity

[a] The first, second, and third regimes correspond to the periods April 1991–June 1995, June 1995–December 2003, and January 2003–March 2004, respectively

[b] The results for the combined sample, when obtained, are not reported in the table

[c] The study also covers Australia

[d] The results from estimating the conventional reaction function are similar and are not reported in the table

average of the implied volatility of foreign currency options to find that volatility had no statistically significant influence on intervention decisions. Frenkel et al. (2003), in an event study that used the generalized autoregressive conditional heteroskedasticity (GARCH) errors from an exchange rate equation as a measure of volatility, found that volatility had a *negative* influence on intervention. The weaker (or perverse) impact of volatility in the latter two studies may to some extent be an artifact of the event study methodology because the sensitivity of a discrete variable to a marginal change in volatility—however it is measured—cannot be high.

Was the reaction function symmetric with respect to large and small interventions? Frenkel et al. (2004) used an ordered probit model to find that, under the first and second regimes, large interventions were mainly motivated by contemporaneous deviations from ¥125 and that, under the first regime, small interventions were influenced more by contemporaneous deviations from the twenty-five-day moving average. These results suggest that intervention became more determined when the yen's depreciation or appreciation was carried too far, but they should not be taken to imply that authorities were defending a particular level of exchange rate for any length of time. The authors defined *large* or *small* in relation to the subsample mean so that large interventions under the first regime could be much smaller than small interventions under the second regime. This may explain the absence of statistical significance for deviations from the twenty-five-day moving average in explaining small interventions under the second regime.

6.3.2. Attempts to Stem the Tide of Yen Appreciation: 1994–5

The yen experienced a prolonged phase of appreciation from early 1993 to the spring of 1995. This occurred in an environment where the new US administration of President Bill Clinton focused on Japan's large current account surplus with the United States, intimating that a higher yen would be desirable for helping to close the imbalance. The yen, starting from around ¥125 per dollar at the beginning of 1993, appreciated to nearly ¥100 in the middle of August. After edging back somewhat, the yen renewed its upward trend in early 1994. The yen–dollar exchange rate fell below ¥100 in June 1994, moved toward ¥90 in early March 1995, and edged further down toward ¥80 in April 1995.

The sustained appreciation of the yen was linked to the tension between the two countries over bilateral trade issues, and many in the market expected the yen to continue to appreciate as long as Japan's current account surplus remained large and the United States made an issue of it (Sakakibara 2000). When bilateral trade talks collapsed in February 1994, the exchange rate reacted violently, despite the fact that economic fundamentals were moving in favor of strengthening the US dollar. From this time on, the US Federal Reserve began to tighten monetary policy. The federal funds rate, which had been 3 percent, was raised by 0.25 percentage points in early February and would eventually reach 6 percent a year later. When the US Government tried to force Japan to set numerical targets for buying American automobiles and components in early 1995, the yen appreciated from ¥100 to ¥80 per dollar (McKinnon and Ohno 1997).

The year 1993 saw the Japanese economy trapped in recession. Real GDP grew by a mere 0.9 percent for the year. While the economy would eventually grow by nearly 2 percent in 1994, a strong yen could have derailed the nascent recovery by putting the brakes on net exports. It was against this background that authorities made determined attempts to stem the tide of yen appreciation from April 1993 through 1995. The intervention in April 1993 was the first sale of yen in the foreign exchange market in nearly five years. Although the US Government took a tough stance on trade issues, US officials were not prepared to see a free fall of the dollar, either. They participated in coordinated intervention with their Japanese counterparts to defend the dollar on a number of occasions, including five times during April–August 1993 and another five times during April–November 1994. Coordinated intervention in defense of the dollar took place again in 1995, twice in early March, and twice more in early April.

Despite these efforts, the yen's rise was unstoppable. The yen–dollar exchange rate briefly fell below the ¥80 mark to reach the then post-World War II high of ¥79.75 during morning trading on 19 April 1995.[13] At this stage, authorities from major industrial countries shared the view that yen appreciation had gone too far. The Group of Seven (G7) finance ministers and central bank governors, meeting in Washington on 25 April 1995, issued a statement expressing their "concerns" that "recent movements [had] gone beyond the levels justified by underlying economic conditions in the major countries" and calling for an "orderly reversal of those movements." Any reaction of the exchange rate to this announcement was short-lived. On 31 May 1995, monetary authorities from twelve advanced countries jointly intervened in the foreign exchange market; US authorities purchased 500 million dollars against approximately 42.3 billion yen, while Japanese authorities sold 63.5 billion yen for approximately 750 million dollars. The exchange rate hardly moved (see Figure 6.5). The unilateral intervention of ¥43 billion (approximately $510 million) by Japanese authorities on 28 June 1995 did not seem to make a difference, either.

---

[13] Chinn (1997), by estimating the quarterly real yen–dollar exchange rate in terms of productivity and fiscal policy differentials between Japan and the United States, finds that the yen was overvalued by some 16 percent in mid 1995 when it was ¥85 to the dollar.

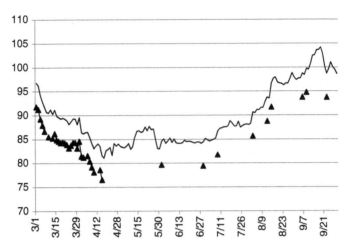

Figure 6.5. Japanese foreign exchange intervention and yen–dollar exchange rate, March–September 1995[a]

[a] A triangle indicates a day of intervention
Source: Spot closing rates from WEFA Group

The yen finally turned the corner after the Japan–US coordinated intervention of 7 July 1995, which involved a sale of 57.9 billion yen (for approximately 667 million dollars) by Japanese authorities and a purchase of 333.3 million dollars (for approximately 29 billion yen) by US authorities. This was accompanied by a BOJ decision to guide the overnight call rate to the then historic low of 0.75 percent, below the official discount rate. The next intervention, on 2 August, was of the LATW kind. Japanese authorities intervened just as Finance Minister Masayoshi Takemura announced a package of foreign investment promotion measures for Japanese institutional investors.[14] As Japanese and US authorities jointly intervened in the New York market, the yen depreciated from ¥87 to ¥90 per dollar. According to a participant, the MOF kept intervening all night until the ¥90 mark was crossed (Sakakibara 2000). On 15 August, they were joined by German authorities. The yen fell to ¥94.50 during midday trading, helped also by the release of lower-than-expected Japanese trade surplus numbers (FRB, December 1995).

The final interventions of this episode took place on 6, 8, and 22 September, when the yen evidently reversed the depreciating trend. The interventions of 8 and 22 September were well-planned, well-coordinated, and well-executed operations. First, on 8 September, the intervention took place just as the BOJ

---

[14] The measures consisted of (1) liberalization of foreign currency-denominated external lending by insurance companies, (2) relaxation of rules governing yen-denominated external lending by insurance companies, (3) elimination of restrictions on the repatriation of nonresident Euroyen bonds, (4) revision of the valuation method for foreign bonds held by institutional investors, and (5) promotion of purchases of foreign bonds by banks by relaxing foreign exchange position controls.

announced that it was cutting the discount rate from 1.0 to 0.5 percent, an action welcomed by US Treasury Secretary Robert Rubin within thirty minutes, in accordance with a prior arrangement. Sakakibara (2000) says that he had conveyed to the BOJ, then under government oversight, his desire to coordinate the intervention with an interest rate cut. Second, on 20 September, the intervention took place just as the government announced a ¥14 trillion economic stimulus package. By this time, the yen had already depreciated to ¥104.68, in anticipation of the unveiling of the fiscal package. It appears that, on both of these occasions, the purpose of the intervention was to make sure that the yen–dollar exchange rate stayed above the ¥100 mark.

6.3.3. Stemming the Free Fall of the Yen: 1998

In 1998, Japanese authorities faced the opposite problem—a sustained depreciation of the yen, which had begun in 1995 but accelerated in the summer of 1997. The yen, which stood at ¥114 per dollar at the end of June 1997, depreciated close to ¥130 toward the end of the year and moved in June 1998 above the ¥140 mark. The depreciation occurred against the background of a weak financial sector, which had been hit hard by prolonged economic stagnation. With slow growth, deflation, and a collapse of asset prices, especially in the real estate market, the balance of nonperforming loans held by banks had risen sharply, putting a large number of banks in difficulty (Hoshi 2001). The problem was compounded by the onset of the Asian financial crisis in July 1997, which caused international investors to reassess the health of the Japanese banking sector, given its large exposure to the region. As foreign investors began to pull out of the equity market, especially out of financial sector stocks, the Nikkei stock average fell precipitously (e.g., from more than 20,000 in June to less than 16,500 in October).

This was a bleak moment for the Japanese economy, as it had become evident that growth was decelerating. As it turned out, real GDP would fall by 2 percent in 1998, and negative growth would continue for another year. It was under these circumstances that, in November 1997, three major financial firms—Sanyo Securities, Hokkaido Takushoku Bank, and Yamaichi Securities— failed, bringing down the stock prices of other major financial firms. At the end of the month, the so-called Japan premium, a premium that Japanese banks faced in raising funds in the international wholesale market, reached 1 percent, virtually squeezing them out of the market (Sakakibara 2000).[15] On the other hand, the yen

---

[15] The difference in three-month Euroyen interest rates between Tokyo (TIBOR) and London (LIBOR) was 0.39 percent in December 1997 (Iwata 2010). The Japan premium virtually disappeared in April 1999 following the injection of ¥7.5 trillion into major banks and the commencement of ZIRP in February.

funding costs for foreign financial institutions edged closer to zero (and reached below zero occasionally). This started the process of foreign financial institutions borrowing yen in the domestic market and investing the proceeds abroad in what became known as the global carry-trade, placing further downward pressure on the yen.[16]

On 16 February 1998, the Japanese Diet passed a set of laws to address the banking crisis, including an appropriation of ¥13 trillion for the resolution of failed banks. The euphoria turned to disappointment, however, when the injection of public money in March 1998, at a mere ¥1.8 trillion, was perceived to be miniscule compared to the magnitude of the nonperforming loans in the banking sector (Sakakibara 2000). The exchange rate, which stood at ¥126 in mid February, reached ¥135 in early April (as the new Foreign Exchange Law came into force). On 9 April 1998, Japanese authorities purchased 196 billion yen in the foreign exchange market just as Prime Minister Ryutaro Hashimoto announced a ¥16-trillion economic stimulus package, actions immediately welcomed by US authorities.[17] On the following day, Japanese authorities intervened again on a much larger scale, buying 2.62 trillion yen. The yen appreciated to ¥127.38, but the impact was short-lived (see Figure 6.6). The banking crisis flared up again in June 1998 as the difficulty of the Long-Term Credit Bank of Japan (LTCB) was reported in the press (LTCB, along with the Nippon Credit Bank, would be nationalized toward the end of the year) and the Japan premium started rising sharply.

As the yen edged closer to ¥145, the MOF approached the US Treasury about the possibility of a joint intervention (Sakakibara 2000). Tough negotiations ensued during 13–17 June. In the event, the US Government agreed on joint action, in exchange for Japan's pledge to implement further fiscal stimulus measures along with a decisive plan to deal with the banking crisis.[18] The coordinated intervention, which took place immediately following announcement of the agreement on 17 June, involved a purchase of 231 billion yen (approximately $1.6 billion) by Japanese authorities and a sale of $833 million dollars by US authorities, as Secretary Rubin announced: "In the context of Japan's plan to strengthen its economy, the U.S. monetary authorities operated in the exchange market this morning in cooperation with the monetary

---

[16] This would happen again under the quantitative easing policy of the early 2000s when, given the lower dollar funding costs for foreign financial institutions, they could occasionally borrow yen funds at negative interest rates from Japanese banks (Iwata 2010).

[17] Finance Minister Hikaru Matsunaga confirmed the intervention, announcing that Japan had taken "decisive action" in the foreign exchange market. US Treasury Secretary Rubin welcomed Prime Minister Hashimoto's announcement of "steps to stimulate the Japanese economy" and noted: "we share the concern expressed by the Japanese Prime Minister about recent weakness in the yen, and in that context we welcome the action undertaken by the Japanese authorities in the exchange market to support the value of the yen" (FRB, September 1998).

[18] This agreement was made at the highest political level, between President Clinton and Prime Minister Hashimoto (Sakakibara 2000).

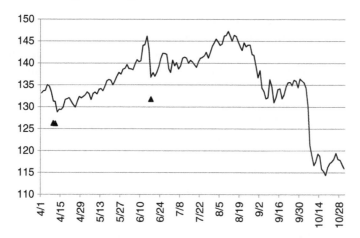

Figure 6.6. Japanese foreign exchange intervention and yen–dollar exchange rate, April–October 1998[a]

[a] A triangle indicates a day of intervention
Source: Spot closing rates from Bloomberg

authorities of Japan. We are prepared to continue to cooperate in exchange markets, as appropriate." This caused the yen, which had declined to a new low of ¥146.78 on the previous day, to appreciate to ¥136.51 at the close of New York trading (FRB, September 1998). This was Japan's last intervention during this episode and the last coordinated intervention with US authorities until 2011.

The impact of the 17 June intervention was short-lived. The yen drifted downward again, reaching the pre-intervention level of ¥146 by early August, and the exchange rate hit the post-bubble peak of ¥147.64 during midday trading on 11 August. It was only in the latter part of the month that downward pressure on the yen finally began to subside as Western financial institutions, hit hard by the Russian default, evidently started to reverse the yen carry-trade (Sakakibara 2000). The yen exchange rate, which was ¥147 on 17 August, fell temporarily below the ¥130 mark on 11 September, helped by a 9 September decision of the BOJ to cut the call rate from 0.5 to 0.25 percent while at the same time announcing that it would reduce the rate further toward zero.[19] Then, the yen saw an unprecedented volatility on 7 October when the exchange rate moved from about ¥134 to ¥120 in one day; on the next day, this was followed by an erratic movement between ¥111 and ¥123 (Cai et al. 2001).

---

[19] This was the first policy change effected under the new Bank of Japan Law. The minutes of the Policy Board meeting suggest that the decision was influenced by the outcome of the 4 September meeting between the US treasury secretary and the Japanese minister of finance in which a deputy governor of the BOJ was also present. The BOJ took note of the direction of globally coordinated monetary easing.

Although the exchange rate remained sporadically volatile through much of the rest of the year, the yen began to stabilize at a more appreciated level amid news of positive developments in the banking sector. On 16 October, the Diet passed legislation to allow ¥60 trillion of public money to be injected into troubled banks to strengthen their capital. The sum of bad loans and cumulative write-offs, which was estimated at 10 percent of GDP in 1998, continued to rise for some time, but a subsequent wave of nationalization and consolidation gradually restored health to the banking sector.[20] The yen appreciated from ¥135 at the beginning of the month to ¥114 on 19 October, an appreciation of some 15 percent in just over two weeks.

6.4. FOREIGN EXCHANGE INTERVENTION AND MONETARY POLICY: 2001–4

6.4.1. Quantitative Easing Monetary Policy

With interest rates near or at zero, Japanese authorities lost the option to stimulate the economy by further cutting the policy rate. In such an environment, a deflationary shock could even raise real interest rates and deepen the recession. In international policy circles, there was active discussion of the effectiveness of monetary policy when interest rates are near zero. Bernanke and Reinhart (2004), summarizing the past and ongoing debate, argued that monetary policy could still stimulate the economy even under the zero-interest-rate floor by (1) providing assurance that short-term interest rates would be kept lower in the future than currently expected, (2) altering the composition of the central bank's balance sheet to change the relative supplies of securities in the market, and (3) expanding the size of the central bank's balance sheet beyond the level required to set the short-term policy rate at zero (which they called "quantitative easing").[21]

Concerning the policy of quantitative easing, Bernanke and Reinhart (2004) further noted that expansion of the monetary base under the circumstances could be beneficial through several channels. Particularly relevant among them (to Japan) were the portfolio rebalancing effect (which operates by causing the private sector to rebalance its portfolios, thereby lowering yields

---

[20] The newly created Financial Reconstruction Commission and the Financial Supervisory Agency injected about ¥7.5 trillion of public funds into fifteen large banks in March 1999 before recapitalizing five regional banks with about ¥290 billion.

[21] Bernanke et al. (2004) discuss how the three types of policies might work in practice, generally providing supportive evidence for the effectiveness of each based largely on the historical experience of the United States.

on alternative, nonmonetary assets) and the signaling effect (which operates by altering expectations of the future path of policy rates through a visible demonstration of commitment to maintaining a high reserves target). Of the two channels, Eggertsson and Woodford (2003) stressed the signaling effect as the key transmission channel of central bank action by arguing that any direct effect of quantitative easing was limited.

Within the context of Japan, some advocated using yen depreciation as a means of ending deflationary pressure. Orphanides and Wieland (2000) argued that the exchange rate would respond to changes in the relative domestic and foreign money supplies through the portfolio balance effect even when interest rates were near zero. Such an effect may be small under normal conditions, but a drastic expansion of base money might succeed in depreciating the currency and stimulating aggregate demand. In a similar vein, Svensson (2001) advocated a devaluation followed by a temporary exchange rate peg as a "foolproof way of escaping from a liquidity trap." This would raise inflationary expectations and jumpstart the economy. Unlike Orphanides and Wieland (2000), Svensson (2001) did not rely on the portfolio balance channel (which may be small even for a substantial change in base money), advocating instead unsterilized intervention to enforce the peg at a more depreciated exchange rate (see also McCallum 2000).[22]

The magnitude and intractableness of the economic problem in Japan required extraordinary action. In March 2001, the BOJ, going beyond the ZIRP of February 1999–August 2000,[23] adopted what became known as quantitative easing monetary policy (QEMP). The decision was made against the background of falling stock prices, collapsing exports and industrial production, and a press report about large losses by major Japanese banks for the accounting period ending in March 2001.[24] QEMP consisted of three pillars: (1) the central bank supplied ample liquidity by using current account balances (commercial bank deposits held at the central bank) as the main operating target; (2) it publicly committed itself to maintaining ample liquidity

---

[22] Coenen and Wieland (2003) discuss yen depreciation as a way to ameliorate the effect of the zero-interest-rate bound and simulate the impact of such a policy in a macroeconomic model consisting of the United States, the euro area, and Japan, finding that aggressive liquidity expansions would offset the effect of the zero bound in raising inflationary expectations and thereby stimulating output.

[23] On 12 February 1999, the BOJ cut the overnight call rate initially to 0.15 percent, with the intention of reducing it further down to zero. The virtual zero interest rate was achieved in early March when the call rate reached 0.04 percent (Ueda 2005). In August 2000, with signs of economic recovery and diminished prospects for deflation, the BOJ lifted the ZIRP and raised the overnight call rate to 0.25 percent. In late 2000, the economy began to decelerate again, prompting the BOJ to cut the call rate to 0.15 percent. This rate was maintained until the new framework of quantitative easing (with the implied zero policy rate) was adopted in March 2001.

[24] The Nikkei average fell below 13,000 at the end of February, while real exports declined by 3.1 percent and industrial production by 3.9 percent in January from the previous month.

until core CPI inflation became zero or higher on a sustained basis; and (3) it increased the purchases of JGBs to inject liquidity (Maeda et al. 2005; Oda and Ueda 2007). During the period of QEMP, from March 2001 to March 2006, the BOJ raised the CAB target nine times and the monthly amount of JGB purchases four times to increase the monetary base (see Table 6.3). An inspection of the BOJ balance sheet indicates that about half of the increase in base money was made possible by open-market purchases of JGBs (see Figure 6.4), with the other half coming from purchases of other assets.

Because maintaining the CAB beyond the required reserves would keep the call rate near zero, QEMP was nothing but a version of ZIRP. The policy not only concerned the price of money but also involved a "zero rate commitment." In April 1999, Masaru Hayami, governor of the BOJ, articulated at a press conference that the central bank would maintain the zero short-term interest rate "until deflationary concerns are dispelled." Policymakers at the BOJ believed that such a commitment would assure markets that short-term interest rates in the future would be kept lower than currently expected. This corresponds to the first channel of monetary policy under the conceptual framework of Bernanke and Reinhart (2004), which BOJ economists called the "policy duration" effect. Fujiki and Shiratsuka (2002) provide evidence that ZIRP, during February 1999–April 2000, had the effect of flattening the yield curve.

QEMP was more than ZIRP in one potential respect. By altering the relative supply of assets through massive JGB purchases (Bernanke and Reinhart's second channel) as well as by expanding the central bank's balance sheet through successive CAB increases (the third channel), quantitative easing

Table 6.3. Bank of Japan's policy decisions under quantitative easing, March 2001–January 2004

Policy Board meeting where decision was made	Targeted current account balances (CAB)	Monthly purchases of Japanese government bonds (JGBs)
19 March 2001	About ¥5 trillion	¥400 billion
14 August 2001	About ¥6 trillion	¥600 billion
18 September 2001	Over ¥6 trillion	—
19 December 2001	About ¥10–15 trillion	¥800 billion
28 February 2002	—	¥1 trillion
30 October 2002	About ¥15–20 trillion	¥1.2 trillion
25 March 2003	About ¥17–22 trillion[a]	—
30 April 2003	About ¥22–7 trillion	—
20 May 2003	About ¥27–30 trillion	—
10 October 2003	About ¥27–32 trillion	—
20 January 2004	About ¥30–5 trillion	—

[a] Effective 1 April 2003; this was explained as a technical adjustment necessitated by the conversion of the Postal Services Agency (in charge of postal savings) into Japan Post Public Corporation
Source: Bank of Japan

could possibly further reduce yields on nonmonetary assets and depreciate the currency to raise inflationary expectations. In retrospect, evidence provided by Oda and Ueda (2007) suggests that the portfolio rebalancing effect of the type described above was not very strong. Rather, QEMP worked much the same way as ZIRP, by lowering the expectations components of interest rates through the zero-interest-rate commitment. The authors further show that successive upward CAB revisions were perceived by the markets as a signal of greater commitment to monetary accommodation.[25] Broad empirical evidence shows that QEMP reduced long-term government bond yields and the risk premium component of the funding costs faced by individual financial institutions (Ueda 2005).

6.4.2. Intervention and Monetary Policy Decisions

The great intervention of 2003–4, which took place under quantitative easing, was massive indeed. The cumulative amount came to 7 percent of Japan's annual GDP and exceeded the corresponding period's external current account surplus. Ito (2005) suggests the possibility that Japanese authorities were responding to speculative pressure in the foreign exchange market. By regressing the size of daily intervention on the short-term net speculative currency futures positions at the Chicago Mercantile Exchange's International Money Market (IMM), the author shows that the coefficient was statistically significant but only for long positions, suggesting that authorities only attempted to counter appreciation pressure against the yen. Fatum and Hutchison (2010), dividing the fifteen-month period of the great intervention into two subperiods, find that the standard explanatory variables were significant determinants of intervention decisions during 2003 but not during 2004. Taylor (2007: pp. 288 and 291) intimates that Japanese authorities were defending the ¥116 line from January to July 2003 and that the defense line later shifted to ¥110.

The fact that the great intervention in particular, and the intervention of the 2001–4 period more generally, took place when the monetary base was expanding under quantitative easing raises a question about the relationship between intervention and monetary policy. In fact, from 2001 to 2004, the increase in the CAB of over ¥44 trillion almost exactly corresponded to a cumulative sale of ¥42 trillion in the foreign exchange market (see Table 6.4,

---

[25] Jung et al. (2005) show in a theoretical model that optimal monetary policy—when the central bank faces a weak economy and the zero-interest-rate bound—is to make a credible commitment to maintain zero interest rates even after the natural rate of interest returns to a positive level, since this would lead to higher expected inflation, lower long-term interest rates, and a weaker domestic currency.

Table 6.4. Change in current account balances (CAB) at Bank of Japan and cumulative interventions by Ministry of Finance (in trillions of yen)

	Change in CAB (A)	Net cumulative sum of interventions (B)	A/B
January 2003–March 2004 ("great intervention" only)	17.9	35.1	0.51
March 2001–March 2004 (quantitative easing)	43.5	42.3	1.03

Sources: Bank of Japan; Ministry of Finance

bottom row). The intervention can therefore be said to have been entirely "unsterilized." If we instead focus on the great intervention of 2003–4 alone, about half was unsterilized (top row). How should the BOJ balance sheet expansion during this period be interpreted? If the intervention (by the MOF) caused monetary policy to be eased, it might be said that the BOJ compromised its independence. On the other hand, if the intervention had no impact on monetary policy decisions, the monetary impact of intervention in Japan was entirely at the whim of its independent central bank, the scale of the intervention notwithstanding.

Lambson et al. (2014) present a game-theoretic model of interaction between the MOF and the BOJ during the quantitative easing period, where the two agencies' objectives may differ (e.g., full employment versus price stability). The MOF effects money growth through intervention in the foreign exchange market, while the BOJ does so through open market operations in the domestic asset market. The CAB of commercial banks changes, not only when the government intervenes in the foreign exchange market but also when it engages in transactions with the private sector or when the public's demand for central bank notes changes. In this environment, the central bank is shown to react symmetrically to foreign exchange intervention and Treasury operations, but intervention can still lead to an increase in CAB if it raises the central bank's target or the political costs of sterilization (given that intervention could represent a net injection of liquidity while Treasury receipts and purchases tend to cancel each other out).

To be sure, the BOJ was under intense political pressure in the early 2000s, when public dissatisfaction was so strong that politicians—who thought the central bank was not cooperative enough—were openly proposing to abrogate its independence by revising the Bank of Japan Law (Umeda 2011).[26] Given

---

[26] Yoshikawa (2009), a member of the prime minister's Council on Economic and Fiscal Policy during 2001–5, reviews the internal debate between the government and the BOJ on the causes of deflation. The government took the view that monetary policy was the cause of deflation, while the BOJ repeatedly argued that deflation was an outcome of economic

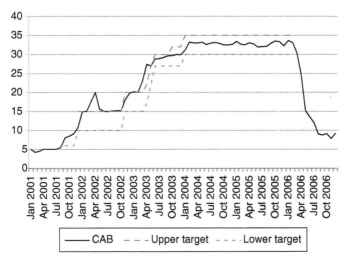

Figure 6.7. Bank of Japan's current account balances (CAB) and targets under quantitative easing (in trillions of yen; end of month figures)

Source: Bank of Japan

the tense political climate, the costs of undoing every effort of the government to inject liquidity through intervention could have been enormous. Watanabe and Yabu (2013), making a distinction between intervention and other government payments, use a dynamic regression model to show that, during the period of the great intervention, the BOJ did not respond symmetrically to intervention and other Treasury payments. They show that the BOJ allowed the monetary impact of intervention on the CAB to remain longer than that of Treasury purchases. If true, this was probably made possible by a leeway provided in the CAB target on a daily basis, as it was defined from December 2001 as a range, not a single number (see Figure 6.7; see also Table 6.2).

Remarkably, there was a complete absence in the Monetary Policy Board minutes of any reference to foreign exchange market intervention. It is possible that, given the operational independence of the BOJ, the central bankers conscientiously avoided any appearance of their decisions being influenced by government actions by keeping complete silence about intervention; it is unimaginable that they would have admitted yielding to political

---

stagnation. In the fall of 2001, the government made it a central pillar of macroeconomic policy to fight deflation and subsequently included *monetary policy* (the exclusive domain of the central bank) in a package of measures to be implemented immediately. In the 15 February 2002 council meeting (during which this policy was discussed), Economy and Industry Minister Takeo Hiranuma called for additional monetary easing, to which BOJ Governor Masaru Hayami replied that sufficient monetary easing was already in place and that the central bank could do little to increase the money supply as long as the economy remained stagnant. According to Yoshikawa (2009), this BOJ position would remain until the fall of 2006, when deflation ceased to be an overriding policy issue.

pressure even if they had in fact done so. A detailed analysis of each of the nine decisions to raise the CAB target under QEMP reveals that board members often disagreed with the proposed decisions, leading to a split vote in six of the nine cases. Only in one case (20 May 2003) was there a passing reference to exchange rate volatility (but not foreign exchange market intervention) as background to the decision (Umeda 2011). Compelled in a press conference to explain the relationship between foreign exchange market intervention and the just-announced decision to raise the CAB target, on 10 October 2003, BOJ Governor Toshihiko Fukui categorically denied any connection between the two (Umeda 2011: p. 151).

A closer look at daily data reveals that, during the period of quantitative easing, the central bank reacted differently from day to day in response to intervention (see Table 6.5). The central bank fully accommodated or fully sterilized the reserve change arising from intervention with almost equal probability. Given the operational framework in place during the period of QEMP, it is reasonable to conjecture that the BOJ was reluctant to fully accommodate the reserve increase associated with a large intervention, as it did not wish to allow the CAB target to be exceeded by a large margin. Only rarely did the BOJ fully sterilize the reserve change when the intervention involved more than ¥500 billion. On the other hand, the central bank may have been more willing to accommodate the reserve inflow when the prevailing CAB level was well below the target. These conjectures are supported by an econometric analysis of Lambson et al. (2014).[27] This means that, although the

Table 6.5. Settlement-day reaction of base money to intervention episodes under quantitative easing in Japan[a]

	Fully sterilized	Partially sterilized	Fully accommodated	Total
Greater than ¥500 billion	5	17	2	24
Greater than ¥300 billion but less than ¥499 billion	10	3	9	22
Less than ¥299 billion	42	9	40	91
Total number of intervention episodes	57	29	51	137

[a] This differs from Table 6.1 in that the sample excludes days when the Japanese market was closed for trading and that the amount also includes the purchases of euros on twelve days; based on a comparison of intervention size (at time *t*) to the subsequent change in current account balances (CAB) from *t*+1 to *t*+2 (when settlement takes place)
Sources: Ministry of Finance; Bank of Japan; and author's estimates

[27] Lambson et al. (2014) show that, depending on where the sum of intervention and Treasury operations stood in relation to the CAB target, the BOJ differentiated its reaction to daily intervention. The central bank fully sterilized the intervention when the CAB would exceed the target if it went unsterilized, while fully accommodating when there would be a shortfall in meeting the target if sterilized.

BOJ may have been more willing to accommodate intervention when the resulting monetary increase remained well within the CAB target range, it did not wish to allow the range to be violated substantially.[28]

Fatum and Hutchison (2005), estimating the monthly balance of base money as a function of twelve lags of base money, the call rate, and intervention during the period December 1991–September 2004, find that intervention did not help predict the growth of base money. If anything, a structural break was at the beginning of 2001 and not in 2003, as might be expected. The authors conclude that the great intervention of 2003–4 did not cause monetary policy to be eased beyond what would otherwise have been the case. This is a rather mechanical exercise that ignores the discrete nature of BOJ decisions to raise the CAB target, but the more formal ordered probit model of Lambson et al. (2014) comes to a similar conclusion. In explaining the nine discrete Monetary Policy Board decisions to raise the CAB target, their maximum likelihood estimate of the coefficient of cumulative intervention was positive but statistically not significant.

Part of the lack of strong quantitative evidence supporting causality from intervention to monetary policy reflects the fact that Monetary Policy Board decisions to raise the CAB target were concentrated in the first half of the period while a greater part of the intervention took place toward the end (see Figure 6.8). Only once did a Policy Board decision coincide with a large-scale intervention operation (following which, as noted, Governor Fukui denied the

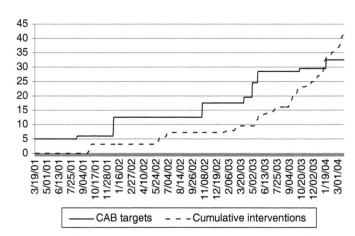

Figure 6.8. Bank of Japan's current account balance (CAB) targets and cumulative interventions by Ministry of Finance under quantitative easing (in trillions of yen)

Sources: Bank of Japan; Ministry of Finance

[28] The BOJ allowed the upper limit to be violated whenever there was upward pressure on the call rate, for example in the face of a seasonal demand for central bank reserves (Shirakawa 2008).

connection between the two). Two alternative interpretations are possible. First, the BOJ created additional room for unsterilized intervention (Ito 2005), possibly in *anticipation* of future intervention operations. Second, the relationship between intervention and monetary growth was a coincidence brought about by two autonomous agencies acting independently of each other.[29] In either case, the monetary effect of intervention was equivalent to unsterilized intervention.

6.5. A NEW MANNER OF INTERVENING IN THE FOREIGN EXCHANGE MARKET: 2010–11

6.5.1. Structural Changes in Japan's External Sector

The intervention operations of the early 2000s evidently caused the yen to depreciate during the coming years. Although the yen's secular depreciation is not so clearly evident when it is valued against the US dollar (see Figure 6.3), it becomes more apparent in effective terms. IMF measures of the yen's real and nominal effective exchange rates declined by 40 and 22 percent, respectively, from early 2001 to mid 2007 (see Figure 6.9); likewise, BIS indices (not shown

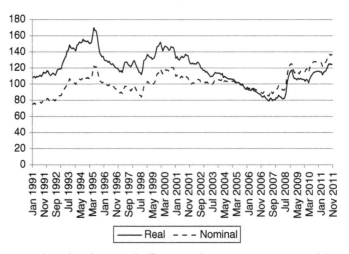

Figure 6.9. Yen's real and nominal effective exchange rates, 1991–2011[a] (2005=100)

[a] In terms of unit labor costs

Source: IMF, *International Financial Statistics*

---

[29] Iwata (2010), BOJ deputy governor during 2003–8, stressed that it was a coincidence but welcomed it as equivalent to central bank purchases of foreign bonds if government purchases of foreign assets were consolidated with central bank acquisition of JGBs.

in the Figure) show a depreciation of 33 and 23 percent, respectively, in real and nominal terms. Fukao (2005) shows that the yen during this period was undervalued relative to the level implied by a long-run portfolio balance model. Although the empirical literature is generally skeptical about the short-term effectiveness of daily intervention during 2003–4 (see Takagi 2014b for a survey), the great intervention not only was effective in putting the brakes on the yen's further appreciation but also pushed the value of the yen downward as it was accompanied by significant monetary easing (Iwata and Takenaka 2012).

Against the background of a weaker yen, three important structural changes took place in Japan's external sector. First, not only did the GDP share of exports increase, from around 10 percent in the early 2000s to over 17 percent in 2008, but Japan's overall openness (the value of exports and imports divided by GDP) rose from about 20 percent to 35 percent during the same period. Partly corresponding to the greater openness of the Japanese economy was a declining share of the nontradable goods sector. During the "lost decade," the share of the nontradable goods sector expanded, in a way consistent with a real exchange rate level that was higher than the historical average. As the yen's real effective exchange rate returned to a level more consistent with the long-run average, however, the share of nontradable goods in Japanese output began to decline from a peak achieved in 2002 (Kawai and Takagi 2011).[30]

Second, Japan's trade integration with Asia deepened as China overtook the United States in 2007 as the nation's biggest trading partner. In 2008, Asia's share in Japan's total trade (nearly 40 percent) far exceeded the combined shares of North America and Europe (28 percent). This was achieved as part of a larger trend of regional integration within Asia, where the share of intraregional trade rose from 30 percent to more than 50 percent of total trade over two decades. Closely related to intraregional trade was intraregional foreign direct investment (FDI), which has recently accounted for more than 30 percent of the region's total FDI. Direct investment in plants and equipment created production networks and supply chains in industries such as electronics, automobiles, and other machinery products that cut across national borders—a flipside of the growing intraregional trade. As the center of these expanding production networks, over 90 percent of Japan's exports consisted of highly income-elastic products, including industrial supplies and capital goods, not to mention consumer durables.

Third, as part of these developments, the composition of Japan's external current account surplus changed (see Figure 6.10). While the value of both

---

[30] Kawai and Takagi (2011) define the nontradable goods sector to include construction, electricity, gas, water, wholesale and retail trade, banking and insurance, real estate, transportation, telecommunication, and services.

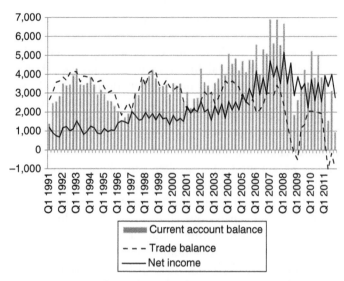

Figure 6.10. Components of Japan's external current account balance, Q1 1991–Q4 2011[a] (in billions of yen)

[a] Not seasonally adjusted

Source: Ministry of Finance

exports and imports expanded substantially, the country's chronic surplus in its trade balance saw a sharp decline after 2007. In the immediate aftermath of the global financial crisis, from the third quarter of 2008 to the first quarter of 2009, Japan even recorded a deficit in its trade balance for the first time in nearly twenty years. In contrast, the surplus on net income from abroad rose steadily from ¥3.5 trillion in 1991 to ¥16.5 trillion in 2007. In 2011, the income surplus was about ¥14 trillion, more than enough to offset the trade balance deficit of ¥1.6 trillion. Higher costs of production in Japan, exacerbated by a higher value of the yen beginning in the late 1980s, encouraged Japanese manufacturing firms to shift their production activities abroad. Japanese firms increasingly exported parts and components to their production sites and subsidiaries in the rest of Asia while importing finished products or re-exporting them to third markets in North America and Europe. The compositional changes in the external current account reflected these developments.[31]

These structural changes explain why Japan was hit so hard by the global financial crisis in late 2008, despite the fact that its financial system was relatively free of toxic assets. Industrial production contracted sharply in the fourth quarter of 2008 and the first and second quarters of 2009: by 15.0, 34.0,

---

[31] The shutdown of nuclear power plants following the Great East Japan Earthquake in March 2011, which increased the country's reliance on imported fuels, added to the structural deterioration of Japan's trade balance.

and 27.6 percent (year-on-year), respectively. Although the fall in output was attributable to a confluence of factors—including stock price declines that eroded the capital base of commercial banks as well as the lagged impact of a sharp rise in oil and other commodity prices in the summer of 2008—the primary cause was the contractionary effect of global deleveraging on world trade. In this environment, Japan was particularly vulnerable because output had become much more responsive to demand shocks coming from abroad (Kawai and Takagi 2011). Given Japan's strong trade links to Asia, the collapse of Asian exports to North America and Europe had a ripple effect on Japan's export of industrial supplies and capital goods to the region.

6.5.2. Monetary Policy Actions after the Global Financial Crisis

The yen began to appreciate moderately against the US dollar following the onset of the subprime loan crisis in early August 2007, from the high 110s. The pace of appreciation then accelerated after the Lehman failure and, in December 2008, the yen–dollar exchange rate fell below ¥90. The yen gained a renewed upward momentum in the middle of 2010, reaching the low 80s later in the year. The yen likewise appreciated against the euro, rising from about ¥160 per euro before the Lehman failure to the ¥130–40 range toward the end of 2009. The yen traded at around ¥110 against the euro in the middle of 2010 before edging toward the ¥100 mark in late 2011. The yen (along with the Swiss franc) was among the few major currencies that appreciated substantially against most other major currencies during the period, including those in Asia.[32] From the middle of 2007 through early 2009, for example, the yen appreciated by more than 70 percent against the Korean won, more than 40 percent against the Indonesian rupiah, and about 20 percent against the New Taiwan dollar and the Singapore dollar.

Macroeconomic fundamentals do not explain the sharp appreciation of the yen during this period. In fact, Japan was the only major advanced economy that experienced negative economic growth for the year 2008 as a whole. Although most advanced countries experienced recession in 2009, Japan's economic contraction (of 5.5 percent) surpassed the contractions experienced by the United States, the euro area, and the United Kingdom, where the financial crisis for the most part had originated. Japan recovered part of the output loss in 2010 by growing by 4.7 percent but experienced negative growth again in 2011. In contrast, most of Asia's major economies fared much better, notably with China, India, and Indonesia maintaining positive growth during

---

[32] According to De Bock and de Carvalho Filho (2013), the Japanese yen and the Swiss franc have been virtually the only currencies that tend to appreciate against the US dollar whenever global investors attempt to reduce their risk exposure simultaneously.

2009. Although Singapore and Taiwan were initially hit hard, they recovered rather quickly, as did Korea. The yen's strength during this period at least in part reflected the perception that it was a safe haven currency (Botman et al. 2013),[33] combined with the unwinding of the global yen carry-trade as American and European investors repatriated their investments from Asia and other emerging regions (Iwata 2010).

Sharp appreciation of the yen coming against the backdrop of a collapsing economy defined the challenges faced by Japan's policymakers. Authorities in principle refrained from intervening in the foreign exchange market to stem the tide of appreciation. When the whole world was engulfed by a crisis, Japan as a major industrial country did not have the option to devalue out of the recession. Instead, authorities eased fiscal and monetary policies, initially in coordination with the other Group of Twenty (G20) countries. Although the public debt-to-GDP ratio was already high (at nearly 150 percent), the government expanded fiscal policy substantially, with the deficit widening from 2.0 percent of GDP in 2007 to 5.1 percent in 2008 and further to 7–8 percent in 2009–11 (see Figure 6.1). The stimulus measures, amounting to 2.6 and 2.2 percent of GDP in 2009 and 2010, respectively, included cash payments, public works, subsidies for energy-efficient purchases, a higher gift tax exemption to support spending, and vocational training.

By this time, the BOJ had exited from quantitative easing (in March 2006), and the CAB balance had returned to a normal range (by July 2006). The BOJ had also raised the overnight call rate in two steps from 0 to 0.5 percent (in February 2007).[34] Part of the reason given for the interest rate increases was to curtail the yen carry-trade, which had become quite active since 2005. At this time, not only hedge funds and other institutional investors but also major foreign investment banks and Japanese individual investors, including housewives, were participating in this interest rate arbitrage scheme (BIS 2007; Iwata 2010; Umeda 2011).[35] Following the Lehman failure, however, the stance of monetary policy shifted in the direction of easing.[36] On 31 October 2008, three weeks after coordinated interest rate cuts by European and US monetary

---

[33] Botman et al. (2013) show how this safe haven feature of the yen is related, not to capital inflows, but to derivatives trading.

[34] When the BOJ terminated quantitative easing, it initially kept the overnight call rate at near zero. This was lifted in July 2008 when the call rate was raised to 0.25 percent; in February 2007, this was raised again, to 0.5 percent.

[35] Hattori and Shin (2007) show that yen liabilities were funding not only pure currency carry-trades but also a general increase in the balance sheets of hedge funds and financial institutions beginning in about 2005. Kato (2010) speculates that the peak was in April 2007 when the balance of call market borrowing by foreign banks reached ¥13.2 trillion.

[36] The first steps were taken on 14 October 2008, when the range of eligible JGBs for repo operations was expanded and the minimum fee for the Security Lending Facility reduced from 1.0 to 0.5 percent. It was announced that the frequency and size of CP repo operations would be increased; the range of ABCP acceptable as collateral would be broadened; and US dollar funds-supplying operations would be expanded.

authorities went into effect, the BOJ cut the call rate by 20 basis points to 0.3 percent and the discount rate (now renamed the basic loan rate under the complementary lending facility) by 25 basis points to 0.5 percent. Because the BOJ had not participated in the earlier coordinated interest rate cuts, the yen appreciated sharply from about ¥100 to about ¥90 toward the end of the month. The call rate and the basic loan rate were further cut to 0.1 and 0.3 percent, respectively, on 19 December, again following similar actions by the other advanced country central banks.

Although the BOJ did not participate in the coordinated interest rate cuts, it responded quickly to the Federal Reserve's action to pay interest on excess reserves. On the same day (8 October 2008), the BOJ issued a statement announcing that the governor had instructed the staff to consider ways to improve the working of monetary policy operations, including the CAB. In a press conference, the central bank spokesman added that what they had in mind was the measure just introduced by the Federal Reserve to pay interest on excess reserves. On 31 October, the BOJ announced that, along with a cut in the call rate, a measure would be introduced to pay interest on excess reserves at 0.1 percent, ensuring that the call rate would not fall below that level regardless of the amount of liquidity injection.

Additional easing measures ensued. In early December, the central bank raised its monthly purchases of JGBs from ¥1.2 trillion to ¥1.4 trillion and introduced a time-bound measure to provide unlimited liquidity to financial institutions against relaxed collateral requirements. In January 2009, it began outright purchases of CP and ABCP up to ¥3 trillion and, in February, reinstated the program of purchasing stocks held by financial institutions (through April 2010) and started outright purchases of corporate bonds up to ¥1 trillion. In March, the BOJ further raised monthly purchases of JGBs to ¥1.8 trillion. Similar actions to introduce additional mechanisms of liquidity provision were announced in 2009 and 2010, including the 30 April 2010 announcement to provide lending at the policy interest rate to financial institutions extending loans in support of "growth" industries.

6.5.3. Decisive Actions to Calm the Disorderly Markets

The MOF intervened in the foreign exchange market only on four occasions during 2010–11 (see Table 6.6). Unlike many of the previous intervention episodes during 1990–2004, each of these episodes was a measured response to what authorities perceived to be disorderly movement in the exchange rate. Each intervention was also characterized by decisiveness and involved an accompanying measure to enhance the credibility of the intervention as a signal of judgment and determination. The first intervention of the post-global financial crisis period took place on the afternoon of 15 September 2010, when the

Table 6.6. Characteristics of intervention episodes in Japan, 2010–11

Dates	Background	Size	Accompanying measure
15 September 2010	Yen–dollar exchange rate moved from ¥90 toward ¥83 in three months	¥2,124.9 billion	Announcement of support by Bank of Japan (BOJ) governor
18 March 2011	Exchange rate falls temporarily below ¥77 in aftermath of 11 March Great East Japan Earthquake	¥6,925 billion	Decision on 14 March by BOJ to increase size of asset purchase fund by ¥5 trillion; coordinated intervention by British, Canadian, European and US authorities following G7 statement
4 August 2011	Exchange rate hovers in range of ¥77–8 for one month	¥4,512.9 billion	Decision on 4 August by BOJ to increase size of asset purchase fund by ¥5 trillion; followed on 8 August by G7 statement of general support
31 October 2011 (followed by successive interventions on 1–4 November 2011)	Exchange rate appreciates to postwar record by falling below ¥76	¥8,072.2 billion (followed by ¥1,019.5 billion)	Decision on 27 October by BOJ to increase size of asset purchase fund by ¥5 trillion; statement of support by BOJ governor

Sources: Ministry of Finance; author's judgment

yen had appreciated to its then fifteen-year high of ¥82.87. The sale of over 2 trillion yen immediately pushed the value of the yen down to ¥85 per US dollar.

In an unusual gesture by the central bank, BOJ Governor Masaaki Shirakawa immediately issued a statement welcoming the "action by the Ministry of Finance in the foreign exchange market," which he hoped would contribute to exchange rate stability, and he expressed the central bank's determination to continue to provide liquidity to the market (Umeda 2011: p. 224). Two days later, on 17 September, the CAB was allowed to increase by ¥2.06 trillion, almost equal to the size of the intervention. The CAB increased by another ¥1.2 trillion on the next business day (21 September) as the BOJ refrained from fully sterilizing the impact of Treasury purchases. The operation of 15 September effectively amounted to unsterilized intervention, and the BOJ took the unusual action to intimate such an intention publicly. This was made possible by the payment of interest on excess reserves, which ensured that intervention, even if unsterilized, would not cause the overnight call rate to fall below 0.1 percent.

The impact of the intervention was immediate and appeared substantial, but the exchange rate then began to revert back to its original level (see Figure 6.11). In the meantime, the pace of economic recovery was evidently decelerating. Under these circumstances, on 5 October 2010, the BOJ Monetary

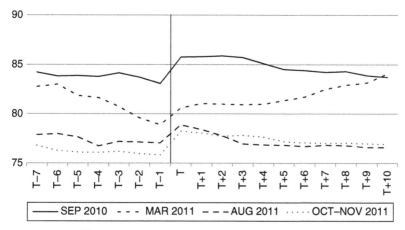

Figure 6.11. Yen–dollar exchange rate movements during Japan's four intervention episodes, 2010–11 (yen per US dollar; T=day[s] of intervention)

Source: Spot closing rates from Bloomberg

Policy Board agreed on a "comprehensive monetary easing policy." This consisted of three pillars: (1) the overnight call rate would be reduced from 0.1 percent to the 0–0.1 percent range, which was understood by the public as ZIRP; (2) ZIRP would be maintained until CPI inflation was judged to remain at about 1 percent (year-on-year) over the medium term;[37] and (3) a ¥5-trillion fund would be established on the BOJ balance sheet to purchase assets—including CP, corporate bonds, exchange-traded funds (ETFs), and J-REITs, while the balance of fixed-rate funds-supplying operations would be raised to ¥30 trillion.[38] The intention of the third pillar was to create a condition whereby the BOJ could begin to increase the holding of JGBs beyond the self-imposed limit equal to the outstanding balance of currency notes (Umeda 2011). Any impact of this announcement on the exchange rate was temporary at best.

The second intervention of the period took place on 18 March 2011, seven days after a devastating magnitude-9.0 earthquake hit the northeast coast of the main island of Honshu on 11 March. The material damage from the earthquake—and the successive waves of tsunami it triggered—was believed to be so large as to create investor expectations that Japanese insurance and nonfinancial firms would need to repatriate a substantial amount of capital

---

[37] The first pillar was an over-advertisement on the part of the BOJ because as long as 0.1 percent interest was paid on excess reserves, the call rate would not be expected to fall below that level. In the event, the call rate did fall below 0.1 percent after the measure was implemented but never declined below 0.085 percent (Umeda 2011). The second pillar was only a reaffirmation of what had been the existing policy.

[38] In the official BOJ statement, *kikin* (fund) is translated into English as *program*. The term *fund* signifies that the assets purchased under the program would be treated separately from the rest on the balance sheet.

from abroad, as had occurred following the earthquake that hit the city of Kobe in January 1995. As the yen strengthened, retail investors with positions in foreign currencies faced margin calls, forcing them to close positions by abruptly purchasing yen, thereby exacerbating yen strength (FRBNY 2011). The yen temporarily hit the then post-World War II high of ¥76.25 in New York trading on 17 March. The MOF intervened in the market to sell nearly 7 trillion yen, the largest single-day amount of intervention yet.

The intervention of 18 March was timed to coincide with a BOJ monetary policy action as well as coordinated actions by the authorities of other major industrial countries. First, on 14 March, the BOJ Monetary Policy Board made a decision to increase the size of the asset purchase fund from ¥5 trillion to ¥10 trillion. This served as a signal that most of the intervention would effectively be unsterilized. Second, on 17 March, the G7 finance ministers and central bank governors issued an unusual statement announcing their intention to intervene in the foreign exchange market jointly on the *following* day.[39] The United States contributed $1 billion to this effort. Yen-selling operations were conducted by each central bank at the start of its respective trading day, beginning in Tokyo. Much of the yen's depreciation occurred immediately following the release of the G7 statement, which nearly coincided with the intervention by Japanese authorities. The yen depreciated from ¥79.20 to ¥82.00 during the course of the day (FRBNY 2011).

The third intervention, which took place on 4 August 2011, involved a sale of more than 4.5 trillion yen. This occurred in an environment where the yen was approaching the then post-World War II high of ¥76.25 as the country was still struggling to recover from the natural disaster of March. There were also expectations that the forthcoming revision of the CPI would push the rate of inflation downward. This intervention also received support from the BOJ. The Monetary Policy Board, which was to meet for two days on 4–5 August, concluded its deliberations on the first day, immediately announcing that the asset purchase fund would be augmented by another ¥5 trillion. This too amounted to saying that the intervention would effectively be unsterilized. Four days later, on 8 August, the G7 finance ministers and central bank governors, while affirming their "support for market-determined exchange rates," stated that "[excess] volatility and disorderly movements in exchange rates have adverse implications for economic and financial stability" and asserted their readiness to "consult closely in regard to actions in exchange markets and . . . cooperate as appropriate."

The yen continued to appreciate, reaching the then postwar high of ¥75.95 on 19 August 2011. On 24 August, the MOF announced a package of

---

[39] The statement read in part: "In response to recent movements in the exchange rate of the yen associated with the tragic events in Japan, and at the request of the Japanese authorities, the authorities of the United States, the United Kingdom, Canada, and the European Central Bank will join with Japan, on March 18, 2011, in concerted intervention in exchange markets."

"emergency" measures to cope with the yen appreciation. First, as a one-year time-bound measure, it set aside $100 billion held in the Foreign Exchange Fund Special Account as official reserves to create a facility to provide lending at the London Interbank Offered Rate (LIBOR) to support outward foreign investment. This would be provided through the government-owned Japan Bank for International Cooperation to support the purchases of foreign firms by Japanese firms as well as to secure the supply of raw materials and energy resources abroad.[40] Second, the MOF strengthened monitoring of speculative activities in the foreign exchange market by requiring major banks to report foreign exchange trading positions. This was a time-bound measure, initially set to expire at the end of September. On the same day, the BOJ issued a statement saying that it expected the measures announced by the minister of finance to contribute to the "stability of the foreign exchange market." These announcements had little impact on the exchange rate.

The last major intervention took place on 31 October 2011 and involved a sale of 8 trillion yen, a record amount. Minister of Finance Jun Azumi immediately confirmed the intervention and stated that its purpose was to counter excessive speculation. BOJ Governor Masaaki Shirakawa issued a statement welcoming the action. This was followed by smaller interventions, totaling about ¥1 trillion, on four consecutive days in November. These operations occurred as the yen had temporarily hit the new post-World War II high of ¥75.31 in morning trading. The yen had been strengthening against the evolving sovereign debt crisis in Europe, but Japanese authorities believed that the strength of the yen had little to do with the economic fundamentals of the Japanese economy, with manufacturing firms barely restoring their production and supply chains from the earthquake-inflicted disruption. Again, the intervention followed a monetary easing measure. On 27 October, the BOJ Monetary Policy Board had raised the asset purchase fund by another ¥5 trillion. The yen depreciated to ¥79.55 but returned to the ¥76–7 range by the end of the year. The historical high of ¥75.31 would not be broken again.

6.6. THE CHANNELS OF INTERVENTION EFFECTIVENESS

6.6.1. Effectiveness in Influencing Daily Exchange Rate Returns

Given the LATW intervention strategy, the question of whether yen sales (purchases) had the intended effect of depreciating (appreciating) the yen—or

---

[40] The press reported in February 2012 that Sony and Toshiba had taken advantage of this scheme; in July 2012 it was reported that Japanese firms had taken out $8.9 billion in fifteen dollar-denominated loans from the scheme.

at least moderating the pace of appreciation (depreciation)—against the US dollar has received considerable attention in the literature on Japanese intervention (see Takagi 2014b for a survey). Recent studies based on official daily intervention data for 1991–2004 have employed three methodological approaches: (1) a GARCH model or its variant to estimate the impact of intervention on daily exchange rate returns, jointly with the impact of the absolute value of intervention on conditional variance; (2) use of the predicted value from a separately estimated intervention reaction function as an instrumental variable for a single equation regression model; and (3) non-parametric methods, including event study and propensity score matching techniques. As expected, reflecting the variety of methodologies employed, the literature reports a wide range of results, which also depend on the subsample and the particular characteristic of the intervention—for example, whether it was coordinated or unilateral, public or secret, a sale or a purchase.

Some broad generalizations are possible. First, the estimates from the second regime (roughly corresponding to June 1995–December 2002) and the third regime (corresponding to the great intervention, January 2003–March 2004) as well as from the entire sample period (April 1991–March 2004) tend to support effectiveness, while those from the first regime (roughly corresponding to April 1991–May 1995) or from the combined first and second regimes tend to support effectiveness only when intervention was coordinated. Second, when a distinction was made between interventions contemporaneously detected ("public") and those not detected ("secret"), the former type was more likely to be found effective. Third, when one–day-lagged intervention was used to control for the potential feedback from the exchange rate to intervention[41] or when weekly data were used, effectiveness was not supported (Beine 2004; Beine et al. 2003). This may mean that a substantial portion of any impact of intervention was consummated within the same day the intervention occurred, an interpretation consistent with the efficient market hypothesis. Fourth, effectiveness was more likely to be supported by those employing an event study methodology, which treats interventions that take place on successive days as a single event, but any effectiveness found therein tends to diminish as the pre/post-event window is lengthened. Whatever the correct reading of the literature, however, the magnitude of any impact was numerically very small, with the most

---

[41] Simultaneity could operate on two levels. First, Japanese authorities may be prompted to intervene when the exchange rate moves in an adverse direction, and the greater the adverse movement, the larger the intervention. Second, authorities may continue intervening until they see a favorable turnaround in the exchange rate. The second problem is particularly relevant for event studies that treat a cluster of interventions on succeeding days as a single event. Most studies do not control for the simultaneity problem (Neely 2005).

favorable point estimate of 0.14 percent (¥0.11–17, depending on the level of the exchange rate) in response to an average-sized intervention (Takagi 2014b).[42]

6.6.2. Impact on Daily Exchange Rate Volatility

Impact on volatility is another topic that has received attention in the literature (see Takagi 2014b for a survey). Although the majority of the studies seem to support, at least conditionally, the emerging conventional wisdom that intervention increases volatility (Dominguez 1998), evidence must be weighed carefully. Studies that unequivocally support that emerging consensus (Nagayasu 2004; Kim and Sheen 2006; Hoshikawa 2008) all employed a GARCH-type specification in which the impact of intervention on volatility is obtained from the conditional variance equation estimated jointly with a conditional mean equation. Conditional variance is an unobservable measure, which may not have a direct counterpart in real life. It is not certain that authorities and traders recognize an increase in jointly estimated conditional variance as a rise in actual market volatility. Other GARCH-type studies conditionally support the conventional wisdom—for example, when the first regime is included in the sample or when intervention was public or coordinated (e.g., Beine 2004; Hillebrand and Schnable 2006; Hassan 2012).

Any evidence of positive impact could be an artifact of the GARCH-type methodology. Watanabe and Harada (2006) argue that, as shocks to exchange rate volatility are persistent, inclusion of intervention in the conditional variance equation presupposes persistence in the effects of intervention. In order to control for such a volatility clustering bias, the authors assumed that volatility consisted of short-term and long-term components with shorter and longer degrees of persistence and estimated a system of three (instead of two) equations. With this correction, their results show that intervention had either no impact or negative impact on short-term variance. Likewise, Beine et al. (2003), using a Markov regime-switching model, find that evidence of positive impact disappeared when two states of volatility (high and low) were considered; interventions had little impact on the conditional variance of *weekly* exchange rate returns for 1991–5. Any evidence of positive impact could also reflect the positive feedback from volatility to intervention, which is not controlled for by most GARCH-type studies (Kim 2007).

Evidence is mixed but weighs somewhat toward finding no impact when other measures of volatility are used. When the second moment of the risk-neutral density (RND) of expectations drawn from option prices was used

---

[42] This translates to 0.7 percent for an intervention of ¥1 trillion.

(this may be better characterized as a measure of uncertainty), studies find a wide range of results, from positive impact, to no significant impact, and to negative impact (e.g., Galati et al. 2005; Morel and Teiletche 2005). The event study of Fatum and Hutchison (2006) is the only empirical work on Japan that has employed a directly observable measure of market volatility, namely, the daily variance of the yen–dollar exchange rate calculated from ten minute-frequency returns over forty-eight hours preceding and succeeding each event. The authors find no systematic link between intervention and volatility for April 1991–December 2000, with volatility declining in twenty-three of the forty-three events and rising in the remaining twenty.

6.6.3. The Portfolio Balance and Signaling Channels

While recent literature generally supports the effectiveness of daily intervention in influencing daily yen–dollar exchange rate returns during 1991–2004, especially when such intervention was coordinated or large and infrequent, any effectiveness of intervention appears to have been numerically small and short-lived. Dominguez (2003) contends that the impact of intervention lasted no more than eight hours. The martingale property of the daily yen–dollar exchange rate (Takagi 1988c) implies that any impact should be permanent, but evidence suggests otherwise. There is no evidence of impact in *weekly* data. Effectiveness or impact typically found in an event study tends to weaken or even disappear when the pre/post-event window is lengthened. A study shows that about 40 percent of the impact of intervention was reversed the next day (Castren 2004), a number that is corroborated by Evans and Lyons (2005) in the context of the response of daily exchange rate returns to the arrival of macroeconomic news.[43] The transitory nature of intervention impact is consistent with the larger empirical literature on intervention (e.g., Edison 1993; Dominguez 2006).

Although the literature has conventionally identified portfolio balance and signaling as the two main channels of influence, it is difficult to believe that either of these is important in Japan, at least when effectiveness is measured in daily frequency. For one thing, any intervention-induced portfolio adjustment is miniscule in relation to the stocks of Japanese and US government debt, even if substitutability between the two can be shown to be sufficiently imperfect. For example, the outstanding stock of FBs was 11 and 14 percent, respectively, of the total stock of JGBs in 2000 and 2004. Even the largest monthly portfolio adjustment during 1991–2004 amounted to a small fraction

---

[43] Evans and Lyons (2005) show that part of the initial impact of macroeconomic news on the daily euro–dollar rate was systematically reversed over several days during April 1993–June 1999.

of these. This is not to deny the portfolio balance effect over the medium term when there is a large, sustained intervention in which domestic and foreign assets are exchanged, as might have been the case during the period of the great intervention.[44] But such would be a rare event indeed.

Second, the signaling effect, as the term is normally used in the literature, refers to an intervention-induced change in market expectations about the future stance of monetary policy. For this to be operational there must be (1) a link between intervention and actual future monetary policy and (2) a link between intervention and market expectations of future monetary policy. Unless the first of the two links is consistent, an observation of intervention would not convey meaningful information about monetary policy. Humpage (2003) argues that central banks are not likely to use intervention as a signaling device for monetary policy because if they validate the signals, the intervention is no longer sterilized. In countries like Japan and the United States, moreover, the central bank could even lose its independence if it altered monetary policy systematically in response to interventions by fiscal author-ities.[45] Any signaling effect that may have existed in Japan before April 1998 is no longer operative, except when the central bank deliberately cooperates with the government in pursuit of common objectives. This might have been the case during 2010–11.

The signaling effect of intervention can be understood more broadly as a channel through which any information is conveyed to market participants. Then, given the convention of $t+2$ settlements, it is almost a truism that signaling operates in Japan and can even be the dominant channel. There is plenty of evidence to support this claim. For example, when a dummy variable is included for intervention, the impact of size on volatility disappears (Frenkel et al. 2005), and first-day interventions are more effective when they are separated from subsequent interventions on successive days (Castren 2004; Ito 2005). The signaling effect does not mean that any announcement would do the trick. Fatum (2009) finds that a dummy variable for false reporting did not affect the exchange rate during 1999–2003, nor did the dummy variables for official intervention announcements. It is possible that, given the scale of intervention during this period, false reports or official announcements did not contain much new information beyond what market participants had already been expecting.

---

[44] The increase in foreign exchange reserves from 2000 to 2004 amounted to 44 percent of the corresponding increase in Japan's total external portfolio assets.

[45] Studies of the signaling effect of US intervention are mixed. While Lewis (1995b) identifies Granger causality from intervention to future monetary policy, Kaminsky and Lewis (1996) and Klein and Rosengren (1991) report conflicting or negative findings (see also Fatum and Hutchison 1999).

6.6.4. The Microstructure Channel

The transitory nature of any impact of intervention, combined with the finding that secret interventions could be effective in some cases, lends support to the validity of the market microstructure channel (Evans and Lyons 2002, 2005). In this view, intervention if perceived by the market acts like any other information about fundamentals (Ehrmann and Fratzscher 2005). Regardless of whether or not it is perceived, intervention always affects order flows (i.e., the net of buyer-initiated and seller-initiated orders),[46] which may in turn trigger portfolio rebalancing or convey information. The finding that public or coordinated interventions can sometimes increase market volatility is consistent with the microstructure view of intervention working through the aggregation of new information by the market (Beine et al. 2009).[47] If the intervention conveyed no new information, after the traders adjusted their positions and quotes in response to a new pattern of order flow, the exchange rate would return to the original level. It is possible that an initial move in the exchange rate could set in motion the herd-like behavior of traders who follow a chartist strategy. Cai et al. (2001) show that order flow was the most important cause of the unprecedented volatility of the yen–dollar exchange rate observed during 1998 (see Section 6.4.3).

In a market inhabited by chartists, intervention might succeed in breaking up the exchange rate's self-propelling drift. Documenting the chartist behavior of traders in the yen–dollar, pound–dollar, and euro–dollar markets from August 1999 to April 2000, Osler (2003) shows that take-profit orders were clustered at round numbers, while stop-loss orders were clustered just below or above those numbers depending on whether they were sales or purchases. Once the exchange rate crosses the "support and resistance levels," herd behavior typically sets in to accelerate movement of the exchange rate in one direction. In such an environment, intervention could conceivably be effective in preventing the exchange rate from trending further downward or upward by creating two-way trades at or around the support and resistance levels. Intervention could even reverse order flow dynamics and trigger herd behavior in the opposite direction. As we saw, this is what may have happened in mid 1995, when the new intervention tactic introduced by Eisuke Sakakibara evidently reversed the yen's sharp and steady appreciation.

The diversity of results reported in the literature suggests that the effectiveness and the impact of intervention depend not only on such characteristics as

---

[46] Evans and Lyons (2002), discussing the critical role of order flow, show that it explained more than 40 percent of daily changes in the yen–dollar exchange rate between May and August 1996.

[47] Obtaining daily volatility from the realized hourly returns for the day, they find that, during 1989–2001, only coordinated intervention increased the volatility of the daily deutsche mark–dollar (or euro–dollar after 1999) exchange rate.

size and frequency, but also on the environment in which it takes place. Intervention can also be used to signal information about different things, not just monetary policy.[48] Fratzscher (2008) shows, for the euro–dollar and yen–dollar markets, that intervention tends to be more effective during periods of high volatility and uncertainty. Beine et al. (2003), using a Markov regime-switching model (capturing high and low volatility), show that coordinated intervention during 1991–5 was destabilizing in a low volatility state but stabilizing in a high volatility state (see Beine et al. 2009 for a similar result on the deutsche mark–dollar market). This may to some extent reflect what Sarno and Taylor (2001) call the "coordination channel." When uncertainty is high, intervention could stabilize the market by anchoring exchange rate expectations at a level consistent with fundamentals (see also Morel and Teiletche 2005).

All of this means that some interventions can be effective while others are not. Dominguez (2003) identifies for the yen–dollar market during 1991–2002 that 47 percent of the daily returns on 218 days had a correct sign. That is, intervention was effective at most about half the time. This conforms to our observation from Japan's selective intervention episodes. Because each intervention episode is unique, econometric tests of the *average* impact of intervention can only yield mixed results, while event studies could find more instances of effectiveness.[49] Shirakawa (2008), governor of the BOJ during 2008–13, stated that the only meaningful assessment of intervention was that of intervention in a specific, exceptional circumstance. While expressing general skepticism about the average effectiveness of intervention, he argued that monetary authorities should intervene only when in their view the probability of success was high (p. 290). The intervention episodes of 2010–11 support the view that Governor Shirakawa practiced what he preached by cooperating with the government to create a condition in which intervention was more likely to succeed.

---

[48] At the time of the European Exchange Rate Mechanism (ERM) crisis in the early 1990s, US authorities are said to have intervened to sell deutsche marks to signal that the United States was not practicing benign neglect toward the dollar's weakness. Their intention was not to signal that the Federal Reserve was about to tighten monetary policy (Truman 2003).

[49] Galati and Melick (2002), using the same data set, find effectiveness during 1991–6 with an event study, but their econometric analysis fails to find any impact on yen–dollar exchange rate returns or volatility.

7

Retrospective and Prospective Issues in Japanese Exchange Rate Policy

7.1. INTRODUCTION

The preceding chapters, in reviewing Japan's exchange rate policy since 1945, have discussed, among other things, how authorities established a single exchange rate for the yen, achieved current and capital account convertibility, and used various instruments to manage exchange-rate or balance-of-payments developments. The trajectory of Japan's policy shift was clearly in the direction of letting market forces play a greater role. Starting from a system of draconian controls over trade and payments, authorities progressively liberalized the system until they ultimately surrendered virtually all state control, even including foreign exchange market intervention. More recently, they have felt greater freedom from external considerations to conduct macroeconomic policies for domestic purposes. In an increasingly interdependent world, the exchange rate and the balance of payments will likely continue to remain relevant, but Japanese exchange rate policy will not be the same.

This concluding chapter provides a summary, draws lessons, and discusses outstanding issues. The chapter first characterizes, with broad strokes, the contour of Japanese exchange rate policy over the past sixty-plus years. In drawing overarching lessons from the Japanese experience, it identifies major errors in exchange rate policy, including the protracted pace of capital account liberalization (CAL) and the failure to liberalize the domestic financial system early, ideally before the currency was floated. It then identifies current and prospective issues, including the impact of Asian monetary cooperation on the historical focus of Japan's exchange rate policy on the US dollar, the new modality of market intervention, what to do with the country's large foreign exchange reserves, and government–central bank cooperation. The chapter concludes by discussing the latest episode of monetary easing as evidence of a fundamental change in the nature of Japanese exchange rate policy.

7.2. CHARACTERIZING JAPANESE EXCHANGE RATE POLICY

As a natural consequence of exchange rate-based stabilization, Japan entered the world trading system with an overvalued currency. The literature advises countries attempting an exchange rate-based stabilization to make a timely devaluation or exit to a more flexible exchange rate regime. Otherwise, currency overvaluation—a product of successful stabilization—could create competitiveness concerns and balance-of-payments difficulties. But timely devaluation rarely occurs (Bird and Willett 2008); exit from a peg is usually disorderly (Eichengreen et al. 1998). Argentina provides a recent, dramatic example of this. Following the successful exchange rate-based stabilization of 1991 (the "Convertibility Plan"), the country was unbending in maintaining its peg against the US dollar until it experienced a currency crisis and a debt default in 2001–2 (Takagi 2013). This did not happen to Japan, however. For one thing, Japan was protected by extensive exchange and capital controls. For another, it used the overvalued exchange rate as an extra incentive to improve productivity. As a result, the yen was no longer overvalued by the late 1960s.

The overvalued yen helped perpetuate the restrictive system of trade and payments. Komiya and Itoh (1988) argue that, if the exchange rate had been set at a level that would have permitted maintaining a favorable balance of payments without imposing restrictive measures, special schemes would not have been necessary to promote exports and discourage imports. Ideally, Japan would have benefited from devaluation soon after the US military procurement boom of the Korean War ended. Instead of devaluation, however, Japan obtained assistance from the International Monetary Fund (IMF) to manage balance-of-payments crises through financing and adjustment. Few among the Japanese elite believed in the price mechanism, preferring to operate a disequilibrium system. From 1957 to 1970, Japan had barely enough foreign exchange reserves to cover just a few months of imports (see Figure 7.1). This explains why, when authorities under foreign pressure began to liberalize imports in 1960, they felt compelled to liberalize short-term capital inflows by allowing nonresidents to open free-yen accounts.

Japan faced a hostile world. Asia did not welcome exports from Japan, requiring authorities to use foreign aid to open up the region's reluctant markets. Most of the major trading nations acted the same. When Japan acceded to the General Agreement on Tariffs and Trade (GATT) in 1955, fourteen countries—which collectively accounted for about 40 percent of Japan's exports to GATT members—refused to give Japan most-favored-nation (MFN) status by invoking Article 35 (Komiya and Itoh 1988).[1] Even when many of these

---

[1] Among the major countries, only Canada, Italy, the United States, West Germany, and the Scandinavian countries accorded Japan MFN status, at least formally. Italy, West Germany, and the Scandinavian countries retained discriminatory import practices against Japan.

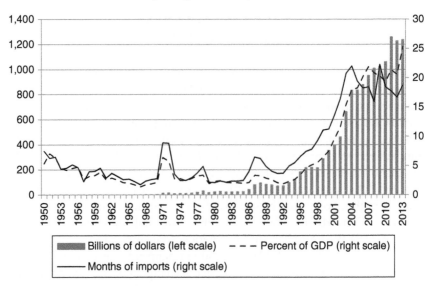

Figure 7.1. Japan's official foreign exchange reserves, 1950–2013[a] (in billions of US dollars; percent of gross domestic product; months of imports)

[a] Year-end figures; fiscal-year gross national product figures were used for 1950 and 1951 in place of calendar-year gross domestic products (GDPs)

Source: IMF, *International Financial Statistics;* ECB (1953); author's estimates

countries withdrew the application of Article 35 in the 1960s, they required Japan to accept as a condition the continuation of discriminatory practices against its products and to agree not to bring the case to GATT. With pervasive exchange controls in place throughout the world, limited foreign exchange reserves in the environment of a fixed exchange rate, and a sense of being ostracized, it is not difficult to understand why authorities took special measures to promote exports and discourage imports. Unfortunately, this created the image of Japan as an unfair mercantilist nation.

Those who lived through this period as junior officials rose up in the hierarchy to become Japan's senior policymakers in the late 1960s. They carried the same sense of victimization, saw the country's new prosperity as fragile, and failed to recognize that Japan, as an important player in the international monetary system, now had a responsibility to help ensure its stability. Desperate attempts to defend the yen's fixed exchange rate, even after it had become obvious to almost everyone that they would be futile, served to cement the perception of Japan as a mercantilist nation. This experience further created the view that Japan was prone to use an undervalued currency to promote its exports, although in reality the yen had been overvalued during most of its post-World War II existence. The subsequent history of Japanese exchange rate policy should dispel any notion that Japanese authorities deliberately attempted to depress the value of the yen to gain commercial advantage. To the contrary, the yen appreciated precipitously both against the US dollar and in effective terms over the coming decades.

Haruhiko Kuroda (2003), vice minister of finance for international affairs from July 1999 to January 2003, stated that the Japanese Government had never used a weaker yen as a tool of macroeconomic policy, with exchange rate policy designed to ensure that the exchange rate move in a stable manner consistent with economic fundamentals (p. 159). Econometric studies of Japanese intervention confirm that it was symmetric with respect to appreciation and depreciation. From the 1970s through the 1990s, authorities were at times found to intervene massively in support of the yen; most of the Japan–US or Group of Five/Seven (G5/7) coordinated actions involved pushing the value of the yen upward. In these instances, Japan agreed to implement measures to appreciate the yen out of fear that its trading partners, especially the United States, would impose trade sanctions. Although the end result was always a higher yen, Japanese authorities were often seen to acquiesce reluctantly to foreign demand. The reality of what happened hardly altered the perception of Japan as a nation intent on using a weaker yen to gain commercial advantage.

Japanese exchange rate policy, following the emergence of Japan as an economic superpower, can only be understood within the broader context of escalating Japan–US bilateral economic problems (Bergsten and Cline 1987; Lincoln 1988). In particular, Japan's large bilateral current account surplus with the United States remained a dominant international economic issue from the 1970s through the 1990s. Throughout this period, McKinnon and Ohno (1997) argue, the United States pursued a policy of coupling protectionist threats with demand for yen appreciation. No matter how much the dollar fell, some in the US Government still observed the Japanese trade surplus and saw further room for yen appreciation. The markets, on their part, began to incorporate these expectations, causing Japanese interest rates to stay perennially below US rates. Japanese authorities countered the yen's appreciation pressure with market intervention, but their reaction was a passive one of the lean-against-the-wind kind. In the end, they almost always allowed the yen to appreciate.

This meant that, because the real exchange rate is endogenous over the medium term, Japan's inflation rate needed to be permanently lower. This was fine as long as the United States was experiencing a relatively high rate of inflation. As soon as US inflation stabilized, the "ever-higher yen" (McKinnon and Ohno 1997) meant deflationary pressure in Japan. For example, as US producer price inflation declined from 9.1 percent during 1975–80 to 2.7 percent during 1981–90, Japanese producer price inflation fell from 4.6 percent to −0.4 percent. As a result of lower inflation in Japan, although the yen's nominal exchange rate against the US dollar appreciated by 184 percent

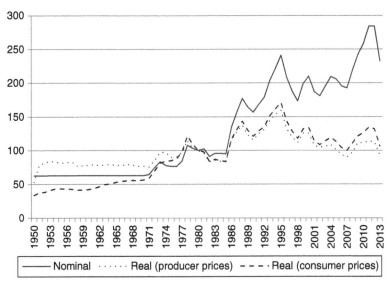

Figure 7.2. Yen's nominal and real exchange rates against US dollar, 1950–2013[a] (1980=100)

[a] An increase means an appreciation of the yen; annual averages; there are discontinuities in the Japanese price data in 1970 for producer (wholesale) prices and 1957 for consumer prices
Source: IMF, *International Financial Statistics*; Bank of Japan; author's estimates

from 1980 to 2012, the real appreciation was only 12 percent on the producer price index (PPI) basis and 32 percent on the consumer price index (CPI) basis; substantial depreciation under *Abenomics* (see Section 7.5), however, caused the CPI- and PPI-based real exchange rates both to approach the 1980 level in 2013 (see Figure 7.2). Deflation in Japan did not start with the bursting of the asset price bubble. Producer prices were already falling in the middle of the 1980s.

Throughout the sixty-plus years since the occupation, Japanese policymakers lacked a long-term strategy to define the pace, sequence, and end goal of trade and payments liberalization. Neither did they have a clear vision for Japan's international economic relations or firm principles to guide their decisions. As a result, they could only be reactive to external events. Even the yen internationalization efforts were half-hearted, with parts of the bureaucracy dragging their feet to protect their turfs. The 1998 revision of the Foreign Exchange Law, implemented as part of the broader financial big bang, may be one of the few exceptions to this generalization. With the Foreign Exchange Law revision, the national bureaucracy had a vision, a strategy, and clear principles; the prime minister even showed strong leadership, a rare event in Japan's consensus-based decision-making system. Unfortunately, this came too late to influence events that had already taken place. In all fairness, it must be acknowledged that Japanese authorities were treading unknown territory. Little empirical literature was available to predict the impact of their actions, let alone to prescribe their policies. International economics (both normative and positive) has been evolving, and the pendulum of best practices or expert opinion has swung a few times.

7.3. LESSONS FROM THE JAPANESE EXPERIENCE

Lessons can be gleaned from the Japanese experience in the form of five policy errors, some of which have already been alluded to in the preceding account.

7.3.1. Failure to Devalue the Yen

The yen should have been devalued in the mid 1950s. This would have allowed Japan to accumulate sufficient foreign exchange reserves and spared it the need to tighten macroeconomic policies each time rapid growth led to a surge in imports. An appropriately priced yen would have prompted Japan to ease controls on trade and payments more quickly, weakened the arbitrary regulatory power of the national bureaucracy, and lessened the chance of Japan being labeled as an unfair mercantilist by its trading partners. Changing the par value of the yen, however, was never considered an option because authorities did not believe in the market mechanism. Neither is there any guarantee that, if the yen had been devalued as suggested, they would have consented to revaluation as soon as productivity gains strengthened the country's external position. It is possible that devaluation in the mid 1950s would have only hastened the inevitability of the currency turmoil by a few years. Even so, Japan would have achieved a more liberal trade and payments regime early and avoided the type of foreign criticism it received in later years. How history played out in the 1980s might then have been different.

7.3.2. Politicizing the Japan–US Trade Balance

Lincoln (1988), commenting on the Japan–US economic problems of the 1970s and 1980s, echoed the view of many observers that US officials, politicians, and businessmen erred in overemphasizing the importance of the bilateral trade balance, in asserting that current account balances should be zero, and in linking the imbalances to Japan's trade barriers. Using the threat of protectionism, US authorities pushed Japan to open its market. To the extent that trade barriers existed, they needed to be removed—for Japan's own sake and perhaps also for the benefit of a few exporters to Japan. But the mistake was to think that removing the barriers would eliminate the bilateral trade imbalance, with little appreciation of the fact that Japan's current account surplus reflected its saving surplus and that the US deficit was a reflection of low saving. The logic became even more dangerous when the bilateral imbalance was linked to a supposed undervaluation of the yen. Because Japanese authorities were desperate to avoid the rise of protectionism abroad, they allowed the yen to appreciate each time a trade dispute flared up.

The extent of what the Japanese Government did to promote the import of finished products is considerable. Numerous "emergency" economic measures included government purchases of foreign products ranging from foreign-language books to Boeing aircraft. From 1983 to 1995, government-affiliated financial institutions introduced low-interest financing schemes for the import of industrial products. From 1990 to 1997, the government introduced an import promotion tax measure whereby business firms could deduct a portion of the costs of imported industrial products from taxable profits. From 1993 to 2000, it established Foreign Access Zones (FAZs) in twenty-three ports and airports, in order to facilitate the distribution of imports. In 1978, it tasked the Japan External Trade Organization (JETRO, a government-affiliated agency established in 1958 to promote Japanese exports) to dispatch import-promotion missions abroad and to assist foreign firms marketing their products in Japan. In the same year, the business community created a Manufactured Imports Promotion Organization (MIPRO) whose mandate was to promote the import of finished products in close collaboration with the Ministry of International Trade and Industry (MITI).

In retrospect, some of the specific measures implemented during this period even look amusing. From October to December 1978, a 13,000-ton cruise ship, packed with American consumer goods, was used as a floating department store (named "Baotique America") to promote the sale of American products; half a million people made purchases amounting to about ¥1 billion across thirteen port cities in fifty days. In April 1985, Prime Minister Yasuhiro Nakasone appeared on national television asking each Japanese citizen to purchase $100 in foreign products. This was followed by an advertising blitz, which included the formation of a "cheerleading group" of one hundred celebrities and the placement of the prime minister's poster on twenty-five major commuter rail lines in the Tokyo and Osaka metropolitan areas, while the minister of international trade and industry personally asked the chief executive officers of sixty major firms to formulate a specific plan to increase purchases of foreign finished products.[2] From April

---

[2] The MITI also held a series of meetings with representatives from 341 firms to ask them to expand purchases of imported products (Abe 2013).

to May, various import-promotion events took place at more than 20,000 locations throughout Japan (Abe 2013).

The sincerity of the attempts by Japanese authorities to reduce the current account surplus by expanding imports cannot be disputed. Has there been another country in the history of the world that has expended government resources more generously to promote imports from abroad than Japan? As long as the savings–investment imbalance remained fundamentally the same, however, these measures had little chance to eliminate Japan's current account surplus. To placate the Americans and minimize the threat of a costly trade war, the Japanese Government accommodated a higher yen. But the higher yen, too, did little to eliminate the trade or current account surplus. The bilateral trade or current account balance should not have been politicized as a target of bilateral negotiations. Given the sense of debt owed to the United States since the occupation, Japan's senior policymakers could not rebuff a US demand even when it was unreasonable.

Japan no longer has a trade imbalance problem. Profound demographic change has caused its current account surplus to shrink; structural changes, such as a shift of production abroad and a relative decline in competitiveness, have created a deficit in the trade balance (see Figure 7.3). Although the 2011 shutdown of nuclear power plants (which required Japan to import large amounts of mineral fuels) has been a contributing factor, the secular deterioration of the trade balance was already evident long before 2008 (see Section 6.6.1 in Chapter 6). The year 2013 saw a trade deficit of ¥11.5 trillion, the largest annual deficit ever recorded, widening from the deficits of ¥6.9

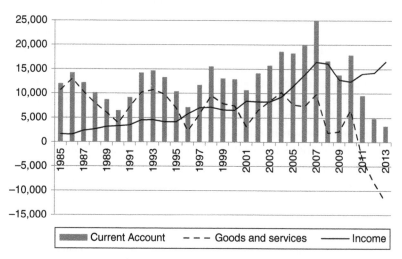

Figure 7.3. Components of Japan's quarterly current account balance, Q1 1985–Q4 2013 (in billions of yen)

Source: Ministry of Finance

trillion in 2012 and ¥2.6 trillion in 2011. In contrast, the surplus in the investment account has been increasing, reflecting the returns on Japan's growing investment positions abroad. The investment income surplus now amounts to more than 3 percent of gross domestic product (GDP). In 2011–13, the current account remained in surplus only because the investment surplus more than offset the trade deficit.

7.3.3. Subordinating Domestic to External Objectives

Focus on external objectives led Japanese authorities to sacrifice domestic stability. The outcome was particularly adverse on two occasions: the high inflation of 1973 and the asset price bubble of 1986–8 (Kuroda 2004). In the first instance, part of the problem was authorities' failure to understand the constraint of the "impossible trinity."[3] As the expansion of global activities by Japanese firms necessitated progressive easing of cross-border transactions, maintaining the fixed exchange rate meant giving up monetary policy independence or accepting a higher rate of inflation than the authorities preferred. To avoid higher inflation, they had no choice but to allow the yen to float, but it took them time to come to this realization. After the collapse of the peg, moreover, authorities eased monetary and fiscal policies substantially in an attempt to mitigate the adverse real impact of the higher yen. Consumer price inflation was already running at double digits when Japan was hit in late 1973 by a quadrupling of oil prices.

The second instance paralleled the first. Following the Plaza Agreement, macroeconomic policies were substantially eased, in part to mitigate the adverse impact of the higher yen. Although the appreciation-induced recession was short-lived, policies remained easy in order to expand domestic demand and thereby to increase imports. Because consumer prices remained stable, authorities did not recognize that the economy was overheating. All of this was done in the name of G5/G7 international macroeconomic policy coordination. Monetary tightening was delayed until May 1989, by which time asset price inflation was in full swing. The government's mistake was to allow external considerations to dictate the stance of fiscal and monetary policies. The world has since learned that international policy coordination could be counterproductive (Feldstein 1988; Bergsten and Siebert 2003).

---

[3] The "impossible trinity" refers to the proposition in international economics that an open economy cannot simultaneously achieve (1) exchange rate stability, (2) free capital mobility, and (3) monetary policy independence. Although domestic and foreign assets must be perfect substitutes for the proposition to hold strictly, Japanese and US assets are believed to be highly substitutable to make the constraint sufficiently binding on the conduct of exchange rate policy.

7.3.4. Protracted Capital Account Liberalization

The process of CAL was unnecessarily protracted. It took the government thirty years to achieve capital account convertibility for the yen and an additional twenty to dismantle all restrictions on cross-border capital transactions. First, inward foreign direct investment (FDI) should have been liberalized in the 1950s. Although approval was routinely given to FDI inflows deemed beneficial to the country, potential foreign investors did not find the capital control regime welcoming. Even if Japanese authorities wanted to protect certain industrial sectors, there was no reason to subject all sectors to prior approval and strict ownership limits. An earlier FDI liberalization would have eased the foreign exchange constraint on the rate of economic growth and thereby allowed Japan to liberalize restrictive trade and payment practices more quickly.

Second, floating the yen without fully liberalizing capital flows led to wide swings in the exchange rate. Fukao (2003) argues that the sharp appreciation of 1977–8 was caused by the rapid growth of exports when private capital outflows were tightly controlled. Given Japan's passive, lean-against-the-wind intervention strategy, a large portion of the current account surplus was left unfinanced, causing the exchange rate to appreciate sharply. In contrast, in the 1980s, greater capital mobility allowed a large balance-of-payments imbalance to be accommodated without pressure on the exchange rate. Authorities did not sufficiently understand the accounting identity relating a current account surplus to the sum of capital outflows and an accumulation in foreign exchange reserves. The alternative to faster CAL was to intervene more forcefully in the foreign exchange market (Eichengreen and Hatase 2005), but this would have subjected Japan to criticism by trading partners as a dirty floater (as happened in 1971 and 1973 following the collapse of the Bretton Woods and Smithsonian regimes, respectively).

7.3.5. Delayed Financial Liberalization

Large exchange rate swings in the early part of the floating period reflected not only restrictions on capital flows, but also underdeveloped domestic capital markets. Japan had barely begun to develop a deep secondary market in Japanese government bonds (JGBs) by the late 1970s. The markets for more sophisticated instruments, such as options and futures, only emerged in the 1980s. Without deep debt markets in which investors can park their long-term funds, active two-way capital flows cannot be expected to take place. Without such flows, foreign exchange markets lack the depth necessary to keep exchange rates stable. Fukao (2003) argues that the exchange rate volatility of the 1970s was due to a lack of sufficient two-way long-term capital flows, given Japanese authorities' passive intervention strategy. Financial liberalization, along with the development of financial markets and instruments, should have been completed much earlier, ideally before the yen was allowed to float.

In the event, financial liberalization was protracted because authorities wanted to maintain the existing financial sector segmentation. According to Mabuchi (1990), this resulted from the longstanding agreement between the Ministry of Finance (MOF) and the banking sector, which limited the involvement of politicians in financial policymaking. The "apolitical" pact meant that, even though market players desired a faster pace of financial deregulation, they refrained from lobbying the politicians. This suited both. The apolitical pact protected the MOF's autonomy, elite status, and jurisdictional boundaries, while the banks had no incentive to politicize financial policymaking as long as the existing system secured them sufficient rents. The pace of capital account and financial liberalization was therefore dictated by the imperative to maintain the domestic regulatory order.[4] The pact was broken only by foreign pressure to open up the Japanese financial system.

7.4. CURRENT AND PROSPECTIVE ISSUES

7.4.1. Asian Monetary Cooperation

Japanese exchange rate policy has almost exclusively focused on the yen's nominal bilateral exchange rate vis-à-vis the US dollar. For the most part, this has been a natural choice. The US dollar was the anchor currency to which most currencies were pegged under the Bretton Woods system. The United States was by far Japan's single most important trading partner during much of this period, although Asia as a region was just as important. Asia's share has steadily risen in recent years and now accounts for about half of Japan's trade, with China having become the country's single most important trading partner (see Table 7.1). Even so, more than half of Japanese exports to Asia and more than 70 percent of Japanese imports from Asia are still invoiced in US dollars. Many of the region's currencies have also been managed in reference to (if not pegged to) the US dollar. The United States also remains far more important than Asia as the destination for outward investments and

---

[4] For example, in 1974, the MOF's Banking, Securities, and International Finance Bureaus agreed (in what is known as the Three-Bureau Agreement) to limit the underwriting activities of Japanese banks in foreign markets to maintain the separation of commercial and investment banking in the domestic financial system. Also, ordinary banks were prohibited from using in Japan funds acquired by issuing long-term liabilities in foreign markets to preserve the status of long-term credit banks in domestic financial markets.

Table 7.1. Asia versus United States in Japan's external transactions (in percentage shares)

Type of transaction(s), year(s)		Asia[a]	Of which, China	United States
Trade, average for 2008–12	Exports	53.44	18.14	16.52
	Imports	42.83	20.81	9.33
Dollar (yen) invoicing, average for 2012–3	Exports	52.48	N.A.	85.85
		(44.30)		(14.10)
	Imports	72.43	N.A.	77.77
		(25.60)		(21.68)
Foreign direct investment, end of 2012	Assets	27.77	8.96	27.54
	Liabilities	13.53	0.27	29.94
Debt securities, end of 2012	Assets	1.61	0.02	31.22
	Liabilities	31.42	21.14	8.88
Equities, end of 2012	Assets	7.09	1.43	43.24
	Liabilities	8.36	4.97	44.34
External bank claims, end of 2012		6.06	1.25	33.09

[a] The definition of Asia follows the statistical definitions of the respective reporting agencies
Sources: Ministry of Finance; Bank of Japan (for external bank claims)

the source of inward investments, in part reflecting the underdevelopment of Asia's financial markets.

Japan's dollar-focused policy may have to be modified if Asian regional monetary cooperation moves forward. Since May 2000, when the leaders of ten Association of Southeast Asian Nations (ASEAN) countries, China, Japan, and the Republic of Korea met in Chiang Mai, Thailand, monetary cooperation has become increasingly institutionalized, including the establishment of the Chiang Mai Initiative (CMI), a network of bilateral swap agreements designed to reduce the risk of currency crisis and to manage a crisis if it occurs. In 2009, the ASEAN Plus Three (ASEAN+3) finance ministers made a decision to multilateralize the CMI by pooling reserves subject to a single contractual agreement and agreed on the amount of member contributions, the borrowing limits, and the allocation of voting powers (see Table 7.2). A decision was also made to establish an "independent surveillance unit" to monitor and analyze regional economies to support decision-making in the CMI Multilateralization (CMIM), which the ministers agreed in 2010 to call the ASEAN+3 Macroeconomic Research Office (AMRO) and to locate in Singapore. It is understood that AMRO is monitoring intraregional exchange rate movements.

At present, there appears to be little appetite in Asia to further strengthen these institutional arrangements. The existing political reality makes it difficult to imagine any closer economic policy cooperation emerging in the near future. At the same time, Asian economies are deepening their trade and investment integration, irrespective of political constraints. Although financial integration has lagged behind, given the limited size and developmental stage

Table 7.2. Financial contributions and voting power under Chiang-Mai Initiative Multilateralization (as agreed in 2012)

	Contributions		Maximum swap limit (in billions of US dollars)	Voting share (in percent)
	In billions of US dollars	In percent of total		
Plus Three countries	**192.000**	**(80.00)**	117.30	71.59
China	76.800	(32.00)	40.50	28.41
China, People's Republic of	68.400	(28.50)	34.20	25.43
Hong Kong SAR	8.400	(3.50)	6.30	2.98
Japan	76.800	(32.00)	38.40	28.41
Korea, Republic of	38.400	(16.00)	38.40	14.77
Association of Southeast Asian Nations (ASEAN)	**48.000**	**(20.00)**	126.20	28.41
Brunei Darussalam	0.060	(0.03)	0.30	1.16
Cambodia	0.240	(0.10)	1.20	1.22
Indonesia	9.104	(3.79)	22.76	4.37
Lao PDR	0.060	(0.03)	0.30	1.16
Malaysia	9.104	(3.79)	22.76	4.37
Myanmar	0.120	(0.05)	0.60	1.18
Philippines	9.104	(3.79)	22.76	4.37
Singapore	9.104	(3.79)	22.76	4.37
Thailand	9.104	(3.79)	22.76	4.37
Vietnam	2.000	(0.83)	10.00	1.85
ASEAN+3	240.000	(100.00)	120.70	100.00

Source: ASEAN+3 Macroeconomic Research Office (www.amro-asia.org)

of most national financial markets (Takagi 2014a), intraregional trade now accounts for more than 50 percent of total trade; intraregional FDI accounts for about 35 percent. Asia's political leaders appear less hostile to the idea of creating a regional trade bloc, with negotiations underway for the Regional Comprehensive Economic Partnership (RCEP) among the ASEAN+3, Australia, India, and New Zealand. The weight of Asia is bound to rise in Japan's external transactions. Japanese authorities will need to pay greater attention to the yen's exchange rate against other Asian currencies (especially the Chinese renminbi) as they become more flexible.

7.4.2. The New Modality of Market Intervention

Kumakura (2012) argues that there is a built-in propensity for yen-selling intervention in Japan by describing the accounting framework of the Foreign Exchange Fund Special Account. When the government intervenes in the foreign exchange market by selling yen, it raises the yen funds by issuing short-term financing bills (FBs). The balance of FBs appears on the liabilities side of the Foreign Exchange Fund Special Account, while the balance of foreign assets acquired through the intervention is carried on the assets side. Although the special account has incurred a substantial capital loss from the yen's secular appreciation over the years (about ¥35 trillion in March 2011), accounting rules require only realized losses or gains to be included in the income statement. Because interest rates on the foreign assets of various maturities held by the special account are higher than the funding rate, this means that the government earns a sizable accounting profit year after year (nearly ¥2 trillion in FY 2012). Part of this is transferred to the national budget.[5]

The historical cost accounting of the Foreign Exchange Fund Special Account explains the lack of aversion to yen-selling intervention but not why authorities in the past followed the lean-against-the-wind intervention strategy. The fact is that, whatever the adverse incentive of the system may be, authorities have all but ceased to intervene in the foreign exchange market since March 2004. In August 2007, when the yen appreciated against the dollar from ¥120 to ¥114 within a matter of days, they remained unengaged. Nor did they intervene when the yen, along with the Swiss franc, displayed a sustained appreciation following the global financial crisis of 2008 (De Bock and de Carvalho Filho 2013). Swiss authorities, alarmed by the negative impact of the soaring franc on the real economy, set the floor of SF1.2 per euro in September 2011, but Japanese authorities remained unmoved. A senior MOF official, when asked whether Japan would follow suit, dismissed such a possibility as unrealistic. On the few occasions that authorities did intervene during 2011–12, however, they did so with size and decisiveness (see Chapter 6).

It appears that Japanese authorities have now given up market intervention as a standard instrument of exchange rate policy. The events of 2011–12 suggest that, in the future, they will only intervene when markets are highly disorderly and in a manner calculated to maximize the impact. Small, frequent smoothing operations are a thing of the past. In this intervention philosophy, Japanese authorities have finally come to agree with the longstanding stance of the United States and other G7 countries. If there is a difference, it is that Japanese intervention, when it does take place, will likely be larger. The country's considerable foreign exchange reserves allow Japan to intervene massively if necessary to defend the yen; the accounting rules of the Foreign Exchange Fund Special Account virtually eliminate authorities' aversion to massive yen-selling intervention. In either case, the infrequency of intervention and the likely larger size will certainly politicize each intervention decision. As was the case in 2011–12, the minister of finance or even the prime

---

[5] Because returns from investments are reinvested, the government issues new FBs equal to the amount of the net annual income. Part of the proceeds is then transferred to the general account of the national budget.

minister will increasingly be making intervention decisions. Interventions will no longer be tactical decisions of a few MOF bureaucrats.

7.4.3. What to do with Foreign Exchange Reserves?

As a result of foreign exchange market intervention, which has involved more purchases than sales of dollars, Japan has accumulated a large amount of foreign exchange reserves, surpassed only by China. Because Japan's policy is to reinvest any returns on foreign assets, the balance of reserves has increased steadily even when there was no intervention. At the end of 2013, the balance of foreign exchange was over $1.2 trillion (see Figure 7.1), which was more than six times the amount held by the second largest industrial country holder of official reserves (Germany). It was eight to nine times the amount held by the United States or the United Kingdom. If we view official reserves as a form of insurance against the contingency in which a country loses access to international capital markets, it is difficult to understand why Japan (a reserve currency country) should find it necessary to hold such a large amount of low-yielding assets in its national portfolio. Because nearly all of the foreign exchange reserves are held under the Foreign Exchange Fund Special Account, the foreign assets have, as their counterparts, liabilities to the Japanese public. Ideally, the government should withdraw from intermediating the public's portfolio investment abroad.

One way to go forward would be to determine the optimal level of reserves for the country (say, a third of the current amount) and to divest the excess amount over time according to preannounced rules so as not to disturb the market. Some have proposed that a portion of the foreign exchange reserves be used to create a sovereign wealth fund, which in turn would be invested in high-yielding, long-term assets. Kawai and Takagi (2009), however, argue that the world would not look kindly on the government of a large G7 economy making commercial investments in foreign private firms, especially if it began to exert its influence on their business decisions. It would become scandalous if speculative investments in stocks and real estate went sour. But these and other radical reforms are unlikely to happen soon. In the meantime, the government is aware of the need to maximize returns while maintaining the safety and liquidity of the underlying assets. In October 2013, the law was revised to allow private firms to manage foreign exchange reserves beginning in April 2014, subject to certain eligibility criteria. The government has also extended foreign currency loans to private firms through the Japan Bank for International Cooperation, a government financial institution, in part as a way to maximize returns on foreign exchange reserves (see Section 6.6.3 in Chapter 6).

7.4.4. Government–Central Bank Cooperation

In a system where the government is responsible for exchange rate policy while the central bank is given operational independence to pursue monetary policy objectives, a conflict could arise if the objectives—or the judgment of prevailing economic and financial conditions—of the two entities differed. Under normal conditions, it makes little sense for the government to intervene in the foreign exchange market against the judgment of the central bank because the central bank can undo everything the government does. Without the central bank's support, intervention would have no monetary policy effect on the exchange rate. On the other hand, if the two entities share the same objectives and judgment, a case can be made for eliminating the duplication by transferring intervention authority to the central bank, as is already the case in many countries. As Lambson et al. (2014) argue, however, endowing the government with the authority to intervene could be an additional channel of checks and balances when the central bank is independent. It could also protect the central bank's credibility from political pressure to intervene when there is a strong trade lobby.

The period of about five years after the 1998 Bank of Japan Law took effect—which roughly corresponds to the term of Governor Masaru Hayami (March 1998–March 2003)—may have been an aberration in the government–central bank relationship. The Bank of Japan (BOJ) appeared so protective of its newly acquired independence that an open conflict with the government emerged over the conduct of monetary policy (see Section 6.5.2 in Chapter 6). The government considered monetary policy insufficiently accommodative, while the central bank viewed deflation to be a result of economic stagnation, not of monetary policy. The great intervention of 2003–4 was a last-resort attempt by the MOF to inject liquidity into the domestic money market when the BOJ appeared reluctant. Okina (2011) observes that the situation was exacerbated by the personality of Governor Hayami, who had in his earlier BOJ career experienced two bouts of high inflation and therefore held a strong personal conviction that a higher yen was in the national interest. And he acted to advocate his own views, not the central bank's best collective judgment.

The government–central bank relationship improved with the appointment as governor of Toshihiko Fukui (March 2003–March 2008), who is believed to have agreed to cooperate with the government as a condition for his nomination by the prime minister. The relationship matured under the governorship of Masaaki Shirakawa (April 2008–March 2013), who no longer believed that cooperating with the government in pursuit of common national interests meant a compromise of central bank independence. During his brief stint as an academic, Shirakawa (2008) had stated that authority to make intervention decisions should ideally be given to the central bank in order to allow it to send a consistent signal about monetary policy; and that authorities should intervene only when the probability of success is high. The Bank of Japan's cooperative attitude during the interventions of 2011–12 possibly reflected Shirakawa's view that government–central bank cooperation was essential to maximize the signaling effect of intervention (see Section 6.7.4 in Chapter 6). Government–central bank cooperation in Japan is now much closer to what is observed in other advanced countries with similar institutional arrangements, such as Canada and the United States (see Section 7.5).

7.5. MONETARY POLICY UNDER *ABENOMICS*

The rhetoric and substance of economic policies adopted by Prime Minister Shinzo Abe following his party's landslide victory in Lower House elections on 16 December 2012 have been called *Abenomics* by the press. *Abenomics* supposedly consists of (1) aggressive monetary easing, (2) fiscal policy mobilization (public works), and (3) growth strategies (structural reforms). In practice, the limited fiscal space, given the large balance of public debt, has not allowed the government to expand fiscal policy in a substantive way. The modest increase that did take place in debt-financed spending in 2013 (the net impact of which was an estimated 0.5 percent of GDP on the structural primary balance (IMF 2013)) is expected to be followed by fiscal consolidation efforts over the coming years. The national consumption tax was already raised from 5 to 8 percent in April 2014, and another 2 percentage-point increase is expected (initially planned for October 2015, but now targeted for April 1917). In the area of structural reform, few specific measures have been announced, let alone implemented, to promote inward FDI, labor market flexibility, and the labor force participation of women as regular workers. *Abenomics* therefore has so far almost exclusively relied on monetary easing, which is a curiosity given the independence of the BOJ.

As an opposition party politician, Abe had been known as an ardent critic of the BOJ and an advocate of inflation targeting. He made vague but inflammatory remarks about the need to revise the Bank of Japan Law, requiring the BOJ to purchase government bonds to finance public works, giving it the dual mandate of price stability and full employment (as is the case in the United States), or even getting the government involved in monetary policymaking. The public increasingly came to anticipate that aggressive monetary easing would be forthcoming if Abe were to become prime minister, especially given that the term of the incumbent governor was coming to an end in April 2013. When it was announced on 14 November 2012 that the Lower House of the Diet would be dissolved, the yen immediately depreciated and crossed the ¥80 mark against the US dollar. The yen edged downward during the election campaign, and the pace accelerated after Abe took office as prime minister. The yen, which was trading around ¥80 in November, hit the ¥100 mark in May 2013. Nothing really substantive or different took place during this period except for the announcement and expectations of aggressive monetary easing.

The transformation of monetary policy under *Abenomics* was more evolutionary than revolutionary. As discussed in Chapter 6 (Section 6.6.3), the BOJ introduced "comprehensive monetary easing" in October 2010, involving a cut in the overnight call rate from "around 1 percent" to "0 to 0.1 percent" and the Asset Purchase Program. The Japanese word *kikin*, translated as "program" in the BOJ's official translation, really means "fund," indicating the idea that the assets purchased under the program would be at least conceptually treated separately from other items on the balance sheet. As a further step in monetary easing, on 14 February 2012, the BOJ Monetary Policy Board announced that: (1) it had defined the "price stability goal in the medium to long term" as a "positive range of 2 percent or lower in terms of the year-on-year rate of change in the consumer price index"; (2) it had set the price stability goal of 1 percent "for the time being"; and (3) in order to achieve this goal, the BOJ would raise the size of the asset purchase "fund" from ¥55 trillion to ¥65 trillion.

To critics, what appeared to be the BOJ's adoption of inflation targeting was unsatisfactory. First, the Japanese word *medo*, officially translated as "goal," can be construed as such only in the sense that perfection is a goal. To native speakers, the word more likely connotes "prospect, hope, or estimate." When the BOJ stated that the goal was to achieve 2 percent inflation in the long run and 1 percent inflation for the time being, many took it to mean that the BOJ was deliberately avoiding commitment; it said the goal was something desirable to aim for but not likely to be achieved. Second, at least for open market purchases of JGBs, the idea of an asset purchase "fund" was intended to circumvent the self-imposed rule that the balance of JGBs should not exceed the amount of bank notes outstanding, a rule adopted in 2001 to avoid the appearance of the BOJ financing fiscal deficits. Although subject to seasonality, the amount of bank notes outstanding is relatively stable in Japan (see Figure 7.4). This meant that the amount of bank notes constrained the expansion of the monetary base through JGB purchases.

The first thing the new Abe cabinet did was to press the BOJ to define what it meant by its price stability goal. On 22 January 2013, the MOF and the Cabinet Office issued a joint statement with the BOJ titled "Overcoming Deflation and Achieving Sustainable Economic Growth." In this landmark government–central bank accord (1) the parties agreed to strengthen their policy coordination, (2) the BOJ set a price stability target (*mokuhyō*) of 2 percent in terms of the year-on-year change in the consumer price index, and (3) the government agreed to aim to achieve fiscal sustainability. The

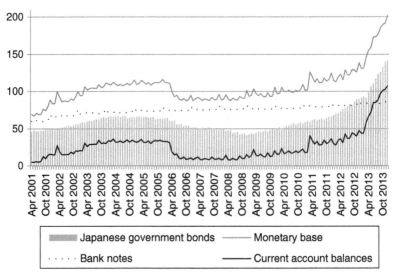

Figure 7.4. Major components of Bank of Japan balance sheet, April 2001–December 2013 (in trillions of yen)

Source: Bank of Japan

word *mokuhyō* explicitly conveys the sense in which the expression inflation targeting is used in the literature. The prime minister then began to select a candidate to succeed the incumbent governor whose term was about to end, stating that he would pick someone sympathetic to his views, including his commitment to the inflation "target" of 2 percent. By so doing, the prime minister effectively instituted inflation targeting without revising the Bank of Japan Law. The only missing element of a formal inflation-targeting regime is the government's ability to hold the central bank governor accountable once appointed.

The second constraint on monetary easing—the self-imposed bank note principle—was removed when in March 2013 the prime minister's own man, Haruhiko Kuroda, was installed as governor of the Bank of Japan.[6] On 4 April 2013, it was agreed at the first Monetary Policy Board meeting held under the new governor that: (1) the BOJ would "achieve the price stability target of 2 percent in terms of the year-on-year rate of change in the consumer price index at the earliest possible time, with a time horizon of about two years"; (2) it would change the main operating target for money market operations from the uncollateralized overnight call rate to the monetary base; (3) it would double the monetary base and the holding of JGBs while lengthening their

---

[6] Shirakawa stepped down a few weeks before the end of his term when the two deputy governors' terms ended to allow the new leadership team to assume office on the same day.

Table 7.3. Bank of Japan's actual and projected balance sheets, 2012–14 (in trillions of yen)

	End of 2012 (actual)	End of 2013 (actual)	End of 2014 (projected)
Monetary base, of which:	138	202	270
Bank notes	87	90	90
Current account balances (CAB)	47	107	175
Japanese government bonds (JGBs)	89	142	190

Source: Bank of Japan

average maturity. The Asset Purchase Program would be terminated, and the bank note principle would be suspended. Governor Kuroda called this package "quantitative and qualitative easing" (QQE). The central pillar of QQE was to double the monetary base from ¥138 trillion at the end of 2012 to ¥270 trillion at the end of 2014 (see Table 7.3). At the end of October 2014, the annual pace of monetary base expansion was further raised by ¥10–20 trillion, with a planned increase in JGB purchases of ¥30 trillion per year.

The monetary base became the operating target under QQE, whereas under the previous program of quantitative easing (2001–6) it had been the current account balances (CAB) of financial institutions, or the monetary base minus the balance of bank notes. The difference is inconsequential because, as noted, the balance of bank notes is relatively stable. This portion of the monetary base was excluded from the target under quantitative easing because the central bank considers it demand-determined and stands ready to supply whatever amount is demanded by the public. Under QQE the monetary base was chosen as the target because it is a more transparent measure. In explaining the logic of QQE, Governor Kuroda criticized the previous phase of monetary easing for its lack of transparency and clarity, with the use of multiple instruments subject to constant revisions. The opaque system was replaced with a simple one—the deployment of whatever means available to double the monetary base in two years. The suspension of the self-imposed bank note principle allowed the balance of JGBs to exceed the balance of bank notes outstanding by more than ¥50 trillion by the end of 2013 (see Table 7.3).[7]

The consequence of aggressive monetary easing under QQE, especially when the US Federal Reserve was widely expected to begin tapering its asset purchases, has been a substantial depreciation of the yen against the US dollar and other major currencies. On an annual average basis, the yen depreciated by more than 22 percent from 2012 to 2013. Japan's senior policymakers have repeatedly stated that the purpose of monetary easing was not to depreciate

---

[7] The amount of JGBs has exceeded the amount of bank notes since August 2012, thanks to the Asset Purchase Program, but only by a moderate amount (e.g., ¥2 trillion at the end of 2012).

the yen but to end deflation. This stance has received a measure of support from the international community. For example, the communiqué from the Group of Twenty (G20) meeting of finance ministers and central bank governors in April 2013 only tersely noted: "Japan's recent policy actions are intended to stop deflation and support domestic demand." After two decades of deflation, Japan now enjoys the world's sympathy. Japan no longer poses a large external imbalance. The rise of China has diminished the political intensity of any remaining Japan–US bilateral economic issues. All this has given Japan, at least for now, breathing space to reflect upon the lessons learned from the experience of subordinating domestic to external objectives. Japan's quest to overcome the fear of freedom has now led to the ultimate form of freedom—freedom to use macroeconomic policies for domestic purposes.

References

Abdelal, Rawi. 2007. *Capital Rules: The Construction of Global Finance*. Cambridge, MA: Harvard University Press.

Abe, Takeshi, ed. 2013. *Tsūshō Bōeki Seisaku, 1980-2000*. Tokyo: Keizai Sangyō Chōsakai.

Alexander, Sidney S. 1952. "Effects of a Devaluation on a Trade Balance." *International Monetary Fund Staff Papers* 2: 263-78.

Angel, Robert C. 1991. *Explaining Economic Policy Failure: Japan in the 1969-1971 International Monetary Crisis*. New York: Columbia University Press.

Asai, Yoshio. 2012. "Sengo Kawase Kanri no Seiritsu." *Seijō Keizai Kenkyū* 195: 93-140.

Asako, Kazumi and Takatoshi Ito. 1991. "The Rise and Fall of Deficit in Japan, 1965-1990." *Journal of the Japanese and International Economies* 5: 451-72.

Baba, Naohiko. 1995. "On the Cause of Price Differentials between Domestic and Overseas Markets: Approach through Empirical Analyses of Markup Pricing." *Bank of Japan Monetary and Economic Studies* 13: 45-74.

Bacchetta, Philippe and Eric van Wincoop. 2005. "A Theory of the Currency Denomination of International Trade." *Journal of International Economics* 67: 295-319.

Bahmani-Oskooee, Mohsen and Scott W. Hegerty. 2009. "The Japanese-U.S. Trade Balance and the Yen: Evidence from Industry Data." *Japan and the World Economy* 21: 161-71.

Bahmani-Oskooee, Mohsen and Gour Gobinda Goswami. 2004. "Exchange Rate Sensitivity of Japan's Bilateral Trade Flows." *Japan and the World Economy* 16: 1-15.

Baishō Mondai Kenkyūkai. 1963. *Nihon no Baishō*. Tokyo: Sekai Jānarusha.

Balassa, Bela. 1964. "The Purchasing Power Parity Doctrine: A Reappraisal." *Journal of Political Economy* 72: 584-96.

Baldwin, Richard E. 1988. "Hysteresis in Import Prices: The Beachhead Effect." *American Economic Review* 78: 773-85.

Bank for International Settlements (BIS). 2008. "Currency Internationalisation in Asia: Evidence from the Foreign Exchange Market." Hong Kong: Representative Office for Asia and the Pacific, Bank for International Settlements.

Bank for International Settlements (BIS). 2007. *Seventy-Seventh Annual Report*. Basel: Bank for International Settlements.

Bank of Japan (BOJ). 1988. "Sengo Kawase Kanri no Suii." Tokyo: Bank of Japan.

Bank of Japan (BOJ). 1986. "Structural Changes in the Secondary Market for Bonds and the Recent Trends in Yields on Long-Term Bonds." Special Paper No. 132. Tokyo: Bank of Japan.

Bank of Japan (BOJ). 1985. *Nihon Ginkō Hyakunenshi*, Volume 5. Tokyo: Bank of Japan.

Bank of Japan (BOJ). 1982. "Recent Developments in the Secondary Market for Bonds." Special Paper No. 103. Tokyo: Bank of Japan.

Bank of Japan (BOJ). 1973. *Money and Banking in Japan.* London: Macmillan.

Bank of Tokyo (BOT). 1960. *Gaika Yosan Seido no Kaisetsu.* Tokyo: Bank of Tokyo.

Bayoumi, Tamim and Gabrielle Lipworth. 1998. "Japanese Foreign Direct Investment and Regional Trade." *Journal of Asian Economics* 9: 581–607.

Beine, Michel. 2004. "Conditional Covariances and Direct Central Bank Interventions in the Foreign Exchange Markets." *Journal of Banking and Finance* 28: 1385–411.

Beine, Michel, Sebastien Laurent, and Franz C. Palm. 2009. "Central Bank FOREX Interventions Assessed Using Realized Moments." *Journal of International Financial Markets, Institutions, and Money* 19: 112–27.

Beine, Michel and Oscar Bernal. 2007. "Why Do Central Banks Intervene Secretly? Preliminary Evidence from the BOJ." *Journal of International Financial Markets, Institutions and Money* 17: 291–306.

Beine, Michel and Christelle Lecourt. 2004. "Reported and Secret Interventions in the Foreign Exchange Markets." *Finance Research Letters* 1: 215–25.

Beine, Michel, Sebastien Laurent, and Christelle Lecourt. 2003. "Official Central Bank Interventions and Exchange Rate Volatility: Evidence from a Regime-Switching Analysis." *European Economic Review* 47: 891–911.

Bergsten, C. Fred. 1982. "What to Do about the US–Japan Economic Conflict." *Foreign Affairs* 60: 1059–75.

Bergsten, C. Fred. 1981. "The Costs of Reaganomics." *Foreign Policy* 44: 24–36.

Bergsten, C. Fred and Horst Siebert. 2003. "Should G7 Policy Coordination be Revived?" *The International Economy* (Fall): 18–23.

Bergsten, C. Fred and William R. Cline. 1987. "The United States–Japan Economic Problem." Policy Analysis in International Economics No. 13. Washington: Institute for International Economics.

Bernanke, Ben S. and Vincent R. Reinhart. 2004. "Conducting Monetary Policy at Very Low Short-Term Interest Rates." *American Economic Review* 94: 85–90.

Bernanke, Ben S., Vincent R. Reinhart, and Brian P. Sack. 2004. "Monetary Policy Alternatives at the Zero Bound: An Empirical Assessment." *Brookings Papers on Economic Activity* 2: 1–100.

Bernanke, Ben S. and Mark Gertler. 1999. "Monetary Policy and Asset Price Volatility." *Federal Reserve Bank of Kansas City Economic Review* (Fourth Quarter): 17–51.

Bilson, John F. O. 1983. "The Choice of an Invoice Currency in International Transactions." In *Economic Interdependence and Flexible Exchange Rates*, edited by Jagdeep S. Bhandari and Bluford H. Putnam, 384–401. Cambridge, MA.: MIT Press.

Bird, Graham and Thomas D. Willett. 2008. "Why Do Governments Delay Devaluation? The Political Economy of Exchange Rate Inertia." *World Economics* 9: 55–73.

Black, Stanley W. 1991. "Transactions Costs and Vehicle Currencies." *Journal of International Money and Finance* 10: 512–26.

Bomberger, William A. and Gail E. Makinen. 1983. "The Hungarian Hyperinflation and Stabilization of 1945–1946." *Journal of Political Economy* 91: 801–24.

Borden, William S. 1984. *The Pacific Alliance: United States Foreign Economic Policy and Japanese Trade Recovery, 1947–1955.* Madison, WI: University of Wisconsin Press.

Bordo, Michael D., Owen F. Humpage, and Anna J. Schwartz. 2010. "U.S. Foreign-Exchange-Market Intervention during the Volcker–Greenspan Era." Working Paper 10/07. Cleveland, OH: Federal Reserve Bank of Cleveland.

Botman, Dennis P. J., Irineu de Carvalho Filho, and W. Raphael Lam. 2013. "The Curious Case of the Yen as a Safe Haven Currency: A Forensic Analysis." IMF Working Paper 13/228. Washington: International Monetary Fund.

Breuer, Janice Boucher and Leianne A. Clements. 2003. "The Commodity Composition of US–Japanese Trade and the Yen/Dollar Real Exchange Rate." *Japan and the World Economy* 15: 307–30.

Bronfenbrenner, Martin. 1975. "Inflation Theories of the SCAP Period." *History of Political Economy* 7: 137–55.

Bronfenbrenner, Martin. 1955. "Monopoly and Inflation in Contemporary Japan." *Osaka Economic Papers* 3: 41–8.

Bronfenbrenner, Martin. 1950. "Four Positions on Japanese Finance." *Journal of Political Economy* 58: 281–8.

Cagan, Phillip. 1956. "The Monetary Dynamics of Hyperinflation." In *Studies in the Quantity Theory of Money*, edited by Milton Friedman, 25–117. Chicago: University of Chicago Press.

Cai, Jun, Yan-Leung Cheung, Raymond S. K. Lee, and Michael Melvin. 2001. "'Once-in-a-Generation' Yen Volatility in 1998: Fundamentals, Intervention, and Order Flow." *Journal of International Money and Finance* 20: 327–47.

Calvo, Guillermo A. and Carlos A. Vegh. 1994. "Inflation Stabilization and Nominal Anchors." *Contemporary Economic Policy* 12: 35–45.

Campbell, John Y. and Yasushi Hamao. 1992. "Predictable Stock Returns in the United States and Japan: A Study of Long-Term Capital Market Integration." *Journal of Finance* 47: 43–69.

Cargill, Thomas F., Michael M. Hutchison, and Takatoshi Ito. 2000. *Financial Policy and Central Banking in Japan*. Cambridge, MA: MIT Press.

Cargill, Thomas F., Michael M. Hutchison, and Takatoshi Ito. 1997. *The Political Economy of Japanese Monetary Policy*. Cambridge, MA: MIT Press.

Casella, Alessandra and Barry Eichengreen. 1993. "Halting Inflation in Italy and France after the Second World War." In *Monetary Regimes in Transition*, edited by Michael D. Bordo and Forrest Capie, 312–45. Cambridge and New York: Cambridge University Press.

Castren, Olli. 2004. "Do Options-Implied RND Functions on G3 Currencies Move Around the Times of Interventions on the JPY/USD Exchange Rate?" Working Paper No. 410. Frankfurt: European Central Bank.

Chen, Ho-Chyuan, Kuang-Liang Chang, and Shih-Ti Yu. 2012. "Application of the Tobit Model with Autoregressive Conditional Heteroscedasticity for Foreign Exchange Market Interventions." *Japan and the World Economy* 24: 274–82.

Chinn, Menzie David. 1997. "Whither the Yen? Implications of an Intertemporal Model of the Dollar/Yen Rate." *Journal of the Japanese and International Economies* 11: 228–46.

Cho, Yoon Je. 2001. "The Role of Poorly Phased Liberalization in Korea's Financial Crisis." In *Financial Liberalization: How Far, How Fast?* edited by Gerard Caprio,

Patrick Honohan, and Joseph E. Stiglitz, 159–87. Cambridge and New York: Cambridge University Press.

Chōgin Sangyō Kenkyūkai. 1970. *En Kiriage to Nihon Sangyō no Jitsuryoku*. Tokyo: Tōyō Keizai Shinpōsha.

Clark, Don P. 1994. "Non-tariff Measures Use in Japan and the United States." *Japan and the World Economy* 6: 53–60.

Coenen, Gunter and Volker Wieland. 2003. "The Zero-Interest-Rate Bound and the Role of the Exchange Rate for Monetary Policy in Japan." *Journal of Monetary Economics* 50: 1071–101.

Cohen, Benjamin J. 1967. "Reparations in the Postwar Period: A Survey." *Banca Nazionale Del Lavoro Quarterly Review* 20: 268–88.

Danne, Christian and Gunther Schnabl. 2008. "A Role Model for China? Exchange Rate Flexibility and Monetary Policy in Japan." *China Economic Review* 19: 183–96.

Das, Dilip K. 1993. "The Yen Appreciation and the Japanese Economy." *Japan and the World Economy* 5: 243–64.

De Andrade, Joaquim Pinto, and Jose Angelo Divino. 2005. "Monetary Policy of the Bank of Japan—Inflation Target versus Exchange Rate Target." *Japan and the World Economy* 17: 189–208.

De Bock, Reinout and Irineu de Carvalho Filho. 2013. "The Behavior of Currencies during Risk-off Episodes." IMF Working Paper 13/8. Washington: International Monetary Fund.

Dekle, Robert. 1998. "The Japanese 'Big Bang' Financial Reforms and Market Implications." *Journal of Asian Economics* 9: 237–49.

Destler, I. M. and C. Randall Henning. 1989. *Dollar Politics: Exchange Rate Policy-making in the United States*. Washington: Institute for International Economics.

Destler, I. M. and Hisao Mitsuyu. 1982. "Locomotive on Different Tracks: Macroeconomic Diplomacy, 1977–1979." In *Coping with US–Japanese Economic Conflicts*, edited by I. M. Destler and Hideo Sato, 243–69. Lexington, MA: Lexington Books.

Detragiache, Enrica and A. Javier Hamann. 1999. "Exchange Rate-Based Stabilization in Western Europe: Greece, Ireland, Italy, and Portugal." *Contemporary Economic Policy* 17: 358–69.

Dixit, Avinash. 1994. "Hysteresis and the Duration of the J-Curve." *Japan and the World Economy* 6: 105–15.

Dominguez, Kathryn M. E. 2006. "When Do Central Bank Interventions Influence Intra-Daily and Longer-Term Exchange Rate Movements?" *Journal of International Money and Finance* 25: 1051–71.

Dominguez, Kathryn M. E. 2003. "Foreign Exchange Intervention: Did It Work in the 1990s?" In *Dollar Overvaluation and the World Economy*, edited by C. Fred Bergsten and John Williamson, 217–45. Washington: Institute for International Economics.

Dominguez, Kathryn M. E. 1998. "Central Bank Intervention and Exchange Rate Volatility." *Journal of International Money and Finance* 17: 161–90.

Easterly, William. 1996. "When Is Stabilization Expansionary? Evidence from High Inflation." *Economic Policy* 11: 66–107.

Edison, Hali J. 1993. "The Effectiveness of Central-Bank Intervention: A Survey of the Literature after 1982." *Special Papers in International Economics* No. 18. Princeton, NJ: International Finance Section, Princeton University.

Eggertsson, Gauti B. and Michael Woodford. 2003. "The Zero Bound on Interest Rates and Optimal Monetary Policy." *Brookings Papers on Economic Activity* 1: 139–233.

Ehrmann, Michael and Marcel Fratzscher. 2005. "Exchange Rates and Fundamentals: New Evidence from Real-Time Data." *Journal of International Money and Finance* 24: 317–41.

Eichengreen, Barry and Mariko Hatase. 2005. "Can a Rapidly-Growing Export-Oriented Economy Smoothly Exit an Exchange Rate Peg? Lessons for China from Japan's High-Growth Era." NBER Working Paper No. 11625. Cambridge, MA: National Bureau of Economic Research.

Eichengreen, Barry, Paul Masson, Hugh Bredenkamp, Barry Johnston, Javier Hamann, Esteban Jadresic, and Inci Ötker. 1998. "Exit Strategies: Policy Options for Countries Seeking Greater Exchange Rate Flexibility." IMF Occasional Paper No. 168. Washington: International Monetary Fund.

Esaka, Taro. 2000. "The Louvre Accord and Central Bank Intervention: Was There a Target Zone?" *Japan and the World Economy* 12: 107–26.

Esaka, Taro and Shinji Takagi. 2013. "Testing the Effectiveness of Market-Based Controls: Evidence from the Experience of Japan with Short-term Capital Flows in the 1970s." *International Finance* 16: 45–69.

Evans, Martin D. D. and Richard K. Lyons. 2005. "Do Currency Markets Absorb News Quickly?" *Journal of International Money and Finance* 24: 197–217.

Evans, Martin D. D. and Richard K. Lyons. 2002. "Order Flow and Exchange Rate Dynamics." *Journal of Political Economy* 110: 170–80.

Fatum, Rasmus. 2009. "Official Japanese Intervention in the JPY/USD Exchange Market: Is It Effective and Through Which Channel Does It Work?" *Bank of Japan Monetary and Economic Studies* 27: 75–98.

Fatum, Rasmus and Michael M. Hutchison. 2010. "Evaluating Foreign Exchange Market Intervention: Self-Selection, Counterfactuals and Average Treatment Effects." *Journal of International Money and Finance* 29: 570–84.

Fatum, Rasmus and Michael Hutchison. 2006. "Effectiveness of Official Daily Foreign Exchange Market Intervention Operations in Japan." *Journal of International Money and Finance* 25: 199–219.

Fatum, Rasmus and Michael Hutchison. 2005. "Foreign Exchange Intervention and Monetary Policy in Japan, 2003–04." *International Economics and Economic Policy* 2: 241–60.

Fatum, Rasmus and Michael Hutchison. 1999. "Is Intervention a Signal of Future Monetary Policy? Evidence from the Federal Funds Futures Market." *Journal of Money, Credit and Banking* 31: 54–69.

Federal Reserve Bank of New York (FRBNY). 1963 (January)–1976 (October). *Monthly Review.*

Federal Reserve Bank of New York (FRBNY). 2011. "Treasury and Federal Reserve Foreign Exchange Operations: January–March 2011."

Federal Reserve Bank of New York (FRBNY). 1976 (Winter)–1994 (Summer–Fall). *Quarterly Review.*

Feldstein, Martin S. 1988. "Thinking about International Economic Coordination." *Journal of Economic Perspectives* 2: 3–13.

Fischer, Stanley, Ratna Sahay, and Carlos A. Vegh. 2002. "Modern Hyper- and High Inflations." *Journal of Economic Literature* 40: 837–80.

Flath, David. 2014. *The Japanese Economy* (3rd Edition). Oxford: Oxford University Press.

Frankel, Jeffrey A. 1990. "The Making of Exchange Rate Policy in the 1980s." Working Paper No. 3539. Cambridge, MA: National Bureau of Economic Research.

Frankel, Jeffrey A. 1984. "The Yen/Dollar Agreement: Liberalizing Japanese Capital Markets." Policy Analyses in International Economics No. 9. Washington: Institute for International Economics.

Fratzscher, Marcel. 2009. "How Successful Is the G7 in Managing Exchange Rates?" *Journal of International Economics* 79: 78–88.

Fratzscher, Marcel. 2008. "Oral Interventions versus Actual Interventions in FX Markets: An Event-Study Approach." *Economic Journal* 118: 1079–106.

Fratzscher, Marcel. 2005. "Strategies of Exchange Rate Policy in G3 Economies." *Economics Letters* 89: 68–74.

Freedman, Charles. 2000. "Recent Developments in the Framework for the Conduct of Monetary Policy in Canada." *Canadian Business Economics* 8: 3–6.

Frenkel, Michael, Christian Pierdzioch, and Georg Stadtmann. 2005. "The Effects of Japanese Foreign Exchange Market Interventions on the Yen/US Dollar Exchange Rate Volatility." *International Review of Economics and Finance* 14: 27–39.

Frenkel, Michael, Christian Pierdzioch, and Georg Stadtmann. 2004. "On the Determinants of 'Small' and 'Large' Foreign Exchange Market Interventions: The Case of the Japanese Interventions in the 1990s." *Review of Financial Economics* 13: 231–43.

Frenkel, Michael, Christian Pierdzioch, and Georg Stadtmann. 2003. "Modeling Coordinated Foreign Exchange Market Interventions: The Case of the Japanese and US Interventions in the 1990s." *Review of World Economics* 139: 709–29.

Friberg, Richard. 1998. "In Which Currency Should Exporters Set Their Prices?" *Journal of International Economics* 45: 59–76.

Fujiki, Hiroshi and Shigenori Shiratsuka. 2002. "Policy Duration Effect under the Zero Interest Rate Policy in 1999–2000: Evidence from Japan's Money Market Data." *Bank of Japan Monetary and Economic Studies* 20: 1–31.

Fujino, Shozaburo. 1988. "Sengo Nihon no Kokusai Shūshi." *Keizai Kenkyū* 39: 97–108.

Fukao, Mitsuhiro. 2005. "Kakudaisuru Sekai Keizai no Fukinkō Risuku to Seisaku Chōsei." Kinyū Kenkyū No. 12. Tokyo: Japan Center for Economic Research.

Fukao, Mitsuhiro. 2003. "Capital Account Liberalization: The Japanese Experience and Implications for China." In China's Capital Account Liberalization: International Perspectives, 35–61. BIS Papers No. 15. Basel: Bank for International Settlements.

Fukao, Mitsuhiro. 1990. "Liberalization of Japan's Foreign Exchange Controls and Structural Changes in the Balance of Payments." *Bank of Japan Monetary and Economic Studies* 8: 101–65.

Fukao, Mitsuhiro. 1983. *Kawase Rēto to Kinyū Shijō*. Tokyo: Tōyō Keizai Shinpōsha.

Fukao, Mitsuhiro, and Kunio Okina. 1989. "Internationalization of Financial Markets and Balance of Payments Imbalances: A Japanese Perspective." *Carnegie-Rochester Conference Series on Public Policy* 30: 167–220.

Fukao, Mitsuhiro, and Masaharu Hanazaki. 1987. "Internationalisation of Financial Markets and the Allocation of Capital." *OECD Economic Studies* 8: 35–92.

Fukao, Mitsuhiro, and Takashi Okubo. 1984. "International Linkage of Interest Rates: The Case of Japan and the United States." *International Economic Review* 25: 193–207.

Fukuda, Shin-ichi, and Ji Cong. 1994. "On the Choice of Invoice Currency by Japanese Exporters: The PTM Approach." *Journal of the Japanese and International Economies* 8: 511–29.

Funabashi, Yoichi. 1988. *Managing the Dollar: From the Plaza to the Louvre.* Washington: Institute for International Economics.

Galati, Gabriele and William Melick. 2002. "Central Bank Intervention and Market Expectations." BIS Papers No. 10. Basel: Bank for International Settlement.

Galati, Gabriele, William Melick, and Marian Micu. 2005. "Foreign Exchange Market Intervention and Expectations: The Yen/Dollar Exchange Rate." *Journal of International Money and Finance* 24: 982–1011.

Galbraith, John K. 1946. "Reflections on Price Control." *Quarterly Journal of Economics* 60: 475–89.

Garber, Peter M. 1996. "The Use of the Yen as a Reserve Currency." *Bank of Japan Monetary and Economic Studies* 14: 1–21.

Giovannini, Alberto. 1988. "Exchange Rates and Traded Goods Prices." *Journal of International Economics* 24: 45–8.

Gowa, Joanne. 1983. *Closing the Gold Window: Domestic Politics and the End of Bretton Woods.* Ithaca, NY: Cornell University Press.

Grassman, Sven. 1973. "A Fundamental Symmetry in International Payments Patterns." *Journal of International Economics* 3: 105–16.

Green, David Jay. 1990. "Exchange Rate Policy and Intervention in Japan." *Journal of Asian Economics* 1: 249–71.

Grimes, William W. 2001. *Unmaking the Japanese Miracle: Macroeconomic Politics, 1985–2000.* Ithaca, NY: Cornell University Press.

Gultekin, Mustafa N., N. Bulent Gultekin, and Alessandro Penati. 1989. "Capital Controls and International Capital Market Segmentation: The Evidence from the Japanese and American Stock Markets." *Journal of Finance* 44: 849–69.

Hadley, Eleanor M. 1970. *Antitrust in Japan.* Princeton, NJ: Princeton University Press.

Hamada, Koichi and Munehisa Kasuya. 1993. "The Reconstruction and Stabilization of the Postwar Japanese Economy: Possible Lessons for Eastern Europe?" In *Postwar Economic Reconstruction and Lessons for the East Today,* edited by Rudiger Dornbusch, W. Nolling, and R. Layard, 155–88. Cambridge, MA: MIT Press.

Hamada, Koichi and Hugh T. Patrick. 1988. "Japan and the International Monetary Regime." *The Political Economy of Japan, Vol. 2: The Changing International Context,* edited by Takashi Inoguchi and Daniel I. Okimoto, 108–37. Stanford: Stanford University Press.

Hamada, Koichi and Fumio Hayashi. 1985. "Monetary Policy in Postwar Japan." In *Monetary Policy in Our Times,* edited by Albert Ando, Hidekazu Eguchi, Roger Farmer, and Yoshio Suzuki, 83–121. Cambridge, MA: MIT Press.

Hamann, A. Havier. 1999. "Exchange Rate-Based Stabilization: A Critical Look at the Stylized Facts." IMF Working Paper 99/132. Washington: International Monetary Fund.

Hartmann, Philipp. 1998. *Currency Competition and Foreign Exchange Markets: The Dollar, the Yen and the Euro.* Cambridge: Cambridge University Press.

Hasegawa, Sukehiro. 1975. *Japanese Foreign Aid: Policy and Practice.* New York: Praeger.

Hassan, Marwa. 2012. "Japanese Foreign Exchange Intervention: A Tale of Pattern, Size, or Frequency." *Japan and the World Economy* 24: 184–92.

Hattori, Masazumi and Hyun Song Shin. 2009. "Yen Carry Trade and the Subprime Crisis." *International Monetary Fund Staff Papers* 56: 384–409.

Hattori, Masazumi and Hyun Song Shin. 2007. "The Broad Yen Carry Trade." Discussion Paper No. 2007-E-19. Tokyo: Institute for Monetary and Economic Studies, Bank of Japan.

Hayashi, Fumio. 1992. "Explaining Japan's Saving: A Review of Recent Literature." *Bank of Japan Monetary and Economic Studies* 10: 63–77.

Helleiner, Eric. 1994. *States and the Reemergence of Global Finance: From Bretton Woods to the 1990s.* Ithaca, NY: Cornell University Press.

Hickok, Susan. 1989. "Japanese Trade Balance Adjustment to Yen Appreciation." *Federal Reserve Bank of New York Quarterly Review* 14: 33–47.

Hillebrand, Eric and Gunther Schnable. 2006. "A Structural Break in the Effects of Japanese Foreign Exchange Intervention on Yen/Dollar Exchange Rate Volatility." Working Paper No. 650. Frankfurt: European Central Bank.

Hollerman, Leon. 1967. *Japan's Dependence on the World Economy: The Approach toward Economic Liberalization.* Princeton, NJ: Princeton University Press.

Horne, J. 1985. *Japan's Financial Markets: Conflict and Consensus in Policymaking.* Sydney: Allen & Unwin.

Horsefield, J. Keith. 1969. *The International Monetary Fund 1945–1965: Twenty Years of International Monetary Cooperation,* Volume I: Chronicle. Washington: International Monetary Fund.

Hoshi, Takeo. 2001. "What Happened to Japanese Banks?" *Bank of Japan Monetary and Economic Studies* 19: 1–29.

Hoshikawa, Takeshi. 2008. "The Effect of Intervention Frequency on the Foreign Exchange Market: The Japanese Experience." *Journal of International Money and Finance* 27: 547–59.

Houthakker, Hendrik S. 1978. "The Breakdown of Bretton Woods" In *Economic Advice and Executive Policy: Recommendations from Past Members of the Council of Economic Advisers,* edited by Werner Sichel, 45–64. New York: Praeger.

Hsing, Han-Min. 2005. "Re-examination of J-Curve Effect for Japan, Korea and Taiwan." *Japan and the World Economy* 17: 43–58.

Hu, The-Wei. 1971. "Hyperinflation and the Dynamics of the Demand for Money in China, 1945–1949." *Journal of Political Economy* 79: 186–95.

Humpage, Owen F. 2003. "Government Intervention in the Foreign Exchange Market." Working Paper 03/15. Cleveland, OH: Federal Reserve Bank of Cleveland.

Hunsberger, Warren S. 1964. *Japan and the United States in World Trade.* New York: Harper and Row.

Hutchison, Michael M. 1988. "Monetary Control with an Exchange Rate Objective: The Bank of Japan, 1973–86." *Journal of International Money and Finance* 7: 261–71.

Hutchison, Michael M. and Nirvikar Singh. 1997. "Equilibrium Real Interest Rate Linkages: The United States and Japan." *Journal of the Japanese and International Economies* 11: 208–27.

Imai, Hiroyuki. 2010. "Japan's Inflation under the Bretton Woods System: How Large Was the Balassa–Samuelson Effect?" *Journal of Asian Economics* 21: 174–85.

Independent Evaluation Office (IEO) of the International Monetary Fund. 2005. "The IMF's Approach to Capital Account Liberalization." Evaluation Report. Washington: International Monetary Fund.

Independent Evaluation Office (IEO) of the International Monetary Fund. 2003. "The IMF and Recent Capital Account Crises: Indonesia, Korea, Brazil." Evaluation Report. Washington: International Monetary Fund.

Institute for International Monetary Affairs (IIMA). 2002. "Report of the Study Group on the Promotion of the Internationalization of the Yen." Tokyo: Ministry of Finance.

International Monetary Fund (IMF). 2013. "Japan: 2013 Article IV Consultation." IMF Country Report No. 13/253. Washington: International Monetary Fund.

International Monetary Fund (IMF). 2012. "The Liberalization and Management of Capital Flows: An Institutional View." Washington: International Monetary Fund.

International Monetary Fund (IMF). 2007. *Selected Decisions and Selected Documents of the International Monetary Fund*, Thirty-First Issue. Washington: International Monetary Fund.

International Monetary Fund (IMF). 1950–66. *Annual Report on Exchange Restrictions*. Washington: International Monetary Fund.

Inuta, Akira. 2000. *Wagakuni Sengo no Gaikoku Kawase Seisaku to Chōki Tanki Shihon Torihiki Kisei no Kanwa*. Tokyo: Chūo Kōron Jigyō Shuppan.

Ishii, Shogo, Karl Habermeier, Jorge Ivan Canales-Kriljenko, Bernard Laurens, John Leimone, and Judit Vadasz. 2002. "Capital Account Liberalization and Financial Sector Stability." Occasional Paper No. 211. Washington: International Monetary Fund.

Isobe, Asahiko. 1966. "The Japanese Foreign Exchange Market." *International Monetary Fund Staff Papers* 13: 256–81.

Ito, Masanao. 2009. *Sengo Nihon no Taigai Kinyū*. Nagoya: Nagoya University Press.

Ito, Takatoshi. 2007. "Myths and Reality of Foreign Exchange Interventions: An Application to Japan." *International Journal of Finance and Economics* 12: 133–54.

Ito, Takatoshi. 2005. "Interventions and Japanese Economic Recovery." *International Economics and Economic Policy* 2: 219–39.

Ito, Takatoshi. 2003. "Is Foreign Exchange Intervention Effective? The Japanese Experience in the 1990s." In *Monetary History, Exchange Rates and Financial Markets*, Vol. 2, edited by Paul Mizen, 126–53. Cheltenham, UK: Edward Elgar.

Ito, Takatoshi. 1987. "The Intradaily Exchange Rate Dynamics and Monetary Policies after the Group of Five Agreement." *Journal of the Japanese and International Economies* 1: 275–98.

Ito, Takatoshi. 1986. "Capital Controls and Covered Interest Parity between the Yen and the Dollar." *Economic Studies Quarterly* 37: 223–41.

Ito, Takatoshi, Satoshi Koibuchi, Kiyotaka Sato, and Junko Shimizu. 2013. "Choice of Invoicing Currency: New Evidence from a Questionnaire Survey of Japanese Export

Firms." Discussion Paper No. 13-E-034. Tokyo: Research Institute of Economy, Trade and Industry.

Ito, Takatoshi and Tomoyoshi Yabu. 2007. "What Prompts Japan to Intervene in the Forex Market? A New Approach to a Reaction Function." *Journal of International Money and Finance* 26: 193–212.

Ito, Takatoshi and Michael Melvin. 1999. "Japan's Big Bang and the Transformation of Financial Markets," NBER Working Paper No. 7247. Cambridge, MA: National Bureau of Economic Research.

Ito, Takatoshi, Peter Isard, and Steven Symansky. 1997. "Economic Growth and Real Exchange Rate: An Overview of the Balassa–Samuelson Hypothesis in Asia." NBER Working Paper No. 5979. Cambridge, MA: National Bureau of Economic Research.

Ito, Takatoshi and Tokuo Iwaisako. 1996. "Explaining Asset Bubbles in Japan." *Bank of Japan Monetary and Economic Studies* 14: 143–93.

Itoh, Motoshige and Kazuharu Kiyono. 1988. "Foreign Trade and Direct Investment." In *Industrial Policy of Japan*, edited by Ryutaro Komiya, Masahiro Okuno, and Kotaro Suzumura, 155–81. Tokyo and San Diego: Academic Press.

Iwata, Kazumasa. 2010. *Defure tono Tatakai*. Tokyo: Nihon Keizai Shimbun Shuppansha.

Iwata, Kazumasa and Shinji Takenaka. 2012. "Central Bank Balance Sheet Expansion: Japan's Experience." BIS Papers No. 66, 132–59. Basel: Bank for International Settlements.

James, Harold. 1996. *International Monetary Cooperation Since Bretton Woods*. Washington: International Monetary Fund; and Oxford: Oxford University Press.

Japanese Economic Counsel Board (ECB). 1953. *Sengo no Kokumin Shotoku*. Tokyo.

Japanese Economic Stabilization Board (ESB). 1952. *Bukka Yōran*. Tokyo.

Japanese Ministry of Finance (MOF). 2003a. "Promoting the Internationalization of the Yen." Chairman's Summary of the Study Group on the Promotion of the Internationalization of the Yen. Tokyo: Ministry of Finance.

Japanese Ministry of Finance (MOF). 2003b. "Toward Increasing the Status of Japan as an International Financial Center." Chairman's Summary of the Study Group on the Internationalization of the Japanese Financial and Capital Markets. Tokyo: Ministry of Finance.

Japanese Ministry of Finance (MOF). 2001. "Report of the Study Group for the Promotion of the Internationalization of the Yen." Tokyo: Ministry of Finance.

Japanese Ministry of Finance (MOF). 1999a. "Internationalization of the Yen for the 21st Century." Report of the Council on Foreign Exchange and Other Transactions. Tokyo: Ministry of Finance.

Japanese Ministry of Finance (MOF). 1999b. *Shōwa Zaiseishi: Shōwa 27–48*, Volume 11. Tokyo: Tōyō Keizai Shinpōsha.

Japanese Ministry of Finance (MOF). 1998. "Internationalization of the Yen." Report of the Subcouncil on the Internationalization of the Yen. Tokyo: Ministry of Finance.

Japanese Ministry of Finance (MOF). 1997. "Concerning the Amendment of the Foreign Exchange and Foreign Trade Control Law." Report of the Council on Foreign Exchange and Other Transactions. Tokyo: Ministry of Finance.

Japanese Ministry of Finance (MOF). 1992. *Shōwa Zaiseishi: Shōwa 27–48*, Volume 12. Tokyo: Tōyō Keizai Shinpōsha.

Japanese Ministry of Finance (MOF). 1982. *The Financial History of Japan: The Allied Occupation Period, 1945–1952*, Volume 20, English Documents. Tokyo: Tōyō Keizai Shinpōsha.

Japanese Ministry of Finance (MOF). 1977–1996. *Kokusai Kinyūkyoku Nenpō*. Tokyo: Kinyū Zaisei Jijō Kenkyūkai.

Japanese Ministry of Finance (MOF). 1976a. *Shōwa Zaiseishi: Shūsen kara Kōwa made*, Volume 12. Tokyo: Tōyō Keizai Shinpōsha.

Japanese Ministry of Finance (MOF). 1976b. *Shōwa Zaiseishi: Shūsen kara Kōwa made*, Volume 15. Tokyo: Tōyō Keizai Shinpōsha.

Japanese Ministry of Finance (MOF). 1952. *Mikaeri Shikin no Kiroku*. Tokyo.

Japanese Ministry of International Trade and Industry (MITI). 1949–83. *Tsūshō Sangyōshō Nenpō*.

Japanese Ministry of International Trade and Industry (MITI). 1990. *Tsūshō Sangyō Seisakushi*, Volume 6. Tokyo.

Johnston, R. Barry, Salim M. Darbar, and Claudia Echeverria. 1997. "Sequencing Capital Account Liberalization: Lessons from the Experiences in Chile, Indonesia, Korea, and Thailand." IMF Working Paper No. 97/157. Washington: International Monetary Fund.

Jorgenson, Dale W., Masahiro Kuroda, and Mieko Nishimizu. 1987. "Japan–U.S. Industry-Level Productivity Comparisons, 1960–1979." *Journal of the Japanese and International Economies* 1: 1–30.

Jung, Taehun, Yuki Teranishi, and Tsutomu Watanabe. 2005. "Optimal Monetary Policy at the Zero-Interest-Rate Bound." *Journal of Money, Credit, and Banking* 37: 813–35.

Kaminsky, Graciela L. and Karen K. Lewis. 1996. "Does Foreign Exchange Intervention Signal Future Monetary Policy?" *Journal of Monetary Economics* 37: 285–312.

Kashiwagi, Yusuke. 1972. *Gekidōki no Tsūka Gaikō*. Tokyo: Kinyū Zaisei Jijō Kenkyūkai.

Kasuya, Munehisa. 1995. "Sengo Fukkōki no Kakuchōteki Keizai Seisaku nitsuite." *Kinyū Kenkyū* 14: 63–100.

Kato, Izuru. 2010. "Tanki Kinyūshijō no Genba de Nani ga Okitaka." *Finansharu Rebyū* 99: 115–51.

Kato Izuru and Toru Nakakita. 2010. "Kokkokin Kanri no Sokumen kara Mita Ryōteki Kanwasaku no Igi nitsuite," *Finansharu Rebyū* 99: 152–78.

Kawai, Masahiro and Shinji Takagi. 2011. "Why Was Japan Hit So Hard by the Global Financial Crisis?" In *The Impact of the Economic Crisis on East Asia: Policy Responses from Four Economies*, edited by D. Shaw and B. J. Liu, 131–48. Cheltenham, UK and Northampton, MA.: Edward Elgar.

Kawai, Masahiro and Shinji Takagi. 2009. "Kawase Rēto to Kokusai Shūshi." In *Kokusai Kankyō no Henka to Nihon Keizai*, edited by Motoshite Itoh, 235–75. Tokyo: Keio University Press.

Kawai, Masahiro and Shinji Takagi. 2005. "Towards Regional Monetary Cooperation in East Asia: Lessons from Other Parts of the World." *International Journal of Finance and Economics* 10: 97–116.

Kearns, Jonathan and Roberto Rigobon. 2005. "Identifying the Efficacy of Central Bank Interventions: Evidence from Australia and Japan." *Journal of International Economics* 66: 31–48.

Keizai Dōyūkai. 1948. "Tanitsu Kawase Rēto Settei to Sono Eikyō." Tokyo.

Kenen, Peter B. 1969. "The International Position of the Dollar in a Changing World." *International Organization 23*: 705–18.

Kiguel, Miguel A. and Nissan Liviatan. 1992. "The Business Cycle Associated with Exchange Rate-Based Stabilizations." *World Bank Economic Review* 6: 279–305.

Kim, Soyoung, Sunghyun H. Kim, and Yunjong Wang. 2001. "Capital Account Liberalization and Macroeconomic Performance: The Case of Korea." Policy Analysis 01-01. Seoul: Korea Institute for International Economic Policy.

Kim, Suk-Joong. 2007. "Intraday Evidence of Efficacy of 1991–2004 Yen Intervention by the Bank of Japan." *Journal of International Financial Markets, Institutions, and Money* 17: 341–60.

Kim, Suk-Joong and Anh Tu Le. 2010. "Secrecy of Bank of Japan's Yen Intervention: Evidence of Efficacy from Intra-daily Data." *Journal of the Japanese and International Economies* 24: 369–94.

Kim, Suk-Joong and Jeffrey Sheen. 2006. "Interventions in the Yen-Dollar Spot Market: A Story of Price, Volatility and Volume." *Journal of Banking and Finance* 30: 3191–214.

Klein, Michael, Bruce Mizrach, and Robert G. Murphy. 1991. "Managing the Dollar: Has the Plaza Agreement Mattered?" *Journal of Money, Credit, and Banking* 23: 742–51.

Klein, Michael and Eric S. Rosengren. 1991. "Foreign Exchange Intervention as a Signal of Monetary Policy." *New England Economic Review* (May/June): 39–50.

Knetter, Michael M. 1993. "International Comparisons of Pricing-to-Market Behavior." *American Economic Review* 83: 473–86.

Kojima, Kiyoshi. 1985. "Japanese and American Direct Investment in Asia: A Comparative Analysis." *Hitotsubashi Journal of Economics* 26: 1–35.

Kojima, Kiyoshi. 1973. "A Macroeconomic Approach to Foreign Direct Investment." *Hitotsubashi Journal of Economics* 14: 1–21.

Komiya, Ryutaro and Motoshige Itoh. 1988. "Japan's International Trade and Trade Policy, 1955–1984." In *The Political Economy of Japan*, Volume 2, edited by T. Inoguchi and D. I. Okimoto, 173–224. Stanford, CA: Stanford University Press.

Komiya, Ryutaro and Kazuo Yasui. 1984. "Japan's Macroeconomic Performance since the First Oil Crisis: Review and Appraisal." *Carnegie–Rochester Conference Series on Public Policy* 20: 69–114.

Komiya, Ryutaro and Miyako Suda. 1983. *Gendai Kokusai Kinyūron: Rekishi Seisaku-hen*. Tokyo: Nihon Keizai Shimbunsha [English translation: *Japan's Foreign Exchange Policy, 1971–1982*, Sydney: Allen and Unwin, 1991].

Koo, Richard C. 1993. "International Capital Flows and an Open Economy: The Japanese Experience." In *Japanese Capital Markets: New Developments in Regulations and Institutions*, edited by Shinji Takagi, 78–129. Oxford: Blackwell.

Kosai, Yutaka. 1988. "The Reconstruction Period." In *Industrial Policy of Japan*, edited by Ryutaro Komiya, Masahiro Okuno, and Kotaro Suzumura, 25–48. Tokyo and San Diego: Academic Press.

Krause, Lawrence B. and Sueo Sekiguchi. 1976. "Japan and the World Economy." In *Asia's New Giant: How the Japanese Economy Works*, edited by Hugh Patrick and Henry Rosovsky, 383–458. Washington: Brookings Institution.

Krugman, Paul R. 1987. "Pricing to Market When the Exchange Rate Changes," In *Real-Financial Linkages among Open Economies*, edited by S. W. Arndt and J. D. Richardson, 49–70. Cambridge, MA: MIT Press.

Kumakura, Masanaga. 2012. "Reforming Japan's Foreign Exchange Policy." *World Economics* 13: 83–98.

Kurihara, Kenneth K. 1946. "Post-war Inflation and Fiscal–Monetary Policy in Japan." *American Economic Review* 36: 843–54.

Kuroda, Akio. 1982. *Nihon no Kinri Kōzō*. Tokyo: Tōyō Keizai Shinpōsha.

Kuroda, Haruhiko. 2004. "The 'Nixon Shock' and the 'Plaza Agreement': Lessons from Two Seemingly Failed Cases of Japan's Exchange Rate Policy." *China & World Economy* 12: 3–10.

Kuroda, Haruhiko. 2003. *Tsūka Gaikō*. Tokyo: Tōyō Keizai Shinpōsha.

Lambson, Val, Shinji Takagi, and Issei Kozuru. 2014. "Foreign Exchange Intervention and Monetary Policy: A Tale of Two Agencies with Conflicting Objectives." *Review of International Economics* 22: 976–91.

Lewis, Karen K. 1995a. "Occasional Interventions to Target Zones." *American Economic Review* 85: 691–715.

Lewis, Karen K. 1995b. "Are Foreign Exchange Intervention and Monetary Policy Related and Does It Really Matter?" *Journal of Business* 68: 185–214.

Lincoln, Edward J. 1988. *Japan: Facing Economic Maturity*. Washington: Brookings Institution.

Mabuchi, Masaru. 1990. "The Politics of Financial Deregulation in Japan: The Concept of Apolitical Pact." *Osaka University Law Review* 37: 1–18.

Maeda, Eiji, Bunya Fujiwara, Aiko Mineshima, and Ken Taniguchi. 2005. "Japan's Open Market Operations under the Quantitative Easing Policy." Working Paper No. 05-E-3. Tokyo: Bank of Japan.

Magee, Stephen P. and Ramesh K.S. Rao. 1980. "Vehicle and Nonvehicle Currencies in International Trade." *American Economic Review* 70 (Papers and Proceedings): 368–73.

Maisel, Sherman J. 1973. *Managing the Dollar*. New York: W. W. Norton.

Maki, Atsushi. 1998. "How High Consumer Prices Are in Japan!" *Japan and the World Economy* 10: 173–86.

Mann, Catherine L. 1986. "Prices, Profit Margins, and Exchange Rates." *Federal Reserve Bulletin* 72: 366–79.

Martin, Edwin M. 1948. *The Allied Occupation of Japan*. New York: American Institute of Pacific Relations.

Marston, Richard C. 1990. "Pricing to Market in Japanese Manufacturing." *Journal of International Economics* 29: 217–36.

Masuda, Hiroshi, ed. 1998a. *GHQ Minseikyoku Shiryō 4: Kōshoku Tsuihō I*. Tokyo: Maruzen.

Masuda, Hiroshi. 1998b. *Kōshoku Tsuihō Ron*. Tokyo: Iwanami Shoten.

McCallum, Bennett T. 2000. "Theoretical Analysis Regarding a Zero Lower Bound on Nominal Interest Rates." *Journal of Money, Credit, and Banking* 32: 870–904.

McKinnon, Ronald I. 1982. "The Order of Economic Liberalization: Lessons from Chile and Argentina." *Carnegie-Rochester Conference Series on Public Policy* 17: 159–86.

McKinnon, Ronald I. and Kenichi Ohno. 1997. *Dollar and Yen: Resolving Economic Conflict between the United States and Japan.* Cambridge, MA: MIT Press.

Meade, Ellen E. 1988. "Exchange Rates, Adjustment, and the J-Curve." *Federal Reserve Bulletin* 74: 633–44.

Mizoguchi, Zenbei. 2004. "Kawase Zuikan." Tokyo: Japan Center for International Finance (available at: www.jcif.or.jp/docs/20040917.pdf).

Moffett, Michael H. 1989. "The J-Curve Revisited: An Empirical Examination for the United States." *Journal of International Money and Finance* 8: 425–44.

Morel, Christophe and Jerome Teiletche. 2005. "Do Interventions in Foreign Exchange Markets Modify Investors' Expectations? The Experience of Japan between 1991 and 2003." Working Paper 2005-04. Paris: University of Paris Dauphine.

Moser-Boehm, Paul. 2005. "Governance Aspects of Foreign Exchange Interventions." BIS Papers No. 24. Basel: Bank for International Settlements.

Nagayasu, Jun. 2004. "The Effectiveness of Japanese Foreign Exchange Interventions during 1991–2001." *Economics Letters* 84: 377–81.

Nakai, Shozo. 1961. *Jiyūka no Bōeki to Gaikoku Kawase.* Tokyo: Kanshōinshinsha.

Nakajo, Seiichi. 1980. "Japanese Direct Investment in Asian Newly Industrializing Countries and Intra-Firm Division of Labor." *The Developing Economies* 18: 463–83.

Nakamura, Takafusa. 1986. *Shōwa Keizai Shi.* Tokyo: Iwanami Shoten [English translation: *Lectures on Modern Japanese Economic History 1926–1994*, Tokyo: LTCB International Library Foundation, 1994].

Narvekar, P. R. 1961. "The Cycle in Japan's Balance of Payments, 1955–58." *International Monetary Fund Staff Papers* 8: 380–411.

Narvekar, P. R. 1960. "The Role of Competitiveness in Japan's Export Performance, 1954–58." *International Monetary Fund Staff Papers* 8: 85–100.

Narvekar, P. R. 1957. "The 1954–55 Improvement in Japan's Balance of Payments." *International Monetary Fund Staff Papers* 6: 143–69.

Neely, Christopher J. 2005. "An Analysis of Recent Studies of the Effect of Foreign Exchange Intervention." *Federal Reserve Bank of St. Louis Review* 87: 685–717.

Nihon Keizai Shimbunsha. 1969. *En Kiriage: Sonotoki Dōnaru.* Tokyo: Nihon Keizai Shimbunsha.

Nihon Keizai Shimbunsha. 1967. *Shihon Jiyūka to Nihon Keizai.* Tokyo: Nihon Keizai Shimbunsha.

Nishimura, Kiyohiko G. 1993. "The Distribution System of Japan and the United States: A Comparative Study from Viewpoint of Final-Goods Buyers." *Japan and the World Economy* 5: 265–88.

Noland, Marcus. 1995. "Why Are Prices in Japan So High?" *Japan and the World Economy* 7: 255–61.

Noland, Marcus. 1989a. "Fiscal Policies and the Japan–US Bilateral Current Account." *Japan and the World Economy* 1: 243–53.

Noland, Marcus. 1989b. "Japanese Trade Elasticities and the J-Curve." *Review of Economics and Statistics* 71: 175–79.

Oda, Nobuyuki and Kazuo Ueda. 2007. "The Effects of the Bank of Japan's Zero Interest Rate Commitment and Quantitative Monetary Easing on the Yield Curve: A Macro-Finance Approach." *Japanese Economic Review* 58: 303–28.

Odell, John S. 1982. *U.S. International Monetary Policy: Markets, Power, and Ideas as Sources of Change*. Princeton, NJ: Princeton University Press.

Ogawa, Kazuo and Chung H. Lee. 1995. "Returns on Capital and Outward Direct Foreign Investment: The Case of Six Japanese Industries." *Journal of Asian Economics* 6: 437–67.

Ohno, Kenichi. 1989. "Export Pricing Behavior of Manufacturing: A U.S.–Japan Comparison." *International Monetary Fund Staff Papers* 36: 550–79.

Ohta, Takeshi. 1982. "Exchange-Rate Management and the Conduct of Monetary Policy." In *Central Bank Views on Monetary Targeting*, edited by P. Meed, 126–31. New York: Federal Reserve Bank of New York.

Okamura, Kaoru, Kotaro Suzumura, and Shuya Hayashi. 2009. "Komiya Ryūtarō Kyōju eno Intabyū." Discussion Paper No. 431. Tokyo: Center for Intergenerational Studies, Hitotsubashi University.

Okazaki, Tetsuji and Takafumi Korenaga. 1999a. "Foreign Exchange Allocation and Productivity Growth in Post-war Japan: A Case of the Wool Industry." *Japan and the World Economy* 11: 267–85.

Okazaki, Tetsuji and Takafumi Korenaga. 1999b. "The Foreign Exchange Allocation Policy in Postwar Japan: Its Institutional Framework and Function." In *Changes in Exchange Rates in Rapidly Developing Countries: Theory, Practice, and Policy Issues*, edited by Takatoshi Ito and Anne O. Krueger: 311–40. Chicago: University of Chicago Press.

Okina, Kunio. 2011. *Posto Manetarizumu no Kinyū Seisaku*. Tokyo: Nihon Keizai Shinbun Shuppansha.

Okumura, Takenosuke. 1950. *Gaikoku Kawase Gaikoku Bōeki Kanrihō Kaisetsu to Bōeki no Shinkōsō*. Osaka: US–Japan Friendship Commission.

Olive, Michael. 2004. "Pricing Behaviour in Japanese Manufacturing: A Comparative Study." *Japan and the World Economy* 16: 417–29.

Orphanides, Athanasios and Volker Wieland. 2000. "Efficient Monetary Policy Design Near Price Stability." *Journal of the Japanese and International Economies* 14: 327–65.

Osler, Carol L. 2003. "Currency Orders and Exchange Rate Dynamics: An Explanation for the Predictive Success of Technical Analysis." *Journal of Finance* 58: 1791–819.

Otani, Akira, Shigenori Shiratsuka, and Toyoichiro Shirota. 2003. "The Decline in the Exchange Rate Pass-through: Evidence from Japanese Import Prices." *Bank of Japan Monetary and Economic Studies* 21: 53–82.

Otani, Ichiro and Siddharth Tiwari. 1981. "Capital Controls and Interest Rate Parity: The Japanese Experience, 1978–81." *International Monetary Fund Staff Papers* 28: 793–815.

Ozaki, Robert S. 1972. *The Control of Imports and Foreign Capital in Japan*. New York: Praeger.

Page, S. A. B. 1981. "The Choice of Invoicing Currency in Merchandise Trade." *National Institute Economic Review* 98: 60–71.

Papaioannou, Elias, Richard Portes, and Gregorios Siourounis. 2006. "Optimal Currency Shares in International Reserves: The Impact of the Euro and the Prospects for the Dollar." *Journal of the Japanese and International Economies* 20: 508–47.

Park, Haesik and Chi-Young Song. 2008. "Japanese Vocal Intervention and the Yen/Dollar Exchange Rate." *Japan and the World Economy* 20: 61–81.

Putnam, Robert D. and Nicholas Bayne. 1984. *Hanging Together: The Seven-Power Summits*. London: Heinemann for the Royal Institute for International Affairs.

Quirk, Peter J. 1977. "Exchange Rate Policy in Japan: Leaning against the Wind." *International Monetary Fund Staff Papers* 24: 642–64.

Rao, Ramesh K. S. and Stephen P. Magee. 1980. "The Currency of Denomination of International Trade Contracts." In *Exchange Risk and Exposure: Current Developments in International Financial Management*, edited by Richard M. Levich and Clas G. Wihlborg, 61–79. Lexington, MA: Lexington.

Rogoff, Kenneth. 1996. "The Purchasing Power Parity Puzzle." *Journal of Economic Literature* 34: 647–68.

Rosenbluth, Frances McCall. 1989. *Financial Politics in Contemporary Japan*. Ithaca, NY: Cornell University Press.

Royama, Shoichi. 1986. *Kinyū Jiyūka*. Tokyo: University of Tokyo Press.

Sakakibara, Eisuke. 2000. *Nihon to Sekai ga Furueta Hi*. Tokyo: Chūo Kōron Shinsha.

Sakamoto, Nobuaki. 1960. *En Kawase Seisaku to Kawase Jiyūka*. Tokyo: Gaikoku Kawase Bōeki Kenkyūkai.

Samuelson, Paul A. 1964. "Theoretical Notes on Trade Problems." *Review of Economics and Statistics* 46: 145–54.

Sargent, Thomas J. 1982. "The Ends of Four Big Inflations." In *Inflation: Causes and Effects*, edited by Robert E. Hall, 41–97. Chicago: University of Chicago Press.

Sarno, Lucio and Mark P. Taylor. 2001. "Official Intervention in the Foreign Exchange Market: Is It Effective and, If So, How Does It Work?" *Journal of Economic Literature* 39: 839–68.

Sato, Kazuo. 1988. "The Role of the IS Balance and Its Macroeconomic Implications: The Case of Japan." *Journal of the Japanese and International Economies* 2: 239–58.

Sato, Kiyotaka. 1999. "The International Use of the Japanese Yen: The Case of Japan's Trade with East Asia." *World Economy* 22: 547–84.

Sazanami, Yoko, Fukunari Kimura, and Hiroki Kawai. 1997. "Sectoral Price Movements under the Yen Appreciation." *Journal of the Japanese and International Economies* 11: 611–41.

Scammell, W. M. 1980. *The International Economy Since 1945*. London: Macmillan Press.

Schenk, Catherine R. 1994. *Britain and the Sterling Area: From Devaluation to Convertibility in the 1950s*. London: Routledge.

Schonberger, Howard B. 1989. *Aftermath of War: Americans and the Remaking of Japan, 1945–1952*. Kent, OH : Kent State University Press.

Shavell, Henry. 1948. "Postwar Taxation in Japan." *Journal of Political Economy* 56: 124–37.

Shinjo, Koji. 1993. "Exchange Rate Changes and Pricing Behavior of Japanese Firms: A Cross-Section Analysis." *Journal of the Japanese and International Economies* 7: 157–74.

Shirakawa, Masaaki. 2008. *Gendai no Kinyū Seisaku*. Tokyo: Nihon Keizai Shimbun Shuppansha.

Shōji Keizai Kenkyūkai. 1963. *Garioa Eroa to Tai Tokubetsu En nitsuite*. Tokyo.

Solomon, Robert. 1977. *The International Monetary System 1945–1976: An Insider's View.* New York: Harper & Row.

Strange, Susan. 1976. *International Monetary Relations.* London: Oxford University Press.

Sumitomo Bank. 1960. *Bōeki Kawase no Jiyūka nitsuite,* Osaka: Sumitomo Bank.

Suzuki, Yoshio. 1985. "Japan's Monetary Policy over the Past 10 Years." *Bank of Japan Monetary and Economic Studies* 3: 1–9.

Svensson, Lars E. O. 2001. "The Zero Bound in an Open-Economy: A Foolproof Way of Escaping from a Liquidity Trap." *Bank of Japan Monetary and Economic Studies* 19: 277–312.

Takagi, Shinji. 2014a. "Financial Integration in Asia: Regional and Japanese Perspectives." In *Asian Financial Integration: Impacts of the Global Crisis and Options for Regional Policies,* edited by Yiping Huang and Shiro Armstrong, 163–86. London: Routledge.

Takagi, Shinji. 2014b. "The Effectiveness of Foreign Exchange Market Intervention: A Review of Post-2001 Studies on Japan." *Journal of Reviews on Global Economics* 3: 84–100.

Takagi, Shinji. 2013. "Argentina Default of 2001." In *The Evidence and Impact of Financial Globalization,* edited by Gerard Caprio, Jr., 25–35. London: Elsevier.

Takagi, Shinji. 1997. "Japan's Restrictive System of Trade and Payments: Operation, Effectiveness, and Liberalization, 1950–1964." IMF Working Paper 97/111. Washington: International Monetary Fund.

Takagi, Shinji. 1995. "From Recipient to Donor: Japan's Official Aid Flows, 1945–90 and Beyond." *Princeton Essays in International Finance* No. 196. Princeton, NJ: International Finance Section, Princeton University.

Takagi, Shinji. 1994. "Structural Changes in Japanese Long-Term Capital Flows." In *The Structure of the Japanese Economy,* edited by Mitsuaki Okabe, 435–58. London: Macmillan.

Takagi, Shinji. 1991. "Foreign Exchange Market Intervention and Domestic Monetary Control in Japan, 1973–89." *Japan and the World Economy* 3: 147–80.

Takagi, Shinji. 1988a. "Financial Liberalization and the 'Bills-Only' Doctrine: A Causality Test of Daily Japanese Data, 1978–1985." *Economic Studies Quarterly* 39: 149–59.

Takagi, Shinji. 1988b. "Recent Developments in Japan's Bond and Money Markets." *Journal of the Japanese and International Economies* 2: 63–91.

Takagi, Shinji. 1988c. "On the Statistical Properties of Floating Exchange Rates: A Reassessment of Recent Experience and Literature." *Bank of Japan Monetary and Economic Studies* 6: 61–91.

Takagi, Shinji. 1987. "Transactions Cost and the Term Structure of Interest Rates in the OTC Bond Market in Japan." *Journal of Money, Credit, and Banking* 19: 515–27.

Takagi, Shinji and Hiroki Okada. 2013. "Central Bank Independence and the Signaling Effect of Intervention: A Preliminary Exploration." Discussion Papers in Economics and Business No. 13-04. Osaka: Graduate School of Economics, Osaka University.

Takagi, Shinji, Toshihiko Nagai, Akihiko Kawaguchi, and Shuichi Shimakura. 1994. "Sengo Infurēshion to Dojji Anteika Seisaku." *Finansharu Rebyū* 33: 1–24.

Takemae, Eiji. 1983. *GHQ.* Tokyo: Iwanami Shoten.

Takita, Yoichi. 2006. *Nichibei Tsūka Kōshō: Nijūnenme no Shinjitsu*. Tokyo: Nihon Keizai Shinbunsha.

Tateno, Fumihiko. 1993. "The Foreign Exchange Market in Japan." In *Japanese Capital Markets: New Developments in Regulations and Institutions*, edited by Shinji Takagi, 452–85. Oxford: Basil Blackwell.

Tavlas, George S. and Yuzuru Ozeki. 1992. "The Internationalization of Currencies: An Appraisal of the Japanese Yen." Occasional Paper No. 90. Washington: International Monetary Fund.

Taylor, John B. 2007. *Global Financial Warriors: The Untold Story of International Finance in the Post 9/11 World*. New York: W.W. Norton.

Taylor, John B. 2006. "Lessons from the Recovery from the 'Lost Decade' in Japan: The Case of the Great Intervention and Monetary Injection." Paper presented at a conference held at the Cabinet Office, Government of Japan, 14 September, Tokyo.

Toya, Tetsuro. 2006. *The Political Economy of the Japanese Financial Big Bang: Institutional Change in Finance and Public Policymaking*. Oxford: Oxford University Press.

Tōyō Keizai Shinpōsha. 1954. *Senzen Sengo Bukka Sōran*. Tokyo: Tōyō Keizai Shinpōsha.

Truman, Edwin M. 2003. "Foreign Exchange Intervention: Did It Work in the 1990s?" In *Dollar Overvaluation and the World Economy*, edited by C. Fred Bergsten and John Williamson, 247–65. Washington: Institute for International Economics.

Tsutsui, William M. 1988. *Banking Policy in Japan: American Efforts at Reform during the Occupation*. London: Routledge.

Turner, Philip. 1988. "Savings and Investment, Exchange Rates, and International Imbalances: A Comparison of the United States, Japan, and Germany." *Journal of the Japanese and International Economies* 2: 259–85.

Ueda, Kazuo. 2005. *Zero Kinri tono Tatakai*. Tokyo: Nihon Keizai Shimbun Shuppansha.

Ueda, Kazuo. 1990. "Are Japanese Stock Prices Too High?" *Journal of the Japanese and International Economics* 4: 351–70.

Umeda, Masanobu. 2011. *Nichigin no Seisaku Keisei*. Tokyo: Tōyō Keizai Shinpōsha.

United States Board of Governors of the Federal Reserve System (FRB). 2005. *The Federal Reserve System Purposes and Functions*. Washington: Board of Governors of the Federal Reserve System.

United States Board of Governors of the Federal Reserve System (FRB). 1991 (January) –2001 (December). *Federal Reserve Bulletin*. Washington: Board of Governors of the Federal Reserve System.

United States (US) Department of State. 1969. *Occupation of Japan: Policy and Progress*. New York: Greenwood Press.

Ushiba, Nobuhiko. 1950. "Gaikoku Kawase Kanri Rei nitsuite." *Gaikoku Kawase*, special issue (June), 4–6.

Volcker, Paul A. and Toyoo Gyohten. 1992. *Changing Fortunes: The World's Money and the Threat to American Leadership*. New York: Times Books.

Wakasugi, Ryuhei. 1994. "Is Japanese Foreign Direct Investment a Substitute for International Trade?" *Japan and the World Economy* 6: 45–52.

Wang, Yuan Chao. 1953. "Japan: Controls and Restrictions over Foreign Exchange and Trade." Washington: International Monetary Fund.

Ward, Robert E. and Frank Joseph Shulman, eds. 1974. *The Allied Occupation of Japan, 1945–1952*. Chicago: American Library Association.

Watanabe, Toshiaki and Kimie Harada. 2006. "Effects of the Bank of Japan's Intervention on Yen/Dollar Exchange Rate Volatility." *Journal of the Japanese and International Economies* 20: 99–111.

Watanabe, Tsutomu. 1994. "The Signaling Effect of Foreign Exchange Intervention: The Case of Japan." In *Exchange Rate Policy and Interdependence: Perspectives from the Pacific Basin*, edited by Reuven Glick and Michael M. Hutchison, 258–86. Cambridge and New York: Cambridge University Press.

Watanabe, Tsutomu and Tomoyoshi Yabu. 2013. "The Great Intervention and Massive Money Injection: The Japanese Experience 2003–2004." *Journal of International Money and Finance* 32: 428–43.

Williams, Justin, Sr. 1979. *Japan's Political Revolution under MacArthur: A Participant's Account*. Athens, GA: University of Georgia Press.

Williams, Justin, Sr. 1968. "Completing Japan's Political Reorientation, 1947–1952: Crucial Phase of the Allied Occupation." *American Historical Review* 75: 1454–69.

Yoshikawa, Hiroshi. 2009. "Defurēshon to Kinyū Seisaku." In *Defure Keizai to Kinyū Seisaku*, edited by Hiroshi Yoshikawa 117–54, Tokyo: Keio University Press.

Yoshikawa, Hiroshi. 1990. "On the Equilibrium Yen–Dollar Rate." *American Economic Review* 80: 576–83.

Yoshioka, Masayuki. 1979. "Overseas Investment by the Japanese Textile Industry." *The Developing Economies* 17: 3–44.

Official Statistical Sources on Japan

Bank of Japan (BOJ). 1952–65. *Economic Statistics of Japan*. Tokyo: Bank of Japan.

Bank of Japan (BOJ). *Balance of Payments Monthly*, monthly issues. Tokyo: Bank of Japan.

Bank of Japan (BOJ). *Chōsa Geppō*, monthly issues. Tokyo: Bank of Japan.

Bank of Japan (BOJ). *Economic Statistics Monthly*, monthly issues. Tokyo: Bank of Japan.

International Monetary Fund (IMF). *International Financial Statistics*, monthly issues. Washington: International Monetary Fund.

Japanese Ministry of Finance (MOF). *Fiscal and Monetary Statistics Monthly*, monthly issues. Tokyo: Ministry of Finance.

Author Index

Subject Index